THE RUSSIAN ART OF WAR

How the West Led Ukraine to Defeat

Jacques Baud

THE RUSSIAN ART OF WAR

How the West Led Ukraine to Defeat

Max Milo

1. Introduction

In 1973, while on vacation in Italy with my family, we stopped off at the monastery of Monte Cassino, the scene of a violent battle in 1943. I remember spending long minutes in front of the grave of a young Canadian who died at the age of 18, the same age I was at the time.

Fifty years later, on the occasion of the visit of President Volodymyr Zelensky,[1] the Canadian Parliament gave a *standing ovation* to a survivor of the *14th Grenadierdivision "1. Galizien"* of the Waffen SS, who fought against the Soviets and took part in atrocities against Jews.[2] Anthony Rota, President of the Parliamentary Assembly, pointed out that this veteran *"fought for Ukrainian independence against the Russians and continues to support the truth today."*[3] A few days later, Rota awkwardly tried to justify himself, claiming that he didn't know the background of this soldier, which is a lie, since he had invited him and the other guests had been duly vetted and approved. To top it all off, Justin Trudeau, the Prime Minister, could think of nothing better than to blame it all on *"Russian propaganda and disinformation."*[4] One wonders if they're doing it on purpose, or if they're just totally retarded.

This incident illustrates several things that characterize the Western approach to the conflict in Ukraine.

---

1. https://forward.com/fast-forward/561927/zelenskyy-joins-canadian-parliaments-ovation-to-98-year-old-veteran-who-fought-with-nazis/
2. https://komb-a-ingwar.blogspot.com/2010/10/blog-post_4610.html
3. https://ici.radio-canada.ca/rci/en/news/2012834/house-speaker-anthony-rota-to-address-parliament-amid-ukrainian-veteran-fallout
4. https://www.opindia.com/2023/09/justin-trudeau-blames-russian-propaganda-after-canadas-parliament-faces-global-shame-for-celebrating-nazis/

First of all, Rota's justifications don't change the bottom line: all Canadian parliamentarians glorified those who fought for Canada's Allies in the Second World War! In fact, they spat on the grave of this young Canadian who was fighting the same enemy as the Soviets. In support, Zelensky, who knew full well what it meant to fight the Russians in the Second World War, himself applauded this former Waffen SS man! Let's not forget that 7 million Ukrainians fought the Third Reich on the side of the USSR and the Allies...

Secondly, these parliamentarians gave a former Nazi a standing ovation without even asking questions. Like sheep. By neglecting their duty of care, and acting without knowledge or understanding, they are all, without exception, examples of an ignorant political class, without honor, irresponsible, profoundly incapable of reflection and humanity. They are a disgrace to democracy.

Thirdly, this incident shows the ambiguity of the situation of Ukrainians, who owe their first independence to the Third Reich, which makes the oppressors of Western Europe the liberators of Ukrainians. The problem is that the Manichean world in which we live cannot accommodate these complex relationships. This leads to a form of negationism that has taken hold in our media, among our journalists and our politicians.

Fourthly, Anthony Rota didn't say that the veteran had fought "Soviets" (which would have been a reference to their ideology, since this was the USSR), but "Russians," singling out an ethnic group. The parliamentarians gave this a standing ovation, highlighting the common ground between the Nazis of yesteryear, the neo-Nazis of today, the Canadian parliamentarians and the rest—hatred of Russians, the driving force behind the Ukrainian conflict. For *not one of* our journalists has spoken out against the sanctions targeting the Russian population, the murders and assassinations of Russian personalities, the actions targeting Russian art and artists, even to the point of renaming paintings in our museums! *All* mainstream media journalists, without exception, have accepted a practice that seemed to have been forgotten since the Holocaust—condemning individuals for what they are, not for what they do.

Paradoxically, I don't associate the vast majority of Ukrainians with this hatred, because many of them don't share it, even though the war

8

polarizes people's minds. I also note that the Ukrainian press often contradicts what our journalists say.

That's why the incident at the Canadian parliament is more than an anecdote—it's the image of a Western political class adrift; of media without faith or law; of politicians and journalists who live off the blood of others, and, as we shall see, in particular that of Ukrainians.

This book—like its predecessors—is not about giving good points to one side or the other. It does not seek to justify either side in the conflict, but to explain what they are doing and why they are doing it.

Naturally, in an intellectual context where everything the Russians do is considered wrong, stupid and bad, explaining what they do is enough to be cast as an "apologist."

Like all conflicts, Ukraine was the scene of unbridled disinformation. The phenomenon is not unusual, but here it took on an almost cartoonish quality. From the outset, the Western narrative revolved around the idea that *"Russia cannot, and must not, win this war."*[5]

This is demonstrated by the hearing of Michel Goya, a colonel in the French army, before a committee of the French Senate in November 2022.[6] Without the slightest knowledge of Russian military doctrine, with a very limited understanding of the art of operations and even of the inner workings of the Atlantic Alliance, he analyzed the war in terms of what a French soldier would do. Beyond navel-gazing, he illustrates a very Western way of understanding war based on our own logic, not on that of our adversary. This is what led to the disasters of 1914 and 1940 in France, and to the failure of operations in the Middle East and Sahel.

At the hearing of General Bruno Clermont on December 7, 2022, Senator (LR) Cédric Perrin perfectly illustrated our inability to understand war in any other way than the way we do:[7]

The Russians made a monumental mistake at the outset... by not operating as Western doctrine would have it, i.e., by bombing the areas which today allow the Ukrainians to respond to them.

---

5. https://www.assemblee-nationale.fr/dyn/16/rapports/cion_def/l16b1111_rapport-informa-tion.pdf
6. https://youtu.be/CvAYOHc8sv4
7. "War in Ukraine: "It's a 20th-century war"", *Public Sénat/YouTube*, December 7, 2022 (https://youtu.be/kIJtZmzK1mc)

In other words, he was surprised that Russia doesn't apply our operational principles. The inability to imagine several solutions to the same problem, and to understand that *others* may have a different, or even more effective, solution, is an expression of Western ethnocentrism. This is exactly why Mali and Niger have asked French troops to leave their territory.

The particularity of this conflict is that, on the Western side, the aim was not to help Ukraine "win" it, but to force Russia to "lose" it. The ultimate aim is not so much to win back territory, as to bring about Vladimir Putin's downfall.

That's why, in August 2023, Ukraine's inability to carry out its counter-offensive made the West fear that it was *"losing control of its narrative."*[8] Worse, as the *New York Times* noted, *"U.S. officials say they fear Ukraine has become reluctant to take casualties."*[9]

This is what Andrés Manuel López Obrador, President of Mexico, summed up so lucidly in June 2022 about NATO and EU policy towards Ukraine[10]:

We supply the weapons; you supply the corpses! It's immoral!

For, from the Western point of view, the course of the conflict depends on the narrative. From the outset of the Russian operation in Ukraine, Western discourse created a false sense of superiority, leading Ukraine to underestimate the reality of the Russian threat.

We will seek to restore a balance to the information that our media and their so-called journalists have deliberately falsified. Deeply dishonest and bloodthirsty, they manage to contradict information that even Ukrainian journalists have given. In this conflict, by rejecting the deontology of the Munich Charter, our media have abandoned their ethics and their honor. Comfortably ensconced in their editorial offices, they have

8. Dan De Luce & Phil McCausland, "Is Ukraine's counteroffensive failing? Kyiv and its supporters worry about losing control of the narrative", *NBC News*, August 4, 2023 (https://www.nbcnews.com/news/investigations/ukraine-war-counteroffensive-russia-success-failure-rcna98054)
9. Helene Cooper, Thomas Gibbons-Neff, Eric Schmitt & Julian E. Barnes, "Troop Deaths and Injuries in Ukraine War Near 500,000, U.S. Officials Say," *The New York Times*, August 18, 2023 (https://www.nytimes.com/2023/08/18/us/politics/ukraine-russia-war-casualties.html)
10. "Mexican president slams NATO policy in Ukraine," *AP News*, June 13, 2022 (https://apnews.com/article/russia-ukraine-mexico-caribbean-nato-b9aaddc8e3da3ad2b2cc013a6e8ff4bb)

done everything in their power to ensure that the conflict is prolonged and lives wasted. And this responsibility predates February 24, 2022.

Our media and "experts" have literally pushed Ukraine into a conflict, denying it any negotiating option, but convincing it that Russia is an adversary, one that it is capable of defeating. They are the most detestable, and I hope this book will help make Ukrainians and Russians realize how dishonest they have been with them.

The misunderstanding of the conflict in Ukraine is partly the result of the intellectual and semantic muddle with which we try to explain it. Notions of strategy, tactics and—newly—"operative art" are boldly mixed together, making it possible to castigate the Russian approach and explain its impending "defeat"—which the West is still waiting for!

Today, the Western narrative has gradually collapsed before the reality of the facts, and what was described as conspiracism in 2022 has become reality.

As with any conflict, it can only be understood by trying to grasp the perceptions and logics of the protagonists. In the pages that follow, we will return to the way Russia sees and wages war. Our military's inability to understand the reality of the situation in Ukraine is not only worrying for the future of our armies, it is literally one of the main reasons for the Ukrainian defeat.

2. Russian Military Thought

Throughout the Cold War period, the Soviet Union saw itself as the spearhead of a historical struggle that would lead to a confrontation between the "capitalist" system and "progressive forces." This perception of a permanent and inescapable war led the Soviets to study war in a quasi-scientific way, and to structure this thinking into an architecture of military thought that has no equal in the Western world.

The problem with the vast majority of our so-called military experts is their inability to understand the Russian approach to war. It's the result of an approach we've already seen in waves of terrorist attacks— the adversary is so stupidly demonized that we fail to understand his way of thinking. As a result, we are unable to develop strategies, articulate our forces, or even equip them for the realities of war. The corollary of this approach is that our frustrations are translated by unscrupulous media into a narrative that feeds hatred and increases our vulnerability.[11] We are thus unable to find rational and effective solutions to the problem.

The way Russians understand conflict is holistic. In other words, they see the processes that develop and lead to the situation at any given moment. This explains why Vladimir Putin's speeches invariably include a return to history. In the West, we tend to focus on the immediate moment X and try to see how it might evolve. We want an immediate response to the situation we see right now. The idea that *"from the understanding of how the crisis arose comes the way to resolve it"* is totally foreign to the West. In September 2023, an English-language journalist even pulled out the

---

11. https://oumma.com/jacques-baud-lancien-espion-qui-aimait-poutine/

"duck test" for me: *"if it looks like a duck, swims like a duck and quacks like a duck, it's probably a duck."* In other words, all they need is an image that matches their prejudices to assess a situation.

The reality is far more subtle than the duck model. In *Newsweek*, an analyst at the *Defense Intelligence Agency* (DIA)—the American equivalent of France's *Direction du Renseignement Militaire* (DRM)—notes:[12]

> *The way in which Russia is waging this brutal war differs from the widely held view that Vladimir Putin wants to destroy Ukraine and inflict maximum civilian casualties, but rather reveals the Russian leader's strategic balancing act.*

The reason why the Russians are better than the West in Ukraine is that they see the conflict as a process, whereas we see it as a series of separate actions. The Russians see events as a film; we see them as photographs. They see the forest, while we focus on the trees. That's why we place the start of the conflict on February 24, 2022, or the start of the Palestinian conflict on October 7, 2023. We discard the contexts that bother us and wage conflicts we don't understand. That's why we lose our wars.

---

12. William M. Arkin, "Putin's Bombers Could Devastate Ukraine but He's Holding Back. Here's Why", *Newsweek*, March 22, 2022 (https://www.newsweek.com/putins-bombers-could-devastate-ukraine-hes-holding-back-heres-why-1690494)

Architecture of Russian military thought

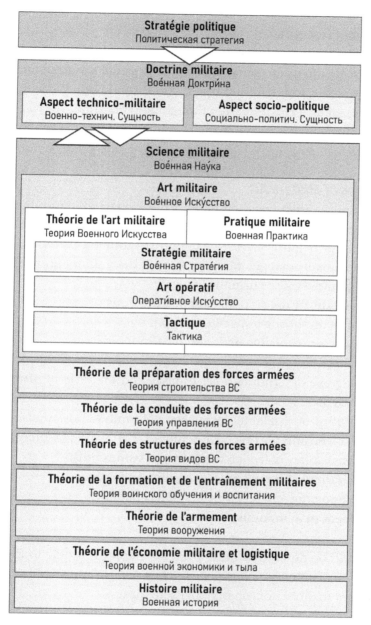

Figure 1—Current Russian military thinking is strongly influenced by the thinking that has been going on since the 1920s. It remains very logically constructed and is established in a quasi-scientific manner based on acquired experience.

Russian Military Doctrine

Doctrinal Elements

Russian military doctrine is the subject of a great deal of study and debate in Russia itself. Our Western perception of this thinking is extremely simplistic and distorted by the American prism. We will not deal here with all aspects of Russian thought and doctrine. We will concentrate on that which is linked to the Ukrainian conflict and the lessons we can learn from it.

Principles of Military Art

All countries articulate their military thinking or policy around general principles which guide the design of their defense and operations. The number of principles varies from country to country, and is very similar. In Russia, unsurprisingly, the principles of the military art of the Soviet forces[13] inspired those currently in use:[14]

- **availability** to carry out assigned missions;
- **focus** on solving a specific mission;
- **surprise** (unconventionality) of military action vis-à-vis the enemy;
- **purpose** determines a set of tasks and the level of resolution of each task;
- **totality** of available **resources** determines how the mission is resolved and the objective achieved (correlation of forces);
- **consistency** of leadership (**unity of command**);
- **economy of forces**, resources, time and space;
- **supporting** and restoring combat capability;
- **freedom to maneuver**.

It should be noted that these principles apply not only to the implementation of military action as such. They are also applicable as a system of thought to other non-operational activities.

---

13. https://irp.fas.org/doddir/army/fm100-2-1.pdf
14. Васильев Е.В. "О некоторых принципах военного искусства", *Военная мысль*, 2005, № 4. pp. 23-29

An honest analysis of the conflict in Ukraine would have identified these various principles and drawn useful conclusions for Ukraine. But none of the self-proclaimed experts on TV were intellectually able to do this.

Thus, Westerners are systematically surprised by the Russians in the fields of technology (e.g., hypersonic weapons), doctrine (e.g., operative art) and economics (e.g., resilience to sanctions). In a way, the Russians are taking advantage of our prejudices to exploit the principle of surprise. We can see this in the Ukrainian conflict, where the Western narrative led Ukraine to completely underestimate Russian capabilities, which was a major factor in its defeat. That's why Russia didn't really try to counter this narrative and let it play out—the belief that we are superior makes us vulnerable.

Force Correlation

Russian military thought is traditionally linked to a holistic approach to warfare, which involves the integration of a large number of factors in the development of a strategy. This approach is embodied in the concept of *"correlation of forces" (Соотношение сил)*. Often translated as "balance of forces" or "ratio of forces," this concept is understood by Westerners only as a quantity of a quantitative nature, limited to the military domain. However, in Soviet thought, the correlation of forces reflects a more holistic reading of war:[15]

> *There are several criteria for assessing the correlation of strengths. In the economic sphere, the factors usually compared are gross national product per capita, labor productivity, the dynamics of economic growth, the level of industrial production, particularly in high-tech sectors, the technical infrastructure of the production tool, the resources and degree of qualification of the workforce, the number of specialists and the level of development of theoretical and applied sciences.*
>
> *In the military field, the factors compared are the quantity and quality of armaments, the firepower of the armed forces, the fighting and moral qualities of the soldiers, the level of staff training, the organization of the troops and their combat experience, the*

---

15. Shakhnavzarov, G., "On the problem of Correlation of Forces in the World", *Kommunist*, No 3 (February 1974), p. 86

character of the military doctrine and the methods of strategic, operative and tactical thinking.

In the political sphere, the factors that come into consideration are the breadth of the social base of state authority, its organization, the constitutional procedure for relations between the government and legislative bodies, the ability to make operational decisions, and the degree and character of popular support for domestic and foreign policy.

Finally, in assessing the strength of the international movement, the factors taken into consideration are its quantitative composition, its influence with the masses, its position in the political life of each country, the principles and norms of relations between its components and the degree of their cohesion.

In other words, the assessment of the situation is not limited to the balance of forces on the battlefield, but takes into account all the elements that have an impact on the evolution of the conflict. Thus, for their Special Military Operation, the Russian authorities had planned the ability to support the war effort through the economy, without moving to a "war economy" regime. Thus, unlike in Ukraine, there was no interruption in the tax and welfare mechanisms.

This is why the sanctions applied on Russia in 2014 had a double positive effect. The first was the realization that they were not only a short-term problem, but above all a medium- and long-term opportunity. They encouraged Russia to produce goods it had previously preferred to buy abroad. The second was the signal that the West would increasingly use economic weapons as a means of pressure in the future. It therefore became imperative, for reasons of national independence and sovereignty, to prepare for more far-reaching sanctions affecting the country's economy.

In reality, it has long been known that sanctions do not work.[16] Logically enough, they had the opposite effect: acting as protectionist measures for Russia, which was thus able to consolidate its economy, as had been the case after the 2014 sanctions. A strategy of sanctions might have borne fruit if the Russian economy had indeed been the equivalent of the

16. https://elgar.blog/2022/02/11/do-sanctions-work/

Italian or Spanish economy, i.e., with a high level of debt; and if the entire planet had acted in unison to isolate Russia.

The inclusion of the correlation of forces in the decision-making process is a fundamental difference from Western decision-making processes, which are linked more to a policy of communication than to a rational approach to problems.

This explains, for example, Russia's limited objectives in Ukraine, where it is not seeking to occupy the entire territory, as the correlation of forces in the western part of the country would be unfavorable to it.

At each control level, force correlation is part of situation assessment. At the operational level, it is defined as follows:[17]

> *The result of comparing the quantitative and qualitative charac-teristics of the forces and resources (sub-units, units, weapons, military equipment, etc.) of one's own troops (forces) and those of the enemy. It is calculated on an operational and tactical scale throughout the area of operations, in the main and other directions, in order to determine the degree of objective superiority of one of the opposing camps. Assessing the correlation of forces enables you to make an informed decision about an operation (battle), and to establish and maintain the necessary superiority over the enemy for as long as possible when decisions are redefined (modified) during military (combat) operations.*

This simple definition is the reason why the Russians committed themselves with forces inferior to those of Ukraine in February 2022, or why they withdrew from Kiev, Kharkov and Kherson in March, September and October 2022—we'll come back to this later.

Nuclear War

Ongoing Evolution

In 1945, the USSR won the race to Berlin. It emerged victorious from the war, but unlike the United States, it was bloodless. In the United States and Great Britain, some leaders saw this as an opportunity to resume

---

17. https://encyclopedia.mil.ru/encyclopedia/dictionary/details.htm?id=10162@morfDictionary

the offensive towards Moscow, since it was thought that Stalin had the same intention towards the Atlantic. But the time was not ripe for the resumption of hostilities, and the Cold War began.

Today, those who claim that Russia has expansionist intentions are simply transposing—without taking the context into account—the Marxist thinking that guided Soviet policy. In this scheme, the USSR saw itself as the spearhead of the class struggle, engaged in a permanent and systemic war with the West as part of a historical process of struggle against capitalism. Until Stalin's death, the USSR's strategic military thinking was dominated by the idea that its security would only be guaranteed by a victory of socialism over capitalism, and that confrontation between the two systems was inevitable. Soviet strategists spoke of the principle of the *"inevitability of war"* (неизбежность *войны*). This idea remained until the 20th Congress of the Communist Party of the Soviet Union in February 1956, when, under the impetus of Nikita Khrushchev, the USSR adopted the principle of "peaceful coexistence." From then on, this was known as the "non-inevitability of war."

This did not prevent Westerners from preparing for possible Soviet aggression, although American documents, now declassified, show that the Soviets had no intention of invading Europe:[18]

> *Recently declassified Soviet documents, articles and minutes of meetings indicate that the Soviet leadership had no intention of invading Europe[19].*

In the USSR, on the other hand, the fear of new Western invasion attempts on its territory remained very real, prompting it to adopt a policy of dissuasion:[20]

---

18. Dr. Mahir J. Ibrahimov, Mr. Gustav A. Otto & Col Lee G. Gentile, Jr, "Cultural Perspectives, Geopolitics & Energy Security of Eurasia: Is the Next Global Conflict Imminent?", *US Army Command and General Staff College Press*, Fort Leavenworth, 2017 (https://www.armyupress.army.mil/Portals/7/combat-studies-institute/csi-books/cultural-perspectives.pdf)

19. Raymond Garthoff, Deterrence and the Revolution in Soviet Military Doctrine, *The Brookings Institute*, Washington D.C., 1990, p. 11

20. Vladislav Zubok, *The Kremlin's Cold War: From Stalin to Khrushchev*, Harvard University Press, Boston, 1997, p. 20

However, the experiences of the First and Second World Wars gave rise to fears that the West would invade the USSR if it appeared militarily weak.

In 1949, the USSR acquired nuclear weapons. This led to the creation of NATO the same year, with the aim of placing Western Europe under the US nuclear umbrella. At this stage, nuclear war was mainly considered at the strategic level, and tactical nuclear weapons were not yet on the agenda. The risk was that the two nuclear powers would be pushed towards direct confrontation and nuclear exchange resulting in *Mutual Assured Destruction* (MAD).

The Indivisibility of Safety

One of the special features of nuclear weapons is that they can cause considerable, even existential, damage, leaving no time to find a response, or even to exploit a final negotiating space.

The asymmetrical situation of the USA and Russia means that the former can use Europe as a "buffer zone," while Russia could very quickly find itself faced with an existential problem. This is why, since the end of the Second World War, a constant feature of Russia's defense policy has been to maintain a "buffer zone" between NATO and its territory (also known as the "*glacis*" in French and the "*Vorfeld*" in German), the aim being to give more space to a conventional conflict and prevent it from becoming nuclear too quickly.

During the Cold War, the Warsaw Treaty Organization (known in the West as the "Warsaw Pact") constituted this space. With NATO's eastward expansion and the progressive denunciation of disarmament treaties by the United States since 2002, this space has disappeared. For this reason, Russia has modified its doctrine of nuclear engagement, enabling it to make more rapid use of nuclear weapons.

It's important to emphasize here that Russia is less afraid of NATO's expansion than of the United States' exploitation of it.

In 1952, Turkey's accession to NATO brought the Alliance close to the USSR, alarming the Soviets. However, they did not react. It was only nine years later, when the Americans deployed PGM-19 JUPITER nuclear missiles in Turkey, that the crisis erupted. At the time, the Americans did not yet have the technology to build intercontinental missiles, and the JUPITERs were only an improved version of the German V2s, with a range of 2,400 to 2,700 km.

Americans don't like it when people do to them what they do to others. The Soviets understood this and began deploying missiles in Cuba, triggering a violent U.S. reaction known as the "Cuban Missile Crisis" in 1962. Eventually, the Americans, caught up in their own game, were forced to withdraw their missiles from Turkey. The USSR won.

Until the early 2000s, new NATO members were accepted with euphoria and without any strategic reflection, because Russia and China were weak. Today, the situation is radically different—the problem is that the legitimate security concerns of European countries are bringing American nuclear power closer to the Russian border, increasing the likelihood of nuclear war in the event of heightened tension. The problems of one country can quickly become those of the whole Alliance, as in 1914.

In 2002, when the USA withdrew from the Anti-Ballistic Missile Treaty (ABM Treaty) and began negotiations with Poland, the Czech Republic and Romania to install dual-use launchers (anti-ballistic and nuclear), the Russians perceived a direct threat. This is what Vladimir Putin said in Munich in 2007, and what he underlined at his press conference with Emmanuel Macron in Moscow on February 7, 2022. The problem is that we're not listening to what he's telling us.

This is not a completely new issue. It was already identified in 1949 by the authors of the Washington Treaty, NATO's founding act, article 10 of which states that

> the Parties may, by unanimous agreement, invite to accede to the Treaty any other European State likely to promote the development of the principles of the present Treaty and to contribute to the security of the North Atlantic area. Any State so invited may become a Party to the Treaty by depositing its instrument of accession with the Government of the United States of America. The latter will inform each of the Parties of the deposit of each instrument of accession.

In other words, countries are "invited," insofar as they can *"contribute to the security of the North Atlantic region."* Clearly, the criterion is not the security of each individual member country, but the collective security of the region.

This is what the "new Europe" countries have failed to understand. They were accepted into NATO at a time when Russia was weakened. Today, NATO offers them a kind of insurance, under whose shelter they pursue ultra-nationalist and discriminatory policies towards their Russian-speaking minorities, with the declared aim of provoking Russia. In fact, their membership of NATO and the EU is fundamentally destabilizing for the European continent. In fact, even within the NATO military, their reputation is particularly bad, as I have seen.

This also means that, potentially, every country in the Euro-Atlantic area can be a member, but that the Alliance is under no obligation to accept every country that wishes to join. This is one of the reasons why Ukraine's entry into NATO is so hotly debated within the Alliance itself.

But an essential principle of Russian security policy is that of the "*indivisibility of security*" (*неделимость безопасности*).[21] It is not exclusively Russian and has been accepted by OSCE members and is enshrined in the *Istanbul Document* (1999)[22] and the *Astana Declaration* (2010):[23]

> *The safety of each participating state is inextricably linked to that of all the others.*

In other words, the security of one country cannot be achieved at the expense of another. One example was the presence of the French tactical nuclear PLUTON missiles, then the HADES, which threatened the existence of "friendly" populations in Germany and Switzerland.[24]

However, when NATO—and the United States in particular—deploys armaments, thereby reducing the warning and early-warning times of a neighboring country (in this case, Russia), this principle is not respected.

What bothers the Russians, therefore, is not so much the proximity of NATO, as the willingness of the Americans to deploy nuclear weapons

---

21. http://www.kremlin.ru/acts/news/70811
22. https://www.osce.org/files/f/documents/0/2/39570.pdf
23. https://www.osce.org/files/f/documents/b/3/74987.pdf
24. "Atomziel Württemberg?", *Der Spiegel*, July 20, 1975 (https://magazin.spiegel.de/EpubDelivery/spiegel/pdf/41458263)

there.[25] This is because the installation of nuclear weapons "point-blank" makes it virtually impossible to implement a bilateral crisis management mechanism. Indeed, it was in the wake of the Cuban crisis that the famous "red telephone" was set up between Washington and Moscow—neither a telephone let alone a red telephone, but an emergency communication channel designed to facilitate crisis management.

What's astonishing is that Westerners don't seem to have perceived this risk. NATO's advance has been seen as a geographical success, but no strategic conclusions have been drawn. And yet, by moving closer to the Russian border, NATO is also removing its own early warning capability. The *RAND Corporation* has clearly warned the US government of this problem:[26]

> *While placing strike assets close to Russia would reduce the time available to Russian military commanders to detect and respond to air and cruise missile attacks, it would leave US and allied commanders even less time to detect and respond to Russian missile attacks against assets currently located at these bases. This combination of mutual vulnerability and risk of surprise attack could be seriously destabilizing in the event of a crisis, particularly if tactical nuclear weapons are also stored at nearby sites.*

Deploying missiles close to the Russian border has nothing whatsoever to do with NATO's defensive—or non-defensive—vocation, as the Alliance runs exactly the same risk. This is what Vladimir Putin tried to explain in his press conference on February 7, 2022, following Emmanuel Macron's visit to Moscow.

On March 25, 2023, on the occasion of Alexander Lukashenko's visit to Russia, Vladimir Putin declared on the *Rossiya 24* channel that the Belarusian president had asked him to deploy "*tactical nuclear weapons*" on its territory.[27] The reason given was Britain's decision to

25. https://www.mid.ru/tv/?id=1744872&lang=ru
26. James Dobbins, Raphael S. Cohen, Nathan Chandler, Bryan Frederick, Edward Geist, Paul DeLuca, Forrest E. Morgan, Howard J. Shatz, Brent Williams, "Extending Russia: Competing from Advantageous Ground", *RAND Corporation*, 2019
27. "Белоруссия давно просит у России ядерное оружие", *Vesti.ru*, March 25, 2023 (https://www.vesti.ru/article/3268612)

supply depleted uranium anti-tank shells.[28] But—as always—the reality is more complex.

First of all, Vladimir Putin is merely repeating Lukashenko's words, as the Russians make no doctrinal distinction between tactical, operational and strategic nuclear weapons. Moreover, the weapons mentioned have ranges in excess of 1,000 km, whereas—traditionally—nuclear weapons with ranges of 150 to 500 km are considered tactical.

The Belarussian request came after a number of events that our media carefully avoided mentioning—notably the attitude of Poland, nostalgic for its past greatness and seeking to reconstitute the Intermarium.[29] It has its sights set on the western part of Belarus, which it considers to belong to it historically, and whose reconquest is part of its security policy.[30] This is why it supports the opposition in Belarus politically, materially and ostensibly, with the blessing of the USA. On January 11, 2023, the signing of a joint declaration by Poland, Ukraine and Lithuania forming the Lublin Triangle, a military mini-alliance linked to NATO, worried Lukashenko.[31]

Moreover, as the situation in Ukraine deteriorated and Russia's predicted collapse faded, the U.S. began to work on "regime change" in Belarus, in order to achieve a small "success." On March 22, 2023, Wendy Sherman, Assistant Secretary of State, met with Svetlana Tikhanovskaya, leader of the Belarusian militant opposition, to coordinate their actions. As the American media outlet *The Atlantic Council*[32] pointed out, the United States is seeking to instrumentalize the Belarusian opposition for the benefit of Ukraine.

But another, more significant event explains the Russian decision—the deployment, at the end of February 2023, of four American strategic nuclear bombers of the B-52H STRATOFORTRESS type at Moron air

28. https://www.rts.ch/play/tv/redirect/detail/13894210
29. Emil Avdaliani, "Poland and the Success of its 'Intermarium' Project," *moderndiplomacy.eu*, March 31, 2019
30. Jacek Bartosiak, "Belarus as a Pivot of Poland's Grand Strategy," *The Jamestown Foundation*, December 16, 2020 (https://jamestown.org/program/belarus-as-a-pivot-of-polands-grand-strategy/)
31. "Presidents of Ukraine, Lithuania and Poland signed the Joint Declaration following the Second Summit of the Lublin Triangle in Lviv", *website of the President of Ukraine*, January 11, 2023 (https://www.president.gov.ua/en/news/u-lvovi-prezidenti-ukrayini-litvi-ta-polshi-pidpisa-li-spilnu-80313)
32. Stephen Nix & Mark Dietzen, "The Belarusian opposition can help defeat Putin in Ukraine", *The Atlantic Council*, February 7, 2023 (https://www.atlanticcouncil.org/blogs/ukrainealert/the-belarusian-opposition-can-help-defeat-putin-in-ukraine/)

2. Russian Military Thought

base (Spain) *"to send a message to Russia."*[33] On March 11, 2023, one of these aircraft (call sign: NOBLE61) carried out a simulated nuclear attack (*missile strike drill*) against the city of St. Petersburg from the Gulf of Finland.[34] Reported by the Russian opposition website *Meduza*[35] on the same day, the information was—obviously—not picked up by any mainstream Western media. Yet it was probably what prompted Vladimir Putin, two weeks later, to accede to President Lukashenko's request to deploy nuclear weapons on Belarusian territory.[36]

Russia's decision was the occasion for further elucidations by our "experts," who played with words. Swiss expert Alexandre Vautravers declared on *RTS* that this was an arms *transfer*, which would contravene the Nuclear Non-Proliferation Treaty (NPT).[37] Not true. As confirmed on the same day by the Russian opposition media *Meduza*, Vladimir Putin clarified that this was not a *transfer* but only a *deployment*.[38] The essential difference is that these weapons remain under Russia's exclusive authority. In other words, Russia is no different from the USA, with its nuclear weapons depots in Germany, Belgium, the Netherlands and Turkey.

Russia is replaying the Cuban missile scenario in Belarus. As the same causes have the same effects, the American administration did an about-face. On June 2, 2023, Jake Sullivan, Joe Biden's National Security Advisor, declared:[39]

---

33. Tom Dunlop, "American B-52 bombers overfly Estonia in message to Russia", *UK Defence Journal*, March 3, 2023 (https://ukdefencejournal.org.uk/american-b-52-bombers-overfly-estonia-in-message-to-russia/)

34. David Cenciotti, "Let's Have A Look At B-52's Mission Over The Baltics And Close To Russia Yesterday," *The Aviationist*, March 12, 2023 (https://theaviationist.com/2023/03/12/lets-have-a-look-at-b-52s-mission-over-the-baltics-and-close-to-russia-yesterday/)

35. "An American B-52 bomber capable of carrying nuclear weapons conducted planned maneuvers over the Baltic Sea," *Meduza.io*, March 12, 2023 (https://meduza.io/en/news/2023/03/12/an-american-b-52-bomber-capable-of-carrying-nuclear-weapons-conducted-planned-maneuvers-over-the-baltic-sea)

36. Jones Hayden, "Putin says Russia to deploy tactical nuclear weapons in Belarus," *Politico*, March 25, 2023 (https://www.politico.eu/article/putin-says-russia-to-deploy-tactical-nuclear-weapons-in-belarus-reports/)

37. https://www.rts.ch/play/tv/redirect/detail/13894210

38. "Путин пообещал разместить тактическое ядерное оружие в Беларуси. ЕС пригрозил санкциями, Украина потребовала созвать заседание Совбеза ООН", *medusa.io*, March 26, 2023 (https://meduza.io/feature/2023/03/26/putin-poobeschal-razmestit-takticheskoe-yadernoe-oruzhie-v-belarusi-v-germanii-zayavili-chto-rossiya-prodolzhaet-yadernoe-zapugivanie)

39. "White House wants to engage Russia on nuclear arms control in post-treaty world," *PBS News*, June 2, 2023 (https://www.pbs.org/newshour/politics/white-house-wants-to-engage-russia-on-nuclear-arms-control-in-post-treaty-world)

The Biden administration is ready to discuss unconditionally with Russia a future nuclear arms control framework.

As in the Cuban crisis, the Americans only understand the hard way: instead of trying to bring about change through cooperation—as was successfully done during the Cold War—they try to do it through confrontation and exclusion.

Russian Nuclear Doctrine

On *France 5* on October 27, 2022, in a program devoted to the "dirty bomb" that Russia accused Ukraine of developing, criminologist Alain Bauer explained that the Russians consider tactical nuclear weapons to be conventional weapons.[40] This is totally false.

In fact, Russian doctrine does not single out *tactical* nuclear weapons. Russia has a range of nuclear weapons of varying strengths, to be used according to circumstances and objectives. But they consider the use of nuclear weapons—whatever their strength—to be of a strategic nature, as they can provoke a nuclear escalation.

In an article on this subject, Diego A. Ruiz Palmer, Head of the Comparative Assessment Section of NATO's Defense Policy and Planning Division, recalled that the Soviets saw the use of nuclear weapons only as a last resort:[41]

As early as 1966, the Central Intelligence Agency had identified a growing Soviet interest in conducting military operations without the use of nuclear weapons.

This was demonstrated by the DNIEPR 67 maneuvers, and confirmed by the *Soviet Union's "growing preference for a purely conventional option."*

The Soviets realized that the use of theater nuclear weapons could only complicate operations. Russia has always favored maneuver and rapid progress as its main operational and tactical principles. They are there-

---

40. Program "C dans l'air", "Bombe sale": que prépare Poutine? #cdanslair 27.10.2022", *France 5/ YouTube*, October 28, 2022 (https://youtu.be/1Ub3buKx-yg?t=153)
41. Diego A. Ruiz Palmer, "The NATO-Warsaw Pact competition in the 1970s and 1980s: a revolution in military affairs in the making or the end of a strategic age?", *Cold War History*, September 3, 2014, (DOI: 10.1080/14682745.2014.950250)

fore gradually abandoning the idea of using tactical nuclear weapons in favor of new conventional weapons.[42] This is what we see today with super- or hypersonic-speed missiles. Russian operative art and tactics are therefore not based on nuclear weapons, but on concepts such as concentration of forces on the main axis, partial victory and economy of forces.[43]

The concept of tactical nuclear weapons was essentially developed by the Americans in the 1960s, in order to distinguish between weapons that could be used on the European continent and those that could affect the United States. To avoid reaching the point of nuclear holocaust (MAD) too quickly, strategies were devised to control a possible nuclear escalation. Both East and West equipped themselves with weapons that would keep the prospect of MAD at bay.

In 1967, NATO adopted the *"flexible response"* strategy. Its purpose was to make it clear to the Soviets that the United States would not move directly and automatically to a strategic nuclear exchange. Indeed, despite its evolution over time and technologies, U.S. nuclear strategy retains one constant element—keeping the use of nuclear weapons off U.S. soil. This is why the Americans advocate a return of these weapons to the European theater,[44] and why they are so insistent on the idea that the Russians are seeking to use tactical nuclear weapons in Ukraine.

The difference in approach between the two superpowers is explained by the profoundly asymmetrical geostrategic situations of the USA and Russia. The USA can reach Russian territory with tactical/operational nuclear weapons, while Russia can only reach American soil with strategic or intermediate-range weapons. So, in the event of a major conflict, to avoid a strategic nuclear exchange affecting their territory, the USA would seek to keep a nuclear conflict in the European theater. To do this, they would carefully avoid directly hitting Russian national soil, so as not to trigger a "strategic duel" with Russia.

Paradoxically, this dissymmetrical situation is also asymmetrical. By keeping the nuclear exchange at a tactical level, Russia can use low-

42. James M. McConnell, *"The Soviet Shift in Emphasis from Nuclear to Conventional"*, Center for Naval Analyses, Department of the Navy, Monterey (CA), June 1983 (CRC490-VOl. II)
43. https://nuke.fas.org/guide/russia/doctrine/intro.htm
44. "Nonstrategic NuclearWeapons," *Congressional Research Service (CRS)*, Washington DC, January 17, 2019 (updated March 7, 2022) (https://fas.org/sgp/crs/nuke/RL32572.pdf)

intensity weapons in Europe, while the United States can only respond by striking the territory of its allies. It was this paradox that led to the Euromissile crisis in the early 1980s, and gave rise to the pacifist and anti-nuclear movement in Germany and Northern Europe. It culminated in the signing of the Intermediate-Range Nuclear Forces Treaty (INF Treaty).

Russian nuclear doctrine short-circuited American reasoning by declaring that no distinction can be made between tactical and strategic. Thus, the use of nuclear weapons on European soil (and *a fortiori* against Russia) could trigger an intercontinental retaliation. This is the essence of Russia's nuclear deterrent.

Russia has adopted the USSR's consistent *no-first-use* policy. On the other hand, it has not specified—as France has—how it intends to deal with an escalation. This is the principle of deterrence.

Russia's nuclear doctrine envisages the use of nuclear weapons only in the event of an existential threat to the Russian state, as specified in the presidential decree of June 2, 2020:[45]

> *The Russian Federation reserves the right to use nuclear weapons in response to the use of nuclear weapons and other weapons of mass destruction against it and/or its allies, as well as in the event of aggression against the Russian Federation using conventional weapons, when the very existence of the State is threatened.*

The problem, in a nuclear exchange over short distances, and therefore with short warning times, is to determine when the country is under existential threat, and therefore when to react. For this reason, the 2020 edition of Russia's nuclear doctrine somewhat lowered the level at which Russia can consider the use of nuclear weapons. Funnily enough, this is what Sweden and Finland have failed to understand—their request to join NATO has been widely applauded, but in the event of war, these countries could be the first to be pre-emptively nuclearized.

---

45. Presidential Decree No. 355 of June 2, 2020 "On the foundations of the state policy of the Russian Federation in the field of nuclear deterrence" (http://www.consultant.ru/document/cons_doc_LAW_354057/752b5672d30c8f49fddf240797c7daca7e53d781/)

This is probably what motivated President Joe Biden's decision, at the end of March 2022, to abandon the *no-first-use* principle for nuclear weapons.[46] Until then, the United States had considered the use of nuclear weapons solely for deterrence purposes (the *sole purpose* policy). But Joe Biden's decision *"leaves open the option of using nuclear weapons not only in retaliation for a nuclear attack, but also to respond to* non-nuclear *threats."*[47] Obviously, no Western media reported this major change in US nuclear policy. For example, the annual *Swiss Security Report*,[48] published in September 2022 by the Swiss Federal Intelligence Service (SRC), says not a word about it!

For the sake of clarity, we use English strategic terminology here, which is more refined than French terminology:[49]

- A *pre-emptive* strike is launched when a confrontation is unavoidable and it is thought that the adversary might strike.
- A *pre-emptive* strike is triggered when there are concrete indications that the adversary is going to strike (in the case of nuclear weapons, based on observations from surveillance satellites).
- *Launch-on-Warning* is a shot fired while the opponent has already launched a missile and it's still in the air.

As Vladimir Putin made clear at the Eurasian Economic Union summit in Bishkek (Kyrgyzstan) in December 2022,[50] the principle of nuclear engagement remains *Launch on Warning* (LOW). In other words, the triggering of nuclear watch systems on alert.

In other words, while the Russians only plan to use nuclear weapons first in the event of an existential threat, the Americans allow themselves to do so at any time. As a result, Russia would use nuclear weapons, if Moscow and the country's institutions were directly threatened. For

46. Daryl G. Kimball, "Biden Policy Allows First Use of Nuclear Weapons," *Arms Control Today*, April 29, 2022 (https://www.armscontrol.org/act/2022-04/news/biden-policy-allows-first-use-nuclear-weapons)

47. Daryl G. Kimball, "Biden Policy Allows First Use of Nuclear Weapons," *Arms Control Association*, April 29, 2022 (https://www.armscontrol.org/act/2022-04/news/biden-policy-allows-first-use-nuclear-weapons)

48. https://www.newsd.admin.ch/newsd/message/attachments/72369.pdf

49. Karl P. Mueller... [et al.], "Striking first: preemptive and preventive attack in U.S. national security policy", *RAND Corporation*, 2006 (https://www.rand.org/content/dam/rand/pubs/monographs/2006/RAND_MG403.pdf)

50. "Putin says Russia could adopt US preemptive strike concept," *AP News*, December 9, 2022 (https://apnews.com/article/putin-moscow-strikes-united-states-government-russia-95f1436d23b94fcbc-05f1c2242472d5c)

example, a Ukrainian attack on Crimea would most likely not be consi-dered existential for the Russian state. On the other hand, the USA could use nuclear weapons if one of its military bases came under attack.

Diagram of nuclear decision and response mechanisms

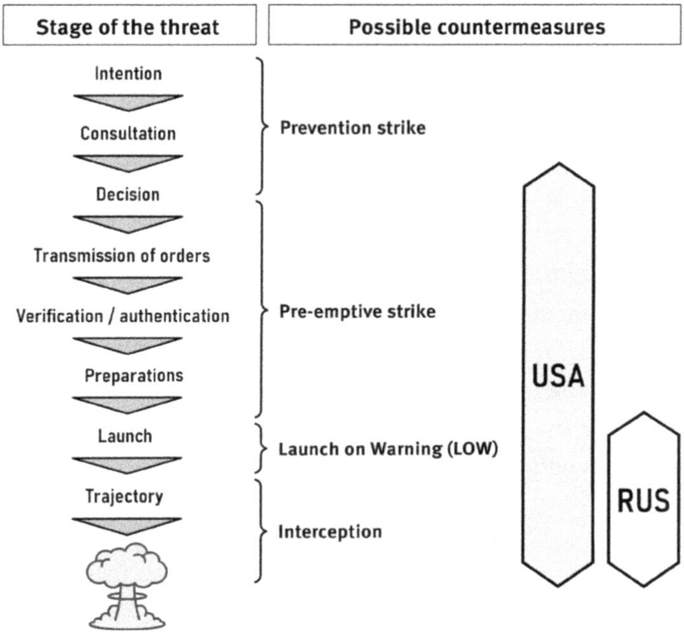

Figure 2—Joe Biden's decision to abandon the no-first-use policy allows the USA to carry out pre-emptive (or even pre-emptive) strikes, while Russia restricts itself to LOW strikes, which some see as part of pre-emptive strikes.

In October 2022, Volodymyr Zelensky inflamed passions by proposing to strike Russia to prevent the use of nuclear weapons:[51]

> *What should NATO do? Make it impossible for Russia to commit nuclear weapons. But the important thing is that I again call on the international community, as before the 24th (February 2022) to strike pre-emptively so that they know what will happen to*

---

51. https://www.newsweek.com/zelensky-nuclear-putin-russia-war-pre-emptive-1749781

them if they use them, and not, on the contrary, wait for Russia's nuclear strikes.

Our media and *fact-checkers* then tried to water down Zelensky's speech. On the media site *20minutes.fr*, the expression *"preventive strike"* (превентивний удар) clearly uttered by Zelensky became *"preventive measures,"*[52] which is literally disinformation. The claim that Zelensky is ready to start a nuclear conflict is denied by stating that he did not mention *"nuclear strikes."* This is true, but irrelevant. It doesn't matter what kind of weapon he had in mind, because Russian nuclear doctrine provides for:[53]

> *19. The conditions determining the possibility of the use of nuclear weapons by the Russian Federation are as follows:*
> *a) receipt of reliable information on the launch of ballistic missiles attacking the territories of the Russian Federation and/or its allies;*
> *b) the use by the enemy of nuclear weapons or other weapons of mass destruction on the territory of the Russian Federation and/or its allies;*
> *c) enemy action on critical state or military facilities of the Russian Federation, the disabling of which would disrupt the response of nuclear forces;*
> *d) aggression against the Russian Federation using conventional weapons, when the very existence of the State is threatened.*

Zelensky's statements clearly fall within the scope of paragraph c). For—probably unaware of the scope of his speech—he called for a strike *"that makes the use of nuclear weapons impossible."* Which, for Russia, could be precisely the reason to use them. Once again, our media are lying.

The problem is that they systematically conceal information that could help us understand the situation. Let's recall here that during the conflict with Ukraine, contrary to what Jean-Philippe Schaller, a Swiss

---

52. https://www.20minutes.fr/monde/ukraine/4004256-20221007-volodymyr-zelensky-appele-utiliser-arme-nucleaire-contre-russie-faux
53. http://kremlin.ru/acts/bank/45562

"journalist" accustomed to conspiracy,[54] claimed, Vladimir Putin never mentioned nuclear weapons before Western leaders threatened to use them, like Liz Truss, then candidate for British Prime Minister, who declared herself ready to unleash a *"global annihilation."*[55] But the same journalist suggested that Russia wanted to use chemical weapons in Ukraine[56] without any evidence. Here, we have the creation of *fake news* for the purposes of influence.

Hybrid Warfare

Russia's hybrid war is a carefully nurtured myth in the West, to which everyone has their own definition. It has become a catch-all "concept,"[57] which our media and politicians (and even our generals!) use to give an apparent coherence to events which, on the face of it, have nothing to do with each other.[58] In technical terms, it's conspiracism.

In 2017, Vladimir Putin told *Le Figaro:*[59]

> *You mustn't invent imaginary threats from Russia, hybrid wars, or other such specters; you've invented them yourselves. You're scaring yourselves, and you're basing your policies on this imaginary data.*

The idea that Russia would have developed such a concept of "hybrid warfare" is based on the interpretation of an article written in 2013 by Valery Gerasimov, Chief of the Russian General Staff, in an article entitled, *"The Value of Science in Foresight."*[60]

In fact, the original article was published in the *Journal of the Academy of Military Sciences* on January 26, 2013 under the title, "Main trends in the development of forms and methods of employing armed forces and

---

54. https://pages.rts.ch/emissions/geopolitis/12938579-armes-la-course.html
55. https://www.independent.co.uk/news/uk/politics/liz-truss-nuclear-button-ready-b2151614.html; https://youtu.be/IvH7cgbdazU
56. https://www.rts.ch/play/tv/redirect/detail/13027609
57. François Heisbourg, "Ukraine: a 'hybrid war', really?", *Ouest-France*, December 22, 2022 (https://www.ouest-france.fr/monde/guerre-en-ukraine/point-de-vue-ukraine-une-guerre-hybride-vraiment-c87142da-813d-11ed-a33c-a84555e230e2)
58. Nathalie Loiseau on "C dans l'air", October 17, 2021 ("Poutine, maître du jeu #cdanslair 17.10.2021", *France 5/YouTube*, October 18, 2021) (1h18'07")
59. https://video.lefigaro.fr/figaro/video/vladimir-poutine-l-interview-exclusive/5453365155001/
60. Герасимов Валерий, "Ценность науки в предвидении," *vpk-news.ru*, February 26, 2013 (https://vpk-news.ru/articles/14632)

the current tasks of military science to improve them."[61] It describes the evolution of wars as waged by the West against the Arab world, and the word "hybrid" does not appear in it.

In fact, the term "hybrid warfare" originated in the West. Pseudo-experts and other journalists have tried to describe it without being able to understand what it might be, giving us a fuzzy, impalpable concept. After the Ukrainian crisis of 2014, Westerners were trying to make sense of a "Russian invasion" without Russian troops; a democratic revolution by far-right nationalist or even neo-Nazi militants; the legitimacy of a government that governed without having been elected, and so on. We then constructed a logic that brought together cyberwarfare, terrorism, clandestine warfare, conventional warfare and, naturally, information warfare. Gerasimov's article then became the key to reading naturally incoherent events.

Our journalists thus artificially created a "doctrinal basis," which *Le Point* magazine claimed was "*validated by Vladimir Putin*" himself.[62] We don't really know whether to condemn the journalist's racism or imbecility.

In fact, the concept of "hybrid warfare" does not exist in Russian military thinking, and Russia has never theorized or invoked it. The problem came from Russia specialist Mark Galeotti, who first commented on Gerasimov's article and deduced from it the existence of a "*Gerasimov Doctrine*," supposedly illustrating the Russian concept of hybrid war.[63] But in 2018, realizing the damage he had unwittingly caused, Galeotti apologized—bravely and intelligently—in an article entitled, "I'm sorry I created the Gerasimov Doctrine," published in *Foreign Policy* magazine:[64]

I was the first to write about Russia's infamous high-tech military strategy. One small problem: it doesn't exist.

---

61. Valeri V. Gerasimov. "Main trends in the development of forms and methods of employment of armed forces and current tasks of military science to improve them" (Основные тенденции развития форм и способов применения Вооруженных Сил, актуальные задачи военной науки по их совершенствованию), *Journal of the Academy of Military Sciences*, No. 1, January 26, 2013
62. Marc Nexon, "Gerasimov, le général russe qui mène la guerre de l'information," *Le Point*, March 2, 2017.
63. Mark Galeotti, "The 'Gerasimov Doctrine' and Russian Non-Linear War," *inmoscowsshadows. wordpress.com*, June 7, 2014.
64. Mark Galeotti, "I'm Sorry for Creating the 'Gerasimov Doctrine," *Foreign Policy*, March 5, 2018.

To understand the idea of hybrid warfare, we need to go back to the typology of warfare. Without going into too much detail, "conventional" warfare is what we've known since the Second World War, and for which our armies have prepared themselves. It's a war that uses a combination of land, air and naval means to achieve objectives. Forces are engaged as a system. This is what is known as third-generation warfare, of which the *Blitzkrieg*, waged by the Germans in 1939—1940, is the archetypal example.

Typology of Wars Based on Technology

Type of war	Brief description
1st generation	Close combat between individuals with simple weapons (sword, shield, etc.)
2nd generation	Use of modern weapons (rifle, machine gun, artillery, aviation), but not yet in an integrated manner (World War I)
3rd generation	Integration of weapons into a combat system (combined arms) (World War II, Blitzkrieg)
4th generation	Non-linear combat by non-state actors (guerrilla, terrorism, etc.) (Iraq, Afghanistan)
5th generation	Non-kinetic combat in the field of information technology and perception management (Ukrainian Army 2022-)

Figure 3—Typology of wars. In Russian military thinking, there is no such thing as a hybrid type of war. On the other hand, the confrontation of two different types of war can result in a "hybrid confrontation." In a way, this is the case in Ukraine, where a 3rd generation war (on the Russian side) and a 5th generation war (on the Ukrainian and Western side) are confronting each other. The "hybrid" character is therefore not a "strategy", but a state of affairs between two war logics.

At the end of the Cold War, when Western armies were engaged in insurgency-type conflicts (against interventions they had themselves created), they were confronted by more rustic forces, even rudimentary guerrillas. These were the wars of the 4th generation.

5th generation wars are said to be "non-kinetic," i.e., they take place without any real contact with the adversary. Cyberwarfare, subversion and information warfare seek to subjugate the adversary by causing the collapse of his system. Although elements of this type of warfare have been present in every conflict since 1939, it remains largely a figment of the imagination. This is the vision of the war Ukraine expected to wage with Russia. Everyone (and common sense) knew that the Ukrainian army was in no position to defeat Russia on its own. The idea was to defeat Russia through a combination of sanctions, political and cultural economic isolation, and a narrative that would turn Russia into a pariah state.

For the Russians, the vision is much clearer: hybrid war is not a form of war that we choose, but the result of confrontation between two countries or entities that use different types of war.[65] Thus, the confrontation between Russia and Ukraine is hybrid in nature, because Ukraine is trying to practice 5th generation warfare, while Russia is in a 3rd generation conflict.

In his article, Gerasimov analyzes the recent evolution of Western-led conflicts and draws lessons on how to integrate them into military thinking. His article is a methodological approach, not a description of how Russia would have incorporated these lessons into its doctrine.

The concept of "hybrid war" offers an indefinite space that allows self-proclaimed "experts" of all stripes to create coherence around (mostly unverified) allegations and give "logic" to actions attributed to Russia. Westerners insist on explaining a conflict by a doctrine that doesn't exist, and our "experts" imagine chimerical conflicts, such as a *"project to destabilize the European Union."*[66]

In November 2022, *TV5 Monde* and *CAP Europe* analyst Christine Dugoin-Clément give us examples of Moscow's "hybrid war."[67] But when we compare these examples with reality, we see that neither the media nor the "researchers" have an integral and honest view of the facts. Our image is more conspiratorial than journalistic or scientific.

---

65. V. B. Andrianov & V. V. Loiko, "Questions on the application of the armed forces of the Russian Federation in crisis situations in peacetime" (Вопросы применения ВС РФ в кризисных ситуациях мирного времени), *Voennaya Mysl*, January 2015, p. 68
66. https://youtu.be/Ft9fQzjky5Q
67. https://youtu.be/aA-yoCdingk

TV5 Monde Conspiracy on Hybrid Warfare

TV5 Monde claims...	In reality...
Illegal immigration from Belarus and the Kaliningrad exclave is described by Poland as "hybrid warfare."	There are no facts to back up this accusation, which is based solely on the Polish government's "fear" after the Russian authorities opened up Kaliningrad airport to international airlines.[68] Not only is there no indication whatsoever, but it's hard to see why Russia would send immigrants by plane to Kaliningrad to come and "invade Poland." In fact, under the pretext of "hybrid war," Poland is legitimizing the construction of a physical barrier between the two countries, which would otherwise have been condemned by the EU.
The attacks on the NORD STREAM 1 and 2 gas pipelines are seen as part of Moscow's hybrid warfare "as Russian troops get into trouble."	At this stage, we don't know, and our contributors are just making things up. After an article by the famous American journalist Seymour Hersh, who pointed the finger at the United States in February 2023,[69] the official version is that these attacks were perpetrated by Ukraine.[70]
The disruption of rail traffic in northern Germany due to the severing of data cables in Berlin-Karow and Herne, North Rhine-Westphalia.	The Russians had nothing to do with it—it was a theft of copper cables by organized gangs.[71]
The breaking of fiber-optic cables linking the Shetland Islands to Great Britain, where "the Kremlin's hand is on everyone's mind."	We already know that the "hand of the Kremlin" is only a fairly frequent damage[72] caused by trawlers[73] and not by sabotage.[74]

68. Claudia Ciobanu, "Fearing New Hybrid War Front, Poland to Build Wall on Kaliningrad Border," *Reporting Democracy*, November 2, 2022 (https://balkaninsight.com/2022/11/02/fearing-new-hybrid-war-front-poland-to-build-wall-on-kaliningrad-border/)

69. Seymour Hersh, "How America Took Out the Nord Stream Pipeline," *Substack*, February 8, 2023 (https://seymourhersh.substack.com/p/how-america-took-out-the-nord-stream)

70. Shane Harris & Souad Mekhennet, "U.S. had intelligence of detailed Ukrainian plan to attack Nord Stream pipeline," *The Washington Post*, June 6, 2023 (https://www.washingtonpost.com/national-security/2023/06/06/nord-stream-pipeline-explosion-ukraine-russia/)

71. "Keine Sabotage, sondern Gier", *Tagesschau.de*, July 27, 2023 (https://www.tagesschau.de/investigativ/bahn-ausfall-sabotage-kabel-diebstahl-100.html)

72. Olivia Solon & Mark Bergen, "Fishing Boats Can't Stop Running Over Undersea Internet Cables," *Bloomberg*, April 24, 2023 (https://www.bloomberg.com/news/articles/2023-04-24/fishing-boats-keep-running-over-ocean-internet-cables#xj4y7vzkg)

73. Derrick Bryson Taylor & Christine Chung, "Shetland Cut Off From the World After Undersea Cable Breaks," *The New York Times*, October 20, 2022 (updated October 21, 2022) (https://www.nytimes.com/2022/10/20/world/europe/shetland-scotland-outage.html)

74. https://therecord.media/fishing-vessel-not-sabotage-to-blame-for-shetland-island-submarine-cable-cut

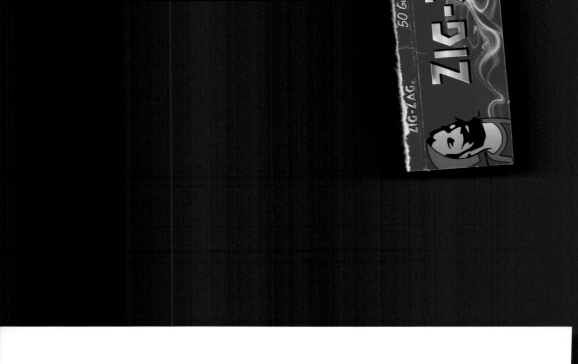

Young Russian arrested in Norway for spying, after using drones.	In reality, he was taking landscape photographs, but he was breaking a new Norwegian law passed in early 2022, which prohibits Russian citizens from using drones[75]—a country that wasn't even able to prevent the NORD STREAM sabotage!

Figure 4—Since the start of SMO, the aim of Europe's state media has shifted from information to propaganda and disinformation. Their journalists are "under orders," so this is logical. What's more surprising is the involvement of people who claim to be academics, who confuse "hypotheses" with "facts," and even assert things that we already know to be false.

Thus, those who trumpeted that the Russians were practicing hybrid warfare (for example, in France, Natalie Loiseau, Generals Dominique Trinquand and Michel Yakovlev, Colonel Pierre Servent, etc.) misled us, as Ofer Fridman explains in *PRISM*:[76]

> *The attempt to use the Western concept of hybrid warfare to define the Russian approach to war has led to an incorrect analysis of the Russian modus operandi.*

As a result, Westerners tend to get lost in concepts that have neither head nor tail, and wage false wars. It's the same phenomenon as with terrorism, against which no Western country has been able to develop a real strategy for over a quarter of a century—we have explained the phenomenon so that it "fits" our discourse, without trying to understand it. By aligning our strategies with our representation of reality, and not with the reality on the ground, we don't solve the problem—we perpetuate it. This is why countries like Mali, Niger and Burkina Faso no longer see our "aid" as a solution, but as a problem.

---

75. "Russian man jailed for 90 days in Norway for illegally flying drone", *Euronews/AP/AFP*, November 23, 2022 (updated November 28, 2022) (https://www.euronews.com/2022/11/23/russian-man-jailed-for-90-days-in-norway-for-illegally-flying-drone)

76. Ofer Fridman, "On the "Gerasimov Doctrine"—Why the West Fails to Beat Russia to the Punch", *PRISM*, Vol. 8, N° 2, Institute for National Strategic Security, National Defense University, 2019, pp. 100-113 (https://ndupress.ndu.edu/Portals/68/Documents/prism/prism_8-2/PRISM_8-2_Fridman.pdf)

The Link Between Politics and War

Clausewitz's principles permeate Russian military thinking. This is nothing new. During the Cold War, the Marxist ideology that underpinned the Soviet system saw war as a continuation of politics by other means. But whereas Clausewitz saw this process in the context of foreign policy, the Soviets saw it in the context of class struggle, which extended from domestic to foreign policy.

Today, class struggle is a very distant concept in Russia, and the links between war and politics are understood, as with Clausewitz, within the framework of foreign policy. This means that military action is not an end in itself, but serves politics:

> *Tactical victories, the achievement of the war's military objectives, lead to political victory.*

Thus, the use of force and the achievement of tactical and operational objectives (*Ziele*) must lead to the political goal (*Zweck*).

This is a very different position from that of Westerners, who wage wars (Afghanistan, Iraq, Syria, Libya, etc.) that are disconnected from a political process. They are even at a loss when we try to associate a political process with them (as in Mali or Niger). Clearly, we are fighting wars for nothing.

The Russian reading of war implies a fluid transition between politics and war. This is why negotiation is part of the process, whereas for Westerners it's a separate process. This explains the latter's reluctance to negotiate solutions (or even to disregard the agreements they have signed!).

For example, in February 2012, faced with the hardening situation in Syria, Russia proposed a three-point plan to Western countries that called for the departure of Bashar al-Assad, as reported by *The Guardian*.[77] It was discussed by Vitalii Churkin, Russian ambassador to the United Nations, and Martti Ahtisaari, Nobel Peace Prize winner and former Finnish president.[78] Thus, from the outset, there was a solution

---

77. Julian Borger & Bastien Inzaurralde, "West 'ignored Russian offer in 2012 to have Syria's Assad step aside'", *The Guardian*, September 15, 2015 (https://www.theguardian.com/world/2015/sep/15/west-ignored-russian-offer-in-2012-to-have-syrias-assad-step-aside)
78. Fanny Arlandis, "En 2012, la France et ses alliés auraient ignororé un plan prévoyant le départ de Bachar el-Assad," *Slate.fr*, September 15, 2015

for the departure of Bashar al-Assad without resorting to violence. But the "P3" (France, Great Britain and the United States) refused: their objective was not to replace Bashar al-Assad, but to dismantle Syria, since Israel—and therefore the United States—perceived this country as an advanced bastion of Iran.

On February 25, 2022, after Ukraine had lost much of its military potential, Volodymyr Zelensky called for negotiations.[79] He contacted Ignazio Cassis, Switzerland's Foreign Minister, to organize mediation and a peace conference.[80] Russia declared itself ready for talks, and a first round of talks was held in Gomel, close to the Belarussian border. But the European Union disagreed. On February 27, it arrived with a 450-million Euro package to finance arms, halt the negotiation process and encourage Ukraine to fight.[81]

In mid-March 2022, Volodymyr Zelensky, realizing that NATO was not ready to accept Ukraine into its fold and declaring that he wanted to give up his candidacy,[82] sent his proposals for the Istanbul negotiations. The prospects for a solution between the Russians and Ukrainians looked good.[83] The European Union immediately released 500 million euros to provide lethal[84] and non-lethal[85] military aid to Ukraine. For his part, Boris Johnson intervened and destroyed all negotiating efforts, as reported by *Ukrainska Pravda*.[86] In fact, "BoJo" did nothing more than blackmail Ukraine during a telephone conversation and then, a week later, during

79. Olga Rudenko, "Ukraine ready to negotiate with Russia", *The Kyiv Independent*, February 25, 2022 (https://kyivindependent.com/national/ukraine-ready-to-negotiate-with-russia/)
80. Arthur Rutishauser, "Schweiz will Friedenskonferenz in Genf organisieren", *Tages Anzeiger*, February 26, 2022 (https://www.tagesanzeiger.ch/schweiz-will-friedenskonferenz-in-genf-organisieren-129475547083)
81. Maïa de La Baume & Jacopo Barigazzi, "EU agrees to give €500M in arms, aid to Ukrainian military in 'watershed' move", *Politico*, February 27, 2022 (https://www.politico.eu/article/eu-ukraine-russia-funding-weapons-budget-military-aid/)
82. Zoya Sheftalovich, "Russia's Lavrov sees hope of 'compromise' with Kyiv as Zelenskyy signals NATO shift", *Politico*, March 16, 2022 (https://www.politico.eu/article/zelenskyy-peace-talks-russia-realistic-accept-compromise-nato/)
83. sobel Koshiw & Daniel Boffey, "Russia and Ukraine 'close to agreeing' on neutral status, says Sergei Lavrov", *The Guardian*, March 16, 2022 (https://www.theguardian.com/world/2022/mar/16/russia-and-ukraine-close-to-agreeing-on-neutral-status-says-sergei-lavrov)
84. https://eur-lex.europa.eu/legal-content/FR/TXT/PDF/?uri=CELEX:32022D0472
85. https://eur-lex.europa.eu/legal-content/FR/TXT/PDF/?uri=CELEX:32022D0471
86. Iryna Balachuk & Roman Romaniuk, "Possibility of talks between Zelenskyy and Putin came to a halt after Johnson's visit", *Ukrainska Pravda*, May 5, 2022 (https://www.pravda.com.ua/eng/news/2022/05/5/7344206/)

his visit to Kiev,[87] he exchanged the withdrawal of his proposal for unlimited Western support.[88]

In mid-August 2022, during his visit to Ukraine, Turkish President Tayyip Erdogan offered to arrange a meeting with Volodymyr Zelensky and Vladimir Putin.[89] After some hesitation, Vladimir Putin declared himself ready for a meeting[90], but Boris Johnson intervened—once again—and warned Ukraine against "frivolous" peace plans.[91] The Turkish initiative was abandoned.

Thus, while the Russians see a fluid, two-way link between war and politics, the West tends to make war an end in itself. That's why Westerners struggle to get out of conflicts, whereas Russians have provided exit routes (in February, March and August 2022). This gives the Russians a more strategic, considered and less impulsive approach to conflict than their Western counterparts.

Doctrine Structure

The Russians have always attached particular importance to doctrine. Better than the West, they have understood that "*a common way of seeing things, thinking and acting*"—as Marshal Foch used to say[92]—gives coherence while allowing infinite variations in the conception of operations. Military doctrine is a kind of "common core" that serves as a reference for designing operations.

Russian military doctrine divides military art into three main components: *strategy* (*strategiya*), *operative art* (*operativnoe iskoustvo*) and *tactics* (*taktika*). Each of these components has its own characteristics, very similar to those found in Western doctrines. Using the terminology of the French doctrine *d'emploi des forces*:

87. https://peoplesdispatch.org/2022/05/09/ukrainian-news-outlet-suggests-uk-and-us-governments-are-primary-obstacles-to-peace/
88. https://www.gov.uk/government/news/pm-call-with-president-zelenskyy-of-ukraine-2-april-2022
89. "Erdoğan suggests to revive negotiations between Ukraine, Russia on the basis of the March agreements", *Ukrainska Pravda*, August 18, 2022 (https://www.pravda.com.ua/eng/news/2022/08/18/7363895/)
90. https://www.cnnturk.com/turkiye/dunyanin-gozu-uclu-zirvede
91. Tom Balmforth & Andrea Shalal, "UK's Boris Johnson, in Kyiv, warns against 'flimsy' plan for talks with Russia", *Reuters*, 24 August 2022 (https://www.reuters.com/world/europe/uks-johnson-kyiv-warns-against-flimsy-plan-talks-with-russia-2022-08-24/)
92. Maréchal Foch, *Des principes de la guerre*, Economica, 2017

- The strategic level is that of *conception*. The aim of strategic action is to lead the adversary to negotiation or defeat.
- The operative level is that of *cooperation and coordination* of inter-force actions, with a view to achieving a given military objective.
- The tactical level, finally, is that of *maneuver execution* at weapons level, as an integral part of the operational maneuver.

Tactical objectives must promote the achievement of operational objectives, which in turn must promote the achievement of strategic objectives of a political or military nature. In fact, in Russian military thinking, each level plays with multiplier factors that should enable the objectives of the higher level to be achieved: the achievement of operational objectives results from the multiplier effect of inter-army synergies, and the achievement of strategic objectives results from the multiplier effect of the achievement of operational objectives.

Unlike Russian military thinking, which is more holistic and networked, Western military thinking tends to be sequential and linear. Whereas Westerners tend to see operational success as the sum of tactical successes, Russians tend to see it as the result of multiplication. This is why, at the end of 2023, the predictable failure of the Ukrainian counter-offensive left the Western halls of power at a dead-end.

In Russia, while strategy is seen as an essentially intellectual activity of a political nature, and tactics as an activity of an essentially technical nature, "operative art" is the art of optimally exploiting the synergies between the forces involved.

These three components correspond to levels of leadership, which translate into leadership structures and the space in which military operations are conducted. For simplicity's sake, let's say that the strategic level ensures the management of the *theater of war (Театр Войны)* (TV); a geographically vast entity, with its own command and control structures, within which there are one or more strategic directions. The theater of war comprises a set of *theaters of military operations* (*Театр Военных Действий*) (TVD), which represent a strategic direction and are the domain of operative action. These various theaters have no predetermined structure and are defined according to the situation. For example, although we commonly speak of the "war in Afghanistan" (1979-1989) or the "war in Syria" (2015-), these countries are considered in Russian terminology as TVDs and not TVs.

The same applies to Ukraine, which Russia sees as a *theater of military operations* (TVD) and not a *theater of war* (TV), which explains why the action in Ukraine is referred to as a *"Special Military Operation"* (*Специальная Военная Операция - Spetsial'naya Voyennaya Operatsiya—SMO*) and not a "war".

The use of the word "war" would imply a different structure of conduct than that envisaged by the Russians in Ukraine, and would have other structural implications in Russia itself. Moreover—and this is a central point—as NATO Secretary General Jens Stoltenberg himself acknowledges, *"the war began in 2014"*[93] and should have been ended by the Minsk Agreements. The SMO is therefore a "military operation" and not a new "war," as many Western "experts" claim.

Organization of the Strategic Space in the Russian Conception

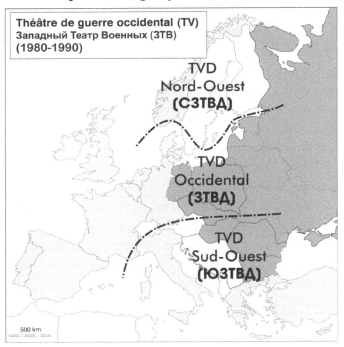

Figure 5—Soviet vision of the Western theater of war during the Cold War. The theater of war (TV) is both a political and military concept, with a very broad scope. It is subdivided into theaters of military operations (TVD). Russia's structuring of its strategic space illustrates why Ukraine is a theater of military operations (TVD) rather than a theater of war (TV).

---

93. https://www.nato.int/cps/en/natohq/opinions_211698.htm

Strategy

Simply and generically speaking, strategy is the way in which we want to achieve a political, military or other objective.

It's a term totally misunderstood by our journalists, who use it indiscriminately, often as a synonym for "tactics" to avoid repetition, or even "doctrine." To their shame, some military personnel also confuse these notions themselves. Anecdotally, this can lead to confusion during presentations, such as Colonel Michel Goya's presentation to a Senate committee on November 2, 2022.[94]

More generally, this confusion is reflected in the military's inability to formulate strategies for conducting a conflict. This confusion stems from another confusion often made by our military between political strategy and military strategy. The military's inability to formulate strategies for fighting in conflicts they know little about leads them to blame politicians. It's a fact that politicians are often incapable of doing strategy. But—and this is an observation I've made personally—our generals are more often than not incapable of formulating strategies. What we call a "strategy" is often no more than a collection of disparate operational measures to which we try to give coherence. This is the case in the Sahel, where French soldiers are literally dying for nothing.

In Russian military thinking, as in most constitutional states, the strategic level is broken down into a political strategy and a military strategy. Political strategy is a function of the decisions taken by the country's political authorities, while military strategy is the translation of these decisions to the military level. Political and military strategies complement each other, and must therefore converge towards the main objective, which is political in nature. The notion of *Grand Strategy*, with which the Americans are familiar, consists in defining a global approach to internal and external problems. It doesn't exist in Russia. In fact, it no longer exists. Only the Soviet Union had a superior form of strategy, determined by the role it wished to assume in its rivalry with the capitalist world.

Today, Russia's strategic approach is extremely pragmatic and much less dogmatic than that of the West. Although political and military strategies are the responsibility of the political power and the military command

---

94. https://youtu.be/aZe5diu87sk

respectively, they must be worked out in consultation and are the result of dialogue. It would be wrong to think that strategies are drawn up in an obscure office in the Kremlin and then imposed on the military. Indeed, strategies are not developed in a vacuum. They have to take into account a number of conditions determined by the context and by our own capabilities. This is the principle of "correlation of forces" seen above, which determines the choice of strategy. As a probable consequence of Vladimir Putin's professional heritage, and unlike in Europe, decisions are taken after a methodical analysis of the facts with the intelligence services.

While the West struggled to convert its military successes into political ones (Algeria, Vietnam, Afghanistan, Iraq, Libya, Sahel, etc.), the Soviets, then the Russians, applied the Clausewitzian principle that *"war is the continuation of politics by other means."* There is therefore a continuum between war and politics. Thus, although NATO's eastward expansion is a matter of concern for Russia, and the possible deployment of nuclear weapons on its border is a major aspect of this, it is *not the* reason for its intervention in Ukraine.

The reason for the intervention was the threat to the population of the Donbass following Volodymyr Zelensky's decision of March 24, 2021 to reconquer Crimea and the Donbass. On the other hand, it is certain that in the minds of the Russian leadership, this intervention was intended to open the door to negotiations that would include the question of Ukraine's membership of NATO. Zelensky himself understood this, as evidenced by his proposal of March 2022.

In other words, it's all about turning operational successes into strategic successes, and strategic successes into political successes. Unlike the West (which struggles to negotiate and doesn't know how), the Russians see the idea of negotiation as consubstantial with war. This is why they were open to the various negotiating proposals made by Volodymyr Zelensky (February 25 and mid-March 2022) and Tayyip Erdogan (August 2022). In November 2022, Zelensky confessed that he had received signals from the Russians that they would be ready for direct negotiations with him, but that he had not followed up.[95]

---

95. "Zelensky admits receiving hints that Putin wanted to negotiate", *The Kyiv Independent*, November 16, 2022 (https://kyivindependent.com/zelensky-admits-receiving-hints-that-putin-wanted-to-negotiate/)

This also explains why Russia has not seen sanctions as a problem, but as an opportunity. Rather like China, it sees the crisis as an opportunity to meet new challenges. Blinded by our discourse, we failed to see that the sanctions applied from 2014 onwards were an opportunity to boost the Russian economy. Not only did they have a protectionist effect, but they also opened up new horizons, as in the case of the agricultural products that Russia was importing then and is exporting today.

Unlike the Russians, the West understands victory only through the total crushing of the adversary. This is why, from 2014 onwards, they gradually sought to exclude Russia from all international forums, and why they forced Ukraine to renege on its compromise proposals.[96] Their inability to understand military strategy in a political context tends to lead them into endless wars (Afghanistan, Iraq, Syria, Sahel, etc.). The total absence of objectives, strategies and therefore perspectives for conflict resolution leads to situations such as Mali or Niger, where local governments have realized that the wars waged by France are leading nowhere.

Unlike the Americans and their NATO allies, the Soviets went into Afghanistan with a strategy and an objective! Unlike the Americans and NATO later on, the Soviets maintained strategic coherence throughout their intervention. They focused on preserving Afghan communist power, not on destroying the resistance forces. Thus, unlike the West, they did not have to carry out air strikes massively affecting the civilian population. Moreover, on the strength of the experience acquired during the Basmachi Revolt in the 1920s, they did not seek to transform Afghan society or its secular and religious traditions. Unlike the Westerners, they only had to fight against combatants, not against Afghan society. Thus, the Soviet army was not forced to leave and the government they supported remained in place for another two years; whereas thirty years later, the Americans were forced to leave and the government they supported lasted only—48 hours!

Generally speaking, since the end of the Cold War, there have been two different decision-making philosophies between Russia and the West. Moscow's decisions are the result of in-depth analysis and a long-term vision, unencumbered by public opinion. In the West, on the other hand,

---

96. Roman Romaniuk, "Possibility of talks between Zelenskyy and Putin came to a halt after Johnson's visit", *Ukrainska Pravda*, 5 May 2022 (https://www.pravda.com.ua/eng/news/2022/05/5/7344206/)

decisions are taken from a short-term perspective, with an eye to communication and public opinion. As a result, factors that might upset the public are excluded from the outset, and dissenting voices are silenced. This is the opposite of a holistic approach, and it's exactly what led to Ukraine's defeat.

In Russia, strategy is adapted to the adversary, not to public opinion. As we have seen in our hearings of military officers before parliamentary committees, they find it difficult to step back from their personal conception of war and military strategy. Their inability to adapt to their adversary's strategy leads to asymmetrical situations that work to their disadvantage. This is why they have lost in Afghanistan, Iraq, the Sahel and elsewhere, and why they will continue to lose.

Operative Art

The Essence of Operative Art—Synergy

As is often the case in France, the prose of Monsieur Jourdain is being reworked, and certain researchers seem to have rediscovered the art of operations. While the term *"art opératif"* is characteristic of Russian military thinking and vocabulary, the art of operations it covers has been known for many decades. Nevertheless, caught up in its "war on terror," the West has forgotten it, and military thinking has remained confined to the tactical realm.

Operative art is neither a type of operation (as some experts have declared[97]), nor a method for *"desubstantiating"* the enemy, nor a way of *"aiming for the collapse of the adversary as a system,[98]"* but the part of military doctrine that governs the level of conduct between the tactical and strategic levels. It is the general framework within which military operations are conceived. It should be noted that it is an "art," i.e., an activity in which imagination and creativity are encouraged, as emphasized by the *Encyclopaedic Military Dictionary* (VES).[99]

There are many reasons for this loss of Western memory. Classical strategic references, such as Clausewitz or Jomini, do not mention the operative level. On the other hand, their use of the word "strategy" evokes the modern notion of "operative art." This apparent absence can be explained by the

---

97. https://www.rts.ch/info/monde/13135499-bernard-wicht-le-succes-de-loperation-russe-cest-davoir-reussi-a-mystifier-tout-le-monde.html
98. https://youtu.be/jWyJgFv88Mk
99. https://encyclopedia.mil.ru/encyclopedia/dictionary/details.htm?id=13724@morfDictionary

nature of warfare in the early 19th century, and probably explains the use of the expression "*stratégie opérationnelle,*" frequently used in French military vocabulary to designate what the Russians call "*art opératif.*"

It was only after the First World War that the combined progress of aviation, artillery, mobility, armor and communications gave new importance to the notions of "time" and "space." This led to the conceptualization of "operative art" between the wars in Great Britain, Germany and Russia.

The archetypal result of this thinking was the so-called *Blitzkrieg* ("lightning war") which the Germans implemented in Europe in 1939-1941. In France, the term *Blitzkrieg* remains associated with the anti-German propaganda of the time, and tends to designate a brutal way of waging war. Today, comparing the SMO to a *Blitzkrieg* tends to suggest an analogy between today's Russia and Nazi Germany.[100] Yet few of the "experts" and "strategists" on our TV screens know what they're talking about. This starts with the fact that the Germans never theorized this type of war as *Blitzkrieg*!

The Blitzkrieg *Principle*

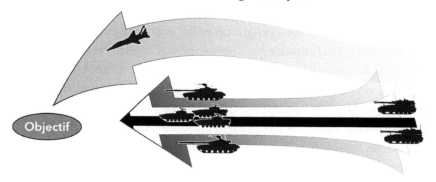

Figure 6—The term "Blitzkrieg" has become widely misunderstood and has become a byword. For specialists, however, "blitzkrieg" remains the model for operative action, enabling quality to overcome quantity. This is what happened in 1940, when the quantitative advantage was clearly on France's side. But as always, where France had a sum of "solos," the Germans knew how to play an orchestra! It's exactly the same problem today... In the Russian vision, operative art is the art of bringing synergies into play between the various components of forces, in order to achieve objectives that can be transformed into strategic successes.

---

100. Luke Harding, "Demoralised Russian soldiers tell of anger at being 'duped' into war", *The Guardian*, March 4, 2022 (https://www.theguardian.com/world/2022/mar/04/russian-soldiers-ukraine-anger-duped-into-war)

This "blitzkrieg" is not a way of waging war, but a way of conducting operations by engaging a numerically superior adversary with inferior manpower. It's a dynamic approach to operations that combines synergies between ground and air forces. Maneuvering creates local and temporary superiorities, enabling us to overwhelm a more powerful force.

Theorized by Sir Basil Liddell Hart in the 1920s and 1930s, then taken up by the Germans in the 1930s, it inspired the Soviets Georgii S. Isserson and especially Mikhail Tukhachevsky, who developed the Russian concept of "Deep Operation" in 1936:[101]

Simultaneous attack of enemy defenses by air and artillery in the depth of the defense, penetration of the tactical zone of the defense by attacking units with extensive use of armored forces, and abrupt conversion of tactical success into operational success in order to completely encircle and destroy the enemy. The main role is played by the infantry, and the mutual support of all types of forces is organized according to its needs.

The final months of the Second World War saw the greatest evolution in operational thinking. On the vast plains of Eastern Europe, the Soviets were able to develop their art of military operations. The Byelorussian Strategic Offensive Operation (June 23—August 29 1944) (also known as Operation Bagration), which enabled the Red Army to extend its advantage over 600 km in two months, was a decisive step in the evolution of Soviet, and later Russian, military thinking.[102]

Immediately after the Second World War, Westerners were caught up in colonial conflicts, where the art of operations (in the sense of joint action) tended to disappear. With the probable exception of the first Gulf War (1991), Westerners fought only tactical wars, against numerically and technologically inferior adversaries.

In the early 1980s, with the gradual elimination of theater nuclear weapons, the prospect of deep operations once again opened up on both sides of the Iron Curtain. The art of operations became the subject

---

101. Jack D. Kem (Ed.), "Deep Operations", *Army University Press*, Fort Leavenworth, Kansas, November 2021
102. https://mil.ru/winner_may/history/more.htm?id=11960765@cmsArticle

of numerous studies and debates within Western intelligence services, which were concerned about Soviet capabilities that had no real equivalent in the West.

Symptomatically, the Americans only really conceptualized the offensive dimension of operations in the 1982 and 1986 editions of their *FM-100-5 Operations* manual. More than 40 years after the Soviets, they understood the importance of interaction between mutually supporting operations in the depths of enemy territory. Their concept was refined in the 1993 version of *FM-100-5*, with the formalization of the operational space.

Experience shows that Westerners tend to confuse the terms "operational" and "operative." Unlike French, German and Russian, the word "operative" does not exist in English as a military term. As a result, NATO terminology uses the word *operational* to designate both aspects, leading to confusion.

Today, Russian forces continue to draw inspiration from the experiences of the Second World War.

Contrary to popular opinion in the West, it is not mass that is the source of success, but the dynamic combination of means:

> *The principle of concentration of effort is not so much quantitative as qualitative, i.e. the ability to find a dynamic form (...) capable of stunning and "saturating" the enemy through its novelty and surprise.*[103]

At the heart of this dynamic approach is maneuver. As an element of combat capability, maneuver cannot be quantified, but it is often as important as firepower in achieving success. It's all about exploiting the enemy's vulnerability (a breach in his front) to penetrate his system and take up a more favorable position to strike.[104]

The Russians see operative art as a multiplier of tactical action to achieve strategic objectives. This is possible thanks to the synergy created a) between the inter-army components and b) between the operative actions themselves. It is this dynamic dimension that gives the concept of *"joint operation"* (общевойсковая *операция*) the meaning of operative art.

---

103. http://tutunnikovnn.ucoz.ru/3710_1.pdf
104. http://tutunnikovnn.ucoz.ru/3710_1.pdf

Operational Control

Whereas Americans see operative art as a juxtaposition of operations within a coherent concept, Russians tend to see operations as a whole, where each component works in support of another. By analogy with the martial arts, Russians perceive it a little like karate—it is agility and speed that give the advantage, more than weight. It is not numbers that confer superiority, but the way in which you engage your forces and create local and temporary superiorities, and pre-empt the deployment of opposing forces.

This is why the Russians seek success in the dynamics of operations. As soon as combat becomes static, the model has to change. This is what we saw at the end of summer 2022.

As in any business, the key to success is to integrate the decision-making process. This is particularly true in Ukraine, where the means of recognition on both sides leave little time for decision-making.

In 1940, the coordination and synchronization of the various weapons relied heavily on radio. It was largely for this reason that French tanks—though technically superior—were unable to exploit their qualities against their German counterparts: only some of them had a radio.

Today, the proliferation of tactical reconnaissance resources (e.g., mini-UAVs) has compressed the loop from observation to target destruction. This is the OODA (*Observe, Orient, Decide and Act*) loop, well known to Western militaries, which is an increasingly automated process, thanks to network connections and artificial intelligence.

In Afghanistan, where relatively small forces were engaged in complicated terrain, the Soviets began working on networked systems. In order to respond quickly and precisely to Mujahideen raids and ambushes, they sought to shorten the time between observation and reaction. Technically, this meant integrating reconnaissance and fire-fighting resources to react in near-real time. In just a few months, the structure of the 40th Army was adapted to this reality by eliminating battle tanks, adding special and air-mobile forces, and increasing artillery and communications resources.

These experiments led to the "ROK/RUK" concept:

- The "*Reconnaissance-Fire Complex*" (*Разведывательно-огневой комплекс—Razvedivatel'no-Ognevoï Kompleks—ROK*) which integrates combat systems at the tactical level (122 and 152 mm artillery, multiple rocket launchers and mortars).[105]

- The *"Reconnaissance-Frappe Complex"* (*Разведывательно-ударный комплекс—Razvedivatel'no-Udarnyy Kompleks—RUK*), which is the joint implementation of the concept for the operational level. It includes theater missile systems (e.g., hypersonic), large-caliber artillery assets, combat helicopters, aviation and electronic warfare assets.[106]

Already discussed in the early 1980s, the concept has been the subject of countless debates in the Russian specialist press. Russian intervention in TVD Syria enabled the validation of technologies that have brought the ROK/RUK to maturity today.

Summary of the Differences between ROK and RUK

	ROK	RUK
Driving level	Tactics	Operational
Driving systems	KRUS STRELETS	AKATSIYA-M SOZVEZDIYE-M2 ANDROMEDA-D
Means of recognition	Razvedchiki Light drones: KUB ORLAN-10/30	Spetsnaz Medium and heavy UAVs: ORION
Means of action (examples)	Artillery (122/152 mm) Suicide drones: GERAN-2 LANCET-3 KUB-BLA	Artillery (152/203 mm) Aviation Missiles: ISKANDER KINJAL ZIRKON Electronic warfare systems (REB)

Figure 7—Examples of ROK and RUK control systems and weapons. The list is not exhaustive, but is intended for illustrative purposes only.

The Ukrainian conflict has brought a new dimension to these concepts, which seem to have taken observers by surprise.

---

105. https://bigenc.ru/c/razvedyvatel-no-ognevoi-kompleks-ba42cf
106. https://bigenc.ru/c/razvedyvatel-no-udarnyi-kompleks-f2079c

Its particularity is not the multiplication of drones, but the emergence of a multitude of ever shorter OODA loops at the lowest tactical levels. This means that not only has the battlefield become "quasi-transparent," but action capabilities can be deployed more rapidly.

In addition, Ukraine's use of weapon systems such as the French CAESAR or the American HIMARS has meant that Russian ROK/RUK systems have had to be drastically adapted. There are two reasons for this: the speed with which these systems can be armed and fired, and—in the case of HIMARS, whose missiles have non-ballistic trajectories—the need to calculate trajectories in order to pinpoint the location of launchers.

The result was two trends that had already begun in Russia:
- ever-greater automation, thanks to the use of artificial intelligence;
- the need for network-centric operational management.

Based on the experience gained on the TVD Syria, the Russians have set up a centralized operations management system to conduct all of Russia's forces, including nuclear forces. Designated the *National Defense Conduct Center (Национальный центр управления обороной—НЦУО)* (NTsUO), it brings together in a single point all the elements enabling the management of operations.[107] It is from this NTsUO that information bulletins on the conflict in Ukraine are issued.

The Russian pipeline is built around several integrated networks:
- AKATSIYA-M, the Russian Armed Forces' operative-strategic and operative control network, is a kind of military Internet, set up back in 2005 as an information platform for connecting unified operative-tactical and tactical control networks;
- Unified operative-tactical and tactical control networks (ESU TZ) for the operational engagement of troops. These are the SOZVEZDIYE-M2 (for ground troops) and ANDROMEDA-D (for airborne troops) systems;
- TZ ESUs for air forces and air defense forces.

All these systems were deployed on the TVD Syria in 2015, and have since been upgraded. They integrate reconnaissance, decision and fire/flight capabilities to shorten response times.

These systems have their extension at the lowest tactical level in the form of a small pocket terminal, which is the real novelty on the TVD

---

107. https://sneg5.com/obshchestvo/armiya/centr-upravleniya-oboronoy-rf.html

2. Russian Military Thought

Ukraine: the Intelligence, Control and Communication System (комплекс разведки, управления и связи, KRUS STRELETS).

The KRUS STRELETS enables combat driving, voice communications, data transmission (coordinates, target identification and designation), and terrain navigation. It is interoperable with all national reconnaissance, surveillance, target designation, radar, rangefinder, inclinometer and UAV systems. It is one of the core elements of the ROK/RUK in the Ukrainian field.

The Lower Tactical Segment of the ROK/RUK

Figure 8—Contrary to popular belief, the Russian armed forces are highly decentralized. Shown here are the UNKV-E terminals of the STRELETS system for lower tactical infantry units down to battle group level.

First engaged on TVD Syria in 2015, the STRELETS system has been connecting Russian tactical drones, mechanized artillery, tanks and infantry since 2017. In particular, it enabled the September 20, 2016 Russian strike on an Islamic State command post (which I mentioned in my book *Governing by Fake News*), where some 30 American, Israeli, Qatari and Turkish officers reportedly died.[108]

---

108. Judah Ari Gross, "Russia: Mossad, other foreign agents killed in Aleppo strike," *The Times of Israel*, September 22, 2016 (https://www.timesofisrael.com/russia-mossad-other-foreign-agents-killed-in-aleppo-strike/)

In Ukraine, according to a Ukrainian commander, a tank is spotted by the Russians in less than 5 minutes, and shot at within 3 minutes. The survivability of a tank would be only 10 minutes.[109] It's hard to say whether these figures are realistic, but they do show that the ROK/RUK complexes work very well. It's (half) surprising that there's no mention of them in the French-language media.

Examples of ROK at Artillery Battalion Level

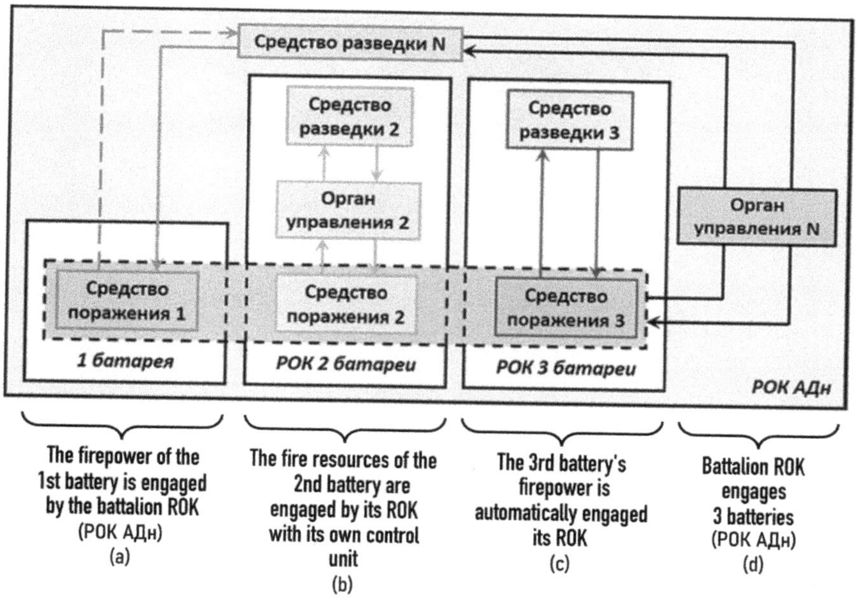

Figure 9—Four examples of ROK integration at artillery battalion level: at artillery battery level (b) and (c) or at battalion level with one battery (a) or with the whole battalion (d) [Source: Russian doctrine documents, submitted by the Ukrainian Army].

That said, in the higher operational segment, Russian intelligence still shows weaknesses. Some Ukrainian successes can be attributed to a lack of detection and long-range battlefield surveillance resources. The size of the TVD means that detection resources must have a corresponding depth.

---

109. Thibault Spirlet, "Tanks and troops out in the open in Ukraine can't go 10 minutes without being spotted and fired upon, Ukrainian official says", *Business Insider*, September 28, 2023 (https://www.businessinsider.com/tanks-troops-in-the-open-are-hit-within-10-minutes-ukraine-official-2023-9)

This was the case for the Ukrainian attacks on the Crimean Peninsula, which could not be anticipated because of the lack of early warning systems.

By comparison, the United States has a global defense architecture. It is the only country in the world to have structured its armed forces around commands for each continent. This structure has implications for intelligence resources for monitoring the situation in each of these commands' areas of responsibility.

The M-55 MYSTIC-B

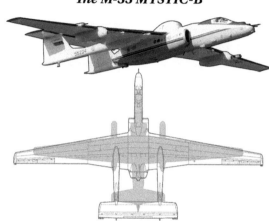

Figure 10—The M-55 MYSTIC-B is the heir to the M-17 STRATOSFERA (MYSTIC-A) project of the 1980s. It is an aircraft capable of operating at very high altitudes (20,000-30,000 m), equipped with sophisticated electronic and optronic sensors to monitor operating depth. It is expected to perform functions similar to those of the famous American U-2R aircraft (silhouette in grey). According to British intelligence services, the first M-55s are currently arriving at the TVD Ukraine.[110]

Russia does not have the same density of observation satellites as the United States. Its intelligence resources are concentrated on Ukraine, but are not sufficiently granular to bridge the gap between strategic intelligence and the higher-level conduct of operations. This explains efforts to speed up production of the A-50U MAINSTAY early warning aircraft, and the reactivation of the M-55 MYSTIC-B spy plane project.[111]

---

110. https://twitter.com/DefenceHQ/status/1726153057971401130
111. https://www.thedrive.com/the-war-zone/soviet-era-m-55-spy-plane-may-be-headed-to-war-in-ukraine

Offensive Operations

Basic Diagram

In the Russian conception, offensive operations are broken down into:

- A *"main thrust"* (основное *направление наступления*) directed at the very objective of the action or operation. In American terminology, this is a *"decisive operation."*
- A *"secondary thrust(s)"* (второстепенное *направление наступления*) whose purpose is to facilitate the implementation of the main thrust, by inducing the adversary to divide his forces. In NATO terminology, this is a *"supporting operation."*

While the decisive operation is generally well understood, the same cannot be said of support operations (secondary thrusts), which most often have the function of attracting part of the opponent's resistance in order to relieve forces in the main thrust. These support operations or secondary thrusts can take a variety of forms. One of these is what the Americans call the *"shaping operation:"*[112]

Shaping operations are operations that use military capabilities to create the conditions necessary to carry out decisive operations. Shaping operations use the full range of military capabilities to reduce the enemy's ability to coherently resist before or while the commander executes a decisive operation. The commander applies the principle of force economy to shaping operations, equipping them with the minimum essential military resources needed to create the conditions for the decisive operation to benefit from overwhelming military capabilities.

Like the decisive operation, shaping operations can be carried out in any depth of the area of operation and by any force. However, the commander must clearly establish how shaping operations contribute to the decisive operation. In offensive or defensive actions, shaping operations may involve preventing the enemy from using an area or the electromagnetic spectrum, destroying or degrading

---

112. Major David R. Moore, "Decisive, Shaping, Sustaining Operations: An Operational Organization For The Contemporary Mission Environment", *School of Advanced Military Studies, United States Army Command and General Staff College*, Fort Leavenworth, Kansas, May 27, 1999 (https://apps.dtic.mil/sti/pdfs/ADA370239.pdf)

his main assets (particularly his command and control, logistics, fire support and air defense assets), or isolating key elements of his forces.

The best illustration of this concept was the Special Military Operation launched on February 24, 2022, consisting of a *main thrust* on the Donbass and a *secondary thrust* towards Kiev. Contrary to the assertions of certain strategists, such as Bernard Wicht on the Algerian channel *AL24*, the push on Kiev was not a *"mystification."*[113] We are not dealing here with disinformation, but with a *"shaping"* operation. The aim was to force Ukraine to deploy its forces in such a way as to prevent it from reinforcing its position against the main Russian thrust towards the Donbass. More on this later.

Another example of a shaping operation was the campaign of strikes against Ukrainian electrical installations between October 2022 and May 2023. The aim was to force the Ukrainians to use their anti-aircraft missiles, so as to enable the Russian air force to operate freely on the front line. Secret US documents "leaked" in April 2023 indicate that Ukrainian SA-10/S-300 and SA-11/BUK anti-aircraft systems and ammunition were depleted in this way between the end of March and the end of May 2023. In April 2023, Colonel Yuriy Ignat, spokesman for the Ukrainian Air Force, noted that this campaign had had *"a perceptible effect,"* and that Ukrainian anti-aircraft capabilities were now insufficient.[114] Our "experts" have come up with every possible explanation—except the right one.

This campaign against electrical infrastructure has enabled Russia to shape the battlefield for the Ukrainian counter-offensive of 2023, which is now unprotected against Russian tactical aviation.[115] As the Indian media reports: *"The Kamov Ka-52 Alligator helicopter gunship seems to have established itself as the best tank killer."*[116] It is to combat these helicopters, which have become one of the major obstacles to its counter-offensive, that Ukraine is seeking to obtain F-16 fighters.

---

113. https://youtu.be/jWyJgFv88Mk
114. Ellie Cook, "Russian Glider Bombs Spark New Air Defence Woes for Ukraine," *Newsweek*, April 13, 2023 (https://www.newsweek.com/russia-glider-bombs-ukraine-air-defense-jdams-1794155)
115. https://air-cosmos.com/article/ukraine-aviation-russe-la-contre-offensive-en-danger-65273
116. https://www.eurasiantimes.com/double-kill-russias-ka-52-alligator-hunts-2-ukrainian-tanks/

The Breakthrough

Widely used in the last major Soviet offensives of 1944 to 1945, and despite its formidable effectiveness, the "breakthrough" concept briefly disappeared from Soviet doctrine in the 1960s to the 1970s. The emergence of tactical nuclear weapons in the European theater made it possible to annihilate large concentrations of forces instantly. But in the early 1980s, after the Euromissile crisis and the abandonment of the idea of deploying theater nuclear weapons in Europe, the idea of the "breakthrough" returned. In 1984, the US Army's *FM 100-2-1* manual on Soviet tactics described Soviet breakthrough operations as follows:[117]

> *For example, in one case, a Guards Infantry Corps was allocated a 22-kilometer-wide advancing spindle, but concentrated 80 to 90 percent of its forces on a width of less than a third of its total spindle width. Thus, over a width of 7 kilometers, the Corps massed 27 battalions, 1,087 artillery pieces and towed mortars, and 156 tanks and self-propelled artillery weapons, giving it a superiority of 4 to 1 for infantry, 10 to 1 for artillery and 17 to 1 for tanks.*

This concentration of forces on a very narrow front seems contrary to common sense. Any infantry corporal knows that to avoid casualties, soldiers need to be dispersed as much as possible. This was the hard-learned lesson of the infantrymen of the First World War. But what is true at the tactical level is not necessarily true at the operational level, because the principle that dominates the notion of breakthrough is the saturation of the enemy's defense. To put it simply—faced with a weapon that can destroy three tanks per minute, the attacker increases his chances of survival by presenting more than three tanks per minute.

The idea of a breakthrough is to create temporary superiority over a portion of the front line. Thus, assuming an average force ratio of 3:1 on the front line as a whole, we gather enough resources to create a local superiority of 5-6:1 on the breakthrough sector. It is from this concept that the myth of "waves of infantry" or "human waves" originated, which misinformed "experts" claimed the Soviets used.

---

117. "Field Manual 100-2-1, The Soviet Army: Operations and Tactics," *Department of the Army* Washington, DC, July 16, 1984 (https://irp.fas.org/doddir/army/fm100-2-1.pdf)

This legend was created by Ukrainian propaganda to explain the need to hold on to Bakhmut in order to wear down the Russian army. In February 2023, the French TV channel *LCI* showed us a *"human wave"* of... 8 men![118] Our "experts" just don't get it. In April 2023, Christopher Perryman, a British veteran fighting for Ukraine, explained in *The Spectator* that he had hardly ever seen a Russian fighter. In fact, the Russians use artillery and then come in to clear the ground. They hardly ever expose themselves to infantry fire. He notes: *"Their artillery teams are really excellent. You can't compare Iraq to this, it's much more intense."*[119]

In fact, the breakthrough concept is only fully effective against a dynamic defense. The early SMO thrusts into the depths of the Ukrainian defenses were not configured as breakthroughs, and the Russians did not really use this concept in Ukraine.

On the other hand, this was the concept recommended by Western strategists to Ukraine for its 2023 counter-offensive. However, when the adversary is solidly anchored in a reinforced defense system, a breakthrough is only possible with clear and massive air superiority. This is the bitter experience of the Ukrainians. We'll come back to this later.

In Ukraine, neither the Ukrainians nor the Russians fight with *"waves of infantry."*

Operations at Depth

To attack a force with inferior means in numbers, the Russians use maneuver to achieve limited superiorities in time and space, sufficient to gain the advantage, before redeploying troops to create another local superiority in another sector. This is the Operative Maneuver Group (OMG) (*Группа оперативного маневра—Gruppa operativnovo manevra*), which is the modern version of concepts theorized in the 1930s in the Soviet Union.

In 1982, the Americans drew on this concept to sketch out *AirLand Battle*, aimed precisely at attacking the Soviet rear. However, unlike the Soviet concept, they did not really seek to engage ground forces. Their objective was to carry out air and artillery strikes in the depths of

---

118. https://youtu.be/pe2khpEykc4
119. Colin Freeman, "'Iraq does not compare to this': the British soldier on Ukraine's front line", *The Spectator*, April 15, 2023 (https://www.spectator.co.uk/article/iraq-does-not-compare-to-this-the-british-soldier-on-ukraines-front-line/)

the enemy (*deep battle*). It's not really an operational art, but a form of long-distance tactical action.

Often confused with the notion of "operative art" by some "experts,"[120] the LDA is an *ad hoc*, highly mobile force that pushes into the depths of the enemy's system. It progresses according to the "flowing water" principle, bypassing enemy strongpoints and major localities, in order to attack the enemy's second echelon and reserves. In fact, the objective of the LDA is not to destroy the opponent, but to prevent him from reinforcing his first echelon forces.

In Ukraine, in the first phase of the SMO, the Russians engaged in a form of LDA in order to position themselves around Kiev and thus carry out a *shaping operation* whose objective was to fix the Ukrainian second echelon in order to prevent it from reinforcing the Donbass position and pushing Zelensky towards negotiation. The aim was to transform an operational success into a strategic one. This was exactly what happened, with its demands for talks at the end of February, then in mid-March 2022.

At the end of March 2022, in response to Volodymyr Zelensky's negotiating proposal, Russian troops withdrew from the Kiev sector. This allowed the Ukrainian army to reinforce the Donbass troops and prepare an offensive towards the south.

Defensive Operations

Although static in appearance, defense derives its effectiveness from the synergy of joint combat. During the Cold War, the Soviet Union always assumed that NATO would make the first decision to attack. The Warsaw Pact's major maneuvers invariably began with a surprise NATO attack, often preceded by a nuclear strike. This was particularly true of the ZAPAD 77 exercise (May-June 1977), which validated the concept of a Theater of Operations Command (TVD).

Towards the end of the Cold War, there were endless debates in the USSR about the nature of operations, whether they were "defensive offensive" or "offensive defensive." The end of the Cold War and Russia's hopes of joining the Western community put an end to these Byzantine quarrels.

---

120. https://www.rts.ch/info/monde/13135499-bernard-wicht-le-succes-de-loperation-russe-cest-davoir-reussi-a-mystifier-tout-le-monde.html

At the time of the SMO, our "experts" preferred to present the Russian army as they wished it to be, rather than as it is. For example, they saw the defensive system put in place by the Russians since October 2022 as essentially static and linear, rather like what we saw in 1914-1918. They saw it exclusively from the point of view of the tacticians they are. Naturally, this simplistic analysis was necessary to ensure that the Ukrainians would succeed in their counter-offensive.

But the reality is very different. The Russians have mastered the art of operations, including defensive operations, as demonstrated by the Ukrainian counter-offensive in the summer of 2023. The maps of the Russian defensive system published in the West are based on data collected by American reconnaissance systems, such as the MQ-9 REAPER or RQ-4 GLOBAL HAWK, cruising over the Black Sea. However, these cannot show the dynamic dimension of Russian defense, and therefore its operative dimension.

Contrary to popular opinion in the West, Russian forces do not operate according to rigid patterns. Quite the contrary, in fact. As we have already seen during the Second World War and the war in Afghanistan, they evolve their operational practices in line with needs and technological developments. This is the task of the Land Forces Military Training and Research Center (VUNts SV).

In April 2023, in an article published by *Voïennaya Mysl'* (*Military Thought*) of the Russian Ministry of Defense, Colonel-General Aleksandr Romanchuk and Colonel A. Shigin present three variants of forms of defense.[121]

Decentralized Defense

The first is a "decentralized defense." It combines a network of support points and an in-between area covered by robotized combat systems (such as URAN-9s, NEREKHTAs or PLATFORM-Ms), guided by drones and artificial intelligence to break up opposing attacks. This concept was tested during the ZAPAD-21 exercise (September 2021) in Belarus. This exercise was mentioned in my book, *Putin: Game Master*, but nobody

---

121. Colonel-General Aleksander Romantchuk & Colonel A. Shiguine, "Перспективы повышения эфективности армейских оборонительных операций" (Prospects for Improving the Efficiency of the Army's Defense Operations), *Voïennaya Mysl'*, No. 4-2023, April 22, 2023 (https://limited-vm.ric.mil.ru/Stati/item/486826/)

paid much attention to it, as Westerners were looking for signs of an offensive operation.

Dynamic Defense

The second variant, known as "dynamic defense," resembles the situation in southern Ukraine in the summer of 2023. It divides the area of operations into three zones:

- A "zone of cover," in which mobile units fight, operating autonomously and making extensive use of the "reconnaissance-fire" (ROK) and "reconnaissance-strike" (RUK) concepts. Their aim is to identify the direction of the enemy's attack, weaken it, prevent it from deploying and prevent it from using its weapons in direct fire against the forces of the main defense zone.
- The "main defense zone," in which the main forces are organized and prepared to contain an attack. Its aim is to halt the enemy's advance. Resources are organized according to the enemy's main efforts, and can be reinforced by elements of the covering forces.
- The "holding zone," in which forces are ready to be engaged in the main defense zone, depending on the attacker's priorities. This zone contains operational support resources, which can be deployed in the other two zones, as well as reserves.

According to Ukrainian Brigadier-General Oleksandr Tarnavskiy, commander of the TAVRIA operational-strategic group, this is the model the Russians are applying in the face of the Ukrainian counter-offensive. The key to this dynamic defense system is the use of ROK in the coverage zone and RUK in the defense and holding zones. This system has been made possible by the proliferation of reconnaissance (ORION, ORLAN-10/30) and strike (LANCET-3 and FPV) UAV systems.

In the Zaporozhye region, for example, the main defense zone is made up of three fortified defense lines that follow one another over a depth of up to 50 km or more.[122]

---

122. https://www.bbc.com/news/world-europe-65615184

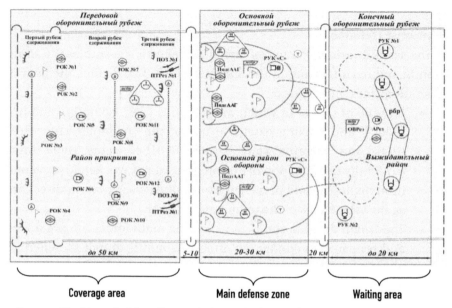

Figure 11—The "dynamic defense" system is the one implemented in Ukraine by General Surovikin since October 2022. Note that the "zone of coverage" makes massive use of ROK/RUK concepts.

Air-Land Defense

The third variant is an "air-land defense," which involves a conventional defensive system, plus a large air-mobile system, enabling one to operate in the depths of the enemy's defenses, and to create main efforts as the situation evolves.

Tactics

In judging an adversary, it is essential to avoid giving in to prejudice. We see the Russians in much the same way as the French see the Germans in *La Grande Vadrouille*. This is why, after declaring *urbi et orbi* that the Russians were ineffective, poorly led, ill-equipped and demotivated, the West must recognize that the Ukrainians—motivated, armed and trained by NATO—were unable to gain the upper hand.

In Russian terminology, tactics is the use of different military formations (tanks, mechanized infantry, artillery, aviation, air defense, etc.) in combat. It is the integration of these elements that leads to operative art. We won't discuss all aspects here, but will concentrate on those relevant to understanding the Ukrainian conflict.

Defense

In October 2022, for a number of reasons that we'll discuss below, Russia switched to a defensive strategy in Ukraine. This implies a more static posture, where superiority is assured by reserves that have to intervene on a front more than 800 km long.

It's not a question of going into all the details of Russian defense, but of understanding the principle. At the tactical level, we find the same logic as at the operational level. The diagram of the Russian battalion defense system[123] shows two main zones: a large surveillance zone, followed by a defense zone.

From the contact line to the first line of defense, a 5 to 10 km-deep surveillance zone is set up to detect and prevent enemy thrusts. For this purpose, there is a first curtain of anti-tank mines. It is normally 120 m deep; but to accommodate the MICLIC assault mine-clearing systems supplied by the West and the Ukrainian UR-77, their depth has been increased to 500 m. However, as the Russians do not always have the quantity of mines required for this change, this has led to irregularities in the structure of the minefields, posing an additional difficulty for the Ukrainians.

Behind this first "curtain" of anti-tank mines, operate fighter units ("*Okhotniki*"), which are highly mobile "*specialized detachments*" (*спецотряд*) specially trained for anti-tank combat.[124] They have no heavy weaponry, but work extensively with ROK/RUK systems to combat the adversary using artillery, anti-tank systems, helicopter gunships or robots.[125]

---

123. "Общая Тактика". *Ministry of Defense of the Russian Federation*, Krasnoyarsk, 2017, p. 90 (vii. sfu-kras.ru/images/pdf/u26_obshhaya-taktika.pdf)
124. https://www.dialog.ua/russia/267455_1675683736
125. https://hromadske.radio/ru/news/2023/02/02/okhotnyky-za-leopardamy-okkupant-zavezly-na-donbass-ustroystva-kotor-e-iakob-mohut-popast-v-tanky-zapadnoho-obraztsa

2. Russian Military Thought

Russian Battalion Defense System

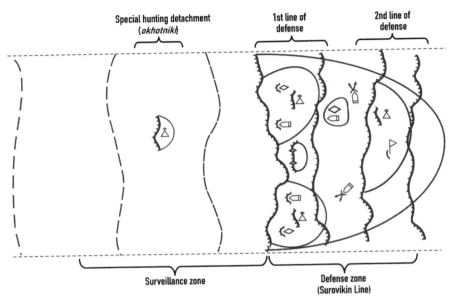

Figure 12—Russian defense structure. The "defense zone" is the area where forces are organized to fight a defensive battle. It comprises ground reinforcements and fortifications stretching along the entire front line. In Ukraine, it is known as the "Surovikin Line." In September 2023, after more than three months of fighting, the Ukrainian counter-offensive had not broken through the "surveillance zone". [Source: "Общая Тактика", 2017, p. 90]

In Ukraine, Russian forces adopted a defensive posture as early as October 2022. The disproportionate attention paid to the battle of Bakhmut led to relative calm on the rest of the front, enabling the installation of a staggered and particularly dense system in depth.

Next comes the defense zone, 10 to 20 km deep, which includes the actual defensive system, with anti-tank obstacles, mines, terrain reinforcements, etc.[126]

In August 2023, with Ukrainian efforts focused on the small village of Robotino, Brigadier-General Oleksandr Tarnavskiy of the Ukrainian army declared that his forces had broken through the first Russian line of defense and reached the second. Western experts suggested that he was lying and that the Ukrainians never actually reached the first line of defense.

---

126. https://studfile.net/preview/7511393/page:4/

In fact, they were probably all right, but they were talking about different things. General Tarnavskiy assumed that the Russians were applying the dynamic defense model described by General Romanchuk. Thus, he considered that his forces had pushed into the zone of cover, to touch the zone of surveillance of the battalions of the Surovikin Line.

Understanding Ukraine's Declarations

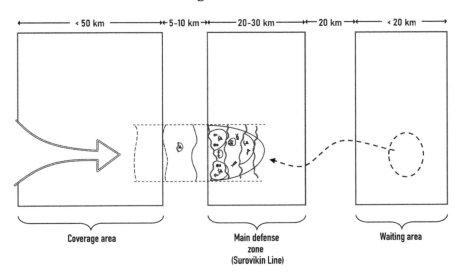

Figure 13—*When Ukrainian General Tarnavskiy claimed that his troops had broken through the Russian first line of defense in the Rabotino sector, he was referring to the Russian operative posture and considered the zone of cover to be a line of defense. This is technically false. For their part, Western commentators—including the author—who asserted that Ukrainian troops did not go beyond the zone of cover, were talking about the Russian tactical set-up. In fact, between the beginning of June and the beginning of September 2023, at no point on the front did Ukrainian troops reach the main defense zone (the Surovikin line).*

It's also important to understand that the Russians see the battlefield as dynamic. Thus, what we call "minefields"—which are generally large rectangles where mines are distributed according to a precise geometric pattern—are understood as a dynamic element of combat by the Russians. Thus, when a detachment manages to enter a mined area with special aircraft, the Russians immediately project new anti-tank mines behind these elements, isolating the advanced detachment and depriving subsequent elements of mine-clearing systems.

67

The "Pocket of Fire"

In February 2021, the Russian military magazine *Zvezda* described the training of the forces of the Southern Military District (to be engaged in Ukraine a year later):[127]

> *During field exercises, sub-units of motorized riflemen carry out a sudden withdrawal from occupied lines to draw the enemy into a pocket of fire, followed by an intensive offensive with artillery fire support.*

This is exactly the scenario that was observed in Kiev (March 2022), Kharkov (September 2022) and Kherson (October 2022), and which was repeated all along the front line during the Ukrainian counter-offensive in 2023. But our "experts" can't read. Seeking to convince themselves and the rest of the world of their prejudices, they helped to propagate a false image of these events, which gave Ukraine the illusion of a possible victory.

This is why, from late summer 2022, as the Russians began to adopt a defensive strategy, there was talk of Ukrainian "counter-offensives." But our media only reported the announcement of their launch, never their outcome.

As State Department advisory panel member and Russia expert Steven Myers told *USA Today*, the Ukrainians report on their "pinpricks" to show the West the progress they've made, but *"they don't talk about the counterattacks of the Russians, who don't care about gaining or keeping ground in the 'pockets of fire' and are experts at setting traps."*[128]

This gives the impression that the Ukrainians are only advancing. However, an examination of the map shows that the front line is constantly fluctuating without changing fundamentally. The problem is that every move results in colossal losses on the Ukrainian side.

---

127. https://zvezdaweekly.ru/news/2021291350-Qy88G.html
128. https://eu.usatoday.com/story/news/world/ukraine/2023/09/07/ukraine-russia-war-live-updates/70783569007/

The "Pocket of Fire" Concept

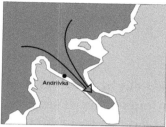

September 2, 2022
Ukrainian forces launch an offensive on the town of Andriivka. The Russians let the Ukrainians make their breakthrough, luring them into a "pocket".

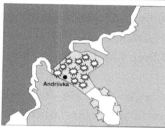

September 2, 2022
Russian forces "close" the pocket with intense artillery fire and fight Ukrainian formations in the fire pocket.

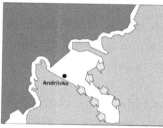

September 3, 2022
The remaining Ukrainian forces are trying to withdraw under Russian fire.

September 4, 2022
The situation is back to normal. Ukrainian forces have suffered heavy losses, but have not gained any territory.

Figure 14—The "pocket of fire" concept consists of withdrawing to push the opponent to make a breakthrough, thus encircling him in a "cauldron" (котел) where he is methodically destroyed. This tactic, which dates back to the Second World War, was used by the Donbass autonomists in 2014-2015, then in Kharkov (September 2022), in Kherson (October 2022), and at multiple points along the front line during the Ukrainian counter-offensive of 2023.

The Russian calculation is that lost ground can be regained, while human lives cannot. Forced into action by their Western sponsors, the Ukrainians have not integrated this factor into their operational thinking.

This is why they suffered considerably higher losses than the Russians, but have to protect a decisive narrative if they are not to discourage the West.

The Battalion Battle Group (BTG)

In Ukraine, tactical action is carried out by Battalion Battle Groups (BTGs). These are small forces the size of a reinforced battalion, bringing together all the components of tactical-level joint combat. These forces of around 600 to 800 men are highly mobile and have an autonomous joint combat capability. The creation of the Battlegroups (BTGs) was the result of the restructuring of the Soviet and then Russian armed forces, which began in the late 1980s.

In Europe, in relatively compartmentalized terrain, the basic combat unit is the company or battalion. But in the Soviet army, designed to operate over vast territories, the maneuver unit was the regiment or battalion. Particularly at a time when means of communication were highly hierarchical, the degree of autonomy of small units was very limited. This explains why the notion of initiative was different in the Soviet and Western armies.

But that all changed with the war in Afghanistan. Contrary to popular belief in the West, in the Soviet Union, and later in Russia, the armed forces and military doctrine have always been the subject of discussion, right down to the lowest levels of command. The war in Afghanistan was no exception. Military personnel could exchange views on tactics and combat techniques in Soviet military magazines such as *Voïenny Vestnik*.

As a result, lessons learned in the field were quickly incorporated into the conduct of operations and doctrines of employment. This explains in particular the complete restructuring of the 40th Army, which entered Afghanistan in 1979 with a "traditional" structure, and which by 1983 had a totally different structure, composed mainly of light infantry, special forces, helicopter-borne units, artillery and signals units.

In February 2023, Swiss expert Alexandre Vautravers asserted that in 2007, Vladimir Putin gave his new Defense Minister Anatoly Serdyukov the task of transforming the Russian army so that it would be *"ready for war in ten years,"* and he saw this as the harbinger of the SMO in 2022. He also claimed that this reform followed the NATO model, so that Russia too can project forces abroad and *"create states in the Balkans... we want to do the same too."*[129] This is the stuff of soap operas.

In fact, according to the pro-Western *Moscow Times*, Serdyukov's mission was to *"clean up the Ministry of Defense and bring transparency and combat readiness to the armed forces."*[130] The Russian army inherited from the Yeltsin period was deeply corrupt, dysfunctional and unwieldy. These observations were confirmed by the leadership and the coordination problems observed in South Ossetia in August 2008.[131] They provided the impetus for the implementation of Serdyukov's reforms.

With Serdyukov, who was a civilian, Vladimir Putin wanted to get away from the *siloviki* system, which made the Ministry of Defense a source of corruption. The aim was to reduce the size of the armed forces to a manageable and affordable size. The Russian army underwent a drastic slimming program. From over a million men in 2008 to 845,000 in 2013, the emphasis was on a professional army: the number of senior officers was cut by 70%, systems were no longer developed but bought "off-the-shelf," and so on.

Basically, the Russian army did exactly the same thing as Western countries had done in the previous decade: reforms were guided not by doctrinal changes, but by the country's economic situation and the priority given to the country's development.

However, the idea of reducing the size of operational units, while maintaining a high firepower capability, dates back long before the Serdyukov reform. Back in 1989, based on the experiences of the war in Afghanistan, the Soviets had perceived the need to break down their forces into smaller modules, endowed with a high degree of operational autonomy:[132]

> *Experience of local wars and conflicts in recent years shows that a battalion, reinforced by artillery, air defense weapons, etc. (in all, up to eight attached sub-units), is the basic tactical entity on the battlefield. To a certain extent, this is because the commander still*

129. https://www.club-44.ch/mediatheque/
130. https://www.themoscowtimes.com/2012/11/13/serdyukov-leaves-big-shoes-to-fill-a19363
131. Michael Kofman, "Russian Performance in the Russo-Georgian War Revisited," *War on the Rocks*, September 4, 2018 (https://warontherocks.com/2018/09/russian-performance-in-the-russo-georgian-war-revisited/)
132. LTC Lester W. Grau, "The Soviet Combined Arms Battalion Reorganization for Tactical Flexibility," *Soviet Army Studies Office*, Fort Leavenworth, Kansas, September 1989 (https://apps.dtic.mil/sti/pdfs/ADA216368.pdf)

has the opportunity to personally observe the situation on his front and react immediately.

The BTG Concept

The idea is to create formations capable of fighting autonomously. Within NATO, similar thinking led to the creation of *Brigade Combat Teams* (BCT) in the United States and *Battlegroups* in Great Britain.[133]

For Russia, the aim was to maintain a high level of firepower while maintaining smaller formations. After trials with brigades at the end of the Cold War, it opted for a battalion structure.

The battalion is the smallest military unit with a staff; so, it has the capacity to analyze the situation, make complex decisions and conduct joint combat. What's more, the battalion is more agile than a regimental structure. It can manage all the combat and support elements required for its action.

What makes BTGs so special is their focus on firepower and mobility. It's a formation designed for dynamic conflict, as imagined during the Cold War and as seen in the first weeks of the SMO.

BTG Structure

BTGs are a form of reinforced motorized or airborne rifle battalion, designed to operate relatively autonomously in dynamic combat. The idea is to be able to push rapidly into the depths of the enemy's territory, bypassing defensive positions requiring sustained combat (such as urban or forest areas).

But this structure has a downside: it's small in terms of the number of combatants. For example, a BTG has only around 200 infantrymen. As a result, when it is forced to fight in urban areas or special terrain, it has to be reinforced by infantrymen. This is why Russian forces had to be reinforced by troops like WAGNER (in Bakhmut) or Chechen formations (in Mariupol).

This chronic shortage of infantrymen apparently led the Russians to engage special forces in some areas where specialized infantry would have sufficed. In the Russian forces, the "special forces" or *spetsnaz* (войска *специального назначения*) are the equivalent of the US Navy

---

133. http://www.armedforces.co.uk/army/listings/l0014.html

SEALs: troops intended for high-risk operations in enemy territory, often for deep operational reconnaissance actions. Today, this latter function has been taken over by drones, leaving the *spetsnaz* a little idle. Engaging them on hot spots was tempting, but suboptimal.

Some "experts" pointed out the weakness of the BTG's logistical capabilities, and laughed at the long columns of immobilized vehicles north of Kiev at the very start of the offensive. If these columns were indeed a malfunction, our "experts" failed to understand the mechanisms behind them.

BTG logistics are organized around the "*push principle*" (or *Bringprinzip* in German). In other words, the aim is to relieve the BTG command of the task, organize its own logistics and bring it what it needs, according to pre-calculated requirements. This system differs from the "*pull principle*" (*Holprinzip* in German), where the unit command fetches what it needs from the rear. The disadvantage of the *push principle* is that logistics efforts can be poorly synchronized with the BTG's operational situation. This is what happened north of Kiev, causing the traffic jams whose images were widely commented on by our "experts."

Composition of a Generic BTG

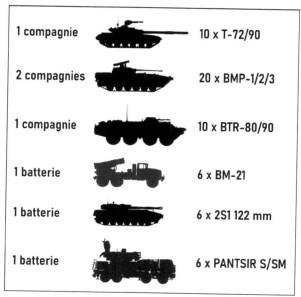

1 compagnie	10 x T-72/90
2 compagnies	20 x BMP-1/2/3
1 compagnie	10 x BTR-80/90
1 batterie	6 x BM-21
1 batterie	6 x 2S1 122 mm
1 batterie	6 x PANTSIR S/SM

Figure 15—The BTG is a small task force with remarkable firepower. Its main weakness is the relative lack of infantry.

2. Russian Military Thought

Respect for Civilian Populations

On March 21, 2022, the Swiss *RTS* reported *"indiscriminate bombings"* [which] *"killed everyone."*[134] But that's not what American analysts saw. The following day, in the American magazine *Newsweek*, a US Air Force officer noted: *"I know the media keeps repeating that Putin is targeting civilians, but there's no proof that Russia is doing it intentionally."* In the same article, a DIA analyst noted that *"the vast majority of airstrikes take place over the battlefield, with Russian aircraft providing 'close air support' to ground forces. The remainder—less than 20%, according to US experts—target military airfields, barracks and support depots."*

The Swiss media thus contradicted the US intelligence analyst who pointed out that *"if we simply convince ourselves that Russia is bombing indiscriminately, or that it is failing to inflict more damage because its personnel are not up to the job or because they are technically inept, then we are not seeing the conflict for what it* is.*"*[135]

In October 2022, Peter Maurer, president of the *International Committee of the Red Cross* (ICRC), declared in the Swiss magazine *Die Weltwoche*:

> *We note that there are genuine efforts on both sides not to allow this conflict to degenerate completely. There are precautionary measures in regards to the civilian population.*[136]

In April 2022, the Swiss state media returned to the subject, declaring that Russia was practicing *"strategic scorched-earth tactics."*[137]

In fact, Russian forces are credited with strategies used by the defenders. For example, the *"scorched earth policy"* is designed to prevent an attacker

---

134. https://www.rts.ch/info/monde/12958379-les-relations-avec-washington-sont-au-bord-de-la-rupture-dit-moscou.html

135. William M. Arkin, "Putin's Bombers Could Devastate Ukraine But He's Holding Back. Here's Why", *Newsweek*, March 22, 2022 (https://www.newsweek.com/putins-bombers-could-devastate-ukraine-hes-holding-back-heres-why-1690494)

136. "Präsident des Roten Kreuzes Peter Maurer sagt: "Der Ukraine-Krieg markiert eine Trendwende." Das humanitäre Völkerrecht werde wieder stärker beachtet. Die Rolle des neutralen Vermittlers bleibe unverzichtbar. Friede sei nur durch Gespräche möglich", *Die Weltwoche*, October 7, 2022 (https://weltwoche.ch/daily/praesident-des-roten-kreuzes-peter-maurer-sagt-der-ukraine-krieg-markiert-eine-trendwende-das-humanitaere-voelkerrecht-werde-wieder-staerker-beachtet-die-rolle-des-neutralen-vermittlers/)

137. "Russian army's future strategy in Ukraine analyzed by experts," *RTS Info*, April 24, 2022 (https://www.rts.ch/info/monde/13040980-la-strategie-future-de-larmee-russe-en-ukraine-analysee-par-des-experts.html)

from exploiting the resources of conquered territories. By withdrawing, infrastructure, fuel depots, etc. are systematically destroyed, so that the attacker cannot use them to his advantage and his "gains" become a handicap. This was the strategy ordered by Stalin during the German advance in 1941-1942.

Using the presence of civilians to prevent an attacker from using his weapons is also a defensive strategy, generally referred to as *"human shielding."* The reality is that Ukrainian forces are trying to compensate for their tactical inferiority by placing their troops close to or in the center of civilian targets. As William Schabas, Professor of International Law at Middlesex University, London, puts it:

> *I'm very reluctant to say that Ukraine is responsible for civilian casualties, because Ukraine is fighting to defend its country against an aggressor, but to the extent that Ukraine brings the battlefield into civilian areas, it increases the danger to civilians.*[138]

Thus, not only are the Russians the attackers now, but they're not out to conquer territory. Their objective is to protect a population. It's hard to understand why they would systematically seek to destroy the infrastructures of these same populations, which are generally favorable to them!

Russian Conduct

A Pragmatic Philosophy of Conduct

In December 2022, General Bruno Clermont's hearing before a Senate committee illustrated the extremely schematic and simplistic vision of Russian conduct held by our generals.[139] Beyond the naïve depiction, the Ukrainian conflict shows that Russian conduct is extremely flexible and

---

138. Sudarsan Raghavan, "Russia has killed civilians in Ukraine. Kyiv's defense tactics add to the danger", *The Washington Post*, March 28, 2022 (https://www.washingtonpost.com/world/2022/03/28/ukraine-kyiv-russia-civilians/)
139. https://youtu.be/INa_9ZzEgfM

very well integrated. Even at the height of the Cold War, the US Army's *FM-100-2* manual on Soviet forces declared:[140]

> *Soviet operations and tactics are not as rigid as many Western analysts think.*

The Soviet army was organized on the basis of the Red Army's experiences during the Great Patriotic War (June 22, 1941 to May 9, 1945): large-scale operations, launched over vast areas with massive forces. The maneuvering unit was the regiment, or even the battalion. That's why the initiative of staff officers was focused on this level. The war in Afghanistan changed everything: the extreme compartmentalization of the terrain, numerous small tactical-level clashes and the impossibility of engaging large military formations gave new importance to the lower tactical level. The 40th Army, articulated as a conventional joint army, was rapidly transformed into a force made up of helicopters and artillery in abundance, capable of supporting a multitude of small independent units very quickly, thanks to plethoric means of transmission.

For Russian forces, the main lesson of this conflict was the promotion of individual initiative at the lower tactical level, with the corollary of lowering the level of application of what they call "*decentralized conduct*" (децентрализация *управления* - ДЦУ) (DTsU). Better known by its German name of *Auftragstaktik*, DTsU is the equivalent of what is called "*conduite par objectifs*" in industry or "*conduite par missions*" (*mission command*) in some armies. It is defined as the:[141]

> *principle of developing a specific solution based on the mission received.*

In France, this concept of "conduct by objectives" is very poorly understood, and is therefore decried by a few historians and military "experts" who have no command experience.[142]

---

140. https://irp.fas.org/doddir/army/fm100-2-1.pdf
141. Цепков И. В. "Терминологические основания выделения терминов-реалий и способы их перевода (рус.)", *Вестник* МГЛУ, № 19-2 (679), 2013
142. https://www.vududroit.com/2022/06/ukraine-le-temps-des-mauvais-generaux/

It's not an element of military tactics, as the term suggests, but a method of leadership (*Führungstil*). This is why, although the term *Auftragstaktik* *is* still widely used in everyday language, the *Bundeswehr* prefers the expression *Führen mit Auftrag* ("leading by mission"). This is in contrast to *Befehlstaktik* (*detailed command*), in which subordinates are given detailed instructions on how to carry out their mission.

With management by objectives, the executive formulates an intention and sets an objective for his subordinate. It's up to the subordinate to find the best solution for achieving this objective, given the situation. Contrary to what some people claim, the subordinate does not have total freedom: he must act within his sphere of competence, within territorial limits (e.g., attack zones) and in the allocation of resources (e.g., air or artillery resources). The interpretation that this means he can "*take initiatives on his own without reference to his superiors*" is simply wrong. The subordinate acts within the framework of his superior's intentions.

Not only does this management system avoid "micro-management," it also allows greater flexibility and is more effective the higher up the hierarchy you go. The problem is that staff officers are generally poorly trained to give subordinates the means and flexibility to make decisions. In the British Army, which adopted this mode of leadership in 1987, an internal study in 2004 showed that the orders issued in Iraq were even more detailed than before. This means that the very principle of leadership by objectives is not understood. The problem is not the method itself, but its application.

On the TVD Ukraine, Ukrainian and Russian forces operate according to the principle of objective-based command. At the start of the Russian operation, Western experts considered the *objective-based approach to* be a decisive advantage for Ukrainian forces over Russian forces, which were reputed to have a more centralized and rigid command system.[143] Experience shows that the opposite is true. In Ukraine, the concept does not seem to have been really assimilated by the troops. On the Russian side, we need to differentiate between the Russian forces, who are sufficiently experienced and trained in the DTsU, and the less experienced Donbass militias, who have suffered a large proportion of the losses attributed to Russia.

---

143. https://www.bbc.com/russian/features-60881647

Grades and Functions

In February 2023, military "expert" Alexandre Vautravers sought to demonstrate the shortage of officers in the Russian army, using the example of a first lieutenant (in France: sous-lieutenant) who was acting as a battalion commander. He had no knowledge of how the Russian army functioned.

In the Russian army, function takes precedence over rank. In other words, commands are awarded on the basis of an officer's actual abilities, not hi rank. This is a phenomenon widely observed during the Second World War and the Cold War, when more capable individuals were promoted to higher positions, despite the availability of *"gradés"* (academy graduates).

As former GRU officer Viktor Suvorov explains in his book, *Inside the Soviet Army*, four principles determine the placement of officers:[144]

1. Seniority does not depend on grade, but on time spent in a position;
2. Eligibility for higher command is determined not by rank, but by suitability for the position;
3. The duration of a command is not fixed, but determined according to need;
4. An executive's position makes him or her eligible for a higher grade, but not vice versa.

There is no automatic correlation between rank and function. Command is not based on bureaucratic criteria, but on results. While it cannot be ruled out that some appointments are influenced by a lack of officers, the Russian army is large enough not to be short of *majors* (in France: *commandants*).

The "Lack of Non-Commissioned Officers"

A criticism often repeated by our "experts," as in the French Senate report of February 2023, to explain the "poor" performance of the Russian army is the shortage of non-commissioned officers.[145] In fact, there are proportionally fewer non-commissioned officers (around 12% in 2010)[146]

---

144. Viktor Suvorov, *Inside the Soviet Army*, Hamish Hamilton, London, 1982
145. "Ukraine: one year of war. What lessons for France?", Information Report No. 334 (2022-2023), *senat.fr*, February 8, 2023 (https://www.senat.fr/rap/r22-334/r22-334_mono.html)
146. https://www.globalsecurity.org/military/world/russia/personnel-nco.htm

than in the French (34% in 2019)[147] or American (45% in 2022)[148] armies. But we must be careful not to jump to conclusions like our senators!

The Russian army traditionally favors the role of officers, especially junior officers (second lieutenants to captains). Officers make up around 30% of the armed forces in Russia, compared with around 12% in France and 18% in the US army. In other words, junior officers perform functions that would be performed by non-commissioned officers in the West. The reason for this is historical.

In Western countries, the NCO corps is largely (but not exclusively) a by-product of the professionalization of the armed forces: the aim is to offer enlisted personnel a career. The Russian army is traditionally a conscript army. It produced junior NCOs who tended to leave the army at the end of their compulsory service. For this reason, officers remain the guarantors of the transmission of experience and technical knowledge. Particularly in Ukraine, Russian officers have less distance from their men than in the West, and are able to take over operational tasks in an emergency. This explains, in particular, the loss rate among Russian officers, which is generally higher than in Western armies.

Conversely, in November 2023, with their forces almost surrounded at Avdiivka, Ukrainian soldiers expressed their disillusionment with their command, which had just been evacuated from the town, leaving the fighters without officers. Trained in the Soviet tradition, they expected their officers to share their fate. But their officers have been trained in the Western school.

That said, one of the elements of the reform of the Russian forces undertaken by Defense Minister Anatoly Serdyukov in 2008 was precisely to professionalize non-commissioned officers and increase their numbers,[149] while reducing the number of officers.[150] However, the Russian army is still strongly officer-led.

In the West, the number of officers in Russia is synonymous with rigidity of command, while the number and role of NCOs is linked to an image of decentralized leadership. This is what the West sought to correct in Ukraine back in 2014, by drastically increasing the number of NCOs and

147. https://fr.wikipedia.org/wiki/Forces_arm%C3%A9es_fran%C3%A7aises
148. https://sgp.fas.org/crs/natsec/IF10684.pdf
149. https://jamestown.org/program/russian-military-plans-new-nco-training-center/
150. https://en.wikipedia.org/wiki/2008_Russian_military_reform

reducing that of officers. This worked to the Ukrainians' disadvantage, as they did not build up a corps of experienced NCOs. During the SMO, Ukrainian officers tended to let NCOs lead actions at the front, while they tended to stay behind. This led to situations where soldiers were lost in the middle of the fighting.

The idea that Russia lacks non-commissioned officers is based on the assumption that a professional army is more efficient than a conscript army. This is not the case. The complexity of weapons systems, often put forward as an argument in favor of a professional army, is a fallacious argument, as this complexity is designed to facilitate the use of weapons and reduce learning times, including for logistics and maintenance activities. In other words, mechanics have been replaced by standard module exchange, and repairs are handled by the weapons supplier. It's the same system as for our cell phones.

However, professionalization remains an asset for activities requiring precise, specialized skills and knowledge.

3. Special Military Operation (SMO) in Ukraine

Calmly, rhythmically, without fuss. This is how Russian troops carry out their tasks, this is how this week of the Special Military Operation begins.
Step by step, towards victory.
Ministry of Defense of the Russian Federation
October 23, 2023[151]

Correlation of Forces

The Russians have a holistic approach to war, taking into account all the factors that directly or indirectly influence the conflict.

Conversely, as we have seen in Ukraine and elsewhere, Westerners have a much more political reading of the war, and end up mixing the two. This is why communication plays such an essential role in the conduct of war: the perception of the conflict plays nearly a more important role than its reality. This is why, in Iraq, the Americans literally invented episodes that glorified their troops.

Russia's analysis of the situation in February 2022 was undoubtedly considerably more pertinent than that of the West. They knew that a Ukrainian offensive against the Donbass was underway and that it could endanger the government. In 2014 to 2015, after the massacres in Odessa and Mariupol, the Russian population was very much in favor of intervention. Vladimir Putin's stubborn clinging to the Minsk Agreements was poorly understood in Russia.

---

151. https://pravda-en.com/world/2023/10/23/149768.html

The factors that contributed to Russia's decision to intervene were twofold: the expected support of Ukraine's ethnically Russian population (which we'll call "Russian-speaking" for convenience), and an economy robust enough to withstand sanctions.

The Russian-speaking population had risen up *en masse* against the new authorities following the coup d'état[152] of February 2014, whose first decision had been to strip Russian of its status as an official language.[153] Kiev tried to backtrack, but in April 2019, the 2014 decision was definitively confirmed.[154]

Since the adoption of the Law on Indigenous Peoples on July 1st, 2021, Russian speakers (ethnic Russians) are no longer considered normal Ukrainian citizens and no longer enjoy the same rights as ethnic Ukrainians.[155] We can therefore expect them to offer no resistance to the Russian coalition in the eastern part of the country.

In terms of sovereignty, Russian Foreign Ministry spokeswoman Maria Zakharova explained:[156]

In Article 1 of the Treaty on the Principles of Relations between the RSFSR and the Ukrainian SSR of November 19, 1990, the two republics recognize each other as "sovereign states". The 1990 treaty was subsequently replaced by the Treaty of Friendship, Cooperation and Partnership between the Russian Federation and Ukraine of May 31, 1997 (article 39), which was denounced by Ukraine and expired on April 1, 2019.

---

152. Jim Rutenberg, "The Untold Story of 'Russiagate' and the Road to War in Ukraine," *The New York Times Magazine*, November 2, 2022 (updated November 7, 2022) (https://www.nytimes.com/2022/11/02/magazine/russiagate-paul-manafort-ukraine-war.html)

153. *Rebels without a Cause: Russia's Proxies in Eastern Ukraine*, International Crisis Group, Europe Report N° 254, 16 July 2019, p. 2

154. https://www.opendemocracy.net/en/odr/ukraine-language-law-en/

155. "Нардеп від 'Слуги народу' Семінський заявив про 'позбавлення конституційних прав росіян, які проживають в Україні'", *AP News*, July 2, 2021 (https://apnews.com.ua/ua/news/nardep-vid-slugi-narodu-seminskii-zayaviv-pro-pozbavlennya-konstitutciinikh-prav-rosiyan-yaki-prozhivaiut-v-ukraini/)

156. https://mid.ru/en/press_service/spokesman/briefings/1890329/

In fact, it was Petro Poroshenko, between the two rounds of the presidential election, who denounced this treaty, which also defines Ukraine's duties towards its Russian minority, in order to "clean up the act" of his rival Volodymyr Zelensky.[157]

Since March 24, 2021, Ukrainian forces have been stepping up their presence around the Donbass and have increased the pressure against the autonomists with their rate of fire.

Process Leading to Ukraine's NATO Membership

Intensification of strikes against the population of Donbass

Russia's intervention

Triggering of massive sanctions against Russia

Economic collapse of Russia

Popular discontent
Revolts and overthrow of Vladimir Putin

Decolonization process of Russia

Membership of Ukraine in NATO possible

Figure 16—On March 18, 2019, Oleksei Arestovitch, Zelensky's advisor, explained that Ukraine's accession to NATO must involve a confrontation with Russia. He outlined the process that would lead to Russia's defeat, thus enabling Ukraine to join the Alliance.

157. http://opiniojuris.org/2019/05/01/termination-of-the-treaty-of-friendship-between-ukraine-and-russia-too-little-too-late-%EF%BB%BF/

Zelensky's decree of March 24, 2021 for the reconquest of Crimea and the Donbass was the real trigger for the SMO. From that moment on, the Russians understood that if there was military action, they would have to intervene. But they also knew that the cause of the Ukrainian operation was NATO membership, as Oleksei Arestovitch had explained. That's why, in mid-December 2021, they were submitting proposals to the USA and NATO for the expansion of the Alliance—their aim then was to remove Ukraine's motive for an offensive in the Donbass.

The reason for Russia's Special Military Operation (SMO) is indeed to protect the population of the Donbass, but this protection was necessary because of Kiev's desire to join NATO through confrontation. NATO's expansion was therefore only an indirect cause of the conflict in Ukraine. The latter could have spared itself this ordeal by implementing the Minsk Agreements, but what was wanted was a defeat for Russia.

In 2008, Russia intervened in Georgia to protect the Russian minority[158] being bombarded by the Georgian government, as confirmed by Swiss ambassador, Heidi Tagliavini, who was in charge of the investigation into this event.[159] In 2014, many voices were raised, in Russia, calling for intervention, as the new regime in Kiev engaged its army against the civilian population of the five autonomist oblasts (Odessa, Dnepropetrovsk, Kharkov, Lugansk and Donetsk) and applied ferocious repression. In 2022, it was to be expected that the Russian population would not understand the government's inaction, after no effort had been made on the Ukrainian or Western side to enforce the Minsk Agreements.

158. https://www.cfr.org/event/conversation-sergey-lavrov
159. Timothy Heritage, "Georgia started war with Russia: EU-backed report", *Reuters*, September 30, 2009 (https://www.reuters.com/article/us-georgia-russia-report-idUSTRE58T4MO20090930)

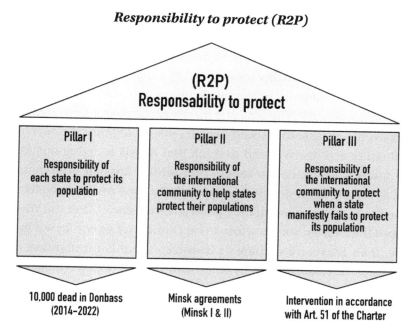

Responsibility to protect (R2P)

(R2P)
Responsability to protect

Pillar I	Pillar II	Pillar III
Responsibility of each state to protect its population	Responsibility of the international community to help states protect their populations	Responsibility of the international community to protect when a state manifestly fails to protect its population
10,000 dead in Donbass (2014–2022)	Minsk agreements (Minsk I & II)	Intervention in accordance with Art. 51 of the Charter

Figure 17—The responsibility to protect, according to the United Nations. As can be seen, neither the United Nations, nor the European Union, nor the diplomacy of Western countries have been able to respect the first two pillars, defended by Russian diplomacy since 2014. Pillar III has become the only possible option for Russia. But it is clear that Russia will use the goal of protecting the Russian population of Ukraine to serve broader national security objectives.

As a result, military intervention would win the support of the ethnic Russian population of Ukraine, and military forces would not have to face "resistance" in the eastern and southern parts of the country.

Right from the start of SMO, it was clear that Russia had no intention of pushing beyond the Russian language areas and trying to establish a lasting presence there. It was Western discourse and our media that added fuel to the fire, attributing to Russia objectives it did not have.

Internationally, however, it was certain that any intervention, however small, would result in sanctions. But, after the experience of 2014, Russia understood the need to prepare the economy for a new shock and make it less dependent on the West. Russian leaders were certainly aware of the project drawn up by the *RAND Corporation* in March 2019, and foresaw the extension of sanctions to which they could be subjected.[160] They knew they didn't have the means to launch an economic retaliation. But they also knew that an economic war against Russia would inevitably backfire on Western countries. Indeed, this eventuality is explicitly mentioned as a risk in *RAND's* strategy.

An important element of Russian military and political thinking is its legalistic dimension. The way our media present events systematically omits events or facts that could explain, justify, legitimize or even legalize Russia's actions. We tend to think that Russia is acting outside any legal framework. Thus, our media present the Russian intervention in Syria as having been decided unilaterally by Moscow,[161] whereas it was carried out at the request of the Syrian government,[162] after the West had allowed the Islamic State to close in on Damascus, as confessed by John Kerry, then Secretary of State.[163] However, there is no mention of the occupation of eastern Syria by American troops, who were never even invited there!

We could multiply the examples, to which our journalists will counter the war crimes committed by Russian forces. This may well be true, but the simple fact that these accusations are not based on any impartial and neutral investigation (as required by humanitarian doctrine), nor on any international one, since Russia is systematically refused participation, casts a shadow over the honesty of these accusations. For example, the sabotage of the Nord Stream 1 and 2 gas pipelines was immediately attributed to Russia, which was then accused of violating international law.[164]

In fact, unlike the West, which advocates a "rules-based international order," the Russians insist on a "law-based international order." Unlike the West, they will apply the law to the letter. No more, no less.

---

160. James Dobbins, Raphael S. Cohen, Nathan Chandler, Bryan Frederick, Edward Geist, Paul DeLuca, Forrest E. Morgan, Howard J. Shatz, Brent Williams, "Extending Russia: Competing from Advantageous Ground", *RAND Corporation*, 2019
161. https://www.lexpress.fr/monde/proche-moyen-orient/intervention-russe-en-syrie_1722867.html
162."Syria: Bashar al-Assad calls for "military aid" from Russia," *Le Point/AFP*, September 30, 2015 (https://www.lepoint.fr/monde/syrie-bachar-el-assad-appelle-a-l-aide-militaire-de-la-russie-30-09-2015-1969436_24.php)
163. John Kerry, recording of a meeting with the Syrian opposition at the United Nations Mission of the Netherlands, September 22, 2016, published by *Wikileaks* ("Leaked audio of John Kerry's meeting with Syrian revolutionaries/UN (improved audio)"), *YouTube*, October 4, 2016)
164. https://www.huffingtonpost.fr/international/article/nord-stream-le-sabotage-des-gazoducs-ne-fait-plus-de-doute-pour-les-europeens_208315.html

The legal framework of Russia's intervention in Ukraine has been meticulously mapped out. As this issue has already been dealt with in one of my previous books, I won't go into detail here, but I will present the chart, which sheds light on the Russian way of proceeding, and is totally absent from Western thinking.

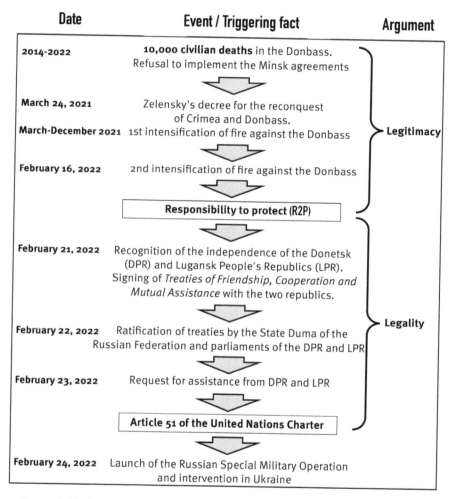

Figure 18—The legal logic of Russian intervention in Ukraine. This process was intended to enable Russia to place the SMO under Article 51 of the UN Charter, so that the self-proclaimed Donbass republics could invoke self-defense. The debates surrounding Israel's invocation of Article 51 against Hamas—which is not a state—demonstrate the relevance of the process initiated by Russia in February 2022.

Russian Forces

The Numbers at the Start of the SMO

In December 2021, the CIA counted 50 Russian Battlegroups (BTGs) on the Ukrainian border, which could be reinforced by a further 50 BTGs. The agency thus estimated the total available potential at 175,000 men,[165] a figure echoed by most commentators. In reality, taking into account the strength of the BTGs (600-800 men), the Russians had at most 60,000 to 80,000 men available for the SMO, figures later confirmed by the Pentagon.[166]

The Russian troops themselves were joined by some 60,000 militia from the Donetsk and Lugansk People's Republics. Thus, the "Russian" force was, in reality, a coalition made up of forces from the army of the Russian Federation, troops from the Donetsk People's Republic (DPR) and the Lugansk People's Republic (LPR) and a contingent from the Chechen National Guard.

While most Russian military personnel are professionals, this is not the case for the troops of the DPR and the LPR, who are "citizens in arms," according to a principle very similar to that known in Switzerland as the "militia system."

With around 40% non-professionals, the Russian coalition is far from being a homogeneous whole. As a result, the quality of its training and weaponry varies widely. Our media and pseudo-military experts have systematically erased these differences in order to attribute to the Russian army the weaknesses of the Donbass militias, particularly when it comes to equipment. We'll come back to this later. What's more, the Donbass militias have different leadership structures, which require "coordination" with the Russian army. This is a problem that Russia undertook to resolve during the second phase of the SMO.

On the other hand, the Donbass militias, however inexperienced, proved to be tough fighters. They fight for the people of "their" region, which they know and in which they have their families and loved ones.

---

165. https://www.washingtonpost.com/national-security/russia-ukraine-invasion/2021/12/03/98a3760e-546b-11ec-8769-2f4ecdf7a2ad_story.html

166. "Senior Defense Official Holds a Background Briefing, April 18, 2022," *defense.gov*, April 18, 2022 (https://www.defense.gov/News/Transcripts/Transcript/Article/3002867/senior-defense-official-holds-a-background-briefing-april-18-2022/)

Let's not forget that under Ukrainian law, ethnically Russian Ukrainian citizens do not have the same rights as "Ukrainian-Ukrainians." This is why these militias feel they are "liberating" their land and why, contrary to what our media have propagated, they have sought to preserve the civilian population in their actions.

*Map published by the **Washington Post** (December 3, 2021)*

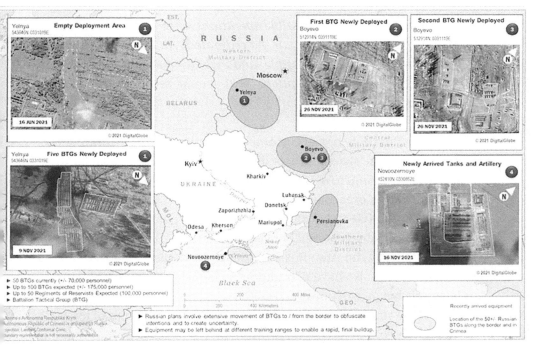

Figure 19—US intelligence map of Russian forces deployed around Ukraine in December 2021. There are no Russian troops in the Donbass. Western politicians—notably the United States, France and Great Britain—have systematically lied about this in order to justify the lack of progress in implementing the Minsk Agreements. France has not played its role as guarantor of the Agreements, and has turned a blind eye to Ukrainian strikes against civilian populations in the Donbass. This is what drove the Russians to the offensive on February 24, 2022. [Source: Washington Post]

The Russian coalition therefore launched the SMO with a force of 90,000 to 140,000 men, depending on the availability of reinforcements. This low number surprised Western observers. Two things are worth remembering here.

89

Firstly, even if the Russian operation had been the subject of "contingency planning," the Russians were probably not fully ready to launch the operation. It was the signs of an imminent Ukrainian offensive that prompted the Russians to put this planning into action and launch the SMO. In other words, the timing was probably not optimal for Russia.

NATO defines the contingency plan as follows:[167]

> *A plan developed for possible operations whose planning elements have been identified or can be estimated. This plan is drawn up in as much detail as possible, and includes the resources required and the deployment options that would serve as a basis for subsequent planning.*

Secondly, Russia is not accustomed to deploying large contingents. "Traditionally," the size of its expeditionary forces is much smaller than what Westerners tend to deploy: in Afghanistan (1979-1989), the Russian contingent never exceeded 115,000 men, and in Syria (2015), 20,000. In South Ossetia (Georgia, 2008), Russian forces peaked at 14,000 men, while the Georgians deployed between 16,000 and 20,000.[168]

Thus, not only do the Russians tend to deploy relatively small contingents, they also have a "tradition" of launching operations with an unfavorable balance of power.

Thus, at the start of the SMO, taking into account the forces of the DPR and LPR, the ratio of forces can be estimated at 0.6:1 in favor of Ukraine on the Donbass front. In May 2022, with the mobilization of Ukraine, 700,000[169] troops faced the 100,000 to 190,000 troops of the Russian coalition (Russia, DPR and LPR). This means a 3-4:1 ratio in favor of Ukraine during phase 1 of the operation.

Our TV strategists keep repeating that the rules of military art call for a superiority of 3 to 1 to be successful in an attack. In fact, this is only

---

167. *NATO Glossary of Terms and Definitions (English and French)*, AAP-6, NATO Standardization Office (NSO), 2021

168. https://warontherocks.com/2018/09/russian-performance-in-the-russo-georgian-war-revisited/

169. "700,000 soldiers defending Ukraine now, Zelenskyy says, as battles rage in the Donbas," *Euronews/AP/AFP*, May 21, 2022 (https://www.euronews.com/2022/05/21/live-sievierodonetsk-shelling-brutal-and-pointless-zelenskyy-says-as-russia-continues-offe)

a planning value, valid for a frontal attack. An examination of the great battles of history shows that in 57% of cases, the attacker achieved victory despite a ratio that was unfavorable to him.[170] The explanation for this apparent contradiction lies in the art of operations: it is maneuver and the succession of actions within an operation that can compensate for an unfavorable ratio. The maneuver must prevent the adversary from regrouping in order to organize his defense. This is what the Ukrainians failed to do in 2022, as they no longer had any maneuvering capability.

Russian Armed Forces Personnel

Knowledge of the Russian system by our so-called "military experts" is extremely fragmentary and tinged with prejudice. From the Russian side, this is a considerable advantage, as these "experts" tend to constantly underestimate Russia's capabilities. In fact, this is a major part of the explanation for Ukraine's defeat by Russia since February 2022. From the point of view of our staffs, these "experts" are very dangerous, because they distort our thinking and lead us to the wrong conclusions.

Since the beginning of the SMO, our media and "experts" have presented the Russian forces as quantitatively and qualitatively insufficient, explaining that they can only lose the war. This narrative led our "experts" to predict a general mobilization for May 9, 2022,[171] which the Russians never mentioned.

Until 2022, the Russian armed forces had a total active manpower of 1,154,000 and 2,000,000 reservists. In December 2022, the Russian government decided to increase the active manpower to 1.5 million by 2026, an increase of around 30%.[172]

It's an increase that affected the whole structure, regardless of what happens in Ukraine, as we do in some Western countries, where we've realized that the potential resulting from the "peace dividend" is no longer in line with the current geopolitical situation.

---

170. T.N. Dupuy, *Numbers, prediction, and war: Using history to evaluate combat factors and predict the outcome of battles*, MacDonald & Jane's, January 1, 1979 (https://www.amazon.com/Numbers-prediction-war-history-evaluate/dp/0672521318) (pp. 12-16)

171. https://www.rts.ch/emissions/infrarouge/13079683-guerre-en-ukraine-la-russie-dans-limpasse.html

172. Julia Shapero, "Russia lays out plans to boost size of military to 1.5 million," *The Hill*, January 17, 2023 (https://thehill.com/policy/international/3816314-russia-lays-out-plans-to-boost-size-of-military-to-1-5-million/)

3. Special Military Operation (SMO) in Ukraine

Partial Mobilization

On September 21, 2022, Vladimir Putin issued a decree for the partial mobilization of 300,000 reservists, ending on October 28. In the West, this mobilization was very poorly presented and understood. There are several reasons for this.

The first reason is the confusion fostered by our pseudo-military experts between "mobilization" and "conscription." Contrary to what Alexandre Vautravers claims, there were no *"different mobilizations"* in Russia of *"reservists, conscripts, or whatever you want to call them."*[173] No, you can't "call it different ways!"

Western discourse presented this "partial mobilization" as a special case of "general mobilization." But for those who know how to read, there is a fundamental difference. General mobilization aims to mobilize all the nation's material and human resources to respond to a state of war. Partial mobilization, on the other hand, is designed to deal with a specific situation requiring certain types of resources only, and results in a call-up of reservists. This is exactly what Vladimir Putin said in his address to the nation on September 21, 2022.[174]

Thus, the people mobilized in September-October 2022 are not inexperienced "conscripts" trained "in a hurry" to reinforce the forces in Ukraine. They were reservists who had already served in the armed forces during the previous ten years and who had specialist functions. They were not, therefore, troops destined to be sent to the front, but personnel with a technical function outside combat zones. This is what Vladimir Putin explained when he said that 41,000 men had been assigned to combat troops and 259,000 to support missions in a wide variety of specialties.[175] Contrary to the claims of some of our "experts", such as Colonel Michel Goya,[176] they were only sent to the area of operations after a six-month "refresher" training course. The first "recalls" arrived on the TVD Ukraine in March-April 2023, and were mostly assigned to the Kherson oblast along the Dnieper, which had not seen any significant combat action.

---

173. https://www.lemanbleu.ch/fr/Emissions/189661-Geneve-a-Chaud.html
174. https://news.sky.com/story/putin-says-he-has-lots-of-weapons-to-reply-to-nuclear-black-mail-of-west-12702322
175. http://kremlin.ru/events/president/news/69730
176. https://youtu.be/CvAYOHc8sv4?t=3263

The second reason is the highly spontaneous and apparently highly improvised nature of his execution, which our journalists and pseudo-experts interpreted as Russia "on the run." A more serious analysis allows for a more nuanced judgment.

Two factors explain the timing of this partial mobilization. Firstly, part of the Russian military was committed to the operation on six-month contracts. It was therefore known that by the end of August 2022, some of them would be returning to civilian life. That's why some Russian generals had asked for recruitment to start in June. Then, apparently, the Russian authorities did not want to mobilize more soldiers until they had a clear picture of the impact of sanctions and the economic situation. At the start of summer, the Russian economy was in convalescence, and Vladimir Putin's concern was not to weaken it in this phase. This is why the decision to mobilize was delayed. In a nutshell, it shows that the Russian economy is doing better than Westerners expected.

In addition to these functional considerations, there are structural consequences. The integration of the four southern Ukrainian oblasts into the Russian Federation extends the Russian border by almost 1,000 kilometers. This implies additional capacities to set up a more robust defense system, build permanent command and logistical facilities, and so on. Consequently, the partial mobilization is the consequence of two phenomena: the shift to a defensive strategy, where numbers rather than maneuver play an important role, and the referendums held in the oblasts of southern Ukraine, which involved the establishment of military infrastructures in this region.

As for the course of this partial mobilization, our picture of the situation is very imperfect, even caricatured. It's true that the decision was not unanimous and was criticized in Russia, including by the official media. Generally speaking, not all young people are enthusiastic about going into battle, and Russians are probably no exception. However, it is interesting that the young people interviewed by our media on the Georgian border did not understand that this partial mobilization concerned only reservists.[177] They were misled by the Western narrative, which shows that Russian society has wide access to Western media.

177. "Thousands of Russians cross borders to flee mobilization," *rts.ch*, September 28, 2022 (https://www.rts.ch/info/monde/13421767-des-milliers-de-russes-traversent-les-frontieres-pour-fuir-la-mobilisation.html); "Russian military call-up sparks major exodus," *DW*, September 24, 2022 (https://www.dw.com/en/russian-military-call-up-sparks-major-exodus/a-63227879)

In fact, this phenomenon reflects the weakness of official communication rather than widespread resistance to the SMO, since at the same time more than 70,000 volunteers (who had not been recalled) spontaneously signed up. It's worth noting that flight from compulsory service is a much more widespread problem in Ukraine, where a large proportion of mobilizable personnel can be seen driving expensive German sports cars in Europe's major capitals. This is why Ukraine has had to make massive use of foreign volunteers, including militants from jihadist movements[178] considered terrorists in the West, such as Hayat Tahrir al-Sham.[179]

That said, the Russians are not accustomed to mobilizing and committing large contingents of troops. In this case, they had to manage the mobilization of 300,000 men, the conscription of 140,000 men (part of the normal routine) and the enlistment of 70,000 volunteers, i.e., over half a million men. Clearly, this caused friction, and the breakdowns observed in the mobilization system were noted and commented on by the Russian authorities.

Volunteers are supernumeraries who have agreed to join the armed forces over and above their mobilization quotas. In preparation for the fighting in Ukraine, volunteer units were formed to reinforce the capabilities of battalions, which are traditionally poor in infantry.

Conscription

In Russia, conscription is open to all young people between the ages of 18 and 27 (soon to be raised to 30). There are two sessions per year (a spring session from April 1st to July 15th and an autumn session from October 1st to December 31st), during which some 140,000 young conscripts are trained and then integrated into the armed forces. In 2022, the autumn session was postponed to November 1st because of the partial mobilization in September.

Our media passed off these routine activities as "mobilizations," in order to support the narrative of a weak Russia suffering huge losses.[180]

---

178. "Hundreds of Al-Qaeda militants arrive in Ukraine from Syria", *The Cradle*, March 8, 2022 (https://thecradle.co/Article/news/7669)
179. https://www.state.gov/executive-order-13224/; https://www.gov.uk/government/publications/proscribed-terror-groups-or-organisations--2/proscribed-terrorist-groups-or-organisations-accessible-version; https://www.publicsafety.gc.ca/cnt/ntnl-scrt/cntr-trrrsm/lstd-ntts/crmt-lstd-ntts-en.aspx
180. "War in Ukraine: Vladimir Putin signs decree to increase army strength", *Euronews / AFP*, August 26, 2022, (https://fr.euronews.com/2022/08/26/guerre-en-ukraine-vladimir-poutine-signe-un-decret-pour-augmenter-les-effectifs-de-larmee)

It's all well and good to criticize the Russian Army, even when it acts exactly like us. Such is the case with the conscription mechanism that goes through the Military Districts *(Военный Округ* - BO) (VO). In February 2023, Alexandre Vautravers, a Swiss military "expert," explained that this system is *"extremely dangerous"* for Russia, taking the example of Great Britain in the First World War. The comparison is irrelevant, because the problem with the British was not the recruitment method, but the fact that they had regiments composed of a single nationality, and sent these regiments to the most dangerous areas. This was the case with the Australians sent to Gallipoli, where they were massacred by the Turks, leaving a bitter taste in the mouths of the surviving Australians. In the Russian army, regiments are composed of several ethnic or national groups to avoid this problem.

The "Wagner" Military and Private Security Company

Private military companies (PMCs) or private military and security companies (PMSCs) tend to excite the imagination. Many journalists and experts talk about the attempt or desire to "privatize war." But this is inaccurate. For neither the Americans nor the Russians is it a question of turning war into a "business" (even if some people ultimately profit from it). It's simply a question of outsourcing a certain number of functions that don't require any particular combat skills (logistics functions, site security, etc.). The advantage of these SMPs is that, unlike increases in the size of the armed forces, which require legal and structural adaptations, their use does not require parliamentary decisions.

The United Nations is a major user of PMSCs (particularly Russian ones), as they enable it to carry out security tasks without depending on the goodwill of troop-contributing countries (TCCs). As PMSCs are not under the authority of a member country's executive, they can be given instructions without reference to their home government. For example, US military personnel—whatever their commitment—are always under the authority of the President of the United States. In a multilateral context, this leads to a duplication of chains of command, resulting in incidents such as the Beirut attacks on France and the United States in 1983, and the deaths of the Rangers in Mogadishu in 1993.

There are several dozen PMSCs in Russia, known by the abbreviation TchVK *(Частная Военная Компания)*. Most have security missions in

Russia and around the world, and a small part has been operating since 2014 on behalf of the self-proclaimed Donbass republics. Made up of ex-officers of the Russian armed forces, particularly the special forces (*spetsnaz*), they have had training tasks for the republics' young militias.

The existence of the SMSP "Wagner" has been talked about for several years. But it was in 2021 that the French media began to take an interest, after the Malian government decided to recruit "Wagner" personnel and demanded the withdrawal of the French military. This decision triggered the ire of then French Foreign Minister Jean-Yves Le Drian and an unprecedented propaganda campaign against Russia, combining anti-African racism, Russophobia, bad faith and lies. For more details, I refer the reader to my book *Putin: Game Master?*[181]

The so-called "Wagner" group is a poorly understood entity. It is described as a *"parallel army of Vladimir Putin."*[182] But such an "army" does not exist and is a pure invention. Some experts even question whether it exists in the form attributed to it. According to one Ukrainian source, it appears to be a constellation of small security companies based in European countries (Hungary, Serbia, Switzerland, Italy, Germany, Greece and Taiwan), which go by several names other than "Wagner"[183] and receive mandates on an ad hoc basis.[184]

Its origins apparently lie in the need to manage the volunteer fighters who came to help the autonomists of the self-proclaimed republics of Donetsk and Lugansk back in 2014. Formed from motley volunteers, with no uniform training, and equipped with light weapons, these formations were only adequate for security missions and infantry work. Wagner, which was just one of such groups, gradually phagocytized the others.

These companies are neither equipped nor trained to replace traditional military combat training, with the exception of urban combat, which is extremely demanding and dangerous. It is personnel-intensive, requiring experienced, tough and hardened fighters, but does not require sophisticated equipment or heavy materials.

181. Jacques Baud, *Putin: Game Master?*, Max Milo, Paris, 2022
182. Charlotte Lalanne, "Centrafrique, Mali... Comment les mercenaires russes de Wagner tissent leur toile", *L'Express*, October 3, 2021 (updated October 4, 2021)
183. Nykolaï Koval, "'Фабрики' наемников: где в России готовят террористов", *obozrevatel.com*, June 12, 2018
184. Amy Mackinnon, "Russia's Wagner Group Doesn't Actually Exist", *Foreign Policy*, July 6, 2021

In France, since the events in Mali, the portrayal of this army by the authorities and the media has been more a matter of misinformation than real analysis. "Documentaries" based more on gossip than journalistic investigation tend to present us with the image of a compact army, a kind of shadow force, described by *CNews* as *"Vladimir Putin's secret army."*[185] According to *Africa Intelligence,* "Wagner's" *"parallel diplomacy" is* a problem for Moscow.[186]

In Russia, as in all countries, the tasks of private companies and the armed forces are strictly separated. There are exceptions, such as the American CIA, but these are rare. Integrating a private combat structure into a military command structure poses multiple problems. The most trivial is that of loyalty. It is generally assumed that soldiers fight out of conviction for their country, as is the case with Russian soldiers fighting for their brothers in the Donbass. "Mercenaries" are often motivated more by money than love of country.

Generally speaking, PMSCs can pose another type of problem: they can contribute to the militarization of situations without having the same legal and political constraints as traditional armies. Other problems, relating to law, confidentiality, training, etc., stand in the way of integration into the armed forces. These private units are therefore most often used for independent actions, outside the normal chain of command.

Thus, at the end of October 2022, General Sergei Surovikin commissioned Wagner to destroy the enemy in Bakhmut, with a six-month contract. The aim was not to seize the city, but to destroy the enemy there,[187] in line with the initial "demilitarization" objective set out by Vladimir Putin on February 24, 2022. This is "Operation Bakhmut Meat Grinder" ("БАХМУТСКАЯ МЯСОРУБКА").

How and why "Wagner" came to be involved in Russian operations in Ukraine remains a mystery. It's not impossible that Evgeny Prigozhin, Wagner's administrator, benefited from the support of Surovikin, who took command of the Russian TVD Ukraine forces in October 2022. This could explain the latter's apparent disgrace at the end of June 2023, after the mutiny led by Prigozhin, which the general had opposed.

185. François Blanchard, "Mali: qu'est-ce que le groupe Wagner, 'l'armée secrète de Vladimir Poutine'?", *CNews*, October 7, 2021 (updated October 11, 2021)
186. "Wagner's parallel diplomacy embarrasses Moscow", *AfricaIntelligence.fr*, October 28, 2021
187. https://dzen.ru/a/ZD5JTKwhFzM0r_oo

On a technical level, the use of Wagner for such an operation is not incongruous. Fighting in urban areas hardly requires any joint action, and can be carried out by an independent formation alongside the main battle plan. Wagner is not a military unit and is therefore not integrated into the Russian command structure. It operated in parallel, with an autonomous mission. It has no artillery, but is assigned fire to fulfill its mission.

Contrary to what Bernard Wicht claims on the Algerian channel *AL24*, Wagner was never integrated into the SMO structure—it could only cooperate with this structure. This is what NATO calls "tactical control" (TACON). In other words, the mission was set by the Russian Ministry of Defense; the TVD force commander facilitates Wagner's mission, notably by providing artillery and logistical support, but he cannot give it another mission.

From the end of 2022, the Russian command was preparing to face the "great" counter-offensive announced by Ukraine for late spring 2023. The Russians were expecting a very large-scale operation. This is why Valery Gerasimov, Chief of the General Staff (*GenStab*), took over command of the SMO on January 11, 2023. What our media and "experts" see as the expression of a problem, is nothing more than a way of allocating more resources to the SMO. But Gerasimov wanted to integrate all his forces into a single command structure based on the principle of *unity of command*. This change probably had an impact on the rules for allocating artillery fire, which angered Prigozhin in February.

Logically enough, on June 10, 2023, following Bakhmut's victory, the Ministry of Defense decided to dismantle all private or semi-autonomous formations and place them under the command of *GenStab*, as explained by the Russian media *Gazeta.ru*:[188]

> *Parallel armies must be dismantled and the strictest vertical chain of command re-established in the military organization of the State.*

Members of all PMSCs operating on TVD Ukraine were to be integrated into the armed forces by July 1, 2023. It was to protest against this decision that Prigozhin wanted to meet "face-to-face" with Defense Minister Sergei Shoigu and Valery Gerasimov in Rostov-on-Don.

---

188. https://www.gazeta.ru/army/2023/06/27/17198912.shtml

Unable to meet them in Rostov, Prigozhin decided, in a spectacular move, to go to Moscow to find them. In fact, all things considered, it was nothing more than the action of employees angry at the general management's decision to close their company. Thanks to the mediation of Alexander Lukashenko, President of Belarus, Prigozhin realized that his action had an international resonance with consequences he had certainly not foreseen, and decided to call off his movement.

As he himself later explained in a voice message:[189]

> *The aim of the march was not to let the PMC Wagner be disbanded, and to hold the military leadership to account for the mistakes made during the war.*

Naturally, our conspiracy theorists saw this as an expression of opposition to Vladimir Putin and the fragility of his power.[190] They even saw it as a further reason to push Ukraine to pursue its counter-offensive.[191] This misjudgment, which illustrates the Western approach of wishful thinking, put Ukraine at odds with its operational capabilities and the promises of Western support. Western youth will pay the price.

Now, "Wagner" fighters had the opportunity to join the Russian armed forces, notably in volunteer battalions. It would be wrong—as some French "experts" have claimed—to see in this the re-emergence of SMSP under another name. The criterion is not the salary or who pays it, but integration into a leadership structure. A fundamental principle of military leadership is not to mix leadership structures. As in all countries, a PMSC can only cooperate with the armed forces, but cannot be integrated into them. A volunteer battalion is a formation integrated into the military structure. For the same reason, the Foreign Legion is a French army formation, not a PMSC.

---

189. https://twitter.com/DAlperovitch/status/1673341994804838402
190. "War in Ukraine: Emmanuel Macron says Russia is 'politically and militarily fragile'", *BFM TV/AFP*, July 12, 2023 (https://www.bfmtv.com/international/asie/russie/guerre-en-ukraine-emmanuel-macron-affirme-que-la-russie-est-fragile-politiquement-et-militairement_AD-202307120583.html)
191. Taras Kuzio, "Putin's Wagner weakness is a signal to support Ukraine's counteroffensive", Atlantic Council, June 29, 2023 (https://www.atlanticcouncil.org/blogs/ukrainealert/putins-wagner-weakness-is-a-signal-to-support-ukraines-counteroffensive/)

Chechen Forces

In the wake of the "Wagner" incidents, commentators and other "experts" followed each other in the media, associating Chechen forces with semi-private structures. This, too, is a misunderstanding of the Russian system. The Chechen forces engaged in Ukraine under the command of Ramzan Kadyrov are not a private structure.

Despite the media coverage of its leader, the Chechen contingent is a formation of the National Guard of the Chechen Republic, and is therefore under the authority of the Russian Ministry of Defense. Commonly referred to as "Kadyrovites," the Chechens are not equipped for open combat. They are better suited to fighting in urban areas and securing the rear. For example, it was Chechens who went to secure the Belgorod area after incursions by far-right fighters from the Free Russia movement, who carry out terrorist actions on behalf of Ukraine.

Integrating Ukrainian Defectors

After the February 23, 2014 decision to abolish the 2012 law on official languages, the whole of southern Ukraine went up in flames. Ukrainian troops sent in to restore order rallied to the side of the rebels with arms and equipment. This is how the Donbass militias emerged. Today, the situation is less clear-cut than in 2014, but many Ukrainians do not share Kiev's policies. This partly explains the high number of defections from the Ukrainian army.

A new phenomenon is the integration of these defectors into the Russian forces. This is the case of the *"Bogdan Khmelnitsky"* volunteer battalion, which was integrated into the Russian KASKAD operative-tactical combat group at the end of October 2023. The battalion was reportedly formed in early 2023, in the Donetsk People's Republic, and was integrated into the Russian forces more than six months later, which corresponds to the training time of the fighters. Ukrainian media suggest that they were "probably forced."[192] This is unlikely. Firstly, the Russians are not short of troops—on the contrary. Secondly, it's risky to integrate fighters who could pose a danger to your own troops. Finally, after the Prigozhin mutiny, it's unlikely that the Russian command would risk a *coup d'éclat*.

---

192. https://zn.ua/war/rossijane-zastavili-ukrainskikh-voennoplennykh-perejti-na-sluzhbu-k-vrahu-isw.html

Russia's Objectives and Strategy

On February 23, 2023, speaking of Russia's objectives in Ukraine, Swiss military "expert" Alexandre Vautravers declared:[193]

> *The aim of the Special Military Operation was to decapitate Ukrainian political and military governance in the space of five, ten, maybe even two weeks. The Russians then changed their plan and their objectives with a number of other failures, and so the Russians change their objectives and their strategic orientations almost every week or every month.*

The problem is that our "experts" themselves define Russia's objectives according to what they imagine, only to be able to say that Russia hasn't achieved them. Thus, we need to get back to the facts.

On February 24, 2022, Russia launched its *"Special Military Operation"* (SMO) in Ukraine *"at the drop of a hat."* In his televised address, Vladimir Putin explained that its strategic objective was to protect the population of Donbass. This objective can be broken down into two parts:

- "demilitarize" the Ukrainian armed forces, regrouped in the Donbass in preparation for the offensive against the DPR and LPR; and
- "denazify" (i.e., "neutralize") the ultra-nationalist and neo-Nazi paramilitary militias in the Mariupol area.

The wording chosen by Vladimir Putin has been very poorly analyzed in the West. It was inspired by the 1945 Potsdam Declaration, which envisaged the development of a defeated Germany according to four principles: demilitarization, denazification, democratization and decentralization.

The Russians understand war from a Clausewitzian perspective: war is the pursuit of politics by other means. This means that they seek to transform operational successes into strategic successes, and military successes into political objectives. Thus, the demilitarization evoked by Putin is clearly linked to the military threat to the populations of

---

193. https://www.radiolac.ch/podcasts/6-minutes-avec-23022023-0917-094529/

the Donbass in application of the decree of March 24, 2021, signed by Zelensky.

But this objective conceals a second objective: the neutralization of Ukraine as a future NATO member. This is what Zelensky clearly understood when he put forward his proposal for resolving the conflict in March 2022. At first, his proposal was supported by Western countries, probably because at this stage they believed that Russia had failed in its bid to take over Ukraine in three days, and that it would not be able to sustain its war effort because of the massive sanctions imposed on it. But at the NATO meeting of March 24, 2022, the Allies decided not to support Zelensky's proposal. As the *Washington Post* explained on April 5:[194]

> *For some NATO members, it is better for the Ukrainians to continue fighting and dying than to achieve a peace that is too early or too costly for Kiev and the rest of Europe.*

Nevertheless, on March 27, Zelensky publicly defended his proposal, and on March 28, as a gesture of support for this effort, Vladimir Putin eased the pressure on the capital and withdrew his troops from the area. Zelensky's proposal served as the basis for the Istanbul Communiqué of March 29, 2022, which was a ceasefire agreement, a prelude to a peace agreement.[195] It was this document that Vladimir Putin presented in June 2023, when an African delegation visited Moscow. Boris Johnson intervened and Zelensky withdrew his proposal, exchanging peace and the lives of his men for support "for as long as it takes."[196]

This version of events—which I have already presented in my previous books—was finally confirmed in early November 2023 by David

194. Michael Birnbaum & Missy Ryan, "NATO says Ukraine to decide on peace deal with Russia—within limits", *The Washington Post*, April 5, 2022 (https://www.washingtonpost.com/national-security/2022/04/05/ukraine-nato-russia-limits-peace/)

195. https://braveneweurope.com/michael-von-der-schulenburg-hajo-funke-harald-kujat-frieden-fur-ukraine

196. Roman Romaniuk, "Possibility of talks between Zelenskyy and Putin came to a halt after Johnson's visit", *Ukrainska Pravda*, 5 May 2022 (https://www.pravda.com.ua/eng/news/2022/05/5/7344206/)

Arakhamia, then chief negotiator for Ukraine.[197] He explained that Russia had never intended to seize Kiev.[198]

In essence, Russia agreed to withdraw to the borders of February 23, 2022, in exchange for a ceiling on Ukrainian forces and a commitment not to become a member of NATO with security guarantees from a number of countries:[199]

> *According to several former US officials we spoke to, by April 2022, Russian and Ukrainian negotiators appeared to have agreed on the broad outlines of a negotiated provisional settlement: Russia would withdraw to its positions of February 23, when it controlled part of the Donbass region and all of Crimea, and, in exchange, Ukraine would promise not to seek NATO membership and would instead receive security guarantees from a number of countries.*

Two conclusions can be drawn:
- Russia's objective was not to conquer territory. If the West hadn't intervened to push Zelensky to withdraw his offer, Ukraine would probably still have its own army.[200]
- While the Russians intervened to ensure the security and protection of the population of the Donbass, their SMO enabled them to achieve a broader objective, which touches on Russia's security.

This means that, although this objective was *not formulated*, the demilitarization of Ukraine opened the door to its neutralization. This is not surprising since, conversely, in an interview with Ukrainian channel *Apostrof'* on March 18, 2019, Volodymyr Zelensky's advisor, Oleksei Arestovitch cynically explained that, because Ukraine wants to join

197. "Interview with David Arakhamia, head of the Ukrainian delegation at the peace talks", *1+1*, November 25, 2023 (https://youtu.be/0G_j-7gLnWU)

198. Olena Roshchina, "Head of Ukraine's leading party claims Russia proposed 'peace' in exchange for neutrality", *Ukrainska Pravda*, November 24, 2023 (https://www.pravda.com.ua/eng/news/2023/11/24/7430282/)

199. Matthew C. Mai, "Could the War in Ukraine Have Been Stopped?", *The National Interest*, September 20, 2022 (https://nationalinterest.org/feature/could-war-ukraine-have-been-stopped-204872)

200. https://twitter.com/ArmchairW/status/1670181878866018304/photo/1

NATO, it will have to create the conditions for Russia to attack Ukraine and be definitively defeated.[201]

The problem is that Ukrainian and Western analysis is fueled by their own narrative. The conviction that Russia will lose has meant that no alternative contingency has been prepared. In September 2023, the West, beginning to see the collapse of this narrative let alone its realization, tried to move towards a "freeze" in the conflict, without taking into account the opinion of the Russians, who nonetheless dominate on the ground.

However, Russia would have been satisfied with a situation such as that proposed by Zelensky in March 2022. What the West wanted in September 2023 was merely a pause for an even more violent conflict, following the rearmament and reconstitution of Ukrainian forces.

What this sad episode demonstrates is that Western governments were (and still are) so obsessed with destroying Russia and bringing about regime change, that they totally overlooked Ukraine's intentions. The Swiss ambassador in Kiev at the time was apparently unaware of these facts, which had already been reported in the Ukrainian press in April 2022.

The Operative Concept and Russian Leadership in Ukraine

The Russians do not communicate about their planning or the progress of their operations. While it is relatively easy to reconstruct with precision the initial concept of their SMO, it is more difficult to identify the subsequent phases of this operation, which evolves—quite logically—with time and the situation on the ground.

It is very likely that the original concept of the operation only included what we describe below as phases 1 and 2, because as we can see, all the objectives defined by Vladimir Putin on February 24, 2022 were achieved in these two phases. Witness the two negotiation attempts initiated by Volodymyr Zelensky and prevented at the last minute by the West. It is likely that Russia planned to withdraw from Ukraine after an agreement, such as the one proposed by Zelensky in March. It is highly unlikely that Russia intended to cross the language barrier and venture into the

---

201. "Predicted Russian—Ukrainian war in 2019—Alexey Arestovich", *YouTube*, March 18, 2022 (https://youtu.be/1xNHmHpERH8)

western part of the country. That's why phase 3 has probably been added, given the West's determination to continue the war.

The available evidence does, however, allow us to draw some conclusions. For, while the phasing of the SMO is open to debate, the logic that emerges from it shows that what our media—and certain intelligence services—presented to us was totally false. Now, on the basis of these mistaken interpretations, our Ministries of Defense are beginning to plan the "rearmament" of our armies.

General concept of Special Military Operation (SMO)

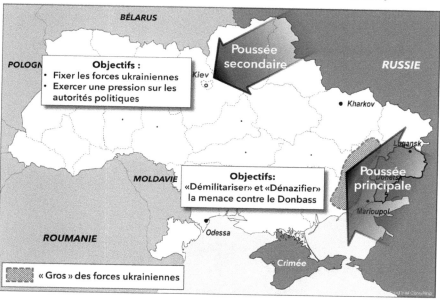

Figure 20—The general mechanics of Russia's special operation faithfully follow its operational doctrine. It consists of a main thrust and a secondary thrust. The role of the secondary thrust is to create favorable conditions for the main thrust. The thrust towards Kiev is not intended to seize the city, but to hold back any reinforcements to the north that might head for the Donbass.

Between phase 2 and phase 3, Russia found itself in a situation similar to that of the Americans in Afghanistan, who gradually had to combine a purely American operation (ENDURING FREEDOM) with a multilateral NATO operation (ISAF). The problem is that our "experts" understood nothing about these issues, and were unable to grasp the situation in Ukraine. Their Russophobia did the rest.

105

Thus, the differences between the Russian army and the Donbass militias were erased, in order to call into question Russian conduct. In this way, the changes at the head of the SMO were interpreted by Western media such as *RTS*[202] in Switzerland, *Figaro*[203] in France, or *BBC*[204] in the UK, as a sign of crisis within the Russian leadership and the "fiasco" of the operation. It's technically a form of conspiracism, which has backfired on Ukraine.

The reality is exactly the opposite. The Russian command has been strengthened and has greater freedom of action than before. Western analyses only led to an underestimation of Russian capabilities and a lowering of Ukrainian guard, as we saw in the days that followed.

Management of SMO (February 24, 2022—October 7, 2022)

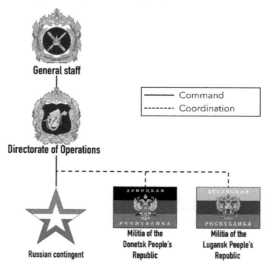

Figure 21—At the start of the SMO, the Russian coalition brought together forces from the Russian Federation and militias from the Donetsk and Lugansk People's Republics. The latter have different equipment, are made up of "citizen-soldiers" and have their own command. This explains the lack of coordination at the start of the SMO, which our media have attributed to the Russian army.

202. https://www.rts.ch/play/tv/redirect/detail/13449035

203. "En pleine mobilisation, la Russie limoge le général chargé de la logistique", *Le Figaro / AFP*, September 24, 2022 (https://www.lefigaro.fr/flash-actu/en-pleine-mobilisation-la-russie-limoge-le-general-charge-de-la-logistique-20220924)

204. Matt Murphy, "Dmitry Bulgakov: Putin fires deputy defence chief amid supply failures," *BBC News*, September 24, 2022, (https://www.bbc.com/news/world-europe-63021117)

Management of SMO from October 8, 2022

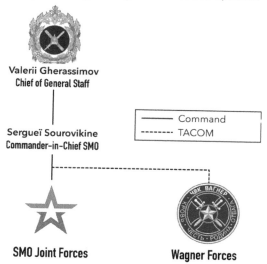

Figure 22—From October 2022, Russian forces integrated troops from the Donbass republics (now part of the Russian Federation). They switched to defensive mode and engaged Wagner's troops for the battle of Bakhmut. This unnatural association was due to the lack of infantry in the Russian structures.

Management of SMO from January 11, 2023

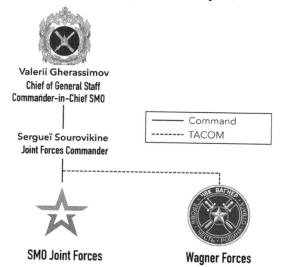

Figure 23—From January 2023, the increase in Ukrainian actions on Russian territory called for an extension of the TVD Ukraine to better coordinate actions on the SMO's rear, particularly for air defense. General Surovikin had not been ousted, as our media have trumpeted, but the area of operation had been enlarged to include certain regions of the territory of the Russian Federation, which is why General Gerasimov became Chief of the SMO.

107

Valerii Gherassimov
Chief of General Staff
Commander-in-Chief SMO

Viktor Afzalov
Joint Forces Commander

SMO Joint Forces

Figure 24—After the battle of Bakhmut, it became difficult to integrate private militias into the Russian system. The Ministry of Defense decided to stop this type of collaboration, in order to simplify the command structure. Colonel-General Surovikin was replaced by Colonel-General Viktor Afzalov.

Phase I

The unfolding of this phase followed exactly the patterns of operative art we have known since the Cold War. This offensive phase was articulated in two thrusts:

- A main thrust (*"decisive operation"*) directed towards the south of the country in the Donbass region[205] and along the coast of the Sea of Azov (Z).
- A secondary thrust (*"support operation"*) on Kiev, led by Russian forces from Belarus (V) and Russia (O).

The mechanics of the operation derived from the fact that the Russian coalition was attacking with an overall inferior force to that of the Ukrainians. If we consider only the Russian forces in Russia, the only ones capable of carrying out joint operations in depth, the ratio of forces was 1 to 3 to 4 in favor of the Ukrainians.

---

205. https://donpatriot.news/ru/article/britanska-rozvidka-nazvala-osnovniy-napryamok-nastupu-okupantiv

The explanation for this apparent contradiction is that the Russians compensated for their inferiority by mastering the art of operations. By pushing deep into Ukrainian territory, they could "break through" by creating superiorities limited in space and time, forcing Ukrainian forces in the west of the country to split up and preventing them from reinforcing the bulk of their forces already deployed in the Donbass.

Surprisingly, this fine mechanics of operational art has not been understood in France, although it is very well described in the doctrine for the use of French forces in 2002.

The Objectives

Targets in the Main Thrust Axis

In line with military doctrine—and quite logically—the main objectives were located in the axis of the main thrust: the neutralization of Ukrainian armed forces that had been regrouped in the Donbass in preparation for the offensive against the DPR and LPR ("demilitarization" objective) and the neutralization of ultra-nationalist paramilitary militias in Mariupol ("denazification" objective).

Targets in the Secondary Thrust Axis

The aim of the secondary thrust towards Kiev was to "fix" Ukrainian forces, preventing them from reinforcing the forces engaged in the main Russian thrust.

Operations Management

In the main thrust axis, the offensive was led by a coalition (Z), comprising of Russian forces from Crimea and Russia's Southern Military District, militias from the Donetsk and Lugansk People's Republics, and a Chechen National Guard contingent for the fighting in the Mariupol urban area.

With Ukrainian forces massed in the south of the country in preparation for an offensive against the Donbass, the Russian-Ukrainian border north of Kharkov was virtually undefended. The V and O forces and the northern grouping of the Z force were able to advance quickly and easily towards Kiev. With phase 1, Russia was seeking to create favorable conditions for achieving its objectives. By preventing the Ukrainians from concentrating their forces on the Donbass and creating main efforts, it enabled its forces to gain a foothold on a front of almost 1,000 km and hold a larger army in check.

On February 24, 2022, Antonov airport in Gostomel was taken by airborne forces. The Swiss newspaper *Neue Zürcher Zeitung* (NZZ) claimed that the Russians wanted to take Kiev, but failed.[206] This is simply not true. An intelligent and honest analysis showed as early as March 2022 that they never deployed sufficient troops to do so. It was therefore logical that they should not achieve a goal they never set for themselves. In fact, the airport was taken in two hours by just 200 paratroopers. It was the same scenario as for the seizure of Prague airport in 1968: a small group seized the critical installations, and was then reinforced by a larger detachment. In Ukraine, this reinforcement of 300 to 400 parachutists arrived on February 26 by road, as Ukrainian artillery prevented airborne reinforcement. As we can see, Russian forces were far from sufficient to take the entire capital.

The function of airborne troops is perfectly described in Russian doctrine: to *"disrupt the deployment of the adversary's reserves."*[207] And that's exactly what they did.

While a ratio of forces of 3 to 1 is generally used to plan an attack, a ratio of 6-12 to 1 is used to carry out an attack in an urban area.[208] At the time, Kiev was defended by around 60,000 men, and under these conditions, the Russians would have had to deploy around half a million men to take it. This would be in the same order of magnitude as the capture of Berlin in 1945.

---

206. https://www.nzz.ch/international/krieg-gegen-die-ukraine/warum-russland-im-kampf-um-kiew-scheiterte-ld.1679477?reduced=true
207. "Вооруженные Силы Российской Федерации: их состав и предназначение," *Армейский Сборник*, 1/2023, January 2, 2023 (https://army.ric.mil.ru/Stati/item/460541/)
208. http://www.dupuyinstitute.org/blog/2018/04/25/u-s-army-force-ratios/

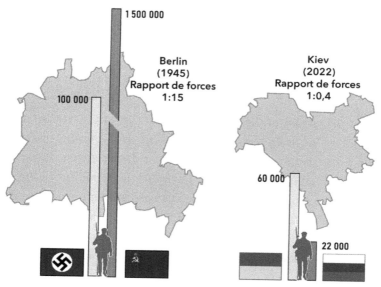

Balance of Power for the Capture of a City

1 500 000

Berlin
(1945)
Rapport de forces
1:15

Kiev
(2022)
Rapport de forces
1:0,4

100 000

60 000

22 000

Figure 25—In 1945, the Soviets took Berlin with a force approximately 15 times greater than that of the Germans. In 2022, for a city of comparable size, the Russians would have had a force ratio 37 times lower. For the city of Mariupol, the Russians had a ratio of 8 to 1 in their favor.

Airborne troops were soon joined by ground forces: some 22 BTGs (i.e., between 13,200 and 17,600 men), according to the Pentagon, around the Ukrainian capital. This left some 20,000 men "threatening" the capital. By creating this pressure, the Russian command was forcing the Ukrainian General Staff to protect Kiev, and thus neglect the reinforcement of its forces in the Donbass region, in line with the main Russian thrust. By comparison, it is estimated that they deployed around 40,000 men to take Mariupol, a considerably smaller city. Thus, the Russians never intended to take the capital.

On March 29, based on a proposal by Zelensky, the Istanbul Communiqué was published. This document was a draft armistice, intended to serve as the basis for a lasting settlement to the crisis. As a sign of goodwill, Vladimir Putin immediately ordered a reduction in military action in the Chernigov and Kiev sectors, as reported by Michael von der Schulenburg, former Under-Secretary of the United Nations, Hajo Funke, Professor of Political Science at the Free University of Berlin, and General

Harald Kujat, former Inspector-General of the *Bundeswehr*,[209] as well as the Russian media *RT*.[210] But hope was short-lived, as once again, under pressure from the West, Zelensky withdrew his proposal, as reported by *Ukrainska Pravda*.[211]

In its press release of March 30, 2022, the Russian Ministry of Defense explained this mechanism:[212]

> *The first phase of the Special Military Operation carried out by the Russian armed forces in the Donbass and Ukraine was designed to force the enemy to concentrate its forces, assets, resources and combat equipment to defend the major urban areas in these zones, including Kiev. The aim was to fix them, without storming the cities, in order to avoid civilian casualties, and to inflict such losses on the Kiev regime's armed forces that it would be unable to use them in our forces' main direction of operation in the Donbass. All these objectives have been achieved.*

The Russian presence in northern Ukraine was not designed to last. It was either to be prolonged by an offensive on the Ukrainian rear, or to be withdrawn. There is no evidence to suggest that the Russian General Staff had considered continuing this thrust. Withdrawal was therefore inevitable, and the Istanbul negotiations gave Russia the opportunity to present this withdrawal as a step in the direction of Ukraine.

The capture of Mariupol allowed the Russians to regroup their forces in the Donbass and focus their efforts on the goal of "demilitarization." Now in a position to enjoy superiority in its decisive zone of operation, Russia was able to withdraw its troops from the Kiev sector and reinforce its position in the south of the country. On March 29, 2022, the negotiations in Istanbul seemed on the verge of becoming a reality. The Russians saw an opportunity to make a gesture of appeasement, as reported by

209. https://braveneweurope.com/michael-von-der-schulenburg-hajo-funke-harald-kujat-frieden-fur-ukraine
210. https://www.rt.com/russia/552910-istanbul-peace-talks-explainer/
211. https://www.gov.uk/government/news/pm-call-with-president-zelenskyy-of-ukraine-2-april-2022
212. https://z.mil.ru/spec_mil_oper/news/more.htm?id=12415372@egNews

the German media *DW*.[213] They announced the withdrawal of Russian troops from the northern sector of Ukraine. To what extent was the Russian withdrawal from Kiev planned, or a gesture of goodwill to mark Zelensky's constructive proposals in Istanbul? This is an open question. In any case, the Russians were able to exploit the withdrawal politically.

Ukraine made the Russian withdrawal look like a victory, which is only fair. More worryingly, the West had not understood the maneuver at all, as demonstrated by General Thierry Burkhard, Chief of Staff of the Armed Forces.[214] In May 2022, Claude Wild, the Swiss ambassador in Kiev, declared on *RTS* that the Russians had *"lost the battle of Kiev."*[215] In reality, the opposite is true. As David Arakhamia, then chief negotiator for Ukraine,[216] confirmed, the aim was to push Ukraine towards negotiation, and this objective was achieved. But the West's entrenchment in a narrative of their own making would push Ukraine towards disaster.

The aim was simply to confirm that *"Russia cannot, and must not, win this war."*[217] Thus, this so-called victory, which is attributed to the know-how of the Ukrainian general staff, is in reality due to the goodwill of the Russians. The problem is that this encouraged Westerners to think:

a) that the Ukrainians are superior in the art of maneuvering and

b) to oppose any attempt by Kiev to negotiate.

One year on, our ambassador's rather simplistic reading, shared by the "experts" and our media, will have cost Ukraine tens or even hundreds of thousands of deaths. When you love, you don't count.

213. "Russia pledges to cut back operations around Kyiv", *DW.com*, March 29, 2022 (https://www.dw.com/en/russia-pledges-to-scale-down-military-activity-near-kyiv-chernihiv-as-it-happened/a-61286047)

214. Laurent Lagneau, "According to General Burkhard, Russia is 'developing a long-term strategy' in Ukraine", *opex360.com*, November 21, 2022 (https://www.opex360.com/2022/11/21/selon-le-general-burkhard-la-russie-developpe-une-strategie-de-long-terme-en-ukraine/)

215. "Nobody would have bet a franc on such resistance", says Swiss ambassador to Ukraine", *RTS Info*, May 24, 2022 (https://www.rts.ch/info/monde/13121067-personne-naurait-parie-un-franc-sur-une-telle-resistance-estime-lambassadeur-suisse-en-ukraine.html)

216. "Interview with David Arakhamia, head of the Ukrainian delegation at the peace talks", *1+1*, November 25, 2023 (https://youtu.be/0G_j-7gLnWU)

217. https://www.assemblee-nationale.fr/dyn/16/rapports/cion_def/l16b1111_rapport-information.pdf

3. Special Military Operation (SMO) in Ukraine

SMO Phase 1 Diagram

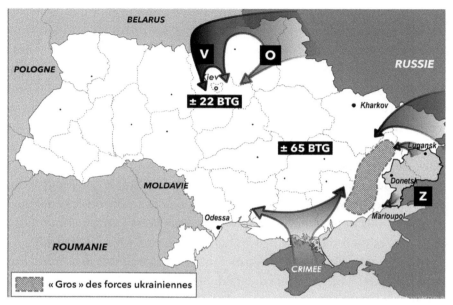

*Figure 26—Phase 1 of the Russian operation from February 24 to March 30, 2022.
The number of troops committed by Russia shows that taking Kiev was never an objective.*

Assessment of Phase 1

Phase 1 is an exemplary example of the application of Russian operative art. Within a month, Russia had achieved most of the objectives defined on February 24:

- By February 25, Zelensky was ready to negotiate with Russia, calling for the opening of negotiations.[218] Initial negotiations were launched in Gomel, but the European Union intervened on February 27 with a 450-million-euro arms package to encourage Ukraine to continue fighting.[219]

- On March 28, with Mariupol (cradle of the AZOV neo-Nazi movement) surrounded, Colonel-General Sergei Rudskoy, head of the Main Operations Directorate of the Russian General Staff (GOU),

218. Olga Rudenko, "Ukraine ready to negotiate with Russia", *The Kyiv Independent*, February 25, 2022 (https://kyivindependent.com/national/ukraine-ready-to-negotiate-with-russia/)
219. Maïa de La Baume & Jacopo Barigazzi, "EU agrees to give €500M in arms, aid to Ukrainian military in "watershed" move", *Politico*, February 27, 2022 (https://www.politico.eu/article/eu-ukraine-russia-funding-weapons-budget-military-aid/)

announced that the objectives of the 1st phase of the SMO had been achieved.[220] The *Financial Times*[221] and *Business Insider*[222] stated that the Russian command considered the goal of "denazification" achieved and it will no longer be subject to negotiations.

It was the Europeans who put an end to attempts at resolving the conflict in late February and late March 2022. The Russians knew that Zelensky was tempted to negotiate, but he was under the sway of the neo-Nazi elements in his entourage, supported by the Western *intelligentsia* and media. The Russians had no interest in trying to overthrow him—on the contrary.

Thus, overall, the Russian objectives had been achieved; but the massive intervention of the West was pushing the two adversaries to play for time. In operational terms, the withdrawal of Russian troops from northern Ukraine and the Kiev region marks the end of Phase 1.

Phase 2

After Phase 1, which aimed to shake up Ukrainian forces, Phase 2 was a transitional phase. It began with Zelensky's constructive proposals at the Istanbul negotiations in March 2022, and ended with the appointment of the new commander of Russian forces in Ukraine, in early October 2022.

During the Istanbul negotiations, a document of proposals signed by the Ukrainian delegation was forwarded to Russia, which saw it as a promising basis for discussion. But at the last minute, under British pressure, Zelensky withdrew his proposal—he had exchanged the possibility of a solution and the tens of thousands of lives of his soldiers for unlimited support and HIMARS systems. None of our media reports this development, which tells Russia that Ukraine now has no choice but to fight.

This phase saw increasing Western involvement to replace the Ukrainian potential destroyed in Phase 1. In a way, the demilitarization of Ukraine, which can be formally declared to have been achieved in May-June 2022, was to begin again. From then on, Ukraine would be entirely dependent

220. "Ukraine: EU doubles military aid to €1 billion—as it happened", *dw.com*, March 23, 2022 (https://www.dw.com/en-ukraine-eu-doubles-military-aid-to-1-billion-as-it-happened/a-61226171; https://p.dw.com/p/48tit)
221. "Russia no longer requesting Ukraine be "denazified" as part of ceasefire talks", *Financial Times*, March 28, 2022 (https://www.ft.com/content/7f14efe8-2f4c-47a2-aa6b-9a755a39b626)
222. Matthew Loh, "Russia is prepared to drop its demand for Ukraine to be 'denazified' from its list of ceasefire conditions", *Business Insider*, March 29, 2022 (https://www.businessinsider.com/russia-nazi-demand-for-ukraine-dropped-in-ceasefire-talks-2022-3?r=US&IR=T)

on the West to fight its battles, as reported by the very anti-Russian British newspaper, *The Guardian*:[223]

> *We're almost out of ammunition and dependent on Western weapons, says Ukraine [...] The deputy director of military intelligence says it's now an artillery war and "everything depends on what the West gives us".*

Contrary to what our media say, Russia has no intention of continuing beyond the Dnieper towards Kiev and the west of the country. It knows that ultra-nationalist forces have been concentrated in this region since the end of the First World War, and thus has no intention of repeating the counter-guerrilla warfare it waged there between 1943 and 1960. The SMO therefore had to change its character and move to a defensive mode.

The Objectives

The objectives of Phase 2 were twofold:

- Reduce the vulnerability of its position in anticipation of the decisive counter-offensive announced by Ukraine. The aim was to tighten the position by reducing the length of the front, in order to increase troop density along the line of contact.
- Continue the "demilitarization" of the threat to the populations of the Donbass.

Operations Management

In Phase 1, the Russians achieved their objectives with a relatively small force, thanks to their ability to maneuver. For Phase 2, two essential factors would determine the course of operations—the prospect of a long conflict (which they did not want) if they continued in an offensive mode; the prospect of a major counter-offensive with a million men.

The Russians therefore had to switch to a more defensive and static mode, where the advantage is given less by maneuver than by the number

---

223. https://www.theguardian.com/world/2022/jun/10/were-almost-out-of-ammunition-and-relying-on-western-arms-says-ukraine

and density of troops. Since February, they have had between 100,000 and 150,000 km2 more territory to defend.

Density of Russian Coalition Forces in Southern Ukraine (July 2022)

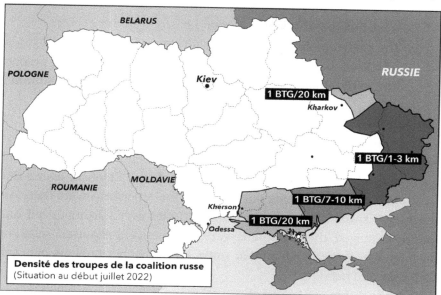

Figure 27—BTG density is an indication of Russian main efforts. As of June 10, 2022, in the Kharkov and Kherson sectors, the density is one BTG per 20 km. In the sector west of Donetsk, the density is one BTG per 10 km. But in the Lyssytchansk sector, the density is one BTG for every 1-3 km of frontage. In other words, the Kharkov and Kherson sectors are not priority areas for Russia.

Less spectacular than the first, this phase was demanding for Russian leadership and staff work. There were several aspects to it:

- The integration of V and O forces withdrawn from northern Ukraine (around 20 BTG) into Force Z, which carries out the main effort in the southeast, namely the "demilitarization" of the threat against the populations of the Donbass.
- Closer focus on the Donbass, while protecting the flanks. As early as spring 2022, it became clear that the Kharkov and Kherson sectors, described as "strategic" in the West, were not a priority for the Russians. The density of troops deployed there (around 1 BTG per 20 km) is far too low for large-scale attacks. What's more, the forces deployed in these areas are cut off from the main

117

Russian forces by the Oskol river in the Kharkov region and by the Dnieper in the Kherson sector.

- Upgrading and integrating troops from the DPR and LPR, as well as volunteers from territories newly integrated into the Russian Federation, into a single leadership structure, so that there is no weak link in the defense system.
- The partial mobilization of 300,000 troops in September 2022, to take account of the enlargement of Russian territory and prepare for the Ukrainian counter-offensive announced since the summer.

The Kharkov Withdrawal

From August 2022, the Ukrainians were under pressure to achieve success on the ground. Joe Biden didn't want to launch his presidential campaign with disaster looming, while Volodymyr Zelensky feared that Western support is running out of steam. The Americans were therefore pushing Ukraine to step up its counter-offensives. Disorganized and poorly managed, the Ukrainians were systematically repulsed, resulting in huge losses in the Ukrainian ranks and creating tensions between Zelensky and his staff.

At the beginning of August, the Russian press was already talking about the possibility of a Ukrainian offensive in the Kharkov sector.[224] This is not a priority sector for the Russians. They have only a small number of troops there, whose function is to flank the decisive zone of operations, which is the Donbass.

Rather than trying to combat Ukrainian thrusts in secondary sectors, the Russians preferred to withdraw their troops to sectors that were more easily defensible, while at the same time increasing the density of their forces. This was the case around Kharkov in early September, and in Kherson a month later. In these two sectors, their presence was not directly useful to the achievement of their objectives, and they found themselves in the same situation as with Snake Island in June—the energy required to defend these territories outweighed their strategic importance.

---

224. Алина Корнеева, "'СП': Президент Украины Зеленский собрал миллионную армию под Харьковом для вторжения в РФ", *RK-News*, August 8, 2022 (https://rk-news.com/2022/08/08/568521166248.html)

Having detected the Russians' departure from the Kharkov region, American intelligence services saw an opportunity for Ukrainian success and passed on the information. The Ukrainians were then busy conducting counter-offensives in the Kherson sector. On September 6, 2022, following American directions, they launched an offensive and recaptured an area that the Russians had abandoned. The huge ammunition depot at Balaklaya was empty when the Ukrainians discovered it, demonstrating that it had already been evacuated in good order several days earlier. The Russians even left areas that Ukraine did not subsequently attack.

Russian troops were therefore withdrawing along a shorter defensive line, protected by the Oskol river. This densification of the front enabled Russia to reinforce its offensive capabilities in the Donbass.

For the Ukrainians, it was a Pyrrhic victory. They advanced to Kharkov without encountering resistance and virtually without a fight. But they entered a huge *"pocket of fire"* ("огневой мешок") (in English, *killing zone*), where Russian artillery was able to destroy an estimated 4,000 to 5,000 Ukrainians (around 2 brigades), while the Russian coalition suffered only marginal losses.

Kherson Withdrawal

Since June 2022, the city of Kherson had been the target of a multitude of Ukrainian "counter-offensives," causing huge losses to Ukrainian forces.[225] Systematically repulsed, none succeeded in breaking through Russian defenses. On November 10, as the Russian forces were in the process of withdrawing, a final Ukrainian counter-offensive was repulsed.

However, on November 8, 2022, the Russian command announced the withdrawal of its troops from the eastern bank of the Dnieper. The issue had been debated in Russia itself since September. The military demanded it, but the politicians were rather opposed.

The Russian General Staff had made the same analysis of the situation as at Kharkov—its objective is not the conquest of territory. The junction between Russian territory and the Crimean Peninsula came about as

---

225. Jeremy Bowen, "Russia-Ukraine war: At the front line of Ukraine's struggle for Kherson", *BBC News*, November 4, 2022 (https://www.bbc.com/news/world-europe-63489081)

3. Special Military Operation (SMO) in Ukraine

Ukrainian forces were destroyed, and we now know that the Russians were ready to negotiate its abandonment in March 2022, before Zelensky withdrew his proposal under pressure from the West.[226]

The Ukrainians had already launched several HIMARS missile attacks against the Nova Kakhovka dam, and the Russian military feared that troops deployed on the western bank of the Dnieper could be totally isolated if the dam gave way. Moreover, by withdrawing these troops behind the river, the general staff wanted to benefit from a natural rampart and shorten the length of the front.

For Russian politicians, the territory concerned, even though it represented only 40% of the Kherson oblast, was formally part of the national territory. They feared—and rightly so—that a withdrawal would give Ukraine an easy victory that would be exploited by Western propaganda. In the end, the military prevailed.

Our media are exultant, but Volodymyr Zelensky was more reserved and rightly feared a trap,[227] because he knew what happened in Kharkov a month earlier—his troops were decimated without a fight. That's what would happen in Kherson, too.

Unlike the Ukrainians, and as General Surovikin made clear, Russia's priority is to preserve the lives of its fighters. In Kherson, in September 2022, the Russians found themselves in the same situation as on Snake Island in June or in Kharkov in August—the energy required to defend these areas was greater than the strategic interest of holding on to them. What the West has trumpeted as a Russian defeat is merely the expression of a balance between the strategic objective and the cost of achieving it. As we have seen since the beginning of the SMO, Russia's conduct of operations is extremely efficient.

This was a withdrawal, not a retreat. A retreat is a movement carried out under pressure and in constant contact with the enemy. A withdrawal is an operation aimed at regrouping forces, tightening a front line or preparing for further action.

226. Matthew C. Mai, "Could the War in Ukraine Have Been Stopped?", *The National Interest*, September 20, 2022 (https://nationalinterest.org/feature/could-war-ukraine-have-been-stopped-204872)
227. https://www.dailymail.co.uk/news/article-11411551/Is-Russias-retreat-Kherson-actually-trap-laid-Ukraine.html

As we had already seen near Kiev six months earlier, Russian troops were not in a state of failure. Russia was withdrawing of its own accord, not under Ukrainian pressure. It should be remembered that Russia's objective is not territorial but security-related, unlike Ukraine, which prioritizes the reconquest of territory over the lives of its men. This makes the withdrawal a victory shared by both sides.

What this withdrawal shows is that Russian management of operations is less political than military—operational and tactical objectives are set by the military. This contrasts with Ukraine, where the conduct of operations is political, which explains the enormous losses and inefficiency. This inefficiency (i.e., the amount of resources used to achieve an objective) can be measured by the speed with which the Ukrainians are losing the equipment supplied by the West. We would see the same phenomenon at Bakhmut in spring 2023 and at Rabotino in summer 2023.

However, Russia's decision was not without consequences for foreign and domestic policy. On the external front, Ukraine and the West were obviously quick to publicize the Ukrainian "victory," with the result that Ukrainian capabilities were overestimated and the idea of negotiations rejected. Domestically, one might have expected disappointment in the form of mistrust of Moscow's leadership. But the Russian general staff had learned the lessons of the Kharkov withdrawal—instead of explaining the reasons for the decision after the fact, General Surovikin communicated in advance. In this way, Russian power did not lose the confidence of public opinion. Even "hawks," such as Ramzan Kadyrov, welcomed the withdrawal.[228]

However, even though its troops had left the western part of Kherson oblast, Russia continued to consider it Russian territory.[229] This left open the possibility of a subsequent offensive to recover it, or to use it as a *bargaining chip* in negotiation.

The problem for Ukraine was that the Western media relayed its propaganda and presented this withdrawal as proof of Russia's weakening and

228. Mark Trevelyan, "Russia's war hawks rally behind decision to abandon Ukrainian city of Kherson", *Reuters*, November 10, 2022 (https://www.reuters.com/world/europe/russias-war-hawks-rally-behind-decision-abandon-ukrainian-city-kherson-2022-11-09/)

229. "Peskov says 'Kherson remains Russian' as Ukrainian forces enter city", *The Kyiv Independent*, November 11, 11 (https://kyivindependent.com/news-feed/peskov-says-kherson-remains-russian-as-ukrainian-forces-enter-city)

the prospect of an imminent final victory. This was the analysis made (among others) by Colonel Michel Goya and General Bruno Clermont before a Senate committee in France, and Alexandre Vautravers in Switzerland, which led to an overestimation of Ukraine's capabilities and pushed the country from defeat to defeat.

To avoid this type of problem, intelligence analysis must remain impartial and free from facile judgments and propaganda. We'll come back to this later.

Assessment of Phase 2

Phase 2 was an unspectacular transition phase. Nevertheless, between late May and early June 2022, Russia achieved its second objective—the "demilitarization" of Ukrainian forces. From then on, Ukraine was dependent on the West for its military supplies.[230]

The Kharkov and Kherson withdrawals can be interpreted in various ways:

- From a military point of view, this was a tactical victory for the Ukrainians, and an operational/strategic victory for the Russian coalition. Vladimir Putin's declared objectives of "demilitarization" and "denazification" are not about gaining territory, but about destroying potential. The Ukrainians are fighting for territory, while the Russians are seeking to destroy capabilities. You can always take back territory, but you can't get back human lives.
- Operationally, the Russians reduced their frontline length to 815 km,[231] giving them greater troop density to respond to the upcoming Ukrainian counter-offensive.
- In strategic terms, the West perceived the Russian withdrawal as a sign of weakening. The "victories" of Kiev, Kharkov and Kherson would recur in the Western narrative to persuade the Ukrainians to engage in their counter-offensive.
- In political terms, this could be seen as a strategic victory for the Ukrainians. This is the first time the Ukrainians recaptured so much territory since 2014. The official rhetoric was one of final victory, raising expectations and hopes that were undoubtedly

---

230. https://www.france24.com/en/live-news/20220610-ukraine-dependent-on-arms-from-allies-after-exhausting-soviet-era-weaponry
231. https://telegraf.com.ua/novosti-rossii/2022-12-22/5726885-vydal-voennuyu-taynu-glava-putinskogo-genshtaba-rasskazal-kakie-strany-bolshe-vsego-pomogayut-ukraine

exaggerated. The problem was not so much that Ukraine was claiming victory, but that the West had convinced itself that Russia is weak. This success was a poisoned chalice for Ukraine, leading our experts to overestimate its capabilities. In mid-September 2022, Ursula von der Leyen declared that the time was "not ripe *for appeasement,*"[232] prompting the Ukrainians to carry out further offensives and reject any idea of negotiation. In September 2022, Volodymyr Zelensky declared that he would only agree to negotiate with Russia on condition that Vladimir Putin was no longer in power[233] and issued a decree a few days later forbidding any negotiations with Russia before Vladimir Putin's departure.[234]

Ultimately, both Ukraine and Russia were counting on some form of success in this phase. But for the Ukrainians, these successes were lethal, but the West was careful not to warn them.

Phase 3

The SMO was a joint action between the Russian armed forces and the forces of the Donbass republics. As the latter were officially independent, they were not subordinate to the Russian command, but coordinated by the Russian General Staff. After the referendums in September 2022, all Russian coalition forces were integrated into Moscow's command structure. This resulted in the creation of a specific command, headed since October 8, 2022 by General Sergei Surovikin, appointed Commander of the Joint Task Force in the area of the Special Military Operation in Ukraine. This was the starting point for Phase 3.

Implementation of the new leadership structures began during Phase 2, conducting complex military operations while setting up new leadership structures and adapting the entire strategic-operational chain of command was a source of vulnerability. This restructuring was therefore the funda-

232. https://www.francetvinfo.fr/monde/europe/manifestations-en-ukraine/guerre-en-ukraine-ursula-von-der-leyen-promet-la-solidarite-avec-kiev-sans-convaincre-tous-les-eurode-putes_5362294.html
233. "Ukraine Will Not Negotiate with Russia as Long As Putin Is In Power: Zelensky," *Barron's/ AFP*, September 30, 2022 (https://www.barrons.com/news/ukraine-will-not-negotiate-with-rus-sia-as-long-as-putin-is-in-power-zelensky-01664548507)
234. Vladimir Socor, "Zelenskyy Bans Negotiations with Putin," *Eurasia Daily Monitor* (Volume 19, No. 147), October 5, 2022 (https://jamestown.org/program/zelenskyy-bans-negotia-tions-with-putin/)

mental reason why the Russians did not attempt to combat the Ukrainian offensive on Kharkov during Phase 2. In so doing, they exchanged territory which was not a priority (and which can be recovered), for the lives of their soldiers and time (both of which cannot be recovered).

Phase 3 marked the transition to a defensive posture, aimed at wearing down the attacking forces.

Several major factors influenced the decisions of the Russian General Staff during this phase:

- Increased Western military supplies to Ukraine and the announcement of a major counter-offensive with a million men by Volodymyr Zelensky[235]
- The contribution of 300,000 reservists, recalled by the partial mobilization of September 2022
- Referendums in the four Russian-occupied oblasts and the integration of DPR and LPR militias into Russian forces. This led to the need to set up local administrations capable of providing services to the inhabitants of the regions newly integrated into the Russian Federation.
- The objectives defined in February 2022 had been achieved, and there was no need to seize new territories. On the other hand, Western aid meant that the new Ukrainian potential had to be fought as it arrived on the TVD. In other words, Russia still needed to be able to operate in the depths of Ukrainian territory.

The shift in Russian strategy towards a more defensive mode was explained on October 18, 2022 by General Surovikin:[236]

> *We have a different strategy… We're not looking for a high rate of advance; we're taking it easy on each of our soldiers and methodically "crushing" the advancing enemy.*

The consequence of this change in strategy and the shift to a more static mode was that superiority was achieved less through maneuver than through the density and flexibility of the defense system.

---

235. https://www.independent.co.uk/news/world/europe/ukraine-million-army-russia-weapons-b2120445.html
236. "Суровикин: российская группировка на Украине методично "перемалывает" войска противника", *TASS*, October 18, 2022 (https://tass.ru/armiya-i-opk/16090805)

This is the strategy that would remain in place throughout 2023.

The Objectives

We do not know what objectives were formally defined for this phase. We can only deduce them from the actions observed in the field.

These are:

- integrate joint forces and consolidate the new unified leadership structures;
- consolidate territorial gains and strengthen the terrain with a view to shifting to a more defensive strategy, capable of withstanding the Ukrainian counter-offensive;
- regain airspace in order to prevent the enemy from gaining the air superiority needed for breakthrough operations.

Operations Management

The battle of Bakhmut was emblematic of Phase 3, and in itself illustrates the strategy outlined by General Surovikin on October 18, 2022: let the Ukrainians advance, and destroy them as they come. The aim was not to take the city, but to destroy the enemy.[237] This is the literal application of what Vladimir Putin said on February 24, 2022, and which derives from Clausewitz's principle:

> *Victory is not simply a matter of conquering territory, but of physically and morally crushing the enemy's armed forces.*

Urban warfare is a special form of combat that doesn't really require inter-army collaboration. It can be carried out by simply armed, but experienced and determined men. This is why, in October 2022, Surovikin commissioned the "Wagner" group to destroy the enemy in Bakhmut— Operation Bakhmut Meat Grinder ("БАХМУТСКАЯ МЯСОРУБКА").

Unlike its French-speaking counterparts, the *New York Times* seems to have understood the Russian maneuver very well. In its November 27, 2022 edition, it described the Battle of Bakhmut very clearly:[238]

---

237. https://dzen.ru/a/ZD5JTKwhFzM0r_oo
238. https://www.nytimes.com/2022/11/27/world/europe/ukraine-war-bakhmut.html

Even if Russia's hopes of expanding its territory have diminished, it can still turn the city into a resource-intensive black hole for Kiev, by withdrawing troops from other priorities, including, potentially, for future offensives.

Encouraged by the Europeans, Zelensky did not listen to his generals and continued to send his men into the slaughterhouse for six months.[239]

On February 17, 2023, Prigozhin accused the Moscow command of wanting the end of Wagner and not allocating him enough artillery ammunition. The British Ministry of Defense intelligence report saw tensions within the Russian leadership because of the difficulty of taking Bakhmut before the SMO anniversary date of February 24.[240] The Western media repeated this analysis, which had no basis in fact.[241]

According to Ukrainian sources, Russian forces had reduced their consumption of artillery shells to 20,000 rounds per day.[242] Difficult to verify, but this could be explained by preparations for the major Ukrainian counter-offensive in the spring. The Russian army was seeking to spread its capabilities, hitherto concentrated in the Donbass region, across the entire front line. Nevertheless, Prigozhin's accusations seemed unfounded.

The Russian Ministry of Defense claimed to have allocated 1,660 rockets for multiple rocket launchers and 10,171 artillery shells to Wagner for the period February 18 to 20,[243] i.e., over 800 rockets and 5,000 shells per day. In other words, Wagner had more artillery ammunition per day in the Bakhmut sector alone than the entire Ukrainian army had in the entire theater of operations.[244]

At the end of April 2023, the six-month contract with Wagner expired and the objective of destroying the enemy at Bakhmut was achieved. The Russian army therefore ceased its artillery and logistical support

239. Kate Tsurkan, "Zelensky, Zaluzhnyi have conflicting views on Bakhmut", *The Kyiv Independent*, March 6, 2023 (https://kyivindependent.com/bild-zaluzhnyi-and-zelensky-have-conflicting-views-on-bakhmut/)
240. https://twitter.com/DefenceHQ/status/1627555726628425728
241. https://www.newsweek.com/wagner-ammo-problem-bakhmut-1783134
242. https://en.defence-ua.com/industries/russia_spends_20000_artillery_shells_per_day_production_cannot_keep_up_with_such_rates_ukraines_intelligence_chief-5312.html
243. https://function.mil.ru/news_page/country/more.htm?id=12455382@egNews
244. https://www.nytimes.com/2022/11/25/us/ukraine-artillery-breakdown.html

for Wagner's troops, who were to be withdrawn and replaced by regular Russian troops. But although Wagner had fulfilled his contract, a small part of the city remained under Ukrainian control. Prigozhin then asked to be allowed to finish the job of reducing the last pockets of resistance and taking control of the whole city.

This was the reason for the psychodrama of early May 2023, when Prigozhin demanded[245] that he be given the means to complete the capture of Bakhmut.[246] His very virulent and aggressive tone against Shoigu and Gerasimov made the Western media fantasize about an internal division within the Russian camp[247] and a possible "coup"[248] against the Moscow "regime."

Russia has no need for controversies that feed Western propaganda. In order to calm the situation, and above all to close the "Bakhmut" file once and for all, the Russian Ministry of Defense agreed to extend Wagner's contract. The contract ended the day after the city was taken, on May 21, 2023, and Wagner's troops were withdrawn from the theater of operations.

Contrary to what some "experts" claimed, the battle of Bakhmut itself had nothing to do with operative art—it was a battle fought exclusively at tactical level with troops that were not integrated into a joint command structure. Such is the difficulty of integrating a private structure into its command structure that the Russian Ministry of Defense decided to discontinue its collaboration with Wagner and offered its members the chance to join the armed forces.

However, in line with Russian military thinking, this battle contributed to the defense strategy adopted back in October 2022. As with the strikes against power plants that forced Ukraine to squander its air defenses, the Russians' aim was to weaken Ukrainian capabilities over the medium and long term.

245. https://t.me/Prigozhin_hat/3251
246. https://www.cnn.com/2023/05/05/europe/wagner-military-group-prigozhin-ammunition-tirade-intl-hnk-ml/index.html
247. https://www.cnn.com/2023/05/05/europe/wagner-prigozhin-russia-ukraine-analysis-intl/index.html
248. https://www.cnn.com/2023/05/24/europe/wagner-prigozhin-russia-manpower-ukraine-intl/index.html

3. Special Military Operation (SMO) in Ukraine

The Aerial Campaign Against Electrical Infrastructure

Our propaganda appropriated the Russian campaign against Ukraine's electricity infrastructure, so that nobody understood a word of it. It was only very (too) late that the West realized this and tried to find a solution.

At the start of the SMO, the Ukrainian air force was quickly grounded by the first Russian strikes, but anti-aircraft capabilities were little affected. These were mainly based on S-300 systems supplied by Russia. Russia's objective was not to take over Ukraine, so it didn't need to control the skies over its entire territory. Its missiles enabled it to operate in depth without having to risk its aircraft and their pilots.

In the summer of 2022, seeing that the West was dragging them into a war of attrition by delivering weapons to Ukraine, the Russians decided to complete the destruction of Ukrainian forces. The aim was to prevent Ukraine from reconstituting its forces for the major offensive it had been promising since the spring.

However, the Russians realized that, when it came to fighting ground targets, aviation bombs are more effective (and probably less costly) than missiles. To do this, they needed to be able to fly freely in Ukrainian skies. The operative objective became the exhaustion of Ukraine's anti-aircraft capabilities, so as to enable front-line bombing missions. This meant hitting targets that the Ukrainians were obliged to protect. This is the reason for the campaign of strikes against the country's electrical infrastructure, which had not been hit until October 2022.

This forced the Ukrainians to use their S-300 and BUK missiles, even firing several of them at a single target. Some of these missiles found themselves without a purpose. Old and poorly maintained, their self-destruct mechanisms often fail. As a result, they end up landing on inhabited sites, as in Dnipro in January 2023,[249] or in Poland, as in Przewodow in November 2022.[250]

Thanks to our "experts" (who found every possible explanation except the right one), the Russian strategy worked. In April 2023, Yuriy Ignat, spokesman for the Ukrainian air force, noted that the Russians had

---

249. https://www.businessinsider.com/zelenskyy-aide-resigns-after-saying-ukraine-shot-down-dnipro-missile-2023-1

250. "Coraz bliżej prawdy o rakiecie w Przewodowie. Wiadomo czyj był pocisk," *Rzeczpospolita*, September 26, 2023 (https://www.rp.pl/kraj/art39165861-coraz-blizej-prawdy-o-rakiecie-w-przewodowie-wiadomo-czyj-byl-pocisk)

launched a vast bombing campaign *"with perceptible effect,"* and that Ukrainian anti-aircraft capabilities were insufficient to respond.[251]

The Russian tactic was to send a first wave of cheap drones or obsolete missiles as decoys, prompting the Ukrainians to activate their radars. Simultaneously, with an A-50U MAINSTAY early warning aircraft monitoring the airspace from Belarus, the Russians analyzed Ukrainian response patterns. They sent a second wave of cruise missiles capable of destroying Ukrainian air defense positions.

By saturating air defenses with a combination of missiles, drones and decoys, the Russians were forcing the Ukrainians to use missiles costing several hundred thousand dollars to reach drones worth a few thousand. According to *Forbes* magazine, Ukraine had 300 SA-10/S-300 systems by February 2022. A year later, classified US documents leaked in April 2023 indicate that Ukraine had only 25 systems left, and that the SA-10/S-300 and SA-11/BUK anti-aircraft systems and their ammunition were depleted between the end of March and the end of May 2023.

Our media trumpeted the fact that the Russians had run out of missiles and were forced to use obsolete ones. What's more, the results announced by the propaganda suggested that Ukrainian air defenses were performing well! Accustomed to understanding strategy only through our own prism, our brilliant "experts" saw nothing of it. Thus, in November 2022, before a Senate committee, Colonel Michel Goya explained that it was simply a matter of *"doing something, because we don't know what to do."*[252] Thanks to them, nobody understood the Russian maneuver.

This explains why the West neglected to supply anti-aircraft weapons before January 2023 and concentrated their efforts on artillery. Ironically, by trying to minimize Russian successes, our media and military expert amplified the effectiveness of Russian strategy and directly contributed to the weakening of Ukrainian resources.

---

251. Ellie Cook, "Russian Glider Bombs Spark New Air Defence Woes for Ukraine," *Newsweek*, April 13, 2023 (https://www.newsweek.com/russia-glider-bombs-ukraine-air-defense-jdams-1794155)
252. https://youtu.be/aZe5diu87sk?t=1520

Ukrainian Air Defense Status

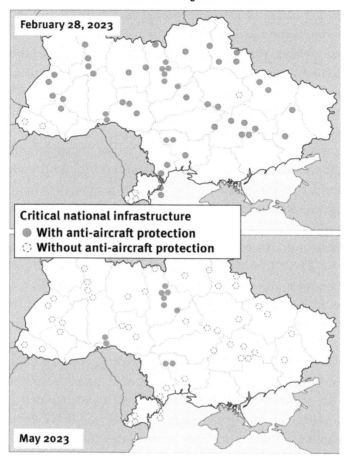

Figure 28—Information from classified documents leaked in early April 2023. They show that, in May, Ukraine no longer had an operational air defense. This was the result of the Russian campaign against the country's electrical infrastructure and the consequence of the claims made by Ukrainian propaganda and our media that Russia no longer had missiles or aircraft.

The Russian strategy has worked well, since between late 2022 and early 2023, the West was urgently required to send anti-aircraft systems to Ukraine. The USA promised a unit of MIM-104 PATRIOTs. In March 2023, France decided to send two CROTALE systems with an 11 km range, and joined Italy in sending a MAMBA SAMP/T system in the summer. Despite the quality of these systems, these efforts were far from sufficient to enable Ukraine to restore its balance.

But here again, the Westerners were not entirely successful. On May 16, 2023, immediately after its deployment, the PATRIOT system supplied by the USA was damaged according to them[253] (or destroyed according to the Russians[254]), as satellite images seem to confirm. More on this later.

Clandestine Warfare

Alongside conventional operations, it seems that very powerful resistance movements are operating in Kiev-controlled territories in the south and east of the country (Odessa, Nikolayev, Zaporozhie, Dnepropetrovsk, Kharkov, Soumy, Chernigov). Little information filters out about them because they disturb the Western narrative, but they are known as the *"Russian Kherson"* (*Русский Херсон*) and appeared in April 2023. In the Kherson, Zaporozhie and Soumy oblasts, eliminations of foreign mercenaries, members of neo-Nazi paramilitary militias, etc., were observed. According to unconfirmed reports, these eliminations amounted to the equivalent of a battalion. Sabotage actions also targeted Ukrainian logistics lines. Ukrainian ammunition depots and military installations were destroyed by plastic-coating.

During the Second World War, on May 30 1942, the Soviet Supreme High Command (VGK) decided to create a Central Staff of the Partisan Movement, responsible for coordinating, supplying, training and equipping partisan movements in Eastern Europe.[255] Did the Russians do the same in Ukraine? We don't know. But it seems that some partisan actions are coordinated with the actions of Russian forces.

It's worth noting that there has been no equivalent movement in Russian-occupied areas, since the majority of the population there is sympathetic to the Russians. Those who remained loyal to Kiev have left.

---

253. https://www.cnn.com/2023/05/16/politics/patriot-missile-damage-ukraine/index.html
254. Elena Teslova, "Russia says it destroyed 5 launchers, radar of US Patriot missile defense system in Ukraine", *aa.tr*, May 18, 2023 (https://www.aa.com.tr/en/russia-ukraine-war/russia-says-it-destroyed-5-launchers-radar-of-us-patriot-missile-defense-system-in-ukraine/2900064)
255. *Vtoraya Mirovaya Voïna—Itogi i uroki*, Moscow, Voenizdat, 1985, p. 161

Assessment of Phase 3

Phase 3 illustrates the asymmetrical dimension into which the Western narrative has pushed Ukraine. Russia's objective is potential, while Ukraine's is territory. In other words, the more Ukraine clings to its objective, the better Russia can achieve its own.

In fact, Russia achieved its goal of "denazification" on March 28, 2022. It achieved its second goal of "demilitarization" for the first time at the end of May 2022—Ukrainians are now dependent on the West for their armaments. It reached it a second time, when the former USSR equipment supplied by Eastern European countries was exhausted by the end of 2022. It reached this point a third time, when Western equipment supplied for the Ukrainian counter-offensive in 2023 was exhausted, and the West found that it could not keep up the pace by the end of 2023.

The supply of weapons by the West has led Russia to wage a war of attrition, in which Ukrainian potential is gradually being eroded. Sacrificing troops to protect territory is the worst strategy in this situation. You can take back territory, but you'll never get back the human lives lost. At present, Westerners are urging the Ukrainians to gamble away their remaining human capital. Our intellectuals see it as a great romantic epic (it's easy to wage war with other people's lives), but we have to remember that Ukraine will have to rebuild itself.

Our media may hail the Ukrainians' heroic defense of Bakhmut, but this solves nothing. The Ukrainians are well aware of this, as there are two opposing approaches—that of General Valerii Zaluzhny, who would have prefered to abandon Bakhmut in order to preserve his troops, and that of Volodymyr Zelensky and General Oleksandr Syrskyi, head of the Ground Forces, who saw in the defense of the town a symbolic dimension, necessary to gain Western support. Zelensky's vision prevailed, because of the Westerners.

As a result, during their counter-offensive, the Ukrainians continued their assault in the hope of retaking Bakhmut.

4. Ukrainian Military Thinking

While Russia's military thinking is perfectly well constructed and documented, Ukraine's is far less structured. Until 2014, the Ukrainian army remained strongly influenced by its Warsaw Pact military tradition. Within the framework of the *Partnership for Peace* (PfP) and the *Euro-Atlantic Partnership Council* (EAPC) (and not NATO, as some "experts" claim), its armed forces were moving closer to Western standards. This influence, which it would put to good use when participating in US operations in Iraq and Afghanistan, locked it into a tactical approach to combat.

This tactical military thinking is struggling to coexist with the more operative military tradition that emerged during the Cold War. It has thus remained in a form of doctrinal transition that deprives it of the intellectual coherence between the strategic, operative and tactical levels that it needs today.

Confronted with the Donbass rebels, it suffered two major defeats that led it to sign the Minsk I (September 2014) and II (February 2015) Agreements. Even then, operations showed a deficit in operative thinking that has persisted to this day—it fights tactically, not operatively. The result is a dissymmetry in the way it fights that would work in the Russians' favor from 2022 onwards.

By the end of 2014, Ukraine had embarked on an *Anti-Terrorist Operation* (ATO) (demonstrating that it was not facing an external threat) for which it was prepared neither doctrinally, structurally nor materially. Western training assistance focused on counter-insurgency. Unfortunately, not only had their know-how failed to bring victory in Iraq and Afghanistan, but it would prove totally unsuited to the nature of the Ukrainian conflict.

The main weakness of the Ukrainian forces stems from this disparate contribution—the absence of a backbone and doctrinal coherence.

The Ukrainian population generally benefits from a very high level of education, and the country is known for its highly skilled hackers. This was all it took for Western countries to see the opportunity to prepare their armies for so-called 5th generation conflicts, with a strong "cyber" component. The image of an enemy (Russia) seeking to "destroy our democracies" by influencing elections in the United States, France, Germany or Great Britain (which has never been proven!) was created. The problem was that this was just a perception, not reality.

But the war being waged by Russia is a 3rd generation war! Thus, we hadn't prepared the Ukrainian army for the right war.

This, paradoxically, the Ukrainian approach to the conflict is totally—hybrid! It is a hasty combination of combat principles dating from the Soviet era, readapted by NATO instructors whose operational experience is totally different from that of Ukraine. From 2022 onwards, this lack of homogeneity was accentuated by equipment from different sources, designed for different doctrines of use, ill-suited to the Ukrainian theater and with composite military and civilian control systems.

Ukrainian Forces

Before 2014, relations between Ukrainian-Ukrainians and Ukrainian-Russians were traditionally good. Particularly among the "educated" population, everyone spoke Russian and Ukrainian indistinctly. Ties between the two ethnic groups were strong and close. The rise to power of a small coterie of extreme right-wing "Kievians," aided by ultra-nationalist fanatics, was completely out of step with the rest of the country. But it was above all the abolition of the Kivalov-Kolesnichenko law on official languages on February 23, 2014, which was felt hardest by the more modest populations in the south of the country and in the Donbass. Russian, previously used for interactions between citizens and the administration and in schools, was replaced by Ukrainian. The whole south of the country went up in flames, and the army was mobilized to quell the demonstrations.

These changes had a profound effect on the armed forces, many of which are sympathetic to the Russian-speaking minority. This led to a massive increase in indiscipline and desertions. Large numbers of army units joined the autonomists with arms and equipment. This explains the rapid arming of the rebels, which our media attributed to Russia.

Traditionally, the Ukrainian army operated on the principle of conscription. In October 2013, President Yanukovych decided to switch to a professional army in 2014. But on May 1, 2014, the new government decided to return to conscription for young people, aged between 18 and 25 in all parts of the country, including the southern regions.[256] In 2015, Ukrainian forces numbered 250,800 men.

In fact, the army was undermined by the corruption of its officers and no longer enjoyed the support of the population. According to a UK Home Office report, in the March-April 2014 recall of reservists, 70% failed to turn up for the first session, 80% for the second, 90% for the third and 95% for the fourth.[257] In October-November 2017, 70% of conscripts failed to show up for the *"Fall 2017"* recall campaign.[258] This is without counting suicides and desertions (often to autonomists), which reached up to 30% of the force in the ATO area.[259]

In 2018, according to Anatoly Matios, Chief Military Prosecutor, after four years of conflict with Donbass autonomists, 2,700 military personnel died *outside* combat situations (accidents, drugs, weapons mishandling, murders and suicides).[260]

256. "Ukraine Enacts Compulsory Military Draft," *NBC News*, May 1, 2014 (https://www.nbcnews.com/storyline/ukraine-crisis/ukraine-enacts-compulsory-military-draft-n94906)

257. *"Country Policy and Information Note—Ukraine: Military service"*, Version 4.0, Home Office, April 2017 (https://www.refworld.org/docid/590748164.html)

258. "В ВСУ заявили о 70% неявки во время осеннего призыва", *iPress.ua*, December 13, 2017 (https://ipress.ua/ru/news/v_vsu_zayavyly_o_70_neyavky_vo_vremya_osennego_pryziva_237367.html)

259. *Fact Finding Mission Report—Ukraine*, Office français de protection des réfugiés et apatrides (OFPRA) and Bundesamt für Fremdenwesen und Asyl (BFA), May 2017 (p. 36); Mikhail Klikushin, "Why Are So Many Ukrainian Soldiers Committing Suicide?", *Observer.com*, June 30, 2017

260. "На Донбассе небоевые потери ВСУ составили 2700 человек,—Матиос", *focus.ua*, October 27, 2018 (https://focus.ua/ukraine/410520-na-donbasse-neboevye-poteri-vsu-sostavili-2700-chelovek--matios)

Ukrainian Army Losses in the Donbass (2014-2018)

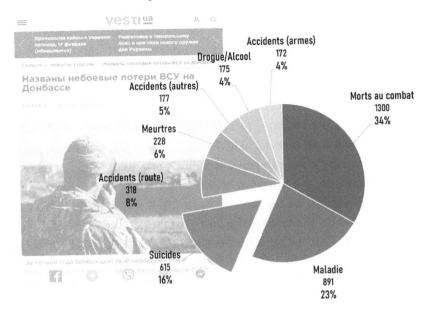

Figure 29—Status of Ukrainian forces between 2014 and 2020. This was why Ukraine is asking for NATO's help to get it back on its feet. NATO would primarily provide assistance in improving the framework conditions of the armed forces. At the same time, NATO countries (notably the USA, Great Britain, France and Canada) were involved bilaterally in training the military and paramilitary (including neo-Nazis and ultra-nationalists). [Source: Vesti.ua]

Desertions to rebel regions were countless. According to the British government, there were 33,000 deserters between 2014 and 2018, and 9,300 in 2019.[261] To deal with this situation, the Ukrainian authorities took a two-pronged approach:

- Request NATO assistance to set up social programs within the armed forces, to facilitate the reintegration of military personnel into civilian life after enlistment, and to combat corruption (BUILDING INTEGRITY program). The aim was to enhance the value of military careers and encourage young people to enlist. It was also in this context that I was involved with Ukraine. The aim

---

261. "Country policy and information note: military service, Ukraine, version 8.0, June 2022 (accessible)", Home Office, June 2022 (updated July 27, 2022) (https://www.gov.uk/government/publications/ukraine-country-policy-and-information-notes/country-policy-and-information-note-military-service-ukraine-june-2022-accessible#preface)

was to revitalize the Ukrainian army by making it more attractive. But this is a long-term activity, which didn't provide an answer to the urgency of the situation.

- The unreliability of the army is prompted the new authorities in Kiev to set up more political paramilitary formations, mainly from the far right (of "neo-Nazi" or "ultra-nationalist" obedience), which brutally suppressed popular revolts throughout the south of the country and provoked the stiffening of the Russian minority. It was a short-term solution, adapted to the urgency of the moment.

This issue has been dealt with extensively in my other books, *Operation Z* and *Ukraine Between War and Peace,* so we won't go into detail here.

Suffice it to recall that, as early as 2014, a series of volunteer units financed by oligarchs such as Igor Kolomoisky (who would become the promoter of Volodymyr Zelensky's artistic, and later political, career) were formed, such as the AÏDAR, AZOV, DNIEPR-1, DNIEPR-2 and DONBASS battalions. Ukrainian forces then needed a sufficient ideological backbone to compensate for the demotivation of soldiers engaged in a war against their own fellow citizens. It should also be remembered that, according to the head of the Ukrainian General Staff, there were no regular Russian troops in the Donbass.[262] This information was confirmed nine months later by the head of the Ukrainian SBU, who stated that only 56 individual Russian fighters had been observed in the Donbass.[263]

Desertion is an endemic problem for Ukrainian forces. So much so that the Ukrainian parliament passed a law authorizing officers to use their weapons against their men if they attempted to desert.[264] In May 2022, an amendment to this law was proposed to the Rada,[265] calling for the deletion of the phrase *"without causing death."* The proposal sparked

---

262. https://www.dw.com/uk/генштаб-україна-не-воює-з-російськими-регулярними-військами/a-18225044
263. https://www.kyivpost.com/article/content/war-against-ukraine/sbu-registers-involvement-of-56-russian-in-military-actions-against-ukraine-since-military-conflict-in-eastern-ukraien-unfolded-399718.html
264. Damien Sharkov, "Ukraine Passes Law Allowing Military to Shoot Deserters," *Newsweek*, February 6, 2015 (https://www.newsweek.com/ukraine-passes-law-shoot-deserters-304911)
265. https://itd.rada.gov.ua/billInfo/Bills/Card/39562

deep indignation on social networks and was withdrawn.[266] However, this proposal did not really modify current legislation. Indeed, commanders are authorized to use their weapons *"to stop a criminal offence, if it is impossible to stop it in any other way."* In combat situations, according to the code of military discipline, these offences are: disobedience, resisting or threatening a leader, violence and desertion.[267] Since the beginning of the Russian SMO, extremist militias have been engaged on the rear of the regular Ukrainian forces, in order to eliminate any combatants who might seek to desert.

Western Disinformation: Russian Troops in Ukraine

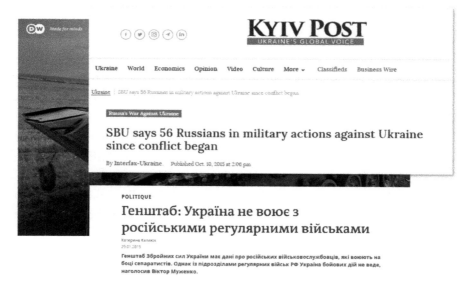

Figure 30—In order to justify sanctions against Russia, an invasion by Russian troops of Ukraine was invented. Yet, according to the head of the Ukrainian General Staff in January 2015, the Ukrainian army was not fighting Russian troops and, in the Kyiv Post of October 10, 2015, the head of the SBU, the Ukrainian security service, stated that only 56 Russian individuals have been involved in combat actions.

---

266. "The Rada will withdraw the bill on the murder of deserters", *The News 24,* May 24, 2022 (https://then24.com/2022/05/24/the-rada-will-withdraw-the-bill-on-the-murder-of-deserters/)
267. Anna Stechenko & Irina Gamaliy, "З Верховної Ради відкликали законопроєкт про розстріл дезертирів", *lb.ua,* May 24, 2022 (https://lb.ua/pravo/2022/05/24/517817_z_verhovnoi_radi_vidklikali.html)

Despite their supporters' attempts to portray them as "extinct," neo-Nazis do exist in the Ukrainian forces[268] and continue to have a mobilizing effect on regular troops.[269]

There are two types of Ukrainian volunteer paramilitary forces: those belonging to the National Guard and those independent of the Ministry of Defense. This is the case of the Ukrainian Volunteer Army (UDA), led by Dmitro Yarosh, which is an offshoot of the Right Sector and a militia that can be described as ultra-nationalist and neo-Nazi. Units of this type were withdrawn from combat zones in the Donbass in summer 2018. This is what our journalists call the "denazification" of the Ukrainian army. But contrary to what they claim, these units have not disappeared. In fact, they were withdrawn because they were difficult to manage, refused to obey the military hierarchy and were responsible for numerous war crimes.[270] Today, the UDA fights alongside the Ukrainian forces, but independently of the decisions of the Ukrainian General Staff.

These units, independent of a centralized command, pose a number of problems. The most obvious is that of operational coordination. Numerous examples show that these units, such as the KRAKEN Battalion, reputed to be particularly brutal, refuse to bow to the decisions of the Kiev general staff. This has led to bloody clashes between these militias and the Ukrainian army. Furthermore, these units, which are not integrated into a hierarchy, do not feel accountable for their actions and tend to commit more war crimes than others.

The Ukrainian Army Faced with Attrition

In January 2022, the Ukrainian armed forces numbered 200,000 to 250,000[271] soldiers, plus up to 900,000 reservists and militiamen. They were preparing for an offensive against the Donbass, knowing that Russia would probably intervene.

---

268. Josh Cohen, "Ukraine's neo-Nazi problem," *Reuters*, March 19, 2018 (https://www.reuters.com/article/us-cohen-ukraine-commentary-idUSKBN1GV2TY)
269. Thomas Gibbons-Neff, "Nazi Symbols on Ukraine's Front Lines Highlight Thorny Issues of History," *The New York Times*, June 5, 2023 (updated June 7, 2023) (https://www.nytimes.com/2023/06/05/world/europe/nazi-symbols-ukraine.html)
270. https://zn.ua/UKRAINE/pravyy-sektor-mozhet-voyti-v-sostav-vsu-lish-kak-otdelnoe-podrazdelenie-171167_.html
271. Prasanta Kumar Dutta, Samuel Granados & Michael Ovaska, "On the edge of war", *Reuters*, January 26, 2022 (https://graphics.reuters.com/RUSSIA-UKRAINE/dwpkrkwkgvm/)

By April-May 2022, the Ukrainian army of February virtually no longer existed, and the West stepped in to keep Ukrainian defenses afloat. It was at this point that Ukraine began to commit territorial troops to counter the Russian coalition. Demonstrations by the wives and mothers of Ukrainian servicemen were violently suppressed.[272]

In July 2022, Zelensky claimed that he wanted to launch an operation to reconquer the lost territories with an army of one million men.[273] But despite these declarations, Ukraine did not manage to muster that many men. This is because young Ukrainians are reluctant to fight. In 2022, the number of male university students increased by 82%, and in some universities this number was multiplied by 12.[274]

In May 2023, while the Russians were talking about raising the *conscription age* from 27 to 30, Ukraine was lowering it from 27 to 25. Oleksiy Reznikov, then Minister of Defense, justified this apparent contradiction by the need to replenish the mobilization reserve. Previously, the maximum age for conscription was 27; so if a man reached 27 and had not served in the army, he could no longer be forcibly mobilized. After the law was amended, men aged between 25 and 60, even those with no military service experience, could be forcibly mobilized.[275]

In June 2023, Swiss military "expert" Alexandre Vautravers declared that the Ukrainian army had a total strength of 960,000 men, including 170,000 "on leave." These figures seemed totally fanciful. In fact, in February 2023, *Statista*'s Research Department had established that Ukraine's maximum potential was 500,000 men (200,000 active, 250,000 reserve and 50,000 paramilitary).[276]

The *Ukrainian Military Pages* media outlet revealed that, according to the Ukrainian General Staff, since May 2023, the situation of the armed forces' new manpower had deteriorated significantly. The personnel

272. Paul Waldie, "In the small Ukraine city Khust, a rare public display of dissent over war with Russia", *The Globe and Mail*, May 2, 2022 (https://www.theglobeandmail.com/world/article-russia-ukraine-war-conscription-protest/)
273. Maxim Tucker, "Ukraine has one million ready for fightback to recapture south", *The Times*, July 10, 2022 (https://www.thetimes.co.uk/article/ukraine-has-one-million-ready-for-fightback-to-recapture-south-3rhkrhstf)
274. https://gordonua.com/ukr/news/society/v-ukrajini-za-rik-vijni-kilkist-cholovikiv-studentiv-platnoji-formi-navchannja-zrosla-na-82-u-dejakih-vishah-u-12-raziv-zmi-1661079.html
275. https://visitukraine.today/blog/1974/conscription-age-cut-to-25-in-ukraine-what-will-change-and-how-will-it-affect-mobilisation
276. https://www.statista.com/statistics/1296573/russia-ukraine-military-comparison/

situation was becoming "particularly critical" because of the increase in combat casualties caused by the Ukrainian counter-offensive in the east and south, and the offensive by Russian troops in the Kharkiv region. By July 2023, only 50 percent of mobilized troops had reported to Ukrainian army training centers.[277] This phenomenon of disaffection was compounded by the ability to serve, which stood at between 50 and 60 percent, and dropped to 10 percent in elite formations, such as the parachute troops.[278] Our "expert" had been talking nonsense.

Despite the fact that they are forbidden to leave the country, thousands of young Ukrainians sought to flee and thus escape mobilization.[279] According to Eurostat figures, 17.7 percent of the 4,114,320 Ukrainians who have found refuge in Europe are between the ages of 18 and 64 and could be mobilized. This represents just under 730,000 men who could join the armed forces, provided they meet the requirements. This is why, in August 2023, Ukraine announced that it would adjust its regulations in August-September 2023 to reduce the number of exemptions, and that it would ask European countries to extradite men of serviceable age. Some countries agreed, such as Poland,[280] but others refused, such as Germany, Austria and the Czech Republic.[281]

While Russia had to deal with a *conscription* problem, because of the increasing size of its army, Ukraine has a *mobilization* problem to deal with, an increasingly tense manpower situation.[282] In fact, the failure of the 2023 counter-offensive, which was supposed to be decisive, only served to accentuate the population's distrust of the Ukrainian government and of Zelensky in particular. In September, a poll showed that

277. https://www.ukrmilitary.com/2023/07/mobilization-buksue.html
278. https://www.ukrmilitary.com/2023/06/50.html
279. "Thousands of Ukrainian men are avoiding military service", *The Economist*, August 31, 2023 (https://www.economist.com/europe/2023/08/31/thousands-of-ukrainian-men-are-avoiding-military-service)
280. "Poland May Start to Extradite Ukrainian 'Draft Dodgers'", *Kyiv Post*, September 4, 2023 (https://www.kyivpost.com/post/21242)
281. Zoltán Kottász, "Ukraine Demands Extradition of Its Draft-Age Men", *The European Conservative*, September 9, 2023 (https://europeanconservative.com/articles/news/ukraine-demands-extradition-of-its-draft-age-men/)
282. Anastasia Stognei, Polina Ivanova & Christopher Miller, "Russia and Ukraine tighten conscription rules ahead of spring hostilities", *The Financial Times*, April 11, 2023 (https://www.ft.com/content/35d34148-32a9-4b95-99da-db2470817329)

over 78 percent of Ukrainians believe he is responsible for corruption in the country.[283]

According to *Time* magazine, the war has decimated the younger age groups and necessitated the mobilization of ever older men, bringing the average age of a Ukrainian soldier to around 43.[284] This means different operational capabilities and a heavier burden on the logistics chain.

Poorly Trained Soldiers

Since the end of the Cold War, Western armies have never had the opportunity to implement the tactical and operational concepts developed during the Cold War to counter the Soviets. Their equipment, doctrines and procedures were adapted to counter-insurgency-type conflicts. This is why, today, what the Ukrainians receive is merely the surplus of what was not used in the "war on terror."

First of all, many units are completely new, created or recreated from the remnants of other units, or made up of newly-incorporated military personnel. This is the case of the 32nd Independent Mechanized Brigade, which did not exist in 2022, and is composed *"mostly of civilians who had never fired on anyone," "many of* whom did *not want to be part of the army,"* and which is engaged against *"experienced and well-equipped* Russians, *with a large number of artillery shells and multiple rockets."*[285]

> *The infantrymen claim to be outclassed by the skilled and apparently fearless Russian military they have seen on this axis of attack.*

This is the exact opposite of what our pseudo-experts and media plumbers tell us.

---

283. Valentyna Romanenko, "Almost 80% of Ukrainians consider Zelenskyy responsible for dealing with corruption in government and military administrations", *Ukrainska Pravda*, September 11, 2023 (https://www.pravda.com.ua/eng/news/2023/09/11/7419343/)

284. Simon Shuster, "'Nobody Believes in Our Victory Like I Do.' Inside Volodymyr Zelensky's Struggle to Keep Ukraine in the Fight," *TIME magazine*, October 30, 2023 (updated November 1, 2023) (https://time.com/6329188/ukraine-volodymyr-zelensky-interview/)

285. Igor Kossov, "New brigade bears heavy brunt of Russia's onslaught in Kharkiv Oblast", *The Kyiv Independent*, September 1, 2023 (https://kyivindependent.com/new-brigade-bears-heavy-brunt-of-russias-onslaught-in-kharkiv-oblast/)

Up to July 2023, Western countries have trained 17 brigades and 63,000 Ukrainian servicemen.[286] The problem is that Western instructors have no experience of the conflict for which they are training Ukrainian officers and servicemen.[287] They often draw on their experience of operations in the Middle East and train Ukrainians in house-cleaning and rebel identification, which have no relevance to the Ukrainian theater.

In fact, the training provided by NATO countries is often out of step with conditions on the ground, highly bureaucratic, and unsuited to the conflict in Ukraine.[288] German and British instructors were unable to communicate effectively with Ukrainian military personnel, and were unable to adapt terminology to their Ukrainian "clients."[289] Ukrainian servicemen undergoing training in Germany told the *Kyiv Independent* that "*the training prepared them for a war that does not exist in Ukraine. They said that NATO officers did not understand the reality on the ground.*"[290]

The intended consequence of this permanent and deceptive underestimation by our media is to push the Ukrainians to fight despite the fact that they know their fight is hopeless. Thus, the morale of the Ukrainian military is very low. Indeed, this has become an argument for Volodymyr Zelensky, who told *CNN* that an invitation to join NATO now "*would be a huge motivation for Ukrainian soldiers.*"[291]

A key issue, but one that has been totally overlooked by our media, is the training of Ukrainian personnel. The destruction of the human military potential of Ukrainian forces has resulted in the gradual disappearance of seasoned servicemen.

---

286. https://www.defense.gov/News/News-Stories/Article/Article/3462714/ukraine-defense-contact-group-members-remain-unified-in-support-to-kyiv/

287. Isobel Koshiw, "NATO training leaves Ukrainian troops 'underprepared' for war", *openDemocracy*, August 8, 2023 (https://www.opendemocracy.net/en/odr/ukraine-russia-training-nato-to-west-military/)

288. Jack Watling, "West must focus on preparing Ukraine's troops—or we will all pay the price", *The Guardian*, July 23, 2023 (https://www.theguardian.com/world/2023/jul/23/west-must-focus-on-preparing-ukraines-troops-or-we-will-all-pay-the-price)

289. Laura Pitel, "Lost in translation: Germany's challenges training Ukrainian soldiers", *Financial Times*, August 28, 2023 (https://www.ft.com/content/5bcb359e-f0ae-475d-9773-b89c0ebe0a1b)

290. https://kyivindependent.com/new-brigade-bears-heavy-brunt-of-russias-onslaught-in-kharkiv-oblast/

291. https://edition.cnn.com/europe/live-news/russia-ukraine-war-news-07-04-23/h_9ffe-d7e97423cb666d3e0079ec06e978?embed=true

Added to this are time constraints, which mean that each stage of training is not consolidated and validated before moving on to the next. The use of drones during training is often difficult, or even forbidden in some NATO countries due to the possibility of accidents with civilians. Only two platoons (around 60-70 men) per battalion are considered to be combat-capable, i.e., around 10 percent of the total strength.

Our military "experts" tell us that the Ukrainian army favors individual initiative and mission-based command. But this doesn't seem to be the reality. According to military journalists who visited the country, "*the Ukrainian armed forces do not encourage personal initiative, mutual trust or mission command.*"[292]

The Russians can bless their hearts that the Ukrainian army was trained by NATO officers.

Ukrainian Conduct

The central problem with the Ukrainian army is that it has not been prepared for a war of movement against a mechanized adversary. Modernized and trained since 2014 by NATO, it has suffered from the lack of experience of Westerners, who have only been confronted with technologically inferior armies in counter-insurgency contexts.

As we have seen in certain operations (such as BARKHANE), Westerners have a clear deficit in understanding the operative level. That's why, since the start of the SMO in February 2022, we haven't seen any major tank battles, like at Kursk in 1943. The Ukrainians are fighting an infantry war, in trenches or in urban areas, as in Mariupol, Severodonetsk or Bakhmut.

We can conclude from this that bringing in tanks, let alone Western ones with which the Ukrainians are not entirely familiar, will not fundamentally change the situation. Even with renewed equipment, Ukraine is no longer in a position to retake the territories taken by the Russians. Let me remind you that while the West talks of territory, the Russians talk of potential.

Another problem stemming from the inexperience of NATO armies is the trend towards "micro-management," which affects the Ukrainian

---

292. https://warontherocks.com/2023/06/what-the-ukrainian-armed-forces-need-to-do-to-win/

army. This trend has increased with the disappearance of experienced commanders and the arrival of hastily-trained officers.

Ukrainian and Western Strategies

Western Strategy

On the face of it, it would appear that Ukraine and Western countries share the same objective and therefore the same strategy. But this is not true. The strategies of Ukraine and the West (i.e., the United States) are sometimes difficult to distinguish from each other, as they feed off each other without succeeding in satisfying very distinct interests.

Since the 2000s, Ukraine's primary interest has been to draw closer to the West in order to guarantee its prosperity. As I have shown in previous books, it sees this rapprochement through NATO membership, which should open the door to the EU, and thus become a "full" member of modern Europe. Until 2014, Russia was a partner and not perceived as a threat. From then on, discriminatory policies against minorities, and in particular the Russian minority, increased tension between the two countries (as with Hungary, incidentally), culminating in the SMO of 2022.

The United States is obsessed with China, whose rapid technological and commercial development—two areas in which it claims world leadership—is still perceived as a threat. The USA's objective is therefore to prevent Russia from becoming China's and Europe's "backyard" for energy and natural resources. Initially, American strategy towards Russia was the subject of two conflicting visions within the White House itself:

- Offer concessions to Russia in order to keep it in the West and thus weaken China;
- Weaken Russia, bring about Vladimir Putin's downfall and a change of power to render it useless to China.

In both approaches, Ukraine played a central role: either for the concessions that could have been made to Russia, or by using it to draw Russia into a conflict. In the end, it was the latter option, defended by Victoria Nuland and Anthony Blinken, the "ultras" of the Biden administration, that was chosen.

It was to be extended by a "decolonization" of Russia,[293] i.e., its dismemberment and the creation of new countries.[294] This was confirmed by Oleksiy Danilov, Secretary of Ukraine's Defense and National Security Council, in March 2022, on the Swiss television channel *RTS*:[295]

> *the West must prepare for the decolonization of Russia. Russia will soon cease to exist within its current borders. This is not up to us. The beginning of Russia's collapse was brought about by Putin on February 24, 2022... The processes that led to the collapse of the USSR are now underway in today's Russia.*

From May 2022, no less than five conferences (including one by videoconference) followed one another in Warsaw (May 2022), Prague (July 2022), Gdansk (September 2022) and Brussels (January 2023). This is a far cry from the "paranoia" proclaimed by the Swiss state media.

To achieve this collapse, a strategy was described very precisely by the *RAND Corporation*, the Pentagon think tank, in March 2019, in a 300-page document entitled, *Extending Russia: Competing from Advantageous Ground*.[296] The Americans scrupulously applied this strategy, which involves pushing Russia into conflict.[297]

This is where Ukraine comes in: it was intended as a kind of bait and switch, enabling the West to mobilize the international community against Russia.

But *RAND* analysts had warned that this strategy could backfire on Ukraine if Russian capabilities were not properly assessed. And that's exactly what happened. Because it was not on the scale of Western economies, it was thought that its economy was fragile and would collapse quickly. Because Vladimir Putin was portrayed as a

---

293. Casey Michel, "Decolonize Russia," *The Atlantic*, May 27, 2022 (https://www.theatlantic.com/ideas/archive/2022/05/russia-putin-colonization-ukraine-chechnya/639428/)
294. https://www.csce.gov/international-impact/events/decolonizing-russia
295. https://www.rts.ch/info/monde/13818312-lukraine-demande-des-armes-des-armes-et-encore-des-armes.html
296. James Dobbins, Raphael S. Cohen, Nathan Chandler, Bryan Frederick, Edward Geist, Paul DeLuca, Forrest E. Morgan, Howard J. Shatz, Brent Williams, "Extending Russia: Competing from Advantageous Ground", *RAND Corporation*, 2019, p. 101.
297. Robert H. Wade, "Why the US and Nato have long wanted Russia to attack Ukraine," *London School of Economics and Political Science*, March 30, 2022 (https://blogs.lse.ac.uk/europpblog/2022/03/30/why-the-us-and-nato-have-long-wanted-russia-to-attack-ukraine/)

"dictator,"[298] we thought the Russian population was just looking for an opportunity to overthrow him. Because we thought the Russian army was ill-equipped and rigidly commanded, we thought it would quickly be defeated on the ground by a NATO-trained Ukrainian army. In other words, Western "strategists" thought that this war would be very short-lived, as the massive sanctions[299] and Russia's international isolation were to ensure that Russia would no longer be able to sustain its war effort, as Ursula von der Leyen imagined before the European Parliament on March 2, 2022.[300]

Evolution of Western Strategy for the Conflict in Ukraine

Approximate Period	Objective	Strategy
February-May 2022	Collapse the Russian economy by targeting the civilian population, in order to cause a social catastrophe that would lead to the overthrow of Vladimir Putin.[301]	Massive sanctions
June-July 2022	Rearm Ukraine so that it is in a better position to negotiate.[302]	Arms deliveries and military assistance
August-December 2022	Engage Russia in a war of attrition to force it to surrender.[303]	Multiple counter-offensives
January-summer 2023	Break through Russian lines and cut Crimea off from Russian territory, in order to cause a panic leading to the overthrow of Vladimir Putin.[304]	Massive Ukrainian counter-offensive

298. "Biden calls Putin a 'dictator' and says Russian army is being 'ridiculed'", *Euronews*, May 4, 2022 (https://fr.euronews.com/2022/05/04/biden-qualifie-poutine-de-dictateur-et-estime-que-l-armee-russe-est-ridiculisee)

299. Paul De Grauwe, "Russia cannot win the war", *London School of Economics and Political Science*, March 2, 2022 (https://blogs.lse.ac.uk/europpblog/2022/03/02/russia-cannot-win-the-war/)

300. https://www.pubaffairsbruxelles.eu/eu-institution-news/speech-by-president-von-der-leyen-at-the-european-parliament-plenary-on-the-russian-aggression-against-ukraine/

301. "Economic sanctions will hurt Russians long before they stop Putin's war in Ukraine," *The Conversation*, March 1, 2022 (https://theconversation.com/economic-sanctions-will-hurt-russians-long-before-they-stop-putins-war-in-ukraine-178009)

302. Joseph R. Biden Jr, "President Biden: What America Will and Will Not Do in Ukraine", May 31, 2022, *The New York Times* (https://www.nytimes.com/2022/05/31/opinion/biden-ukraine-strategy.html)

303. "Why Ukraine is waging a brutal war of attrition against Russia over Bakhmut," *PBS.org*, May 23, 2023 (https://www.pbs.org/newshour/world/why-ukraine-is-waging-a-brutal-war-of-attrition-against-russia-over-bakhmut)

304. Kateryna Tyshchenko, "Russia will panic when Ukraine's counteroffensive begins—Ukraine's Deputy Defence Minister", *Ukrainska Pravda*, May 7, 2023 (https://www.pravda.com.ua/eng/news/2023/05/7/7401067/)

Summer 2023	Gradually and systematically destroy Russian army capabilities.[305]	War of attrition against Russia
August-September 2023	Freeze the conflict on the front lines.	Pushing Zelensky to negotiate
October-November 2023	Find a solution to the strategic losing situation in Ukraine, without losing face.	Push Zelensky to negotiate with Russia and apply a "containment" strategy
December 2023	Reawaken international support for Ukraine	Ensuring Ukraine's survival as a state.

Figure 31—Western objectives fluctuated as events unfolded.

The problem with these different strategies is that they were all based on a *perception of* Russian capabilities, not on the *reality* of the facts. Likely because they have maintained a form of freedom of expression, the Americans are quicker than the Europeans to realize that sanctions will not stop the war.[306] Thus, in April 2022, Janet Yellen, Joe Biden's Treasury Secretary, tried to discourage the Europeans from placing sanctions on Russian oil products so as not to unbalance the market.[307] But there is only one narrative in Europe, and it cannot be disputed. The blind pursuit of a Russian collapse will lead to economic catastrophe and the death of Ukraine and Ukrainians.

The West is convinced that Russia can only lose. But military action won't be enough. The key is to destabilize Russia by creating tension between the population and the Kremlin. This is why the West will support the terrorist campaign waged by Ukraine in Russia and by spreading false information, for example about a possible mobilization in Russia for January 5, 2023.[308]

---

305. http://www.ukrainianjournal.com/index.php?w=article&id=37113
306. Christine Adams, "Can economic sanctions end a war?", *The Washington Post*, March 1, 2022 (https://www.washingtonpost.com/outlook/2022/03/01/can-economic-sanctions-end-war/)
307. "Yellen warns European ban on Russian energy could harm economies", *RFI*, April 21, 2022 (https://www.rfi.fr/en/yellen-warns-european-ban-on-russian-energy-could-harm-economies)
308. Veronika Melkozerova, "Ukraine defense chief warns of new Russian mobilization", *Politico*, December 31, 2022 (https://www.politico.eu/article/ukraine-defense-chief-oleksii-reznikov-warn-russia-mobilization/)

The problem with Western strategy is that it deliberately instrumentalizes Ukraine to satisfy U.S. strategic objectives. As Democratic Senator Richard Blumenthal put it in late August 2023:[309]

Ukraine is the spearhead of our fight for independence and freedom.

He admits that not only is Ukraine doing the job for the U.S., it's doing it at modest cost to Americans:[310]

Let me tell my fellow Americans that you get what you pay for in Ukraine. Russia's armed forces have been weakened by half. Its strength has been reduced by 50% without a single American soldier being killed, and with less than 3% of our military budget. It's a real bargain in military terms.

This cynicism is not exclusively Democratic, but is also fairly widely supported by Republicans, as witnessed, again in August 2023, by Republican U.S. Senator Mitt Romney:[311]

To be able to devote an amount equivalent to around 5% of our military budget... to helping the Ukrainians is, I think, the best national defense expenditure we've ever made. We're not losing any lives in Ukraine, and the Ukrainians are fighting heroically against Russia, which has 1,500 nuclear weapons aimed at us. So we are diminishing and devastating the Russian army for a very small amount compared to what we spend on the rest of defense.

This disregard for the lives of Ukrainians was confirmed by Kajsa Ollongren, Dutch Minister of Foreign Affairs, in early October 2023:[312]

309. Richard Blumenthal, "Zelenskyy doesn't want or need our troops. But he deeply and desperately needs the tools to win", *The Connecticut Post*, August 29, 2023 (https://www.ctpost.com/opinion/article/sen-blumenthal-opinion-ukraine-tip-spear-18335871.php)
310. https://twitter.com/NatalkaKyiv/status/1696759802154614836
311. https://www.youtube.com/watch?v=nXJJw9MV-ak
312. https://www.republicworld.com/world-news/russia-ukraine-crisis/ukraine-a-cheap-way-to-ensure-that-russia-is-not-a-threat-to-nato-says-dutch-minister-articleshow.html

Supporting Ukraine is of course a very cheap way of ensuring that Russia, with this regime, does not pose a threat to the Atlantic Alliance.

The Dutch were said to be parsimonious, but we didn't think that went so far as to describe the Ukrainians' sacrifice as "cheap."

These statements reveal two things about the Western approach:

- No mention is made of the recovery of Ukrainian territories taken by Russia, or of the price paid by the Ukrainians themselves;
- We candidly admit that the United States is exploiting Ukraine to fight Russia at lower cost, so as to be better able to attack China.

Back in March 2019, the *RAND Corporation* had warned the US government that implementing its proposed strategy would have disastrous consequences for Ukraine, risking the loss of territory and countless human lives. The West was therefore well aware of the risks Ukraine was running.

The idea that prolonging the war will weaken Russia is contradicted by the facts. In actuality, the war has boosted the Russian economy and is destroying Ukraine, without even benefiting the West. Quite the contrary, in fact. In January 2023, a report by the *RAND Corporation*, entitled *"Avoiding a Long War,"* warned the USA—once again—against a prolonged war with Russia, as it would turn to the latter's advantage.[313]

In November 2023, I was called out by *RTS* for saying this in my previous books. But now, a year later, Ukrainian general Valerii Zaluzhny is saying it.[314]

Western Strategy: Incoherence at Work

Germany refuses...	But then accepts...
To send LEOPARD 2 tanks to Ukraine[315]	January 25, 2023[316]

313. https://www.rand.org/content/dam/rand/pubs/perspectives/PEA2500/PEA2510-1/RAND_PEA2510-1.pdf

314. "'It was my mistake': Ukrainian Commander-in-Chief on counteroffensive and 'gunpowder' for victory", *RBC-Ukraine*, November 2, 2023 (https://newsukraine.rbc.ua/news/it-was-my-mistake-commander-in-chief-on-counteroffensive-1698929719.html)

315. Holly Ellyatt, "Germany resists intense pressure over tanks for Ukraine, saying 'the situation has not changed," *CNBC*, January 24, 2023 (https://www.cnbc.com/2023/01/24/germany-refuses-to-shift-position-on-tanks-for-ukraine-despite-pressure.html)

316. Arne Delfs & Michael Nienaber, "Germany to Boost Ukraine Firepower With Leopard Battle Tanks," *Bloomberg*, January 25, 2023 (https://www.bloomberg.com/news/articles/2023-01-25/germany-to-send-ukraine-14-leopard-battle-tanks-in-first-step#xj4y7vzkg)

To supply helmets and bullet-proof vests	January 26, 2023[317]
howitzers re-exported by Estonia[318]	February 26, 2023[319]
The United States opposes...	**But then accepts...**
drone attacks on Russian territory[320]	December 9, 2022[321]
supplying M-1 ABRAMS tanks to Ukraine[322]	January 25, 2023[323]
supplying F-16 aircraft to Ukraine[324]	August 18, 2023[325]
supplying ATACMS missiles to Ukraine[326]	September 22, 2023[327]

Figure 32—The West's game of hide-and-seek with weapons for Ukraine shows a total lack of coherent strategy. It is therefore inevitable that the Ukrainians will be unable to achieve coherence. The problem for the Ukrainians is that they have relied totally on Western aid from the very first hours of the SMO.

In September 2023, when the Bundestag had already accepted the idea of supplying Ukraine with TAURUS cruise missiles, the government was

317. Hans von der Burchard, "Germany to send 5,000 protective helmets to Ukraine", *Politico*, January 26, 2022 (https://www.politico.eu/article/germany-export-5000-helmets-ukraine/
318. "Germany blocks Estonia from exporting German-origin weapons to Ukraine -WSJ", *Reuters*, January 21, 2022 (https://www.reuters.com/article/germany-ukraine-arms/germany-blocks-estonia-from-exporting-german-origin-weapons-to-ukraine-wsj-idUSL1N2U123W)
319. Hui Min Neo, "Germany to Send Weapons to Ukraine in Policy Reversal," *The Moscow Times*, February 26, 2022 (https://www.themoscowtimes.com/2022/02/26/germany-to-send-weapons-to-ukraine-in-policy-reversal-a76617)
320. "US 'not encouraging' drone strikes in Russia, State Department says", *France 24*, December 6, 2022 (updated December 7, 2022) (https://www.france24.com/en/europe/20221206-live-ukraine-races-to-repair-power-grid-as-country-enters-peak-frost-period)
321. Michael Evans & Marc Bennetts, "Pentagon gives Ukraine green light for drone strikes inside Russia", *The Times*, December 9, 2022 (https://www.thetimes.co.uk/article/ukraine-drone-warfare-russia-732jsshpx)
322. Jeff Schogol, "The US is sending tanks to Ukraine, just not American ones," *Task & Purpose*, November 4, 2022 (https://taskandpurpose.com/news/ukraine-tanks-military-assistance-russia/)
323. Joe Gould, "In reversal, US to send 31 Abrams tanks to Ukraine," *Defense News*, January 25, 2023 (https://www.defensenews.com/pentagon/2023/01/25/in-reversal-us-to-send-31-abrams-tanks-to-ukraine/)
324. Nicola Slawson, "First Thing: Biden says US will not provide F-16 fighter jets to Ukraine", *The Guardian*, January 31, 2023 (https://www.theguardian.com/us-news/2023/jan/31/first-thing-biden-says-us-will-not-provide-f-16-fighter-jets-to-ukraine)
325. Dan Sabbagh & Helen Sullivan, "US has cleared way for F-16s to be sent to Ukraine, say Denmark and Netherlands", *The Guardian*, August 18, 2023 (https://www.theguardian.com/world/2023/aug/18/us-reportedly-approves-sending-f-16-jets-to-ukraine-from-denmark-and-netherlands)
326. John Ismay, "The Missile Ukraine Wants Is One the U.S. Says It Doesn't Need," *The New York Times*, October 6, 2023 (https://www.nytimes.com/2022/10/06/us/ukraine-war-missile.html)
327. David Martin & Olivia Gazis, "Biden tells Zelenskyy U.S. will provide Ukraine with ATACMS long-range missiles," *CBS News*, September 22, 2023 (https://www.cbsnews.com/news/biden-tells-zelenskyy-u-s-will-provide-ukraine-with-atacms-long-range-missiles/)

still hesitating, before refusing in October. But Ukrainian Foreign Minister Dmytro Kuleba told his German counterpart, Annalena Baerbock:[328] *"You'll do it anyway—it's only a matter of time—and I don't understand why we're wasting time!"* Clearly, the Ukrainians know that the Europeans have no coherence, and end up obeying their narrative.

In the summer of 2023, Zelensky seemed to be beginning to realize that he had been duped by his so-called allies. They kept saying that it's up to Ukraine to decide whether or not to enter into negotiations. But this is obviously not true. Zelensky was forced to withdraw his proposal for a solution in March 2022, which included the withdrawal of Russian troops from Ukrainian territory. But on the other hand, in September 2023, Olaf Scholz declared that there could be no negotiations until the Russians left Ukrainian territory.

Western strategy has two major weaknesses. The first is that our political decisions are based on perceptions and prejudices, not facts. Both the media and the decision-makers apply the "*Coué*" method, which the English-speaking world calls "wishful thinking." Not only have Joe Biden, Ursula von der Leyen, Emmanuel Macron, Olaf Scholz or Alexander de Croo systematically made inadequate decisions, they have deliberately pushed Ukrainians to their deaths. As one Ukrainian soldier put it in an article in *The Times of London*, entitled, "*Our allies are asking us to advance with a gun in our backs*:"[329]

> *Our allies have helped us a lot, but their political leaders are demanding that we take territories in conditions where they wouldn't even think of sending their own soldiers.*

That says it all...

The second weakness is that we are no longer in a rational context. The statements and explanations of our politicians and journalists show that it is not our values, but hatred of the Russian, that dominates Western politics today. The National Gallery's de-baptism of the painting

---

328. "Germany Says Ukraine Belongs in the European Union", *VOA News*, September 11, 2023 (https://www.voanews.com/a/germany-says-ukraine-belongs-in-the-european-union/7263496.html)

329. Maxim Tucker, "'Our allies ask us to advance with a gun at our backs'", *The Times*, October 4, 2023 (https://www.thetimes.co.uk/article/our-allies-ask-us-to-advance-with-a-gun-at-our-backs-vrjdnx2hv)

Degas called *Russian Dancers* in 1899 as *Ukrainian Dancers* is a perfect illustration of the Western approach.[330] It is dominated by an irrational, revisionist dimension where even art is militarized, and an inability to solve problems through intelligent dialogue.

As the *Wall Street Journal* put it in November 2023, we are in the realm of "magical thinking,"[331] which the *Kyiv Post* evokes[332] by referring to a February 2023 article by the *Carnegie Endowment for Peace*:[333]

> *One year on from the start of Russian President Vladimir Putin's war against Ukraine, Russia has suffered a major strategic defeat, Ukraine has won a major strategic victory, and the West has shown a determination, unity and cohesion few expected.*

In other words, both in the United States and in Ukraine, we are aware that we have literally "fantasized" about Ukraine's victory. The question now is how to get back to reality and find a solution without losing face.

The Ukrainian Strategy

The strategic goal of Volodymyr Zelensky and his team is to join NATO, as a prelude to a brighter future within the EU. It complements that of the Americans (and therefore of the Europeans). The problem is that tensions with Russia, particularly over Crimea, are causing NATO members to put off Ukraine's participation. In March 2022, Zelensky revealed on *CNN* that this is exactly what the Americans told him.[334]

Before coming to power in April 2019, Volodymyr Zelensky's discourse was divided between two antagonistic policies: the reconciliation with Russia promised during his presidential campaign and his goal of joining

---

330. https://agauche.org/2022/04/06/nihilisme-anti-russe-un-tableau-de-degas-rebaptise-ukrainien-par-la-national-gallery-de-londres/

331. Eugene Rumer & Andrew S. Weiss, "It's Time to End Magical Thinking About Russia's Defeat," *The Wall Street Journal*, November 16, 2023 (https://www.wsj.com/world/russia/its-time-to-end-magical-thinking-about-russias-defeat-f6d0b8de)

332. Stash Luczkiw, "What the US Means When It Talks About Strategy," *Kyiv Post*, November 20, 2023 (https://www.kyivpost.com/opinion/24363)

333. Eugene Rumer, "Putin's War Against Ukraine: The End of The Beginning," *Carnegie Endowment for International Peace*, February 17, 2023 (https://carnegieendowment.org/2023/02/17/putin-s-war-against-ukraine-end-of-beginning-pub-89071)

334. Chandelis Duster, "Zelensky: 'If we were a NATO member, a war wouldn't have started'", *cnn.com*, March 20, 2022 (https://edition.cnn.com/europe/live-news/ukraine-russia-putin-news-03-20-22/h_7c08d64201fdd9d3a141e63e606a62e4)

NATO. He knows that these two policies are mutually exclusive, as Russia does not want to see NATO and its nuclear weapons established in Ukraine and will seek neutrality or non-alignment.

What's more, he knows that his ultra-nationalist allies will refuse to negotiate with Russia. This was confirmed by *Praviy Sektor* leader Dmitro Yarosh, who openly threatened him with death in the Ukrainian media a month after his election.[335] Zelensky therefore knew from the start of the election campaign that he would not be able to fulfill his promise of reconciliation, and that there was only one solution left—confrontation with Russia.

But this confrontation could not be waged by Ukraine alone against Russia, and it would need the material support of the West. The strategy devised by Zelensky and his team was revealed before his election, in March 2019, by Oleksei Arestovitch, his personal advisor, on the Ukrainian media *Apostrof'*. Arestovitch explained that it would take an attack by Russia to provoke an international mobilization which will enable Ukraine to defeat Russia once and for all, with the help of Western countries and NATO. With astonishing precision, he described the course of the Russian attack as it would unfold three years later, between February and March 2022. Not only did he explain that this conflict is unavoidable if Ukraine is to join NATO, but he also placed this confrontation in 2021-2022! He outlines the main axes of Western aid:[336]

> *In this conflict, we will be very actively supported by the West. Weapons. Equipment. Assistance. New sanctions against Russia. Most likely, the introduction of a NATO contingent. A no-fly zone, and so on. In other words, we won't lose it.*

As we can see, this strategy has much in common with the one described by the *RAND Corporation at the* same time. So much so, in fact, that it's hard not to see it as a strategy strongly inspired by the United States. In his interview, Arestovitch singled out four elements that would

335. Лилия Рагуцкая, "Ярош: если Зеленский предаст Украину—потеряет не должность, а жизнь," *Obozrevatel*, May 27, 2019, (https://incident.obozrevatel.com/crime/dmitrij-yarosh-es-li-zelenskij-predast-ukrainu-poteryaet-ne-dolzhnost-a-zhizn.htm)
336. "UKRAINE 24: Ukrainian Nostradamus who predicted war with russia in 2019 with stunning accuracy", *YouTube*, April 3, 2022 (https://www.youtube.com/watch?v=RZ3GsYPRkv4)

become the pillars of the Ukrainian strategy against Russia, and to which Zelensky would return regularly:

- International aid and arms supplies
- International sanctions
- NATO intervention
- The creation of a no-fly zone.

It should be noted that these four pillars are understood by Zelensky as promises whose fulfillment is essential to the success of this strategy. In February 2023, Oleksiy Danilov, Secretary of Ukraine's Defense and National Security Council, declared in *The Kyiv Independent* that Ukraine's objective was the disintegration of Russia.[337] The mobilization of Western countries to supply Ukraine with heavy weapons then seemed to give substance to this objective, which was consistent with what Oleksiy Arestovich had declared in March 2019.

A few months later, however, it became clear that the equipment supplied to Ukraine was not sufficient to ensure the success of its counter-offensive, and Zelensky requested additional, better-adapted equipment.[338] At the time, Westerners were somewhat annoyed by these repeated demands.[339] Former British Defence Minister Ben Wallace declared that Westerners *"are not Amazon."*[340] In fact, the West does not respect its commitments.

Contrary to what our media and pseudo-military experts tell us, since February 2022, it has been clear that Ukraine cannot defeat Russia on its own. As Obama put it, *"Russia [there] will always be able to main-*

337. Alexander Query, "Danilov: 'Ukraine's national interest is Russia's disintegration'", *The Kyiv Independent,* February 6, 2023 (https://kyivindependent.com/national/danilov-ukraines-natio-nal-interest-is-russias-disintegration)

338. Joe Barnes, "We know West can give us more weapons, says Ukraine's spy chief", *The Tele-graph,* September 18, 2023 (https://www.telegraph.co.uk/world-news/2023/09/18/western-al-lies-are-not-running-out-of-weapons-says-ukraine/)

339. David Averre, "Is the world running out of patience with Zelensky's 'blank cheque' demands? Poland stops giving arms and US gives a fraction of what Ukraine's leader asked for as he visits Canada today to win support", *The Daily Mail,* September 22, 2023 (https://www.dailymail.co.uk/news/article-12548375/Is-world-running-patience-Zelenskys-blank-cheque-demands-Poland-stops-giving-arms-gives-fraction-Ukraines-leader-asked-visits-Canada-today-win-support.html)

340. Dominic McGrath, "UK and other allies 'not Amazon', Wallace tells Kyiv", *The Independent,* July 12, 2023 (https://www.independent.co.uk/news/uk/volodymyr-zelensky-ben-wallace-kyiv-amazon-joe-biden-b2373967.html)

tain its escalation dominance."[341] In other words, Ukraine will only be able to achieve its goals with the involvement of NATO countries. This means that its fate will depend on the goodwill of Western countries. It is therefore necessary to maintain a narrative that encourages the West to maintain this effort. This narrative thus became what we call in strategic terms, its "center of gravity." We'll come back to this later.

As the months went by, the course of operations showed that the prospect of a Ukrainian victory was becoming increasingly remote, as Russia, far from being weakened, was growing stronger militarily[342] and economically.[343] Even General Christopher Cavoli, Supreme American Commander Europe (SACEUR), told a US congressional committee that *"Russia's air, naval, space, digital and strategic capabilities have not suffered significant degradation during this war."*[344]

The West, expecting a short conflict, is no longer able to maintain the effort promised to Ukraine. The NATO summit in Vilnius (July 11-12, 2023) ended in partial success for Ukraine. Its membership was postponed indefinitely. Its situation is even worse than it was at the beginning of 2022, since there is no more justification for its entry into NATO than there was before the SMO.

Ukraine then turned its attention to a more concrete objective: regaining sovereignty over its entire 1991 territory.

Thus, the Ukrainian notion of "victory" is rapidly evolving. The idea of a *"collapse of Russia"* quickly faded, as did that of its dismemberment. There was talk of *"regime change,"* which Zelensky locked in as an objective, by forbidding any negotiations as long as Vladimir Putin was in power.[345] Then came the reconquest of lost territories, thanks to a counter-offensive in 2023. But here too, hopes faded rather quickly. The

341. Jeffrey Goldberg, "Obama Sees Ukraine as Putin's Client State," *The Atlantic*, March 10, 2016 (https://www.atlanticcouncil.org/blogs/natosource/obama-sees-ukraine-as-putin-s-client-state/)

342. Holly Ellyatt, "Russia's military has adapted and is now a more formidable enemy for Ukraine, defense analysts say," *CNBC News*, May 19, 2023 (https://www.cnbc.com/2023/05/19/russias-military-has-adapted-is-now-a-formidable-enemy-for-ukraine.html)

343. https://www.intellinews.com/imf-improves-russia-s-2023-gdp-forecast-from-0-3-to-0-7-275604/

344. https://armedservices.house.gov/sites/republicans.armedservices.house.gov/files/04.26.23 Cavoli Statement v2.pdf

345. "Kyiv decree confirms impossibility of negotiating with Putin", *Reuters*, October 4, 2022 (https://www.reuters.com/article/ukraine-crise-zelensky-poutine-idFRKBN2QZ0ZD)

plan was simply to cut the Russian forces in two, with a thrust towards the Sea of Azov. But by September 2023, this objective had been reduced to the liberation of three cities.[346]

In the absence of concrete successes, narrative remains the only thing Ukraine can rely on to maintain Western attention and willingness to support it. For, as ex-Defense Minister Ben Wallace put it in *The Telegraph* on October 1, 2023: *"the most precious* commodity *is hope."*[347] True enough. But our assessment of the situation must be based on realistic analyses of our adversary. However, since the beginning of the Ukrainian crisis, our analyses have been based on prejudice.

Western Aid

We now know that, in order to convince Zelensky to withdraw the proposal he made to Russia in March 2022, the West pledged to provide arms and ammunition aid for *"as long as it takes."* By the end of May/ beginning of June 2022, the Ukrainian army's material capabilities had been destroyed, and Ukraine was dependent on Western aid.[348] By early 2023, however, it was clear that the West no longer had the capacity to meet its commitments to Ukraine. This explains Zelensky's repeated requests for new equipment. All he's doing is asking the West to respect its commitments!

The problem is that Zelensky still holds out the prospect of victory to his people, whereas, as President Joe Biden confessed in the *New York Times*: it's no longer a question of Ukraine "winning", but simply of fighting.[349]

The problem is that the West deliberately underestimated Russian military power and overestimated Ukrainian capabilities.[350] That's why they thought their weapons could bring victory over Russia. According to the *New York Times*, the weapons supplied are often defective. At the end of March 2023, Volodymyr Zelensky told *Associated Press* that the

---

346. Joe Barnes, "Zelensky vows to liberate Bakhmut and two other cities in secret plan," *The Telegraph*, September 22, 2023 (https://www.telegraph.co.uk/world-news/2023/09/22/volo-dymyr-zelensky-secret-plan-liberate-cities-ukraine/)
347. Ben Wallace, "Ukraine is winning. Now let's finish the job", *The Telegraph*, October 1, 2023 (https://www.telegraph.co.uk/news/2023/10/01/ben-wallace-ukraine-counteroffensive-succeeding/)
348. https://www.france24.com/en/live-news/20220610-ukraine-dependent-on-arms-from-al-lies-after-exhausting-soviet-era-weaponry
349. Joseph R. Biden Jr, "President Biden: What America Will and Will Not Do in Ukraine", May 31, 2022, *The New York Times* (https://www.nytimes.com/2022/05/31/opinion/biden-ukraine-strategy.html)
350. https://youtu.be/hxqIuzn32Fw

systems received *"from a European country"* did not work and had to be repaired several times.[351] This information was also reported by the *Kyiv Independent*.[352] And that's only when the weapons ordered and paid for by Kiev arrive on the front line.[353] Here, as elsewhere, the West sends Ukraine obsolete and often defective equipment.

Testimonies from Ukrainian soldiers[354] report frequent breakdowns and their inability to correctly use overly complicated weapons, designed for professional soldiers and very long training cycles. Poorly trained, Ukrainian soldiers are nevertheless entitled to manuals that are obviously not written in Ukrainian, forcing them to translate them with *Google Translate* in order to understand them.[355]

The challenge for Westerners is to be able to supply the battlefield. It's no longer a question of winning, but of fighting. The idea is that the Russian population, tired by the length of the conflict, could bring about the long-awaited "regime change." As a result, the criterion for supplying arms to Ukraine is not effectiveness, but availability.

Initially, the Westerners collected old Cold War equipment, stored or mothballed in Eastern Europe, and sent it to Ukraine. Often poorly maintained and often in poor condition, they were supplied for want of anything better. But these stocks were quickly exhausted. The Americans were seeking to restart production of 152 mm artillery ammunition in the countries of the former Warsaw Treaty, in Bulgaria, Romania, the Czech Republic and Slovakia.[356] But what is possible for ammunition is more complicated for major equipment. In these cases, deliveries were used to cannibalize surviving Ukrainian equipment. This was the case for the MiG-29 fighters supplied by Poland and Slovakia, which were apparently hardly in working condition and which the Ukrainians could only use

351. Julie Pace, Hanna Arhirova & James Jordan, "Takeaways from AP's interview with Ukraine's Zelenskyy", *AP*, March 30, 2023 (https://apnews.com/article/ukraine-zelenskyy-russia-putin-war-78f55fbf4fb7e57711c2fadaf914fd45)

352. https://www.businessinsider.com/zelenskyy-says-ukraine-received-faulty-air-defense-system-europe-ally-2023-3

353. https://fr.businessam.be/ukraine-armes-achat-livraison/

354. https://t.me/HersonVestnik/5489

355. Thomas Gibbons-Neff & Natalia Yermak, "Potent Weapons Reach Ukraine Faster Than the Know-How to Use Them," *The New York Times*, June 6, 2022 (https://www.nytimes.com/2022/06/06/world/europe/ukraine-advanced-weapons-training.html)

356. "NATO looking at production of Soviet-era weapons used by Ukraine, says Blinken", *The New Voice of Ukraine*, November 30, 2022 (https://english.nv.ua/amp/nato-looking-at-production-of-soviet-era-weapons-used-by-ukraine-says-blinken-50287799.html)

to "cannibalize" their own damaged aircraft.[357] This "2nd generation" Ukrainian army, re-equipped with Soviet and Russian equipment, would also be destroyed by the end of 2022.

Ukraine's Major Land Armaments (October 2023)

	(1) Situation au 24.02.2022 (BBC)	(2) Matériel russe capturé au 01.10.2023 (Oryx)	(3) Fourni par l'Occident au 01.10.2023	(1)+(2)+(3) Total au 01.10.2023
Chars de combat	 987	551	1 135	2 673
Véhicules blindés d'infanterie	 831	972	>2 732	>4 535
Pièces d'artillerie	 1818	204	>967	>2 989
Lance-fusées multiples	 -	52	>101	>153

Figure 33—Major equipment in Ukraine's hands since the start of the SMO. Ukraine's renewed need for equipment shows that Russia has destroyed between 2 and 5 times Ukraine's potential. [Sources: (1) https://www.bbc.com/news/world-60798352; (2) https://www.oryxspioenkop.com/2022/02/attack-on-europe-documenting-equipment.html; (3) https://www.economist.com/zaluzhny-transcript]

In a second phase, the West delivered obsolete equipment from its own reserves to Ukraine. On January 24, 2023, Estonia announced that it was giving away all its 155 mm howitzers, i.e., 24 FH-70s, and 122 mm D-30s of Soviet origin, with their ammunition.[358] This equipment—when operational—is obsolete in the face of Russian weapons. These weapons had been preserved for use in "colonial" wars, in a technologically less demanding environment. This was the case with the venerable M-113 troop transport vehicles, whose 40 mm aluminum armor is equivalent to

357. "Ukraine's top guns need new jets to win the war", *The Economist*, April 23, 2023 (https://www.economist.com/europe/2023/04/23/ukraines-top-guns-need-new-jets-to-win-the-war)
358. Joe Saballa, "Estonia Sending All Its 155-mm Howitzers to Ukraine," *The Defense Post*, January 24, 2023 (https://www.thedefensepost.com/2023/01/24/estonia-sending-howitzers-ukraine/)

10 mm steel, offering precarious protection against today's weapons, as evidenced by the number of their smashed hulks in Ukraine. The equipment supplied at the time enabled Ukraine to fight, but was not sufficient in number or quality to carry out a decisive counter-offensive.

That said, "charity begins at home"—for much of the equipment supplied to Ukraine had been the occasion to give fate a helping hand in forcing our parliaments to increase military spending in order to keep our armies up to date with new equipment.

In a third phase, Westerners had to draw on the equipment of their own forces. This was the case with the CAESAR guns, of which France offered around 30 to Ukraine, taken from its own operational stocks;[359] and Denmark gave Ukraine the 19 pieces ordered from France. The same applied to the 14 British CHALLENGER 2 battle tanks sent to Ukraine. According to Admiral Anthony Radakin, Chief of the Defense Staff,[360] these were taken from the 40 that were actually operational, and reduced the kingdom's operational capacity by 30 percent, pending the arrival of the CHALLENGER 3.[361]

As we can see, they were stripping out their own arsenals to meet Ukrainian demand. For example, according to the *Financial Times*, a British MP claimed that the British army could not last more than 5 days in the event of war.[362] This means that the danger of a Russian attack on Europe is nothing more than war rhetoric designed to create panic among our populations.

In a fourth phase, the West sought to produce the materials needed for Ukraine and supply them on a just-in-time basis. But once again, it was a failure. The Western—and European in particular—arms industry has literally melted away since the end of the Cold War.

---

359. "France to supply Ukraine with twelve additional Caesar guns", *France 24*, January 31, 2023 (https://www.france24.com/fr/europe/20230131-en-direct-macron-reçoit-le-ministre-de-la-défense-ukrainien-kiev-réclame-des-avions-de-combat)

360. https://www.dailymail.co.uk/news/article-12264611/Britain-just-40-tanks-dozen-frigates-destroyers-ready-war.html

361. George Grylls, "Sending British Challenger 2 tanks to Ukraine will weaken UK, general warns", *The Times*, January 16, 2023 (https://www.thetimes.co.uk/article/putin-british-tanks-will-burn-ukraine-war-russia-challenger-2-hsww7wtw9)

362. George Parker & John-Paul Rathbone, "UK armed forces would last just 'five days' in a war, senior MP warns", *Financial Times*, February 10, 2023 (https://www.ft.com/content/4eb1af29-2491-458c-9f69-e065cba58bbb)

In March 2023, the European Union decided on a budget of 2 billion euros to finance ammunition.[363] One billion is to reimburse countries that have drawn on their own stocks to support Ukraine, and one billion is to mobilize European industrial resources to produce 1 million 155 mm shells for Ukraine in 12 months.[364] Sounds like a lot, but it's the equivalent of what Russia fires in 20 to 40 days, according to the *Royal United Services Institute (RUSI)*.[365]

The result of these Western efforts was a 3rd generation Ukrainian army, rearmed and trained in the West, which would be capable of carrying out a decisive operation against Russia.

In September 2023, the West, and the Americans in particular, reached the limit of what they could do. In Belgium, the armed forces had run out of ammunition and were asking for 7 billion euros to replenish their stocks.[366] Admiral Rob Bauer, who chairs NATO's Military Committee, declared that *"we can see the bottom of the barrel"* and that we need to speed up arms production.[367] While the United States was considering reducing its aid to Ukraine, the Europeans were finding that they are unable to compensate for this reduction.[368] In other words, the West cannot keep its promise, and the EU is nothing more than a "paper tiger."

363. "EU agrees 2-billion-euro ammunition plan for Ukraine", *France 24*, March 20, 2023 (https://www.france24.com/en/live-news/20230320-eu-hammers-out-2-bn-euro-ammunition-plan-for-ukraine)
364. "Ukraine updates: EU agrees €2 billion ammo plan for Kyiv", *Deutsche Welle*, March 20, 2023 (https://www.dw.com/en/ukraine-updates-eu-agrees-2-billion-ammo-plan-for-kyiv/a-65045955)
365. Dr Jack Watling & Nick Reynolds, "Meatgrinder: Russian Tactics in the Second Year of Its Invasion of Ukraine", *Royal United Services Institute*, May 19, 2023 (https://rusi.org/explore-our-research/publications/special-resources/meatgrinder-russian-tactics-second-year-its-invasion-ukraine)
366. https://www.rtbf.be/article/defense-et-guerre-en-ukraine-larmee-belge-face-a-une-penurie-de-munitions-7-milliards-deuros-sont-demandes-11250713
367. "NATO's Military Committee head urges boost in arms production," *TVP/Reuters*, October 4, 2023 (https://tvpworld.com/73184483/natos-military-committee-head-urges-boost-in-arms-production)
368. Nicholas Vinocur, Clea Caulcutt & Sarah Anne Aarup, "EU to US: Help, we can't cope without you on Ukraine", *Politico*, October 5, 2023 (https://www.politico.eu/article/josep-borell-eu-ukraine-to-us-help-we-cant-cope-without-you-on-ukraine/)

U.S. Department *of* Defense   ≡

U.S. Department *of* Defense   ≡

RELEASE
IMMEDIATE RELEASE

$775 Million in Additional Security Assistance for Ukraine

Aug. 19, 2022

f 𝕏 ↱

Today, the Department of Defense (DoD) announces the authorization of a Presidential Drawdown of security assistance valued at up to $775 million to meet Ukraine's critical security and defense needs. This authorization is the Biden Administration's nineteenth drawdown of equipment from DoD inventories for Ukraine since August 2021.

Capabilities in this package include:

- Additional ammunition for High Mobility Artillery Rocket Systems (HIMARS);
- 16 105mm Howitzers and 36,000 105mm artillery rounds;
- 15 Scan Eagle Unmanned Aerial Systems;
- 40 MaxxPro Mine Resistant Ambush Protected Vehicles with mine rollers;
- Additional High-speed Anti-radiation missiles;
- 50 Armored High-Mobility Multipurpose Wheeled Vehicles (HMMWV);
- 1,500 Tube-Launched, Optically-Tracked, Wire-Guided (TOW) missiles;
- 1,000 Javelin anti-armor systems;
- 2,000 anti-armor rounds;
- Mine clearing equipment and systems;
- Demolition munitions;
- Tactical secure communications systems;
- Night vision devices, thermal imagery systems, optics, and laser rangefinders.

RELEASE
IMMEDIATE RELEASE

Biden Administration Announces Additional Security Assistance for Ukraine

Aug. 29, 2023

f 𝕏 ↱

Today, the Department of Defense (DoD) announced additional security assistance to meet Ukraine's critical security and defense needs. This announcement is the Biden Administration's forty-fifth tranche of equipment to be provided from DoD inventories for Ukraine since August 2021. It includes additional air defense and artillery munitions, mine clearing equipment, medical vehicles, and other equipment to help Ukraine counter Russia's ongoing war of aggression on the battlefield and protect its people.

The capabilities in this package, valued at up to $250 million, include:

- AIM-9M missiles for air defense;
- Additional ammunition for High Mobility Artillery Rocket Systems (HIMARS);
- 155mm and 105mm artillery rounds;
- Mine clearing equipment;
- Tube-Launched, Optically-Tracked, Wire-Guided (TOW) missiles;
- Javelin and other anti-armor systems and rockets;
- Hydra-70 Rockets;
- Over 3 million rounds of small arms ammunition;
- Armored medical treatment vehicles and High Mobility Multipurpose Wheeled Vehicle (HMMWV) ambulances;
- Demolitions munitions for obstacle clearing; and
- Spare parts, maintenance, and other field equipment.

Figure 34—US aid to Ukraine in August 2022[369] and August 2023.[370] Not only have the amounts changed, but the Administration no longer gives any indication of quantities. In fact, by 2023, the US no longer has the capacity to support Ukraine at the 2022 rate. The PATRIOT missiles, which Ukraine would nevertheless greatly need, are no longer on the list. [Source: US Department of Defense]

This led the United States to juggle the aid it provides to its allies, and redefine their priorities—continue to support a lost cause in Ukraine, or fall back on their main priority: China. No longer able to feed both prio-

---

369. https://www.defense.gov/News/Releases/Release/Article/3134457/775-million-in-additional-security-assistance-for-ukraine/
370. https://www.defense.gov/News/Releases/Release/Article/3509116/biden-administration-announces-additional-security-assistance-for-ukraine/

rities, the aid that was supposed to go to Egypt was diverted to Taiwan, with a perverse effect—the countries of the South now know that they are a negligible quantity, so they look for new, more reliable allies.

As early as June 2022, according to Brigadier General Volodymyr Karpenko, Commander of Land Forces Logistics, Western arms deliveries covered only 10-15 percent of their needs.[371]

In fact, Western countries have grossly underestimated Russia's capabilities. Their support for Ukraine has become more of a communications exercise than an actual aid effort.

The problem is that the West does not have the capacity to wage war against Russia. Even support for Ukraine is pushing NATO countries into a precarious security situation. Which just goes to show that Western countries do not take Russia seriously as a threat to Europe.

In the United States, several mechanisms coexist to support the Ukrainian war effort. The main ones are:

- the *Ukraine Security Assistance Initiative* (USAI), subject to Congressional approval. It concerns equipment purchased on the market or from allied countries;
- the *Presidential Drawdown Authority* (PDA),[372] which authorizes the President of the United States, as supreme commander of the armed forces, to draw down equipment from existing stocks to meet an "*unforeseen emergency.*" It is not subject to congressional approval, but can only be made within existing budgets.

By the end of August 2023, the United States had supplied just under $24 billion worth of equipment under the PDA.[373] In other words, this equipment corresponds to a decline in US operational capabilities—which will therefore have to be reconstituted. In January 2023, the *Center for Strategic and International Studies* (*CSIS*) showed that the time required to reconstitute stocks of some critical equipment will reach 7 years.[374]

---

371. Stew Magnuson, "Ukraine to U.S. Defense Industry: We Need Long-Range, Precision Weapons," *National Defense Magazine*, June 5, 2022 (https://www.nationaldefensemagazine.org/articles/2022/6/15/ukraine-to-us-defense-industry-we-need-long-range-precision-weapons)
372. https://www.state.gov/use-of-presidential-drawdown-authority-for-military-assistance-for-ukraine/
373. https://crsreports.congress.gov/product/pdf/IF/IF12040
374. Mark F. Cancian, "Rebuilding U.S. Inventories: Six Critical Systems," *CSIS*, January 9, 2023 (https://www.csis.org/analysis/rebuilding-us-inventories-six-critical-systems)

Restocking Time for Critical Materials in the United States

	Quantités fournies à l'Ukraine	Unités produites par an	Délai de mise en route (mois)	Temps de production (mois)	Temps de reconstitution des stocks (mois)
Obus 155 mm	1'074'000	93'000	12-18	44	59
Obus 155 mm Excalibur	5'200	2'400	22	23	84
Javelin	8'500	2'100	24	12	56
HIMARS	20	72	26	5	30
Stinger	1600	350?	24	55	79

Figure 35—Table showing the time required to replenish US stocks of weapons given to Ukraine. The table was drawn up by CSIS. For production, only maximum production capacities have been taken into account. [Source: CSIS]

In September 2023, several French military "experts" published an article in the newspaper *La Croix*, calling for an "amplification" of European military equipment production in order to maintain aid to Ukraine.[375]

Yet the United States seemed increasingly embarrassed by this conflict, which was failing to deliver on its promises and turning into a fiasco for American foreign policy. As Volodymyr Zelensky traveled to New York for the United Nations General Assembly, Western enthusiasm appeared to be waning. Zelensky addressed the UN facing a sparse audience, to the extent that the Ukrainian media outlet *1+1* had to "enrich" its report with images from previous sessions—in which Zelensky himself was in the audience, listening to his own speech! But on a more serious note, the United States gave Zelensky a four-page list of tasks to complete, if he wished to continue receiving assistance.[376]

Sanctions

One of the pillars of the Western strategy to defeat Russia was the application of massive and sudden sanctions against Russia. The idea was—as

---

375. https://www.la-croix.com/debat/Guerre-Ukraine-Europeens-doivent-amplifier-leur-pro-duction-materiel-militaire-2023-09-20-1201283537

376. "White House letter sets out reforms that Ukraine needs to implement to receive aid", *Ukrainska Pravda*, September 25, 2023 (https://www.pravda.com.ua/eng/news/2023/09/25/7421354/)

French Economy Minister Bruno Le Maire prophesied—to bring about Russia's collapse, with the idea that if its economy was no longer able to support the SMO, Russia would quickly be forced to surrender.

According to European experts, the effect of the sanctions was to have the effect of a "nuclear bomb"[377] and fuel the narrative of a Ukrainian victory. Yet, very symptomatically, at the end of August 2023, the German magazine *BILD* revealed that Olaf Scholz and Emmanuel Macron, comparing their experiences of dialogue with Vladimir Putin, were surprised to find that at no time did Putin seek to discuss with them the issue of sanctions against Russia.[378] In other words, this was not a matter of concern for Russia.

NATO Intervention

As Oleksei Arestovich announced in March 2019, Ukraine received Western intelligence support right from the start of the SMO.

In July-August 2022, knowing that NATO would not reverse its decision to not establish a *No-Fly Zone* (NFZ) in Ukraine, Zelensky needed to demilitarize or send an international force to the NFZ area. The NFZ was then the target of artillery fire—obviously—attributed to Russia, which has troops stationed there! The Western narrative was that Russia was seeking to create a nuclear threat to Europe (for what purpose?). *France 2* even went so far as to present a damaged chimney on the roof of the ZNPP as a missile![379] In reality, the projectile remains found on site were of Western origin. They included American HIMARS missiles and kamikaze drones[380] and British BRIMSTONE missiles.[381, 382] Their firing was monitored by Westerners, who therefore knew exactly who was carrying out these attacks on the Energodar power plant.

---

377. Gilles Quoistiaux, "Blocage de Swift: la bombe atomique qui n'a pas explosé", *L'Écho*, September 10, 2022 (Updated September 11, 2022) (https://www.lecho.be/dossiers/conflit-ukraine-russie/blocage-de-swift-la-bombe-atomique-qui-n-a-pas-explose/10412813.html)

378. https://www.bild.de/politik/inland/politik-inland/ukraine-krieg-was-scholz-nach-seinem-putin-telefonat-besonders-quaelte-85191144.bild.html

379. Émilie Jehanno, "Guerre en Ukraine: Oui, France 2 a confondé une cheminée endommagée avec un missile dans un sujet", *20minutes.fr*, August 23, 2022 (https://www.20minutes.fr/arts-stars/medias/3340383-20220823-guerre-ukraine-oui-france-2-confondu-cheminee-endommagee-missile-sujet)

380. https://www.telegraph.co.uk/world-news/2022/07/20/ukrainian-kamikaze-drones-strike-russian-controlled-zaporizhzhia/

381. https://mezha.media/en/2022/05/12/brimstone-in-ukraine/

382. https://t.me/milinfolive/88735

The Ukrainian strategy was to place the ZNPP at the center of a battle that would force the international community to intervene in one way or another. That's why, on September 1, 2022, the day an International Atomic Energy Agency (IAEA) mission came to inspect it, Ukraine launched a commando attack on the plant, delaying the deployment of the experts. Several unsuccessful attacks were attempted in September-October 2022, mobilizing 600 men and dozens of barges to cross the Dnieper. These attacks resulted in dozens, if not hundreds, of deaths—and our media saw nothing but Russian disinformation. *RTS* even suggested that Russia was trying to use the plant to *"blackmail the nuclear industry."*[383]

These "attacks" were not confirmed until six months later by the *Times* of London,[384] and then in October 2023 by Kyrylo Budanov, head of Ukrainian military intelligence, who confessed in the Ukrainian press to having carried out three attacks on the plant.[385] In reality, this was a Ukrainian strategy to provoke NATO intervention, as I pointed out at the time. The concrete elements demonstrating Ukrainian responsibility were known, but our media—once again—preferred to develop conspiracy theories in order to preserve their narrative.

On November 15, 2022, a missile exploded near the village of Przewodów, Poland, killing two people. The missile was quickly identified as an S-300 5-V-55K anti-aircraft missile.[386] The next day, Volodymyr Zelensky accused Russia: *"Missiles striking NATO territory... This is a Russian missile attack against collective security! This is a significant escalation. We must react!"*[387] Yet neither the United States, nor NATO, nor Poland accused Russia.[388] This did not stop military "expert" Alexandre Vautravers, on *RTS,* from claiming that it was *"probably a Russian weapon*

---

383. https://www.rts.ch/info/monde/13300261-la-centrale-nucleaire-de-zaporijjia-cristallise-les-inquietudes-internationales.html
384. Maxim Tucker, "Ukraine's secret attempt to retake the Zaporizhzhia nuclear plant", *The Times,* April 7, 2023 (https://www.thetimes.co.uk/article/ukrainian-zaporizhzhia-nuclear-power-plant-russia-putin-war-2023-fx82xz3xz)
385. https://www.rts.ch/info/monde/13300261-la-centrale-nucleaire-de-zaporijjia-cristallise-les-inquietudes-internationales.html
386. https://twitter.com/Osinttechnical/status/1592603808634638336
387. https://youtu.be/26lKZTgSUM4
388. Phil Mattingly, Kevin Liptak, Radina Gigova, Jim Sciutto & Sophie Tanno, "Poland, NATO say missile that killed two likely fired by Ukraine defending against Russian attack", *CNN,* November 16, 2022 (https://www.cnn.com/2022/11/16/europe/poland-missile-russia-ukraine-investigation-wednesday-intl-hnk/index.html)

that strayed and struck across the border."[389] In reality, he knew nothing about it and was making it all up, because it's hard to understand why Russia would fire *anti-aircraft missiles*, let alone at Poland. In fact, in September 2023, Poland published the result of its investigation: it was a Ukrainian S-300 5-V-55 anti-aircraft missile, produced by Russia and sold to Ukraine.[390] Beyond the technical details, this was undoubtedly an accident that Zelensky sought to exploit to obtain a more "physical" involvement of NATO in the conflict.

The No-Fly Zone

The problem in Ukraine is the discrepancy between the reality on the ground and the discourse propagated in the West. Ukraine is fighting a war for which NATO has ill-prepared it. Right from the start of the Russian SMO, Ukraine lost control of its airspace and was no longer in a position to cover counter-offensives on an operational scale. It managed to keep the Russian air force at bay in certain sectors, thanks to its S-300 anti-aircraft systems of Russian origin, but this was not enough to mount a dynamic defense.

That's why, right from the start of the SMO, Zelensky sought NATO's direct involvement in the conflict, repeatedly calling on it to create *"no-fly zones"* or NFZs. But the West is not enthusiastic about directly confronting the Russian air force and its formidable air defenses.

That's why Zelensky will do everything in his power to get the West to take the risk. The situation in Libya in 2011 serves as his model. In this way, real or fictitious events take on a deliberately dramatic importance. In early March 2022, taking advantage of a minor incident at the Zaporizhia nuclear power plant (ZNPP), Zelensky spoke of a danger to Europe[391] and called for the establishment of an NFZ.[392] NATO refused.[393] A few days

---

389. https://www.rts.ch/info/monde/13548963-tir-de-missile-sur-la-pologne-pistes-dexplication-et-consequences.html
390. "Coraz bliżej prawdy o rakiecie w Przewodowie. Wiadomo czyj był pocisk," *Rzeczpospolita*, September 26, 2023 (https://www.rp.pl/kraj/art39165861-coraz-blizej-prawdy-o-rakiecie-w-przewodowie-wiadomo-czyj-byl-pocisk)
391. "Ukraine nuclear plant: Russia in control after shelling", *BBC News*, March 4, 2022 (https://www.bbc.com/news/world-europe-60613438)
392. "Ukraine's Zelenskyy condemns NATO over no-fly zone decision", *dw.com*, March 4, 2022 (https://www.dw.com/en/ukraine-zelenskyy-condemns-nato-over-no-fly-zone-decision-as-it-happened/a-61007081)
393. "Zelensky slams Nato over rejection of no-fly zone", *BBC News*, March 5, 2022 (https://www.bbc.com/news/world-europe-60629175)

later, the incidents at the Mariupol maternity hospital (March 9, 2022) and the Mariupol theater (March 16, 2022)[394] gave Zelensky the opportunity to renew his request, but NATO again refused.[395] In summer 2022, Ukraine tried to provoke a NATO intervention. Shots were fired at the Energodar ZNPP, which was then under Russian control and secured by a Russian National Guard unit. Naturally, our media relayed the Ukrainian accusations without batting an eyelid.[396] In reality, the projectile remains found came from American HIMARS missiles and kamikaze drones[397] and British BRIMSTONE missiles.[398, 399] The *French* state media *France 2* even went so far as to present a damaged chimney on the roof of the ZNPP as a missile.[400]

In June 2023, when Zelensky was under pressure from the West to launch his decisive "counter-offensive," he didn't have enough air cover. Thus, he tried the same ploy, inventing a Russian plot to blow up the ZNPP. In a tweet, he declared that *"it is the responsibility of everyone in the world to prevent it."*[401]

Clearly, the Ukrainians entered this conflict with the assurance that the West would not let them lose. They therefore agreed to provoke Russia[402] with the guarantee that Western support would reduce the Russian response to nothing in a matter of days. At the end of March 2022, Zelensky was forced to withdraw his negotiating proposal in exchange for support "for as long as it takes." His attempts to push the West into setting up an NFZ were nothing more than a way of reminding the West of their promises.

394. Siobhan Hughes, "Zelensky Asks U.S. Again for No-Fly Zone," *The Wall Street Journal*, March 16, 2022 (https://www.wsj.com/livecoverage/russia-ukraine-latest-news-2022-03-15/card/zelensky-asks-u-s-again-for-no-fly-zone-SA6RQHFsz3NUsT9uE4ru)

395. Siobhan Hughes, "Zelensky Asks U.S. Again for No-Fly Zone," *The Wall Street Journal*, March 16, 2022 (https://www.wsj.com/livecoverage/russia-ukraine-latest-news-2022-03-15/card/zelensky-asks-u-s-again-for-no-fly-zone-SA6RQHFsz3NUsT9uE4ru)

396. https://www.rts.ch/info/monde/13291212-la-centrale-nucleaire-de-zaporijjia-bombardee-deux-fois-en-un-weekend-kiev-et-moscou-saccusent.html

397. https://www.telegraph.co.uk/world-news/2022/07/20/ukrainian-kamikaze-drones-strike-russian-controlled-zaporizhzhia/

398. https://mezha.media/en/2022/05/12/brimstone-in-ukraine/

399. https://t.me/milinfolive/88735

400. Emilie Jehanno, "Guerre en Ukraine: Oui, France 2 a confondé une cheminée endommagée avec un missile dans un sujet", *20minutes.fr*, August 23, 2022 (https://www.20minutes.fr/arts-stars/medias/3340383-20220823-guerre-ukraine-oui-france-2-confondu-cheminee-endommagee-missile-sujet)

401. https://twitter.com/ZelenskyyUa/status/1676336904285966336

402. https://www.president.gov.ua/documents/1172021-37533

In fact, this is exactly what Ukrainian Foreign Minister Dmitro Kuleba said in the American magazine *Foreign Affairs*, in an article entitled, "How Ukraine will win."[403] He described a strategy that depends entirely on the supply of modern weapons from the West. It was now June 2022, and our media were relentlessly repeating that Russia is losing,[404] because it no longer has any soldiers or equipment. But the exact opposite was true—the Ukrainian army no longer had the means to carry out a counter-offensive, and is now totally dependent on the goodwill and generosity of the West.

It's a war between the United States and Russia, via Ukraine. As a result, the West is heavily involved in Ukrainian decisions, making it difficult to distinguish between their respective strategies. This poses a number of problems:

- Ukraine's political leadership has only partial control over its strategy, and is largely dependent on the political strategy of Western countries.
- Ukraine's interests collide with those of its partners: its strategy is focused on regaining lost territory, while the West is seeking to bring down the Russian government. Thus, the draft agreement proposed in March 2022, which provided for a return to the borders of February 23, 2022 in exchange for Ukraine's neutrality, and had elicited a positive reaction from Russia, was rejected by the West, which forced Zelensky to withdraw his proposal and engage in an endless conflict.
- Ukraine's military leadership lacks the doctrinal, material and training elements it needs to achieve its objectives.

This situation led to a "back-and-forth" and inconsistencies in Ukrainian conduct that have had to be covered over by a narrative. In the French-speaking world, none of our fanatical media (such as *RTS* in Switzerland, *LCI*, *BFM TV* or *France 5* in France and *RTBF* in Belgium) even mentioned the Ukrainian negotiating initiatives. These media have shown very little compassion for the lives of Ukrainians (and *a fortiori* Russians) and have militated virulently against any possibility of peace, even back since 2014.

---

403. Dmytro Kuleba, "How Ukraine Will Win", *Foreign Affairs*, June 17, 2022 (https://www.foreignaffairs.com/articles/ukraine/2022-06-17/how-ukraine-will-win)
404. https://www.rts.ch/info/monde/13145871-lukraine-affirme-avoir-fait-reculer-les-forces-russes-dans-severodonetsk.html#timeline-anchor-1654233752537

This situation would be the cause of growing tensions between the West and Kiev in 2023. Already in 2014 and 2015, a careful analysis of military operations showed that the Ukrainians were applying "Western-style" schemes, totally unsuited to the circumstances, in the face of more imaginative, flexible rebels with lighter leadership structures. The same thing is happening today.

There are two fundamental reasons for this inconsistency:

- Our media's partial view of the battlefield has left us unable to help the Ukrainian leadership make the right decisions. We saw this with Claude Wild, Switzerland's ambassador to Ukraine until February 2023, whose statements copied from Ukrainian propaganda showed a total ignorance of the real situation on the ground.[405]
- The substitution by our media and self-proclaimed "experts" of Russian military thinking by a "Western" interpretation of operations. Thus, they explained that Russia wanted to take over Ukraine, so it had to take Kiev; that "demilitarization" was aimed at Ukraine's accession to NATO; and that "denazification" was aimed at overthrowing Zelensky.

The media's impact on decision-making is blatantly obvious, as shown by the Swiss *Federal Intelligence Service*'s (SRC) annual report on Switzerland's security situation, which is nothing more than a "copy and paste" of what our media report.

The Spring Counter-Offensive (2023)

First of all, it must be understood that this "counter-offensive" was the heir to the offensive planned and prepared by Ukraine on the basis of Zelensky's decree of March 24, 2021 for the reconquest of Crimea and southern Ukraine.[406] It was to dissuade Ukraine[407] from carrying it out that Russia deployed its troops as early as April 2021 at the border;[408] and

---

405. https://www.rts.ch/play/tv/redirect/detail/13567586?startTime=383
406. https://www.president.gov.ua/documents/1172021-37533
407. Mykola Bielieskov, "The Russian and Ukrainian Spring 2021 War Scare," *National Institute for Strategic Studies*, September 2021 (http://niss.gov.ua/sites/default/files/2021-09/210921_bielies-kov_war_scene.pdf)
408. https://ria.ru/20210214/donbass-1597382842.html

it was to prevent its execution that Vladimir Putin decided to launch his *Special Military Operation* (SMO) on February 24, 2022.

In May 2022, Kyrylo Budanov, head of Ukraine's *Main Directorate of Military Intelligence* (GUR), declared that Russian forces were being greatly weakened and that Ukrainian forces would be able to retake Crimea by the end of the year.[409] But the Ukrainian army had lost most of its equipment and, since June 2022, had been dependent on Western aid to replace its destroyed equipment.[410] In July 2022, Zelensky claimed that he was going to retake Crimea with a million men;[411] but he never managed to muster the necessary manpower.[412] So, despite claiming to have 700,000 men at his disposal,[413] he was unable to launch his operation in the summer of 2022. Numerous "counter-offensives" followed in 2022, but none succeeded in pushing back the Russian coalition.

In September 2022, following the success at Kharkov, Volodymyr Zelensky asked his staff to prepare a counter-offensive. But simulations showed that the prospects of success were slim and that Ukrainian losses would be massive.[414] It was therefore postponed until autumn; then winter 2022; then spring 2023. Classified American documents "leaked" in April 2023 indicate that the offensive should have taken place in late March, early April 2023. As Volodymyr Zelensky would later explain to *CNN*,[415] these successive postponements were due to a lack of manpower and equipment, confirming that Vladimir Putin's demilitarization objective had been achieved.

But the more time passed, the more Zelensky was caught between the Western demand for results and his slim chances of success. That's why

---

409. https://www.5.ua/polityka/do-kintsia-2022-roku-armiitsi-zsu-maiut-zaity-na-terytoriiu-krymu-kerivnyk-hur-budanov-278020.html

410. https://www.lepoint.fr/monde/ayant-epuise-tout-son-armement-l-ukraine-depend-totalement-des-allies-09-06-2022-2478984_24.php

411. https://www.independent.co.uk/news/world/europe/ukraine-million-army-russia-weapons-b2120445.html

412. "Ukraine attacks Russian-held Kherson, plans counterattack", *Al Jazeera*, 12 July 2022 (https://www.aljazeera.com/news/2022/7/12/ukraine-strikes-russian-held-kherson-as-kyiv-plans-counterattack)

413. Emily McGarvey, "Ukraine aims to amass 'million-strong army' to fight Russia, says defence minister", *BBC News*, 11 July 2022 (https://www.bbc.com/news/world-europe-62118953)

414. Julian E. Barnes, Eric Schmitt & Helene Cooper, "The Critical Moment Behind Ukraine's Rapid Advance," *The New York Times*, September 13, 2022 (https://www.nytimes.com/2022/09/13/us/politics/ukraine-russia-pentagon.html)

415. https://youtu.be/gIIexTCdDa0

4. Ukrainian Military Thinking

he's keeping doubt alive as to whether the offensive will be launched at all. From the outset, neither the Americans[416] nor the Ukrainians themselves had any real confidence in the success of their counter-offensive. Yet the offensive was intended to be "decisive," and carried high hopes. A propaganda film was shot to glorify those who would go and kill the "rapists" and "murderers," featuring only equipment supplied by the West.[417]

At the beginning of June 2023, in *Ukrainska Pravda*, Oleksiy Danilov, Secretary of the Ukrainian National Security Council, declared that the launch would not be announced.[418] The idea was to announce it only when combat actions had a prospect of success. For this reason, President Zelensky did not confirm the start of the counter-offensive until June 11.[419]

Western and Ukrainian Objectives

Strategic Objectives

Logically, Ukraine's declared objective is to retake the territories occupied by Russia (in the south and east of the country and in Crimea) and to push its troops back to the borders of 1991, as Mykhaïlo Podolyak declared on *RTS on* February 24, 2023.[420]

(Ironically, when Ukraine became independent in 1991, it had *already* lost Crimea following the January 20 referendum, which made it the *"Autonomous Soviet Socialist Republic of Crimea."* Abolished in 1945, it was re-established on February 12, 1991 by the Supreme Soviet of the Ukrainian SSR.[421] On March 17, Moscow organized a referendum on remaining in the Union, which was accepted by Ukraine. At this stage, Crimea was under the control of Moscow rather than Kiev, while Ukraine *was not yet* independent).

---

416. Alex Horton, John Hudson, Isabelle Khurshudyan & Samuel Oakford, "U.S. doubts Ukraine counteroffensive will yield big gains, leaked document says," *The Washington Post*, April 10, 2023 (https://www.washingtonpost.com/national-security/2023/04/10/leaked-documents-ukraine-counteroffensive/)
417. https://cdn.jwplayer.com/previews/D2aG1luF
418. https://www.pravda.com.ua/eng/news/2023/06/4/7405242/
419. "Ukraine counter-offensive actions have begun, Zelensky says," *BBC News*, June 11, 2023 (https://www.bbc.com/news/world-europe-65866880)
420. https://www.rts.ch/play/tv/-/video/-?urn=urn:rts:video:13813494&startTime=514
421 .Article "1991 Crimean referendum", *Wikipedia* (accessed November 27, 2021)

To achieve this goal, Volodymyr Zelensky requested negotiations with Russia in February, and then put forward a proposal that the Russians were ready to negotiate in March 2022. This provided for the withdrawal of Russian forces from Ukraine (with the exception of the Donbass and Crimea, whose status had yet to be negotiated) in exchange for the country's neutralization. But at the request of the West, he quickly withdrew it, trading a rapid end to the conflict for Western aid for "as long as it takes."

For Westerners, active involvement in the conflict is generally placed under the label of defending our "values." These values are often vague, and everyone understands them as they wish. For example, at the end of February 2022, the *European Union Times* reported that, for the head of the British *Secret Intelligence Service* (*SIS* or *MI-6*), the war in Ukraine was about LGBT rights![422] As we can see, Western objectives remain unclear. This would have consequences for the conduct of operations.

One thing seems clear, however—for the West, the objective is not to recover Ukrainian territory, but to bring about the collapse of Russia. This explains Zelensky's change of policy, which requires a total defeat of Russia to achieve its goal. Thus, in September 2022, he declared that he would only negotiate with Russia on condition that Vladimir Putin was no longer in power,[423] and even issued a decree forbidding any negotiations with Vladimir Putin.[424]

In other words, Volodymyr Zelensky has ruled out the possibility—now admittedly unlikely—of returning to the March 2022 solution, which would have allowed the Russians to leave Ukrainian territory.

For their part, in the absence of any concrete realistic objective, Westerners conjured up the rather bizarre idea that the counter-offensive could create "panic" in the Russian forces, leading to a political crisis and "regime" change.[425] This is why the Prigozhin mutiny (June 2023)

422. https://www.eutimes.net/2022/02/uk-mi6-spy-chief-says-war-in-ukraine-is-about-lgbt-rights/
423. "Ukraine Will Not Negotiate with Russia as Long As Putin Is In Power: Zelensky," *Barron's/AFP*, September 30, 2022 (https://www.barrons.com/news/ukraine-will-not-negotiate-with-russia-as-long-as-putin-is-in-power-zelensky-01664548507)
424. Vladimir Socor, "Zelenskyy Bans Negotiations with Putin," *Eurasia Daily Monitor* (Volume 19, No. 147), October 5, 2022 (https://jamestown.org/program/zelenskyy-bans-negotiations-with-putin/)
425. https://www.independent.co.uk/news/world/europe/ukraine-counteroffensive-russian-losses-putin-b2334687.html

triggered such enthusiasm in the West, as it seemed to demonstrate that this strategy could work. But as usual, the analyses of our pseudo-experts are not built on knowledge and reflection, but on professions of faith. In fact, this incident seems to have strengthened Vladimir Putin.

We've known since June 2022 that neither the quantity nor the quality of the weapons and aid supplied to Ukraine will enable it to achieve victory on the ground. The aim is simply to prolong the conflict, in the hope that this will eventually lead to a political crisis in Russia and "regime change," which would then constitute a total victory for Ukraine.

For its part, Ukraine knows that it will be totally dependent on the West for its foreseeable future. That's why its strategy goes beyond its national interest—it's not a question of satisfying its own short- to medium-term objectives, but the objectives of those who will finance its future.

On November 27, 2022, Mykhailo Podolyak, Zelensky's personal adviser, declared on Ukrainian television that Crimea would be completely liberated by May 2023.[426] But the counter-offensive launched in June 2023 struggled to achieve its objectives. Far from "panicking," the Russian forces resisted very well, as noted by the Ukrainian media *Kyiv Independent*:[427]

> *Soldiers from various brigades told the Kyiv Independent that in this area, the Russians are experienced and well-equipped soldiers, with a large number of artillery shells and MLRS rockets.*
> *The soldiers of the 32nd brigade make no secret of the fact that they often feel overwhelmed. The infantrymen say they are outclassed by the competent and apparently fearless Russian troops they have seen on this axis of attack.*

As a result, this strategic objective was modified. In July 2023, Oleksiy Danilov, who chairs the Ukrainian Security Council, declared that the aim was not to retake territory, but to "demilitarize" Russia.[428] This is

426. https://www.ukrinform.ua/rubric-crimea/3623657-e-tam-u-mene-ulublene-misce-podolak-obicae-cerez-piv-roku-rozpovisti-z-alti-pro-vilnij-krim.html
427. https://kyivindependent.com/new-brigade-bears-heavy-brunt-of-russias-onslaught-in-kharkiv-oblast/
428. https://twitter.com/OleksiyDanilov/status/1676118862998257664

exactly what Podolyak said in August 2023, after the failure of the counter-offensive becomes clear:[429]

The aim is the gradual, systematic destruction of the enemy army's capabilities: its logistics, technical potential, cadres and personnel.

Ironically, in order to disguise the failure of the counter-offensive, they were seeking to redefine its objectives, using almost the same words that Russian General Surovikin had used on October 18, 2022.[430]

At the beginning of September 2023, as the counter-offensive was running out of steam, the Ukrainian leadership was striving to show that it did not want to give up the fight. The strategy was one of gradual "inch-by-inch" reconquest, with the aim of wearing down Russian forces.[431]

In other words, Ukraine was adopting a strategy of attrition against Russia. This new change of strategy was surprising, as one can only hope to win a war of attrition when one has more resources than one's opponent. Here, however, it is clear that if Russia does not have unlimited resources, Ukraine certainly does not have any more.

In fact, in the autumn of 2023, the Ukrainians faced two major obstacles: the West has reached the end of its capacity to provide material support, and the American presidential campaign, in which Joe Biden is unwilling to enter without the beginnings of a solution.[432] In other words, Ukraine lacks the two essential ingredients for a war of attrition: human and material resources, and time.

The problem is how to get out of the conflict without losing face. In mid-December 2023, the *New York Times* reported on efforts by the Biden administration and Ukraine to come up with a new strategy, not to defeat Russia, but to give Ukraine something to negotiate about. To this end, the US deployed a three-star general to work on the issue. It is clear that the Americans are implicitly admitting that Russia is in a position

429. http://www.ukrainianjournal.com/index.php?w=article&id=37113
430. "Суровикин: российская группировка на Украине методично 'перемалывает' войска противника", *TASS*, October 18, 2022 (https://tass.ru/armiya-i-opk/16090805)
431. Roland Oliphant & Julian Simmonds, "Ukraine liberates territory tree by tree after critical tactical shift", *The Telegraph*, September 15, 2023 (https://www.telegraph.co.uk/world-news/2023/09/15/how-ukraine-captured-russian-territory-orikhv/)
432. https://responsiblestatecraft.org/2023/06/13/is-the-us-military-more-intent-on-ending-ukraine-war-than-us-diplomats/

of strength; that they no longer have the capacity to support Ukraine; and that it will have to fight on a tighter budget. The aim was to *"create a sufficiently credible threat for Russia to consider entering into serious negotiations at the end of next year or in 2025."*[433] Clearly, the aim is to maintain the appearance of a possible victory until after the American presidential election.

Operational Objectives

Operationally, the idea was to break through the Russian defensive system and push rapidly towards the Sea of Azov, thus cutting the Russian forces in two, in order to then push towards Crimea on the one hand, and Mariupol on the other.

How Western "strategists" thought such a plan could work with Ukraine's available resources in early 2023 is a mystery—bordering on deliberate crime. In fact, Western and Ukrainian planners ended up believing their own narrative about the Kharkov and Kherson episodes in autumn 2022. In *Foreign Policy* in April 2023, an expert from London's *International Institute of Strategic Studies* (IISS) spoke of a breakthrough within the first 24 hours of the counter-offensive.[434] While our journalists were enthusiastic about the upcoming battle,[435] US intelligence services were far less optimistic about its outcome.[436]

The problem was not simply to break through the Russian system, but to maintain the pace of progress and consolidate successes. The populations of southern Ukraine, discriminated against (notably by the July 1, 2021 law on indigenous peoples[437]) and subjected to numerous abuses

433. Julian E. Barnes, Eric Schmitt, David E. Sanger & Thomas Gibbons-Neff, "U.S. and Ukraine Search for a New Strategy After Failed Counteroffensive," *The New York Times*, December 11, 2023 (https://www.nytimes.com/2023/12/11/us/politics/us-ukraine-war-strategy.html)

434. Franz-Stefan Gady, "Ukraine's Longest Day," *Foreign Policy*, April 18, 2023 (https://foreignpolicy.com/2023/04/18/ukraine-russia-war-counteroffensive-attack-bakhmut-himars/)

435. Timothy Garton Ash, "Why the West must be ready for this moment of opportunity and risk in Ukraine," *European Council on Foreign Relations*, May 12, 2023 (https://ecfr.eu/article/why-the-west-must-be-ready-for-this-moment-of-opportunity-and-risk-in-ukraine/)

436. Julian Borger, Manisha Ganguly, Flora Garamvolgyi & Justin McCurry, "US feared Ukraine could fall 'well short' in spring counter-offensive, leaks reveal," *The Guardian*, April 11, 2023 (https://www.theguardian.com/world/2023/apr/11/us-ukraine-counter-offensive-pentagon-leaks-reveal#:~:text=US intelligence reportedly warned in,trove of leaked defense documents.)

437. "Нардеп від 'Слуги народу' Семінський заявив про 'позбавлення конституційних прав росіян, які проживають в Україні'," *AP News*, July 2, 2021 (https://apnews.com.ua/ua/news/nardep-vid-slugi-narodu-seminskii-zayaviv-pro-pozbavlennya-konstitutciinikh-prav-rosiyan-yaki-prozhivaiut-v-ukraini/)

between 2014 and 2022, probably have no intention of returning to Kiev's authority. This is particularly true in Crimea. There is every reason to believe that the Ukrainians would face strong popular resistance in these regions, as would the Russians if they moved into the western part of Ukraine.

Initial Plan for the Ukrainian Counter-Offensive

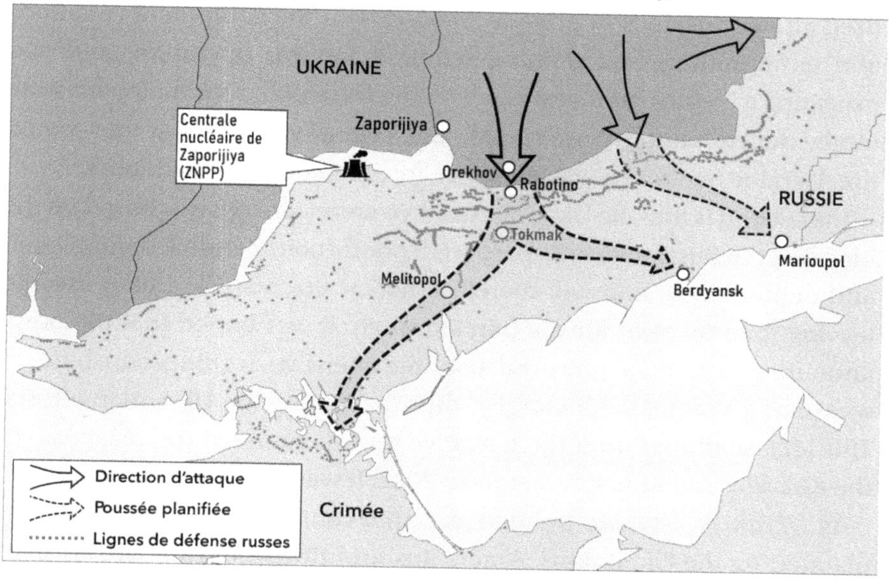

Figure 36—*The Ukrainian counter-offensive appeared to be moving in three directions: a primary direction (virtually imposed by the USA) along the Rabotino—Melitopol axis; a secondary direction along the Staromaïorsk—Mariupol axis; and another secondary direction towards Bakhmut.*

But at the end of September 2023, Ukrainian Brigadier General Oleksandr Tarnavskiy, commander of the TAVRIA strategic-operational group, noted the inadequacy of the Ukrainian forces and declared that the objective of the counter-offensive would be the village of Tokmak, some twenty kilometers from the front line.[438] This fell well short of the announced objectives.

---

438. Vasco Cotovio, Frederik Pleitgen, Daniel Hodge, Konstyantyn Gak & Yulia Kesaieva, "Ukrainian forces have broken through in Verbove, top general says," *CNN*, September 23, 2023 (https://edition.cnn.com/2023/09/23/europe/ukraine-biggest-counteroffensive-to-come-intl-hnk/index.html)

The Conduct of Ukrainian Operations

While the date of its launch has remained confidential, its preparation was widely proclaimed *urbi et orbi* in advance. There are two main reasons for this.

The first is that Westerners were getting impatient, and Volodymyr Zelensky's announcements were designed to reassure them. Even before it got underway, the counter-offensive raised doubts. The West had mobilized all its capacities to provide Ukraine with the equipment (weapons and ammunition) and training required for this operation, and was expecting a "return on investment."[439] The Ukrainians, for their part, were totally dependent on Western aid, and Zelensky feared that they would tire: Ukraine had no choice but to act, forced to do so by its donors.[440]

The second is that the Ukrainian and Western concept was based on the idea that the Russians are ill-prepared, poorly commanded, demotivated and demoralized, and will therefore flee at the first Ukrainian assault, leaving the way clear for the breakthrough. It was hoped that the noisy announcement of a powerful counter-offensive would contribute to weakening the Russians morally, thus facilitating the Ukrainian efforts. This idea stemmed from the narrative that surrounded the recapture of the Kharkov and Kherson sectors in 2022. It was a fatal mistake.

As *Ukrainska Pravda* pointed out, this counter-offensive was jointly planned by the Ukrainians, Americans and British during no less than eight war game sessions.[441] The failure of the operation was therefore also due to the inability of Westerners to plan large-scale offensive operations against a modern adversary:[442]

> *With the troops and armaments at Ukraine's disposal, the American military was convinced that a mechanized frontal attack on the*

439. Tennyson Dearing, "Ukraine's summer counteroffensive is a key moment but long-term resolve remains crucial," *Atlantic Council*, June 6, 2023 (https://www.atlanticcouncil.org/blogs/ukrainealert/ukraines-summer-counteroffensive-is-a-key-moment-but-long-term-resolve-remains-crucial/)

440. https://www.thetimes.co.uk/article/ukraine-isn-t-ready-for-its-big-offensive-but-it-has-no-choice-b7qrq3vcr

441. "Miscalculations, divisions marked offensive planning by U.S., Ukraine," *The Washington Post*, December 4, 2023 (https://www.washingtonpost.com/world/2023/12/04/ukraine-counteroffensive-us-planning-russia-war/)

442. Alona Mazurenko, "US and the West insisted on Ukraine's targeted counteroffensive to cut off Russia from Crimea", *Ukrainskaya Pravda*, December 4, 2023 (https://www.pravda.com.ua/eng/news/2023/12/4/7431593/)

Russian front line was feasible. Further modeling indicated that Kiev's forces could at most reach the Sea of Azov and cut off Russian forces in the south in 60 to 90 days.

This counter-offensive was to be led by 12 brigades, 3 of which were set up by Ukraine and 9 by Western countries. The Americans wanted to launch it in mid-April, to prevent the Russians from further reinforcing their position. But the Ukrainians didn't feel ready, so it was postponed until summer 2023.[443]

The conduct of this counter-offensive seems to have been the subject of major differences between the Americans and Ukrainians at several levels. While the main effort in the direction of Rabotino—Tokmak—Melitopol seems to have been accepted by both sides, it seems that the American military wanted Ukraine to concentrate all its resources on this axis, while General Zaluzhny, commander of the Ukrainian forces, did not want to clear his entire front line for this action. On the other hand, Zelensky insisted on retaking Bakhmut, whereas Zaluzhny, since 2022, has been unwilling to sacrifice his troops for this town.

This may explain the slow fall from grace of General Zaluzhny, accused of involvement in the sabotage of Nord Stream 1 and 2,[444] who is under official investigation for failing to manage the country's defense in early 2022.

A Hesitant Start

In the spring of 2023, the Ukrainians knew they weren't ready, but the West urged them to go for it. This is why, from April onwards, the Ukrainians launched a whole series of attacks, without achieving any decisive success. These actions had only a political function, but they had to be given an operational justification. Alexandre Vautravers, a Swiss military "expert," justified these maneuvers by the impossibility of concealing preparations for a major offensive, and claimed that these

---

443. "Ukrainian counteroffensive could begin in summer, PM says," *The New Voice of Ukraine*, April 11, 2023 (https://english.nv.ua/nation/ukrainian-counteroffensive-could-begin-in-summer-pm-says-war-news-50317188.html)
444. "On the Ukrainian trail of the Nord Stream 2 saboteurs", *Intelligence OnLine*, September 26, 2023 (https://www.intelligenceonline.com/government-intelligence/2023/09/26/on-the-ukrainian-trail-of-the-nord-stream-2-saboteurs,110057638-fac)

repeated announcements were intended to deceive the Russians.[445] *Ukrainska Pravda* confirmed this reasoning, explaining that these are *"shaping operations:"*[446]

> *Ranging from token strikes to more strategically significant attacks, these shaping operations are part of standard military practice. According to defense officials and analysts, their aim is to deceive the enemy, interfere with his mindset and "shape" the battlefield in advance of a large-scale offensive.*

It was nothing more than communicative window-dressing. Readers may wish to compare this "definition" with that of the U.S. Army seen above. We can see that we are simply trying to give coherence to actions that are poorly coordinated, ill-suited to the given mission, and which waste lives and equipment.

This is because a shaping operation does not take place in an operative vacuum—it must be carried out as part of an overall plan and be accompanied, or even rapidly followed, by a decisive operation. Clearly, the Ukrainians didn't have the resources for this kind of complex operation.

As for the idea that it's all about "fooling the Russians," that is based on the idea that, with today's intelligence resources, the battlefield has become totally "transparent." It's a bit simplistic. In August 2023, the Russians launched an offensive in the direction of Kupiansk, which nobody detected and which surprised the Ukrainians, and therefore Western intelligence, which monitors the entire theater for their own benefit.[447]

In fact, until the beginning of June 2023, Ukrainian actions were more akin to "reconnaissance in force," where you go into contact with your adversary to force him to reveal his position. The problem is that to carry out this kind of action, you generally don't use your main resources, but lighter ones—the aim is not to destroy the adversary, but to force him to

---

445. https://www.lemanbleu.ch/fr/Emissions/189661-Geneve-a-Chaud.html
446. Olena Roshchina, "UAV attacks and border breaches are Ukrainian 'shaping operations'—FT", *Ukrainska Pravda*, May 30, 2023 (https://www.pravda.com.ua/eng/news/2023/05/30/7404475/)
447. Dan Sabbagh, "'I couldn't take it any more': holdouts quit Kupiansk after renewed Russian shelling", *The Guardian*, August 29, 2023 (https://www.theguardian.com/world/2023/aug/29/holdouts-quit-kupiansk-after-renewed-russian-shelling-ukraine)

reveal himself. The ideal vehicle for this kind of mission would be one like the French AMX-10RC, but with greater survivability.

The Counter-Offensive Proper

In *The New Voice of Ukraine*, a Ukrainian colonel claimed that the counter-offensive had already begun at the end of April 2023.[448] It is generally accepted that it finally began on June 4, 2023; but Volodymyr Zelensky would not confirm this until a week later, after his forces had seized 7 to 8 small villages, all of which lie within the surveillance zone, well upstream of the Surovikin line.

From the very first days, the images showed a total disaster. According to a Ukrainian informant, in just one attack and a few hours, the Ukrainians lost over 150 vehicles, including 12 LEOPARD 2s (20 percent of what they received) and 15 BRADLEYs (around 15 percent). He also claimed that in the first 72 hours of their attack, 10 LEOPARD 2s were destroyed before they could fire a single shot.[449]

The Russian defense is based on the "dynamic defense" model described above. It's a system that requires the attacker to constantly renew his breakthrough effort. This is something the Ukrainian army is no longer able to do. In the space of three months, the Ukrainians failed to reach the Russians' first line of defense (the Surovikin Line) at any point along the 900 km front.

Ukrainians and Westerners alike were disappointed. The narrative surrounding the Ukrainian "victories" in Kharkov and Kherson propagated by our "experts" (and repeated in official reports in France[450] and Switzerland[451] in particular) led the Ukrainians to underestimate the difficulty of their operation, thus contributing in no small measure to their defeat. As the *Daily Telegraph* noted in July 2023:[452]

---

448. Roman Svitan, "Ukraine's counteroffensive has already started", *The New Voice of Ukraine*, May 1, 2023 (https://english.nv.ua/opinion/ukraine-s-counteroffensive-has-already-started-opinion-50321375.html)

449. https://t.me/resident_ua/18191

450. https://www.assemblee-nationale.fr/dyn/16/rapports/cion_def/l16b1111_rapport-information#

451. https://www.newsd.admin.ch/newsd/message/attachments/72369.pdf

452. https://www.telegraph.co.uk/news/2023/07/21/ukraines-counter-offensive-is-failing-with-no-easy-fixes/

Compare today's laborious and costly progress with the lightning victories of Kharkiv and Kherson last autumn. Back then, Kiev's forces were advancing against an enemy that was retreating to redeploy its troops, trading space for time. Having now reinforced their forces through mobilization and dug in vast defensive lines, the Russians are going nowhere this time.

The problem is that our media only talk about Ukrainian attacks, without ever mentioning Russian retaliation. Thus, we always have the impression that it's the Ukrainians who are advancing. But the reality is far more dramatic for the Ukrainians.

While Western attention was focused on the push towards Melitopol, the Ukrainians were still intent on retaking the town of Bakhmut. In fact, in August-September 2023, this was the sector that suffered the most casualties. Lacking heavy equipment, the troops attempting these attacks were literally decimated by Russian artillery. The reason for this relentlessness is mysterious. One hypothesis is that Zelensky believed this would be a psychological success for Ukraine, which could lead to a political crisis in Russia. In fact, we don't know. But it does show that, contrary to what our "experts" were saying, this city is important to the Ukrainians.

Thus, the Ukrainian capture of the villages of Novodarivka and Rivnopil (located on the Staromayorsk—Melitopol axis) is widely seen as a Russian success. The losses inflicted on the Ukrainians have made it impossible for them to continue pushing along this axis. The British institute *RUSI* noted:[453]

It's also important to recognize that Russian forces are fighting more competently and with reasonable perseverance in defense. Even when they are losing ground, Russian forces are essentially withdrawing from their positions in good order to slow and contain Ukrainian thrusts, while imposing considerable costs on them in terms of equipment.

Apparently, the Western plan used to prepare the counter-offensive was a "breakthrough" with mine-clearing armored vehicles (LEOPARD 2R)

453. Jack Watling & Nick Reynolds, "Stormbreak: Fighting Through Russian Defences in Ukraine's 2023 Offensive, *RUSI*, September 2023 (https://ik.imagekit.io/po8th4g4eqj/prod/Stormbreak-Special-Report-web-final_0.pdf)

advancing under tank support, and mechanized infantry securing the breakthrough corridor to allow a continuous flow of tanks into the breach.

This first breakthrough was to be achieved by the 47th Mechanized Brigade, which was to push on to Tokmak, after seizing the small village of Rabotino. It was then up to the 82nd Airborne Assault Brigade to break through the 47th Brigade's position and push on to Melitopol. The planned pattern was very similar to Russian mechanized operations.

Ukrainian Tactics in the Counter-Offensive

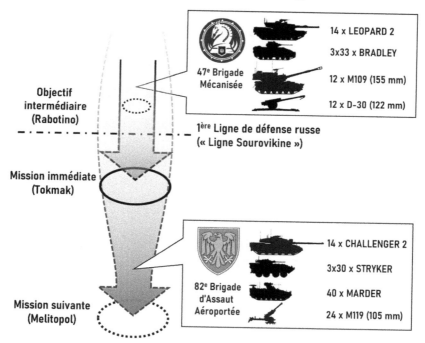

Figure 37—Diagram of the planning of the Ukrainian counter-offensive on the "Rabotino-Tokmak-Melitopol" line of operations. As the New York Times points out, Ukraine has decided to abandon the tactics recommended by NATO and return to those of the former USSR. The action on Rabotino illustrates this change.

The problem was that Russian resistance was tougher than expected. The planning had been done in anticipation of a panic among the Russian military, "poorly commanded, demotivated and weakened." But that's not what happened. In the wake of the unsuccessful 47th Brigade, a dozen other brigades attempted the breakthrough—the 47th mecha-

183

nized brigade; the 65th mechanized brigade; the 116th mechanized brigade; the 117th mechanized brigade; the 118th mechanized brigade; the "SKALA" regiment; the 78th "HERTZ" regiment; the 73rd Special Naval Operations Center; the 46th airmobile brigade; the 71st fighter brigade; the 3rd operational brigade of the National Guard "SPARTAN"; the 14th operational brigade of the National Guard "Chervona Kalyna" and the 82nd airborne assault brigade of the Guard, which was the 2nd echelon formation.

The 82nd Brigade was the 2nd echelon formation, with its CHALLENGER 2 tanks, which the British—proclaimed invincible— feared would be destroyed by the Russians. During its first engagement, at least one of them was destroyed...

By early September 2023, for example, the Ukrainians would have suffered over 50,000 casualties without managing to break through, while, according to Trent Maul, Director of Analysis at the US *Defense Intelligence Agency* (DIA), the Russians hadn't even committed the bulk of their forces.[454]

What's more, while our media were focusing on the imminent victory of the counter-offensive,[455] the Russians were making a breakthrough towards Kupiansk. The Ukrainian media outlet *Kyiv Independent* reported:[456]

> *Soldiers from various brigades told the Kyiv Independent that in this area, the Russians are experienced and well-equipped soldiers, with a large number of artillery shells and MLRS rockets.*
>
> *Like most units, the 32nd was short of vehicles and artillery ammunition. Most of the good equipment is deployed for the counter-offensive on the Zaporizhzhia front.*
>
> *It also lacks battlefield experience, from the lowest ranks to commanding officers... The year 2022 has reduced Ukraine's pool of experienced fighters to such an extent that we can speak of a shortage.*

454. "How the Pentagon assesses Ukraine's progress," *The Economist*, September 6, 2013 (https://archive.ph/1y4tn)

455. "Cédric Mas: "In Ukraine, the time for diplomacy has not yet come"", *rts.ch*, August 23, 2023 (https://www.rts.ch/info/monde/14255857-cedric-mas-en-ukraine-le-temps-de-la-diplomatie-nest-pas-encore-venu.html)

456. https://kyivindependent.com/new-brigade-bears-heavy-brunt-of-russias-onslaught-in-kharkiv-oblast/

The Ukrainian media, confirmed by an analysis by the British *RUSI*,[457] told us exactly the opposite of what our media or the "experts" on our TV sets were saying.[458]

In fact, without sufficient air and artillery support, the Ukrainian army could not use the tactics envisaged by Western planners and break through the Russian system. Contrary to what some "experts" claimed, Ukraine was not "reverting" to Soviet tactics, but was adapting to its adversary, with tactics that had absolutely nothing to do with the USSR.

Thus, from the summer of 2023, the Ukrainian army would attack in small groups of foot infantry, supported by one or two battle tanks, which acted as "assault guns." As Ukrainian Defense Minister Oleksiy Reznikov explained to his American counterpart Lloyd Austin, on June 15, 2023, in Brussels:[459]

Without air support, the only option is to use artillery to hit the Russian lines, dismount targeted vehicles and continue on foot.

This is what the Ukrainians were doing. Their infantrymen were able to slip through the anti-tank minefields and reach the first Russian positions. This is how they were able to claim that they had made progress during the counter-offensive. The problem was that once they came into contact with the Russian lines, they no longer had the means to hold out, let alone make a real breakthrough. The most they could do was engage in close combat with the Russians.

In October 2023, after much prevarication, General Zaluzhny himself acknowledged the failure of the decisive counter-offensive.[460] It had achieved none of its objectives, with neither territorial gains nor the planned

457. Jack Watling & Nick Reynolds, "Stormbreak: Fighting Through Russian Defences in Ukraine's 2023 Offensive", *RUSI*, September 2023 (https://ik.imagekit.io/po8th4g4eqj/prod/Stormbreak-Special-Report-web-final_0.pdf)
458. https://www.lemanbleu.ch/fr/Emissions/189661-Geneve-a-Chaud.html
459. Alona Mazurenko, "US and the West insisted on Ukraine's targeted counteroffensive to cut off Russia from Crimea", *Ukrainskaya Pravda*, December 4, 2023 (https://www.pravda.com.ua/eng/news/2023/12/4/7431593/)
460. Tom Soufi Burridge, "Ukraine general's view of war 'stalemate' appears to be recognition of failed counteroffensive: Reporter's Notebook," *ABC News*, November 3, 2023 (https://abcnews.go.com/International/ukraine-generals-view-war-stalemate-appears-recognition-failed/story?id=104576525)

rout of the Russian army.[461] With the Arab-Israeli conflict attracting the world's attention, Volodymyr Zelensky realized that the lack of results was leading to Western disaffection. He therefore ordered his troops to advance 500 m a day.[462] Once again, operations were conducted by politicians, not soldiers. At no time during the counter-offensive did the Ukrainian forces achieve this pace. To order it at a time when equipment and troops were drying up shows that political leadership is completely out of step with the situation on the ground, since it is unlikely that the Ukrainian military would "want" to advance. It's more realistic to think that they "cannot." This discrepancy is reminiscent of the last days of the Third Reich, when Berlin believed that the retreat of its troops was due to a lack of will.

In October-November 2023, the Ukrainian leadership was forced to "juggle" its units. It moved its units in firefighting exercises across the front line, engaging them in critical areas by drawing on calmer zones.

In reality, the West had never given Ukraine anything to fight for. They gave it something to keep Russia at war, in the hope that this would destabilize that country.

Reasons for Failure

Strategic Reasons

To avoid the media's shortcomings and determine the outcome of the counter-offensive as objectively as possible, we need to analyze it on the basis of the objectives set. The problem is that our journalists play with the latter in order to determine for themselves whether or not they have been achieved. That's what they did with the Russians, and that's what they're doing with the Ukrainians.

At the end of September 2023, the *New York Times* mapped the outcome of the Ukrainian counter-offensive.[463] It noted that over the course of

---

461. Tom Soufi Burridge, "Ukrainian counteroffensive 'shaping-up' amid attempts to destabilize Russian forces," *ABC News*, June 5, 2023 (https://abcnews.go.com/International/ukrainian-counteroffensive-shaping-amid-series-meant-destabilize-russian/story?id=99789793)
462. Kateryna Tyshchenko, "Zelenskyy: We need results every day, to advance at least 500 metres", *Ukrainska Pravda*, October 22, 2023 (https://www.pravda.com.ua/eng/news/2023/10/22/7425232/)
463. Josh Holder, "Who's Gaining Ground in Ukraine? This Year, No One.", *The New York Times*, September 28, 2023 (https://www.nytimes.com/interactive/2023/09/28/world/europe/russia-ukraine-war-map-front-line.html)

the year, the front line had only moved back and forth, with Ukraine gaining around 370 km2 and Russia around 857 km2. This showed that not only had Russia achieved clear success at the operational level, but also at the strategic level. Indeed, its objective was not to take territory, but to weaken Ukraine, as General Surovikin explained in October 2022. Conversely, the Ukrainians' aim was to retake territory.

Ukraine's objective was to retake Crimea and re-establish its sovereignty over the entire territory currently occupied by Russia. In fact, this was the condition Zelensky set for opening negotiations.[464] The problem is that nobody seriously believes that this objective is realistic any more.

So much so that it seems that the Ukrainian army's priorities are no longer focused on these objectives. Since the beginning of September 2023, the main focus has been on strikes against the Black Sea fleet and Crimea. These strikes are of course hailed by our journalists, who gloat over every Russian killed, but the result is a dramatic dispersion of effort. The targets seem to have nothing to do with the course of the counter-offensive, and their sole function is to appear successful for Ukrainian opinion. Volodymyr Zelensky's request for missiles to strike Iran and Syria[465] shows the extent to which Ukraine is seeking success in other theaters to compensate for the failure of its counter-offensive.

This dispersion can be explained by the fact that Ukraine has placed itself in a situation of total dependence on the West. In other words, it has to accommodate both its own objectives and those of its sponsors. In March 2023, Zelensky *had to* trade his proposal for negotiations with Russia for Western support for *"as long as it takes."*[466] In other words, he traded prospects of peace for Western support that precluded any compromise with Russia. As British expert Mark Galeotti put it in *The Times* in April, 2023: Ukraine wasn't ready for its big offensive, but it had no choice.[467] There are always a multitude of reasons for the success or failure of military action. In the case of the Ukrainian counter-offensive, there were two main ones: the inability of the West and the Ukrainians to

464. https://www.cnn.com/europe/live-news/russia-ukraine-war-news-06-16-23/index.html
465. "Ukraine 'Requests Long-Range Missiles to Attack Iranian Kamikaze Drone Production'", *Kyiv Post*, September 27, 2023 (https://www.kyivpost.com/post/22067)
466. https://www.voanews.com/a/biden-us-will-support-ukraine-as-long-as-it-takes-/6953138.html
467. https://www.thetimes.co.uk/article/ukraine-isn-t-ready-for-its-big-offensive-but-it-has-no-choice-b7qrq3vcr

assess Russia's capabilities; and the inadequacy of the strategy adopted. This explains, but does not excuse, the fact that the military offensive never had a real plan, a *sine qua non* for success, as noted by MP Mariana Bezuhla, from President Zelensky's party.[468]

Since the start of the Russian offensive, Westerners and Ukrainians seem to have been relying on a "strategy of hope." Our media claim that the Russians have run out of weapons[469] and personnel; that their ammunition is rusty;[470] that their army is demoralized[471] and badly led.[472] The hope was that the Russian military would "*panic*" and flee;[473] that Russia would lose more men than its adversary; and that Ukraine can only win.

In the French-language media, one military expert after another explained the conflict not from the facts, but from their perceptions and prejudices about Russian forces. Their constant underestimation of Russian capabilities seemed to make possible a strategy of attrition against Russia. Thus, they shifted their focus from a breakthrough to the Sea of Azov, to a strategy of attrition. But knowing that Russia had been applying such a strategy since October, continuing to hold on to the ground and thus exchanging ground for men was a losing strategy from the outset.

The image of the battlefield forged by our media had clearly contributed to pushing Ukraine in the wrong direction. This explains the deep-seated resentment of some Ukrainians, probably the most radical, against our journalists. The latter's moral and intellectual inability to remain within the role defined by the Munich Charter has cost many lives.

468. Alisa Orlova, "MP Fuels Rumors of Zaluzhny-Zelensky Conflict, Calls for Military Leadership Change," *Kyiv Post*, November 27, 2023 (https://www.kyivpost.com/post/24730)

469. https://www.liberation.fr/international/guerre-en-ukraine-a-ce-rythme-les-russes-nont-plus-de-missiles-dans-trois-semaines-20220323_LTACIYGPW5G5XGOKTQL3LJRSQQ/

470. https://www.blick.ch/ausland/ausruestung-immer-schlechter-mit-dieser-rost-munition-muessen-putins-soldaten-kaempfen-id18343393.html

471. https://www.dhnet.be/actu/monde/2022/08/24/la-russie-fait-face-a-une-penurie-de-munitions-de-vehicules-et-de-personnel-leur-moral-est-au-plus-bas-V7KDYW7UAJCH3MNO4B-NJUXBS6E/

472. https://nepassubir.fr/2023/06/18/loperation-de-liberation-de-lukraine-nest-encore-ni-un-echec-ni-un-succes-puisquelle-est-en-cours/

473. Kateryna Tyshchenko, "Russia will panic when Ukraine's counteroffensive begins—Ukraine's Deputy Defence Minister", *Ukrainska Pravda*, May 7, 2023 (https://www.pravda.com.ua/eng/news/2023/05/7/7401067/)

Operative Reasons

As I pointed out in my previous books, the Ukrainians have not mastered the art of operations and joint combat at brigade level and above. Their operations are sequential and insufficiently integrated. In order to be able to denigrate the Russians, our "experts" deliberately concealed the reality of the situation and thus led the Ukrainians to overestimate their possibilities.

In a hearing before a Senate committee in November 2022, Colonel Michel Goya declared that, after the Kharkov and Kherson offensives, the Ukrainians had *"unquestionable superiority."* In fact, this is false. The Ukrainians are victims of their own narrative, which presented the Kharkov and Kherson episodes as a success and proof of the weakness of the Russian forces. Instead of learning from them and making more appropriate operational decisions, our media emboldened our politicians to support a spring counter-offensive on the basis of illusory military superiority.

In early August 2023, the Russian Ministry of Defense reported that 43,000 Ukrainian servicemen had lost their lives in June-July.[474] It's hard to say to what extent this figure reflects reality, although experience shows that the figures given by the Russians are relatively reliable. If verified, this would mean that Ukraine would have lost the same number of soldiers as those trained by NATO to spearhead the counter-offensive. We would then be in a process of accelerated attrition.

At the end of July 2023, more than a month and a half after the start of the counter-offensive, the *Wall Street Journal* confessed:[475]

> *When Ukraine launched its major counter-offensive in the spring, Western military leaders knew that Kiev had neither the training nor the weapons to dislodge Russian forces, from shells to warplanes. But they hoped that Ukrainian courage and ingenuity would save the day.*

---

474. https://www.theinteldrop.org/2023/08/05/ukraines-attrition-rate-suggests-counteroffensive-is-over/

475. Daniel Michaels, "Ukraine's Lack of Weaponry and Training Risks Stalemate in Fight With Russia", *Wall Street Journal*, July 23, 2023 (https://www.wsj.com/articles/ukraines-lack-of-weaponry-and-training-risks-stalemate-in-fight-with-russia-f51ecf9)

In fact, Westerners were pinning their hopes on *"Ukrainian courage and ingenuity."*

In September 2023, during his visit to the United States, Volodymyr Zelensky announced a *"secret plan" to* retake three cities. One of these was identified as Bakhmut, while the other two were the subject of speculation:[476] Tokmak, in the direction of Melitopol, and Soledar on the outskirts of Bakhmut.

But it soon became clear that even these limited objectives were out of reach. In reality, it was the Russians who were on the offensive all along the front line. But they were advancing slowly, with the aim of not exposing their troops.

On December 1, 2023, in an interview with *Associated Press*, Zelensky confessed that the counter-offensive had been a failure and that casualties had been high.[477] This led him to adopt a defensive strategy and order the construction of fortifications.[478]

Tactical Reasons

In September 2023, Volodymyr Zelensky explained that slow arms deliveries were the reason for the slow success of the counter-offensive.[479] This excuse has been disputed in the West, yet it is clearly justified. After all, the West supplied weapons in dribs and drabs, which could be destroyed as they arrived in the theater of operations. In other words, whatever the quality of the weapons supplied, their quantity never reached the critical mass that would enable Ukraine to create sufficient superiority to make a breakthrough. What's more, the weapons often arrive at a time when the Ukrainians no longer needed them, like the M1 ABRAMS.[480] The

476. Joe Barnes, "Zelensky vows to liberate Bakhmut and two other cities in secret plan," *The Telegraph*, September 22, 2023 (https://www.telegraph.co.uk/world-news/2023/09/22/volodymyr-zelensky-secret-plan-liberate-cities-ukraine/)

477. James Jordan, Samya Kullab & Illia Novikov, "The AP Interview: Ukraine's Zelenskyy says the war with Russia is in a new phase as winter looms", *AP*, December 1, 2023 (https://apnews.com/article/zelenskyy-ukraine-russia-war-interview-winter-75f1f785b17452fc23819d459e6ab64b)

478. Matthew Luxmoore, "Ukraine's Zelensky Orders Construction of Defenses to Hold Back Russia," *The Wall Street Journal*, December 1, 2023 (https://www.wsj.com/world/ukraines-zelensky-orders-construction-of-defenses-to-hold-back-russia-9ab87c81?mod=europe_news_article_pos1)

479. https://www.cnn.com/videos/world/2023/09/10/exp-gps-0910-zelensky-on-counteroffensive.cnn

480. Jack Detsch, "Ukraine Is Getting Its Abrams-but Not What It Really Wants," *Foreign Policy*, September 19, 2023 (https://foreignpolicy.com/2023/09/19/ukraine-russia-abrams-military-weapons/)

Ukrainians have failed to understand that the West is not out to win the war for Ukraine, but to prolong it in order to exhaust Russia.

In fact, the Ukrainians were not sufficiently equipped to lead a break-through in a system like that of the Russians. Not only would more demining resources have been needed, but also more troops to secure the bridgeheads after each breakthrough line. In addition, they needed air and artillery superiority in the breakthrough sectors to prevent the arrival of Russian reinforcements.

Lacking these elements, Ukraine has given up on large-scale mechanized breakthrough operations. Its first attempts, in June 2023, ended in specta-cular failure. For such an action cannot be carried out "by halves." It's all or nothing. That's why the Ukrainian command has opted for infantry actions at the lower tactical level (platoon and section), which make it easier to slip through anti-tank minefields and evade Russian artillery.

The Ukrainians' adoption of this new tactic came at precisely the same time as the Americans began supplying them with cluster munitions. The Russians, who had not used this type of weapon—at least in this sector—until then, began to use them. However, cluster munitions were designed to be used by a defender against attacks such as those carried out by the Ukrainians. This has created an asymmetrical situation—what was thought to be an advantage for the Ukrainians has become an additional handicap.

Our media and intelligence services' constant, misleading underes-timation of Russian capabilities seemed to make the promised support for Ukraine sufficient for Zelensky to achieve his goals. Aid for "as long as it takes" therefore seemed to have an end. But the determination of our media, corrupt experts and intelligence services to try to show the irrationality and incompetence of the Russians hid reality from us. They confused information warfare with warfare on the ground. But Russia's capabilities are considerably greater than what corrupt experts were proclaiming. The West therefore trapped itself in a "blank check" that is impossible to honor.

At the end of September 2023, the *Institute for the Study of War* (ISW), an organization headed by Kimberly Kagan, sister-in-law of Victoria Nuland, Assistant Secretary of the State Department, attempted to explain the lack of results from the Ukrainian counter-offensive:[481]

---

481. https://twitter.com/TheStudyofWar/status/1706157492462379203

It is possible that Putin ordered the Russian military command to hold all of Russia's initial defensive positions in order to create the illusion that the Ukrainian counter-offensives had no tactical or operational impact despite substantial Western support.

In other words, the Russians are holding their positions only to give the illusion that they are holding their positions!

Western Critics

As soon as it was launched, it became clear that the great decisive operation they had planned with the help of the United States and trumpeted in our media would not fulfill its promises. The Ukrainians communicate very little about their planning. It is therefore sometimes difficult to determine whether the errors observed result from the concept of the operation or its execution. In the summer of 2023, however, Western criticism of the Ukrainian counter-offensive allow us to draw certain conclusions.

An internal *Bundeswehr* report, published at the end of July 2023 by the *Bild* newspaper,[482] criticized the implementation of the Ukrainian counter-offensive. It insisted that Ukraine was not applying the principles of joint combat advocated by NATO, but was giving precedence to its own operational experience.

But these criticisms of Ukraine were not really justified, for a number of reasons.

The first is that the failure of the Ukrainian counter-offensive was perfectly predictable, even expected. The weapons delivered to Ukraine were insufficient in quality and quantity, as we shall see below. Despite the exaggeratedly optimistic and totally out-of-touch "analyses" of our military "experts," the Ukrainians were only supplied with scrap weapons that we no longer wanted.

The second is that we knew from the outset that the counter-offensive would result in very heavy losses for the Ukrainians, because these losses

---

482. Julian Röpcke, "Bundeswehr kritisiert erstmals die Ukraine-Armee", *Bild*, July 25, 2023 (https://www.bild.de/bild-plus/politik/ausland/politik-ausland/geheim-papier-enthuellt-bundeswehr-kritisiert-erstmals-die-ukraine-armee-84802800.bild.html)

The Russian Art of War

were calculated.[483] Thus, our politicians and media knew perfectly well that the Ukrainians were being sent to their deaths. Such is the perverse role of our media. Instead of presenting the situation correctly and perhaps finding a more reasonable solution, we encouraged Ukraine to carry out this offensive, even though we knew perfectly well that it would be a failure. No serious expert—not even the Ukrainians—is now saying that Ukraine can retake Crimea or go as far as the Sea of Azov.

The third is that—as Zelensky rightly said[484]—weapons arrived in dribs and drabs. As a result, Ukraine was never able to build up sufficient critical mass to be able to carry out operational-level actions. This shows that the Russians have indeed achieved their demilitarization objective, and that the Ukrainian counter-offensive relies *solely* on Western aid. Typically, Ukraine launched its counter-offensive without air capability (or at least air superiority). After months of prevarication, the American agreement for the delivery of F-16 aircraft only arrived at the end of August 2023, two and a half months after the start of the counter-offensive.[485] And to make matters worse, it was decided to lengthen the training of Ukrainian pilots by adding a language course before they could touch the aircraft.[486] Naturally, the official line had to be adapted to convince the Ukrainians that the aircraft were not necessary to guarantee the success of the counter-offensive.[487] Finally, these piecemeal deliveries meant that the arrival of armaments could not be synchronized with operational planning. Thus, by the time the F-16s were announced in October 2023, the question of the counter-offensive was over, and the new aircraft were assigned to the air defense of the western part of Ukraine.

483. https://www.defense.gov/News/Transcripts/Transcript/Article/3433535/deputy-penta-gon-press-secretary-sabrina-singh-holds-a-press-briefing/
484. https://www.cnn.com/videos/world/2023/09/10/exp-gps-0910-zelensky-on-counteroffen-sive.cnn
485. Aamer Madhani & Lolita C. Baldor, "Biden's shift on F-16s for Ukraine came after months of internal debate," *AP News*, August 25, 2023 (https://apnews.com/article/biden-ukraine-f16-deci-sion-russia-64538af7c10489d7c2243dadbad31008)
486. Luis Martinez, "US will help train Ukrainian pilots on F-16s after all," *ABC News*, August 25, 2023 (https://abcnews.go.com/Politics/us-train-ukrainian-16-pilots-after/story?id=102542985)
487. Kateryna Tyshchenko, "Ukraine's counteroffensive may be successful without F-16s", *Ukrainska Pravda*, August 13, 2023 (https://www.pravda.com.ua/eng/news/2023/08/13/7415420/)

4. Ukrainian Military Thinking

Why F-16s are Needed

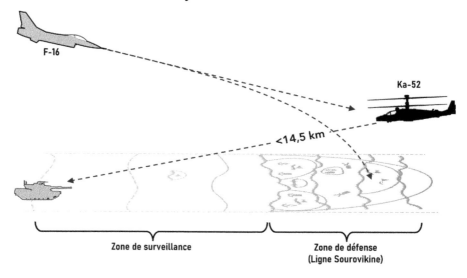

Figure 38—The F-16s are in no position to take on the Russian air force. On the other hand, they could provide cover for breakthrough attempts against Ka-50/52 helicopter gunships, which—according to doctrine—remain cautiously above the Russian defensive system. In addition, the F-16 could attack ground targets at depths of up to 500 km.

The fourth is that the training given to the Ukrainian military is essentially tactical. On the strength of combat experience in the Middle East and Afghanistan, Westerners have taught small tactical formations (group-section-peloton) how to fight. On the other hand, there is an inability to coordinate medium- to high-level joint actions.

The fifth is that, in order to fight a joint battle effectively, you need to have all the various components at your disposal (mainly, intelligence, armor, infantry, artillery, engineers, aviation and air defense). However, not only is the equipment received by the Ukrainians largely unsuited to the Ukrainian conflict, it is also extremely deficient. For example, they lack aviation and effective air defense. In other words, essential components of joint combat are missing.

The sixth is that today, it's no longer enough to coordinate; we need to be able to integrate forces at the operational level. The Ukrainians have the leadership resources needed for coordination, and know how to do it. But a joint force is not simply a collection of systems, but must be a system if it is to function effectively. However, the equipment supplied to Ukraine, of different quality, origin and generation, cannot be made up into a system.

Ultimately, it was the combination of Western impatience for results and their inability to provide Ukraine with the critical mass it needed to lead its counter-offensive that was the main reason for this failure. Upstream, however, it was the inability of Western intelligence services to assess the balance of forces, the underestimation of Russian capabilities and the overestimation of Ukrainian ones that led to this situation.

The Question of Co-Belligerence

The term "co-belligerent" is applied to an actor who takes part in an armed conflict, without being formally bound by a treaty or alliance (such as NATO). Contrary to what some "experts" claim, the term is not defined by international law, which leaves the door open to all kinds of interpretations.

When we deliver weapons to a country and that country engages in a conflict with those weapons, there's no question of co-belligerence. On the other hand, when a country is already engaged in a conflict and we insert ourselves into its logistics chain to support it with weapons, ammunition and repairs, the question takes on a completely different aspect. Thus, the West:

- Fully finances Ukraine's military actions against Russia;
- Supplies arms, on which Ukraine has been totally dependent since June 2022[488];
- Ensures logistical support for Western weapons engaged in combat. Damaged weapons are removed from Ukrainian territory, repaired in border sanctuaries, and then returned to the battlefield. Countries such as France, Germany and Poland are thus fully integrated into Ukrainian operational logistics;
- Ensures the training of combatants for the battlefield;
- Supplies the Ukrainian command with real-time operational intelligence (ISR), with air assets and agents deployed on the battlefield;

---

488. https://www.lepoint.fr/monde/ayant-epuise-tout-son-armement-l-ukraine-depend-totale-ment-des-allies-09-06-2022-2478984_24.php

- Leads an economic war against Russia[489] and its population,[490] with the aim of generating social conflicts and provoking insurrectionary movements (subversion);
- Actively supports and even calls for terrorist actions[491] against the Russian population and authorities.

As the leaked US classified documents of April 2023 demonstrate, France, Sweden, the USA and Britain are providing operational intelligence to Ukrainian forces for targeting and decision-making. Thus, there is clearly a direct involvement in decision-making. This was revealed during the 2023 counter-offensive, when Westerners complained that Ukraine was not following their instructions. We can debate the legal question of this "co-belligerence", but the most serious thing is that we did it badly. With rare incompetence and acting more on the basis of emotion and politics than facts and military rationality, our aid only weakened Ukraine.

Recourse to Terrorism

A notable aspect of the evolution of tactics and methods employed by Ukraine is the use of assassinations and terrorist actions in Russia and Europe. Their particularity is that they are supported by European governments (and parliaments). The idea that we are defending "values" is therefore pure propaganda. We unreservedly condemn the actions of the Palestinians, who have been subjected to violations of international law for 75 years with our approval, but we accept that even less excusable methods are perpetrated on our soil.

That said, the idea of destabilizing Russia from within is consistent with the analysis of its center of gravity. From the outset, Ukraine

---

489. https://www.zeit.de/zustimmung?url=https://www.zeit.de/politik/ausland/2023-01/annalena-baerbock-russland-krieg-aussage
490. "Nous allons provoquer l'effondrement de l'économie russe", lance Bruno Le Maire, *Ouest-France / AFP*, March 1, 2022 (https://www.ouest-france.fr/monde/guerre-en-ukraine/guerre-en-ukraine-nous-allons-provoquer-l-effondrement-de-l-economie-russe-lance-bruno-le-maire-8df620ec-9937-11ec-a65a-8b59a463d3c4)
491. https://lequotidien.lu/politique-societe/jean-asselborn-eliminer-physiquement-vladimir-poutine/

declared that its objective was a change of power in Moscow. So much so that in September 2022, Volodymyr Zelensky himself decreed a law prohibiting any negotiations with Russia as long as Vladimir Putin was in power.[492] However, for such destabilization to be effective, it needs to be backed by discontent or a particularly bad social situation. This is what could have happened if the sanctions against Russia had been effective. On the contrary, they have helped to improve the general situation in Russia.

Attacks on Civilians

The inability to implement and launch the counter-offensive promised in the summer of 2022 prompted the Ukrainian command to carry out raids into Russian territory, reportedly resulting in 13 civilian deaths.[493] The largest of these raids was carried out on May 22, 2023 against villages in Belgorod oblast, close to the Ukrainian border. Its aim was twofold: to show that the Russian population was poorly protected by its government,[494] and more likely—as the Russian government claims—to create a sense of victory after Bakhmut fell.[495]

The media, which disseminate information designed to minimize the role of neo-Nazi movements and nauseating ideologies, have avoided giving details of the nature of the attackers. For example, *RTS* carefully avoided giving any indication of the number of civilian deaths, in order to legitimize an action by extremists to *"put an end to the Kremlin's dictatorship."*[496]

With the eyes of a Swiss, we can probably discuss Russian democracy, like that of France for that matter. But it is surprising that this approach

---

492. "Ukraine Will Not Negotiate with Russia as Long As Putin Is In Power: Zelensky," *Barron's/AFP*, September 30, 2022 (https://www.barrons.com/news/ukraine-will-not-negotiate-with-russia-as-long-as-putin-is-in-power-zelensky-01664548507)
493. https://en.wikipedia.org/wiki/2023_Belgorod_Oblast_incursions
494. "Cross-border incursions from Ukraine take a stab at Russian defences", *Euractiv.com / Reuters*, May 24, 2023 (https://www.euractiv.com/section/global-europe/news/cross-border-incursions-from-ukraine-take-a-stab-at-russian-defences/)
495. "Russian 'clean up' operation after raid on Belgorod from Ukraine", *Al-Jazeera*, May 23, 2023 (https://www.aljazeera.com/news/2023/5/23/ukraine-says-russian-armed-groups-behind-border-raid-on-russia)
496. https://www.rts.ch/info/monde/14042636-des-combattants-font-une-incursion-armee-en-russie-et-frappent-plusieurs-villages.html

accepts and recognizes that opposition to Vladimir Putin is linked to the neo-Nazi far right.[497]

What the Swiss state media fails to mention is that the raids were carried out by two far-right groups, the *"Freedom of Russia" Legion* (LLR) and the *Russian Volunteer Corps* (CVR). The CVR is a neo-Nazi organization whose leader, Denis Kapustin (*nom de guerre*, Denis Nikitin), is considered a neo-Nazi by the *Anti-Defamation League* (ADL).[498] The LLR is also an extreme right-wing organization, but its profile appears less marked.[499]

Initially, the Ukrainian government denied any responsibility for the attacks, claiming that they were carried out by Russian opponents in Ukraine.[500] Although Ukraine is entitled to respond to the SMO by intervening on Russian territory, including with paramilitaries of Russian origin, it immediately chose to disassociate itself from this attack.

Russian Partisans

Légion « Liberté de la Russie »   Corps Volontaire Russe

Figure 39—The formations that have raided Russian territory illustrate the nature of the Western-backed opposition to Vladimir Putin. Whatever one's judgement of the Russian government, the opposition we support has no democratic credentials and conveys nauseating ideologies.

---

497. "Quand des opposants russes à Poutine prennent les armes en Ukraine", *Le Point/AFP*, October 31, 2023 (https://www.lepoint.fr/monde/quand-des-opposants-russes-a-poutine-prennent-les-armes-en-ukraine-31-10-2023-2541503_24.php)

498. https://extremismterms.adl.org/glossary/denis-kapustin

499. https://www.nbcnews.com/news/world/belgorod-raid-russian-volunteer-corps-freedom-russia-legion-rcna86168

500. Yuliya Talmazan, "Who are the anti-Putin groups behind the dramatic raid into Russia?", *NBC News*, May 26, 2023 (https://www.nbcnews.com/news/world/belgorod-raid-russian-volunteer-corps-freedom-russia-legion-rcna86168)

A CVR commander said on May 24 that they had received no assistance from the Ukrainian government *"except for intelligence, fuel, food and medicine."* According to a spokesman for Ukrainian military intelligence (GUR), these groups carried out these operations *"independently, according to their own objectives and plans."*[501] However, these statements are contradicted by the fact that the LLR claims to be officially recognized by the Ukrainian army and to be fighting *"under Ukrainian command."* Moreover, images of the incident showed that the fighters were equipped with American and Ukrainian weapons and vehicles.

The *European Journal of International Law (EIJL)* considered the action of these groups aimed at overthrowing power in Russia to be illegal in itself, but justifiable within the framework of Ukraine's right to self-defense.[502] What the *EIJL* does not analyze is the strategy used. While the actions themselves were clearly not aimed at overthrowing power in Moscow, they were designed to put pressure on the population and incite them to rebel against their government. This strategy is exactly the same as that of the Islamic State for its attacks in France in 2015 and 2016.[503] We can see, then, that our jurists are apologists for terrorism when it doesn't affect us. Terrorism is a method that must be proscribed in *all circumstances*, even if some governments practice it routinely, such as France, the United States, Great Britain and Israel.

These attacks have enabled our media to advance a narrative about the "permeability" of the border and the Russian government's inability to protect its own population. But this assertion needs to be qualified. The border between the two countries is some 2,300 km long, and Russia has chosen not to secure it like the Roman Empire's Hadrian's Wall, or even the Iron Curtain, with a continuous physical barrier. All along the border, at regular intervals, there are rapid intervention forces from the National Guard (Rosgvard), who can act against incursions of this kind. This is what happened, and the Ukrainian incursion was quickly brought under

---

501. https://en.interfax.com.ua/news/general/912407.html
502. Stefan Talmon, "Ukraine's Involvement in Cross-Border Raids by Russian Paramilitary Groups: Illegal Use of Force and Intervention or Lawful Self-Defence?", *European Journal of International Law*, May 29, 2023 (https://www.ejiltalk.org/ukraines-involvement-in-cross-border-raids-by-russian-paramilitary-groups-illegal-use-of-force-and-intervention-or-lawful-self-defence/)
503. Video "France on its knees", *Islamic State*, November 21, 2015

control after penetrating a few hundred meters into Russian territory.[504] However, artillery and drone rocket fire struck deeper into Russian territory, giving the illusion of in-depth action, but this was not the case.

Raid on May 22, 2023 in Belgorod Oblast

Figure 40—The raid by Russian right-wing volunteer units fighting for Ukraine did not go beyond Kozinka. It may have been aimed at the Belgorod-22 site. But the real aim of the operation was to send a signal to the Russian population.

It would appear that the Ukrainians' target was the "Belgorod-22" site, reputed to contain nuclear weapons. In reality, this depot was emptied of its nuclear weapons several years ago, which raises the question of Ukrainian intelligence capabilities.[505]

---

504. Stefan Talmon, "Russian 'clean up' operation after raid on Belgorod from Ukraine", *Al-Jazeerah*, May 23, 2023 (https://www.aljazeera.com/news/2023/5/23/ukraine-says-russian-armed-groups-behind-border-raid-on-russia)

505. Nick Mordowanec, "Russia Removes Nuclear Munitions From Belgorod Amid Conflict: Ukraine", *Newsweek*, May 22, 2023 (https://www.newsweek.com/russia-removes-nuclear-munitions-belgorod-amid-conflict-ukraine-1801940)

Attacks on Infrastructure

On the morning of October 8, 2022, a suicide truck exploded on the Kerch Bridge linking the Crimean Peninsula to Russian territory. Surveillance camera footage of the truck's explosion soon began to circulate. The images are a little too reminiscent of the Islamic State attacks of 2015-2016. This is no doubt why *Radio-Télévision Suisse Romande* modestly described the event as *"a major fire broke out on the vast automobile and railway bridge linking Moscow-annexed Ukrainian Crimea and Russian territory"* and carefully avoided the word "terrorist."[506] Our journalists saw it as an illustration of a special operation *"which is looking more and more like a dead end."*

This attack, which was set up by the Ukrainian SBU special services, according to the *Washington Post*,[507] was a suicide attack designed on the model of Islamic State attacks.[508] Exactly as observed in Syria and Iraq, it is highly likely that the driver of the truck bomb was unaware of the attack and that it was remotely activated without his knowledge.

Crimea remains at the heart of the official Ukrainian narrative. Numerous actions were carried out against the Sevastopol naval base and the Kerch Bridge. On July 17, 2023, a naval drone attack on the bridge's piers caused only minor damage, but showed that Russian infrastructure is vulnerable.

The American investigative media *Grayzone* has made public documents it has obtained, which show that the British at least helped to design and train militants to carry out terrorist attacks, including against the Kerch Bridge.[509]

506. https://www.rts.ch/info/monde/13448785-au-moins-trois-morts-apres-lattentat-contre-le-pont-entre-la-crimee-et-la-russie.html#timeline-anchor-1665255710512

507. Missy Ryan, Natalia Abbakumova & Kostiantyn Khudov, "Amid Ukrainian taunts, Russia scrambles to salvage Crimean Bridge after fiery explosion," *The Washington Post*, October 8, 2022 (https://www.washingtonpost.com/world/2022/10/08/crimea-kerch-bridge-attack-explosion-russia-ukraine/)

508. Isabel van Brugen, "How Ukraine Followed the ISIS Playbook," *Newsweek*, May 31, 2023 (https://www.newsweek.com/what-ukraine-russia-war-learned-isis-surveillance-drones-strikes-videos-1803199)

509. https://thegrayzone.com/2022/10/10/ukrainian-kerch-bridge/

British Planning for the Kerch Bridge Sabotage

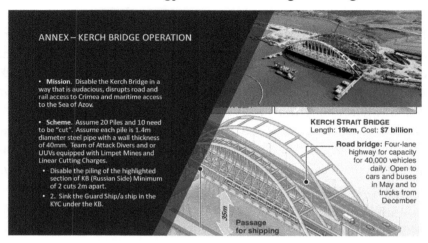

Figure 41—Slide from a British intelligence presentation in April 2022, demonstrating the involvement of Western countries in organizing terrorist attacks [reproduced courtesy of The Grayzone].

The operational impact of these attacks was minimal. There was, of course, material damage, the extent of which was naturally assessed differently on each side. But the Kerch Bridge is not an important logistical artery of the SMO, mainly because of its potential vulnerability. Moreover, between 2014 and 2018, the bridge did not exist, and the Russians have other means of ensuring supplies to the peninsula. Thus, it's more a communications objective than an operational one.

Moreover, as can be seen, the theater of operations is essentially land-based. The Black Sea fleet is not directly involved in the conflict, and in no way constitutes a "center of gravity" for Russia—quite the contrary. Thus, whatever successes Ukraine may have achieved against Russian vessels, they have had no impact on the course of operations. These actions therefore appear more as an alternative to a success that Ukraine is struggling to achieve on the battlefield.

Wet Actions

The call for Vladimir Putin's murder by Western politicians such as Republican Senator Lindsey Graham[510] or Luxembourg Foreign Minister Jean Asselborn in March 2022,[511] shows that our political conduct no longer has any value or honor—for these calls to murder are not just words, they are the expression of a strategy known and widely accepted by our politicians and journalists, until they themselves are directly involved.

Thus, Denis Kireyev, one of the Ukrainian negotiators in Gomel, was assassinated on March 5 by the Ukrainian secret service (SBU) because he was considered too favorable to Russia and thus a traitor.[512] The same fate befell Dmitry Demyanenko, former deputy head of the SBU's Main Directorate for Kiev and its region, who was murdered on March 10, also for being too favorable to an agreement with Russia.[513]

But these actions have continued ever since. As the British magazine *The Economist* explains, Ukraine has activated the 5th Directorate of the SBU, the security service responsible for eliminating Russian citizens or those who support Russia in Ukraine and around the world. Today, these actions are one of Ukraine's main tools in its fight against Russia.[514]

Since February 24, 2022, forty-five Russian citizens have been murdered around the world. We know that this is the work of the Ukrainian special services,[515] as Kyrylo Budanov, head of Ukrainian military intelligence (GUR), confessed in May 2023:[516]

> *All I'll say is that we've murdered Russians and will continue to do so all over the world until Ukraine's complete victory.*

...with the complicity of the countries of the European Union and the United States.

---

510. https://thehill.com/homenews/senate/596843-graham-calls-for-somebody-in-russia-to-take-putin-out/
511. https://lequotidien.lu/politique-societe/jean-asselborn-eliminer-physiquement-vladi-mir-poutine/
512. https://www.timesofisrael.com/ukraine-reports-claim-negotiator-shot-for-treason-offi-cials-say-he-died-in-intel-op/
513. https://www.youtube.com/watch?v=ZWHpVnrwfLY
514. https://www.economist.com/europe/2023/09/05/inside-ukraines-assassination-programme
515. https://www.nytimes.com/2022/10/05/us/politics/ukraine-russia-dugina-assassination.html
516. https://global.espreso.tv/budanov-says-he-does-not-consider-killing-russian-citizens-to-be-terrorism

The bombings of Darya Dugina (August 21, 2022), Nord Stream (September 26, 2022), the Kerch Bridge (October 8, 2022) and journalist-blogger Vladlen Tatarsky (April 1, 2023) were not condemned by any Western media, journalist or politician. For them, there is "good" terrorism (that which affects Russians) and "bad" terrorism (that which affects us).

In October 2023, the *Washington Post* confirmed what we already knew: that Ukrainian services were assassinating their adversaries all over the world.[517] The Ukrainian press picked up on this,[518] but not those in Switzerland or Belgium, for whom the narrative had to be protected. In France, the media hardly mention it at all, except for those who, like *LCI*, promote it.[519] Clearly, it's difficult to admit to supporting practices that come under the heading of terrorism. But the real question is, what are the objectives of this "strategy," which has no impact on the course of operations? Are these the values that Ukraine defends for us?

For example, not a single Western media outlet has condemned the *Mirotvorets* website, which is a kind of digital pillory for those considered traitors. The practice is punishable in many countries,[520] but not in Ukraine.[521] In October 2019, the UN and some European countries called for the closure of the website,[522] but this was refused by the Rada.[523]

In Kherson, just after the arrival of Ukrainian troops in October 2022, a list of *"traitors and collaborators" was posted* online.[524] It includes

517. Greg Miller & Isabelle Khurshudyan, "Ukrainian spies with deep ties to CIA wage shadow war against Russia," *The Washington Post*, October 23, 2023 (https://www.washingtonpost.com/world/2023/10/23/ukraine-cia-shadow-war-russia/)

518. Martin Fornusek, "SBU says 'comments after victory' following media report linking it to assassinations inside Russia", *Kyiv Independent*, October 24, 2023 (https://kyivindependent.com/sbu-says-no-comment-on-media-report-linking-it-to-assassinations-of-high-profile-russians/)

519. "La stratégie d'assassinats ciblés des renseignements ukrainiens", *LCI*, October 25, 2023 (https://youtu.be/otxFFsp5kyk)

520. https://www.mirror.co.uk/news/world-news/dark-website-lists-russian-spies-26051893

521. https://www.refworld.org/docid/58ec89ad13.html

522. *"В ООН настаивают на закрытии сайта 'Миротворец'"* ("UN insists on closing 'Peacemaker' website"), *zn.ua*, October 16, 2019 (https://zn.ua/UKRAINE/v-oon-nastaivayut-na-zakrytii-sayta-mirotvorec-332863_.html); Tetiana Popova, "Benjamin Moreau, deputy head of UN Human Rights Monitoring Mission to Ukraine," *Diplomat*, February 16, 2019 (http://diplomat.media/en/2019/02/16/benjamin-moreau-deputy-head-of-un-human-rights-monitoring-mission-to-ukraine/); "UN demands to close down "Mirotvorets" calling for persecution of UOC", *Union of Orthodox Journalists*, October 17, 2019, (https://spzh.news/en/news/65761-v-oon-potrebovali-zakryty-mirotvorec-prizyvavshij-k-gonenijam-na-upc)

523. *"Разумков ответил на призыв ООН закрыть сайт 'Миротворец'"* ("Razumkov responded to UN call to shut down 'Peacemaker' site"), *zn.ua*, October 17, 2019 (https://zn.ua/UKRAINE/razumkov-otvetil-na-prizyv-oon-zakryt-sayt-mirotvorec-332952_.html)

524. This is the Telegram page: https://t.me/s/Kherson_kolaborant

journalists, teachers, civil servants and others accused of helping Russia. These practices, worthy of the heyday of collaboration with the Nazis, can be found here, too. Public service journalist Jean-Philippe Schaller, for example, openly accuses those who disagree with him of being *"Putin's agents"* on the official Swiss channel (*RTS*).[525]

The Drone Campaign

Since the beginning of 2023, Ukraine has been using drones against Moscow and certain Russian cities. As in Belgorod (close to the border) and Moscow, these attacks target civilians. As reported in the *New York Times*:[526]

> *Although Ukraine's aim in urban areas so far seems to be more to instill fear than to cause bloodshed or large-scale destruction, images of several attacks on oil depots show structures in flames, indicating significant damage.*

"Instilling fear" is indeed a synonym for "terrorizing." The drones are therefore a continuation of the attacks on Darya Dugina and Tatarsky, and the elimination of numerous Russian personalities around the world. This is nothing other than international terrorism, which no Western country has condemned—we condemn it when it comes from the Middle East, but we tolerate it when we practice it.

According to *Newsweek*, these attacks against the civilian population have three objectives:[527]

- Reminding the Russian population that they are at war;
- To show that *"adaptability and ingenuity are increasing in a way that the Russians cannot hope to match, while minimizing the risk of civilian casualties;"*
- To show that the Russian government is incapable of protecting its population.

---

525. https://youtu.be/bEv4-IJsl9k?t=414
526. Christiaan Triebert, Haley Willis, Yelyzaveta Kovtun & Alexander Cardia, "Ukraine's Other Counteroffensive: Drone Attacks on Russian Soil," *The New York Times*, July 31, 2023 (https://the-grayzone.com/2023/07/28/ukraines-baby-factories-profits-war/)
527. https://www.newsweek.com/russia-moscow-drone-strikes-ukraine-beaver-1816990

Similarly, according to Keir Giles, an expert at *Chatham House* in London:[528]

> *Ukraine has identified the opinion and attitude of the Russian population towards the war as one of the key areas it needs to target in order to end the war.*

The aim is therefore to reach Russian public opinion, so that it will act on the government to stop the intervention in Ukraine. This is exactly the same objective that the *Islamic State* (EI) had in France, as evidenced by the EI communiqué after the Nice attack on July 14, 2016:[529]

> *Finally, we say it's up to the French people to decide whether they want to continue waging war against us, or whether they will decide to stop their government's aggression against us? ... We will continue to fight France until it stops meddling in the affairs of Muslims and plundering their wealth directly or indirectly.*

Ukraine finds itself in the same strategic situation as the EI—unable to provide a direct operational response, it is using an indirect strategy, which consists of pushing the civilian population to turn against the decisions of the Russian government.[530] In fact, it's another way of achieving what Western sanctions have failed to do. As the American magazine *Newsweek* notes, Ukraine has followed the example of the Islamic State[531] in Syria.

On the face of it, you might say there's no difference between dropping a bomb on Kiev and dropping it on Moscow. But there is—Kiev is located in a theater of operations, whereas Moscow is not. Assuming that Ukraine has defined the whole of Russian territory as a theater of operations, it's not clear how these actions would impact on the conduct of its own operations.

---

528. Rob Picheta, "Ukrainian drone strikes are bringing the war home to Russia. What does it mean for the conflict?", *CNN*, August 5, 2023 (https://edition.cnn.com/2023/08/05/europe/russia-ukraine-drone-attacks-analysis-explainer-intl/index.html)
529. "*Nice Operation, France," Inspire Guide*, July 17, 2016.
530. Sheikh Hamd bin Hamoud Al-Tameemy, "Rulings on Lone Jihad—Targeting Civilians", section 1, part 2, *Inspire*, no. 17, Summer 2017, p. 23.
531. Isabel van Brugen, "How Ukraine Followed the ISIS Playbook," *Newsweek*, May 31, 2023 (https://www.newsweek.com/what-ukraine-russia-war-learned-isis-surveillance-drones-strikes-videos-1803199)

This is why many countries define terrorist action as deliberately aiming at "non-combatant" targets.[532] Thus, dropping a bomb on a Russian military truck in the Donbass region is not a terrorist act, but targeting a civilian truck in Moscow is.

In fact, the Ukrainian leadership is in a dilemma—it refuses to resume the negotiations it broke off with Russia in March 2022, and must show that it remains active, despite the fact that it no longer has the means to do so in conventional military operations.

No Western media or government has condemned these methods. Quite the contrary. Our official media have glorified them. No more, no less. But there is no such thing as good or bad terrorism. Whatever the reasons, terrorism is... terrorism. It is a method, and it is the use of this method that we must combat. Islamist terrorism and Ukrainian terrorism have in common the reason (foreign intervention), and the method and the objective (driving the population to turn against its authorities). To fight it when it is used against us, but to tolerate it—not to say encourage it—when it is used against others is unacceptable.

By inventing Islamist plots, *our* journalists, paid by the public service, inspire far-right terrorists like Anders Breivik (perpetrator of the Utoya massacre on July 22, 2011).[533] Today, they are apologists for Ukrainian terrorism... there's a logic to it.

Zelensky's Threats

Ukraine, which was said to be victorious, is a long way from winning, and it's a question of avoiding Western disaffection. This explains Volodymyr Zelensky's headlong rush in August 2023, when he declared in the British magazine *The Economist*:[534]

> *Reducing support for Ukraine will only prolong the war, says Zelensky. And it would create risks in the West's own backyard. It's impossible to predict how the millions of Ukrainian refugees*

---

532. https://counterterrorismethics.tudelft.nl/the-problem-of-defining-terrorism-part-1/#_Toc495482520

533. Mattias Gardell, Crusader Dreams: Oslo 22/7, Islamophobia, and the Quest for a Monocultural Europe, *Terrorism and Political Violence*, 26:129-155, 2014

534. https://www.economist.com/europe/2023/09/10/donald-trump-will-never-support-putin-says-volodymyr-zelensky

in European countries would react to the abandonment of their country. Ukrainians have generally "behaved well" and are "very grateful" to those who have taken them in. They won't forget this generosity. But it would not be a "good story" for Europe if it were to "push these people over the edge."

Many saw in this statement that Ukraine would be prepared to use the threat of terrorism to intimidate countries whose support would weaken. It is difficult to predict to what extent such threats are real. But it's not impossible that at some point they concern the journalists who have systematically misled Ukrainians into believing that the Russian threat was negligible—a sort of a fair return.

5. Strategic Analysis

In France, despite the existence of high-quality doctrinal documentation, military commentators—both "pro-Ukrainian" and "pro-Russian"—seem unable to link observations from the field to clear concepts. There is a certain (not to say great) confusion in the terms used, which inevitably leads to an inability to understand the actions of both protagonists. The word "strategic" is used for everything. The notions of "tactics," "operation" and "strategy" are intermingled in pseudo-analyses that are more figures of speech than explanations.

For a long time now, French military managers have not been confronted with concepts that go beyond the tactical level. This phenomenon is also perceptible in armies of the English-speaking world, but to a much lesser extent.

The Center of Gravity

Terminology

In the 19th century, Clausewitz and Jomini had identified the existence of a chain of causality linking the various politico-military actions towards an objective that would lead to victory. But they still had to find criteria for setting this objective. Both strategists had identified a "point" or determining element on which an opponent's strength or effectiveness depended. Jomini described it as a *"strategic decisive point,"* while Clausewitz used the expression *"center of gravity"*[535] defined as:[536]

> *The center of all power and movement, on which everything depends; the characteristic, capacity or location from which enemy and friendly forces derive their freedom of action, physical strength or will to fight.*

Thus, it's not simply a "center of power;" it is a tangible or intangible element from which a protagonist draws his strength and his ability to fight or achieve his objective. Nor is it its strategic objective, as some understand it.

Critical Factors

To enable the center of gravity to exist and be effective, Clausewitz and Jomini identified "points," a kind of gateway to the center of gravity, whose destruction or control would enable the latter to be reached. Clausewitz called them *"neuralgic points,"* while Jomini called them *"decisive points."* They can be military positions, weapon systems, transmission and intelligence facilities, etc.

To take better account of the complexity of the modern battlefield and the interweaving of a wide range of factors, these principles have had to be refined. For example, neuralgic or decisive points have been redefined as a set of tangible or intangible "critical factors," essential for carrying out actions or maintaining freedom of maneuver, the combination of which enables the center of gravity to exist.

These critical factors can be broken down into a combination of critical functions, critical resources and critical vulnerabilities. In the context of the fight against terrorism, their general characteristics can be outlined as follows:

---

535. "*[...] ein gewisser Schwerpunkt, ein Zentrum der Kraft und Bewegung bilden, von welchem das Ganze abhängt, und auf diesen Schwerpunkt des Gegners muß der gesammelte Stoß aller Kräfte gerichtet sein.*", Karl von Clausewitz, *Vom Kriege*, Achtes Buch, Dümmlers Verlag, Berlin, 1832
536. "The hub of all power and movement upon which everything depends; that characteristic, capability, or location from which enemy and friendly forces derive their freedom of action, physical strength, or the will to fight", *Glossary*, FM 100-5 (German: *Schwerpunkt*). Also: "... characteristic(s), capability(ies), or locality(ies) from which a nation, an alliance, a military force or other grouping derives its freedom of action, physical strength, or will to fight", Office of the Joint Staff, *DOD Dictionary of Military and Associated Terms*, Joint Publication 1-02 (Washington DC, 1984) p. 188.

- *Critical functions* are those that are essential for action. They include, for example, communications, command and control capabilities, joint capabilities, etc.
- *Critical resources* are those whose absence compromises the center of gravity. They can include popular support, national cohesion, industrial capacity, and so on.
- *Critical vulnerabilities* are the system's potential weaknesses, its "Achilles heel." They include, for example, the oversizing of a logistics network (as in Somalia in 1993), dependence on popular support in a difficult social context, critical infrastructures that are poorly protected or difficult to protect, and so on.

At the end of the 1990s, American Colonel John A. Warden adapted the principles developed by Clausewitz and Jomini into a model[537] which generically articulates critical factors in five concentric circles, with leadership and direction at its center, followed by critical infrastructure, communications infrastructure, population and, finally, forces deployed in the field. He deduced an air strategy based on a catalog of targets chosen from among the critical factors for reaching an adversary's center of gravity. By deliberately bombing German civilian populations between 1940 and 1945, and the Bulgarian population in 1941, the British had attempted to inflect the support of these populations for the Nazi regime and thus weaken it.[538] The same strategy was applied against Saddam Hussein in 1991 and 2003, and against Serbia in the 1990s.

This was also the strategy of the Islamic State's terrorist campaign in Europe in 2015-2017—the aim was to target the population (critical vulnerability) so that they would demand political power (center of gravity) to withdraw from Syria, along the lines of what happened on March 11, 2004 in Madrid. The terrorist attacks carried out by Ukraine in Russia have exactly the same aim—with the support of the West! In fact,

---

537. Col. John Warden (USAF), "Air Theory for the Twenty-First Century", *Air Power Journal*, 1995
538. Contrary to what history textbooks suggest, it was only after British strikes on German cities and civilians in 1940 that Germany unleashed its Blitz on London (Richard Overy, *The Bombing War: Europe 1939-1945*, Allen Lane, September 26, 2013).

5. Strategic Analysis

this is the same objective behind today's Western sanctions against Iran, Venezuela and Russia.[539] In none of these cases has this strategy worked.

Centers of Gravity in Russia and Ukraine

An analysis of the centers of gravity, i.e., what gives the two protagonists the capacity to maintain their war effort and what they must preserve, shows quite significant differences.

Ukraine's *sine qua non* condition for victory (or even resistance) is international support. This support depends on the West's perception of the conflict. It therefore relies on a narrative that hinges on two axes:

- Ukraine is stronger than Russia, and Russia can only lose.
- The West unreservedly supports Ukraine.

Russia's leaders know that the West is seeking to encourage a break-up of the country through its "decolonization"[540] and economic collapse, in order to destabilize it.[541] Russia's ability to lead the conflict therefore depends on its stability. The aim is to maintain normal economic life within the country and national cohesion.

It can be seen that Ukraine's center of gravity depends very largely on the outside world, whereas Russia's is a function of its domestic policy.

We can also see that the Russian and Ukrainian centers of gravity are different in nature. On the Russian side, we're dealing with very material elements; whereas on the Ukrainian side, we're in the immaterial domain. Russian military thinking is more oriented towards 3rd-generation warfare, while Ukrainian thinking is geared towards 5th-generation warfare. This also confirms the observations made at the start of the SMO, which showed that the Ukrainian political authorities (in this case Volodymyr Zelensky) were more involved in operational decisions than their Russian counterparts.

Our media have thus become a major player in the West's war against Russia. The idea that the narrative would single-handedly provoke an uprising in Russia led Westerners and Ukrainians alike to rely exclusively

---

539. "*Secretary of State* Mike Pompeo's Interview with Hadi Nili of BBC Persian," Washington DC, November 7, 2018; Brendan Cole, "Mike Pompeo Says Iran Must Listen To U.S. 'If They Want Their People To Eat,'" *Newsweek*, November 9, 2018.
540. https://www.csce.gov/international-impact/events/decolonizing-russia
541. https://www.rts.ch/info/monde/13818312-lukraine-demande-des-armes-des-armes-et-encore-des-armes.html

on it. This explains the censorship applied in the West on social networks and in the traditional media. Whereas even during the Cold War, *Pravda* could be found on our newsstands, today anything that might resemble support for Russia is banned.

As a journalist from a major French daily told me: "*The editors forbid us to write the truth, because that would mean we were supporting Putin.*" The reason is simple: narrative had a strategic role to play. That's why our media focused on propagating hatred of Russians, not just Russia.

Our media didn't dare mention the EU policy decided in September 2023, to confiscate the property of Russian citizens traveling in Europe, from cars to toilet paper (!), in order to make them personally bear the brunt of European sanctions.[542] This decision is not very surprising given the family background of Ursula von der Leyen and other European leaders—but it is the first time since the end of the Second World War that a legal device has been adopted that punishes individuals for what they are, not for what they do. Journalists at *LCI, BFM TV, RTS, RTBF and France 5* and elsewhere should ponder this example.

Studying Centers of Gravity

	Russia	Ukraine
Center of gravity	Country stability	Narrative that promotes a perception of success
Critical functions	Maintaining economic and industrial activity.	Maintaining coherence between military action and narrative.
Critical resources	Public support. Importing consumer products and controlling prices.	Major equipment (air defense, tanks, tactical aviation). Human potential. International military and economic support, including foreign investment.
Critical vulnerabilities	Inflationary pressures. Mortality in the field.	Popular support Air defense

Figure 42—Comparison of centers of gravity shows Ukraine's intrinsic weakness.

542. Volodymyr Paziy, "Russians are hysterical over the ban on traveling to the EU with smartphones and other things: what will be confiscated at the border", *Obozrevatel*, September 11, 2023 (https://eng.obozrevatel.com/section-life/news-russians-are-hysterical-over-the-ban-on-traveling-to-the-eu-with-smartphones-and-other-things-what-will-be-confiscated-at-the-border-11-09-2023.html)

Quite logically, both countries focused on protecting their respective centers of gravity and trying to reach the opponent's. This is why the Russians concentrated on destroying Western-supplied equipment ("demilitarization"). This is why the Russians concentrated on destroying Western-supplied equipment ("demilitarization"), and the Ukrainians multiplied spectacular actions on Russian territory, including terrorist actions, with no impact on operations on the ground.

The Russians sought to combat the Ukrainian narrative by confronting it with the reality on the ground.

The Battle of Bakhmut is a good example of how each adversary sought to protect its narrative: the Ukrainians by refusing to cede ground, even to promote an operative maneuver (as General Zaluzhny suggested at the time), and the Russians by causing huge Ukrainian casualties, without using contingent soldiers. It played an essential role in showing the Ukrainians that their official narrative was fallacious. This is why the SMO remains relatively well supported in Russia.

The conduct of the conflict in Ukraine and the actions of Western countries are not based on the actual operational situation, but on the narrative. In other words, Ukraine shares the same center of gravity as Western countries, and therefore does not fully control it. For it is this narrative, so jealously guarded by our media, that is the key to support for Ukraine. This explains the censorship that is *de facto* strictly enforced in Europe and on social networks. As we shall see, this narrative is double-edged and would ultimately prove deadly for Ukraine. For her, victory is determined less by the situation on the ground than by mastery of the narrative, since the latter is decisive in maintaining Western cohesion in support of Ukraine.

Strategically, Ukraine's situation deteriorated rapidly from late spring 2023: its potential had been destroyed in May-June 2022, and its idea of victory (however defined) depended on Western support. The narrative therefore played a central role, but it could no longer mask the failure of the counter-offensive, in a context where the West no longer has the material resources to supply the Ukrainian army.

In August 2023, *NBC News* noted the failure of the counter-offensive and warned that the West was *"losing control of its narra-*

tive."[543] In fact, a *Eurobarometer* poll shows that aid to Ukraine is no longer supported by a majority of European citizens.[544] Thus, those who approve of humanitarian aid have dropped from 64 percent in April 2022 to 47 percent. Support for Ukrainian refugees in the EU has fallen from 55 percent to 36 percent, and approval of EU financial support for Ukraine has dropped from 42 percent to 26 percent. Support for maintaining economic sanctions against Russia has fallen from 55 percent to 46 percent, while only 24 percent approve of arms supplies to Kiev.

In September 2023, when Zelensky was counting on the UN General Assembly to give the Western world a fresh boost, the reception he received was rather cool. For the first time, a major traditional media outlet—the *New York Times*—challenged the Ukrainian narrative by publishing the actual gains of the counter-offensive,[545] showing that Ukraine had lost ground; whereas its objective had been to recapture all the lost territory.

It was to revive the Western narrative, despite the failure of the counter-offensive, that on October 1, 2023 Ben Wallace, former Minister of Defense, wrote an article in *The Telegraph*, in which he declared that Ukraine was "*winning*" and that all it needed was a little more effort from the West to achieve its goal.[546] This was an attempt to resurrect the narrative to encourage the increasingly skeptical West.

The gap between the narrative of victory and the reality on the ground is growing daily. It's also the reason for spectacular actions on peripheral objectives such as the Black Sea fleet, against the Snake Island, against Crimea or against Russian cities. These are what Xavier Moreau calls "Tik-Tok" operations, i.e., military operations whose sole aim is to be published. They have multiplied since the counter-offensive was considered a failure. For example, on October 4, 2023, Ukrainian special

---

543. Dan De Luce & Phil McCausland, "Is Ukraine's counteroffensive failing? Kyiv and its supporters worry about losing control of the narrative", *NBC News*, August 4, 2023 (https://www.nbcnews.com/news/investigations/ukraine-war-counteroffensive-russia-success-failure-rcna98054)

544. https://europa.eu/eurobarometer/surveys/detail/3092

545. Josh Holder, "Who's Gaining Ground in Ukraine? This Year, No One.", *The New York Times*, September 28, 2023 (https://www.nytimes.com/interactive/2023/09/28/world/europe/russia-ukraine-war-map-front-line.html)

546. Ben Wallace, "Ukraine is winning. Now let's finish the job", *The Telegraph*, October 1, 2023 (https://www.telegraph.co.uk/news/2023/10/01/ben-wallace-ukraine-counteroffensive-succeeding/)

5. Strategic Analysis

forces landed on the Crimean coast using jet skis, with the sole aim of disembarking, unfurling a Ukrainian flag and leaving.[547]

The aim of these actions is to give a feeling of success. They show that Ukraine is not giving up the fight, and is seeking to regain the initiative. In reality, these actions, for which men are dying, have absolutely no impact on the course of operations on land. It's all about maintaining a narrative of victory that aims to avoid demobilizing the West.

Russia's strategy has been to preserve its center of gravity, namely the country's stability. This is why, unlike the West, the authorities have avoided making it the focus of their political, economic and diplomatic activities. The resilience of Russia's economy and its immense reserves have enabled a "normal flow" to be maintained; and overall only 50 percent of the population has followed developments in the conflict closely.[548] Paradoxically, the West's relentless application of sanctions, while supporting terrorist activities against Russia, reinforced the feeling of a hostile West and brought the population closer to its leaders.

The official Russian narrative carefully avoids saying who wins and who loses, but focuses on measurable results on the ground. The challenge for the government is to prevent Russian citizens from seeing their daily lives affected by the conflict. There is a remarkable ability to find alternative markets, thanks in particular to links with China. There has also been intense diplomatic activity on Russia's part, including on subjects far removed from the Ukrainian conflict, with successes that have helped maintain public confidence in the country's leadership.

In the West, from the outset, political, economic and diplomatic activities were focused on defeating Russia and forming a global coalition to achieve this. This was wishful thinking, and all these activities were failures. Western diplomacy focused on mobilizing forces against Russia, rather than working for a solution to the conflict and peace. Its obsession has kept it away from other crisis centers, where Russian and Chinese diplomacy has been active and successful.

---

547. "Ukraine war latest: Kyiv says special forces conduct operation in occupied Crimea", *The Kyiv Independent,* October 4, 2023 (https://kyivindependent.com/ukraine-war-latest-kyiv-says-special-forces-conducted-operation-in-occupied-crimea/)
548. https://www.levada.ru/2023/12/08/konflikt-s-ukrainoj-otsenki-noyabrya-2023-goda/

Comparison of Strategic Factors

The lack of systematic strategic analysis leads to a lack of understanding of what's happening on the ground. Particularly in France, so-called "strategic" analysis remains extremely intuitive and seems to be based solely on the latest news published in the media. This inability to read the intentions of others, or to read them only through the lens of one's own logic, stems from an ethnocentrism that is also at the root of France's current tensions with African countries. This ethnocentrism is very perceptible among French journalists, who have a very "metropolitan" culture, even those who have supposedly been abroad.

We need to distinguish between *strategic objectives* linked to national security, which are generally long-term in nature, and the *desired end state*, which is the situation we want to be in at the end of the operation.

This comparison of *centers of gravity* explains the insistence of the West—and the United States in particular—on rallying China, India and the countries of the South behind resolutions condemning and sanctioning Russia. For it is only through this international cohesion that these sanctions can work. The problem is that Western countries act according to what they believe to be their national interests, and the countries of the South also have this right.

Key Players' Strategy (to end 2023)

	Russia	**Ukraine**	**United States**
Strategic objective	Prevent the installation of nuclear missiles near its border.[549]	Bring about state collapse and regime change in Russia.[550]	Weaken China's backyard.[551]

---

549. https://www.mid.ru/tv/?id=1744872&lang=ru

550. Alexander Query, "Danilov: 'Ukraine's national interest is Russia's disintegration'", *The Kyiv Independent,* February 6, 2023 (https://kyivindependent.com/national/danilov-ukraines-national-interest-is-russias-disintegration)

551. Tom O'Connor, "NATO Chief Says Weakening Russia Will Help US Focus on Challenging China," *Newsweek,* September 21, 2023 (https://www.newsweek.com/nato-chief-says-weakening-russia-will-help-us-focus-challenging-china-1828914)

Desired end state	Ukraine's neutrality (non-participation in NATO).[552]	Restoration of its sovereignty within its 1991 borders.[553]	Regime change; dismember of Russia.[554]
Center of gravity	Internal stability.	Narrative of the Ukrainian victory.	Cohesion of the entire international community.

Figure 43—Comparison of the strategic components of the main players in the Ukraine conflict, as defined by the players themselves. The European Union does not appear on this list, as it has not really defined any objectives (other than fighting for "values") and is merely relaying American objectives.

By the end of 2023, Russia's objectives exceeded "denazification" and "demilitarization"—simply because the Russians have achieved both. Western involvement in the conflict in order to prolong it was a new situation that simply pushed the Russians to modify their objectives.

An examination of the various components of the main players' strategy shows that only the Russians have a realistic and attainable goal. Let's recall here that Zelensky's March 2023 proposal satisfied both the Russian strategic objective and its desired end-state. It was only after Western intervention that the Ukrainian president withdrew it.

As for Ukrainian and Western objectives, they are based on assumptions and prejudices that the facts fail to support. These assumptions include the fragility of the Russian economy and Vladimir Putin's unpopularity. For example, there are hopes of a "regime" change in Moscow, but there are no indicators that power has been weakened.

That's one of the reasons for the Ukrainian defeat: our politicians and those who influence them—the media—are the ones doing the planning. They haven't tried to help Ukraine (otherwise they would have done so before 2022); but they are trying to satisfy their prejudices.

552. Max Seddon, Roman Olearchyk, Arash Massoudi & Neri Zilber, "Ukraine and Russia explore neutrality plan in peace talks", *Financial Times*, March 16, 2022 (https://www.ft.com/content/7b341e46-d375-4817-be67-802b7fa77ef1)

553. Pavel Polityuk, "Ukraine says it stands firm on recognition of 1991 borders", *Reuters*, March 17, 2022 (https://www.reuters.com/world/europe/ukraines-president-says-1991-borders-must-be-recognised-adviser-2022-03-17/)

554. https://www.csce.gov/international-impact/events/decolonizing-russia

Support for Vladimir Putin

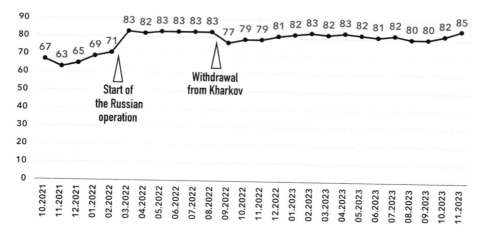

Figure 44—Support for Vladimir Putin's policies has remained stable since the start of the SMO. There is certainly a slight weariness of the conflict, but it does not have sufficient impact to suggest a change of "regime." [Source: https://www.levada.ru/2023/10/03/konflikt-s-ukrainoj-otsenki-sentyabrya2023-goda/]

Support for SMO

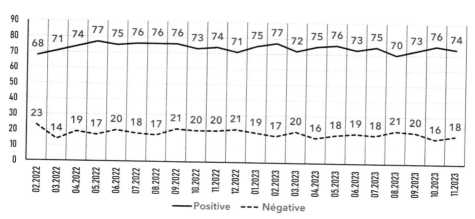

Figure 45—Positive opinion of the SMO remains stable at between 70 percent and 75 percent, as does opposition to military action, which hovers around 20 percent. [Source: https://www.levada.ru/2023/10/03/konflikt-s-ukrainoj-otsenki-sentyabrya2023-goda/]

Support for a Negotiation Process

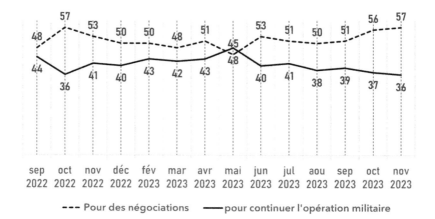

Figure 46—As with the other indicators, support for a negotiation process remains stable. It should be remembered here that this is also the position of the Russian government, as stated by Sergey Lavrov in October 2023. The Russian position has evolved, however, in that it will not enter into a negotiation process with harsher terms than those of 2022, which were rejected by the West. It is certain that, having been deceived by the West with the Minsk Agreements, Russia will also seek very serious guarantees. [Source: https://www.levada.ru/2023/10/03/ konflikt-s-ukrainoj-otsenki-sentyabrya2023-goda/]

Even the final state sought by Ukraine is ambiguous—in 1991, when Ukraine declared its independence, Crimea had already become an *Autonomous Soviet Socialist Republic* under the authority of Moscow, not Kiev. Is this a subtle way for Ukraine to indicate its readiness for a concession without making it too obvious? It's hard to say at this stage.

These figures are from the Levada polling institute (considered a foreign agent in Russia). It is quoted here because it asks the same questions at regular intervals, making it possible to compare the evolution of positions over time. As can be seen, popular support for the special operation is stable and even rising slightly. This seems to contradict the number of supporters of a negotiated solution, which is also on the rise. In fact, there is no real contradiction here, as this is also the position of the Russian government, which has always declared itself open to a negotiated solution. It was the Westerners, in February, March and August 2022, who opposed a negotiation process.

In other words, Russia's center of gravity has remained extremely stable.

For Ukraine, on the other hand, the narrative on which it has relied for Western support is collapsing. Since the summer of 2023, the gap between the narrative put forward by our media and the reality on the ground has been clearly observable. The observations made in my three previous books are proving true, and the Ukrainian military is losing confidence in its authorities. The *Kiev International Institute of Sociology* (KIIS) survey on Ukrainian casualties showed that our politicians and Ukrainian politicians are taking their desires for realities.

In the early November 2023 issue of *TIME Magazine*, Zelensky confessed that:[555]

> *Some front-line commanders, he continues, began refusing orders to advance, even when they came directly from the president's office.*

A Narrative in Decline

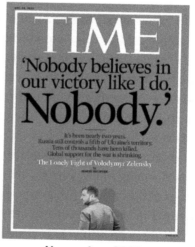

Décembre 2022   **Novembre 2023**

Figure 47—TIME Magazine cover. In one year, Ukraine became synonymous with defeat. To have trumpeted the country's victory, when there was strictly no evidence of it, only accentuated the gap between narrative and reality. Within the country, criticism multiplied and confidence in Zelensky plummeted.

---

555. Simon Shuster, "'Nobody Believes in Our Victory Like I Do.' Inside Volodymyr Zelensky's Struggle to Keep Ukraine in the Fight," *TIME*, October 30, 2023 (updated November 1, 2023) (https://time.com/6329188/ukraine-volodymyr-zelensky-interview/)

When ordered to advance, commanders replied:

With what? "They don't have the men or the weapons," says the officer. "Where are the weapons? Where's the artillery? Where are the new recruits?"

Within the EU, support for Ukraine is no longer unanimous.[556] The emergence of the Israeli-Palestinian conflict has even complicated matters. American weapons destined for Ukraine were redirected to Israel,[557] much to the dismay of Volodymyr Zelensky, who sought to visit Israel, but was refused.[558] In other words, the narrative no longer carries weight, and the support that depends on it is beginning to dry up.

For the United States, international cohesion was the keystone of sanctions against Russia. Yet not only did the US rhetoric against China (supported by its NATO allies) amplify the division between the Western hemisphere and the "rest of the world," but the intemperate statements of Josep Borrell, the EU's foreign policy chief, helped alienate the "global south." As a result, Russia's isolation, a *sine qua non* for its political and economic collapse, never materialized. In fact, it seems that the West, led by the Americans, never thought strategically about this conflict. This is what has allowed Russia to prevail in this conflict.

As a result, neither Ukraine nor the Americans have been able to maintain their center of gravity. The explanation is that Russia has a center of gravity that it is able to control completely, as it depends largely on its domestic politics. Unlike the West, Russia has sought to preserve the well-being of its citizens. This explains why Russians do not feel the impact of the conflict in Ukraine on a daily basis. It also explains Ukraine's attempts to use terrorism to attack Russia's internal stability. However, such actions are unlikely to have a profound impact, as they are not part of a climate of general discontent that they can amplify.

---

556. "Hungary, Slovakia criticise more aid to Ukraine as EU fights over budget", *Euractiv.com/AFP*, October 27, 2023 (https://www.euractiv.com/section/global-europe/news/hungary-slovakia-criticise-more-aid-to-ukraine-as-eu-fights-over-budget/)

557. Barak Ravid, "U.S. to send Israel artillery shells initially destined for Ukraine", *Axios*, October 19, 2023 (https://www.axios.com/2023/10/19/us-israel-artillery-shells-ukraine-weapons-gaza)

558. https://kyivindependent.com/media-israel-refuses-zelenskys-visit-says-time-not-right/

The Ukrainian and American centers of gravity are both externally dependent and not entirely under political control. This critical vulnerability explains why Russia had a strategic advantage over its adversaries. But it also means that the West had badly misjudged the situation.

From the Western point of view, Russia is in a less favorable strategic position than it was before the SMO, so Russia has lost out. But this is only true if we consider Europe as the center of the world. In reality, while European diplomacy has focused on weakening Russia, Russia has focused on creating a new, alternative environment. The key to Russia's success is its holistic approach to warfare.

The Notion of Victory

Russia operates within a framework of Clausewitzian thinking, where operational successes are exploited for strategic ends. Operational strategy ("operative art") therefore plays an essential role in defining what is considered a victory.

As we saw during the battle of Bakhmut, the Russians have adapted perfectly to the strategy that the West has given Ukraine, which prioritizes the defense of every square meter. The Ukrainians thus played into the hands of the attrition strategy officially announced by Russia. Conversely, in Kharkov and Kherson, the Russians preferred to cede territory in exchange for the lives of their men. In the context of a war of attrition, sacrificing potential in exchange for territory, as Ukraine is doing, is the worst strategy of all.

That's why General Zaluzhny, commander of the Ukrainian forces, tried to oppose Zelensky and proposed withdrawing his forces from Bakhmut. But in Ukraine, it's the Western narrative that guides military decisions. Zelensky preferred to follow the path indicated to him by our media, in order to retain the support of Western opinion. In November 2023, General Zaluzhny had to openly admit that this decision was a mistake, because prolonging the war could only favor Russia.[559]

---

559. "'It was my mistake': Ukrainian Commander-in-Chief on counteroffensive and 'gunpowder' for victory", *RBC-Ukraine*, November 2, 2023 (https://newsukraine.rbc.ua/news/it-was-my-mistake-commander-in-chief-on-counteroffensive-1698929719.html)

5. Strategic Analysis

The Importance of Determining a Strategy

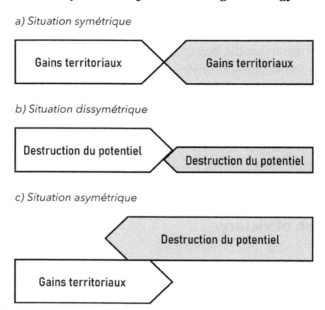

a) *Situation symétrique*

Gains territoriaux — Gains territoriaux

b) *Situation dissymétrique*

Destruction du potentiel — Destruction du potentiel

c) *Situation asymétrique*

Destruction du potentiel

Gains territoriaux

Figure 48—The Western interpretation of Russian strategy in Ukraine is a symmetrical situation in which both Russians and Ukrainians are aiming for Ukrainian territory: one to seize it, the other to defend and reclaim it (a). An asymmetrical situation is one in which the two adversaries pursue similar objectives, but with different potentials (b). When the pursuit of one objective favors the achievement of the opponent's objectives, or when the strategy used favors that of the opponent, we are in an asymmetrical situation. This is the situation into which the West and our media have pushed Ukraine: by holding on to the terrain, the Ukrainians are promoting the objectives defined by Vladimir Putin (demilitarization) and General Surovikin (destruction of potential) (c).

The Ukrainian conflict was inherently asymmetrical. The West wanted to turn it into a symmetrical conflict, proclaiming that Ukraine's capabilities could be enough to topple Russia. But this was clearly wishful thinking from the outset, aimed solely at justifying non-compliance with the Minsk Agreements. Russian strategists have turned it into an asymmetrical conflict.

Ukraine's problem in this conflict is that it has no rational relationship with the notion of victory. By comparison, the Palestinians, who are aware of their quantitative inferiority, have switched to a way of thinking that gives the simple act of resisting a sense of victory. This is the asymmetrical nature of the conflict that Israel has never managed to understand in 75 years, and which it is reduced to overcoming through tactical superiority rather than strategic finesse. In Ukraine, it's the same phenomenon. By clinging to a notion of victory linked to the recovery of territory, Ukraine has locked itself into a logic that can only lead to defeat.

On November 20, 2023, Oleksiy Danilov, Secretary of the National Security and Defense Council, painted a bleak picture of Ukrainian prospects for 2024.[560] His speech showed that Ukraine has neither a plan to emerge from the conflict, nor an approach that would associate a sense of victory with that emergence: he was reduced to linking Ukraine's victory to that of the West. In the West, however, the end of the conflict in Ukraine is increasingly perceived as a military, political, human and economic debacle.

In an asymmetrical situation, each protagonist is free to define his own criteria for victory, and to choose from a range of criteria under his control. This is why Egypt (1973), Hezbollah (2006), the Islamic State (2017), the Palestinian resistance since 1948 and Hamas in 2023 are victorious, despite massive losses. This seems counter-intuitive to a Western mind, but it is what explains why Westerners are unable to actually "win" their wars.

In Ukraine, political leadership has been locked into a narrative that precludes a way out of the crisis without losing face. The asymmetrical situation now working to Ukraine's disadvantage stems from a narrative that has been confused with reality, and has led to a response that is ill-suited to the nature of the Russian operation.

---

560. https://www.rnbo.gov.ua/ua/Diialnist/6714.html

6. A Technological War

The Russian Defense Industry

In June 2023, military "expert" Alexandre Vautravers declared in a Swiss media report that *"Russia's defense industry is a shadow of what the Soviet Union's was"* and that it *"condemns the Russian army to being on the defensive."*[561] He interpreted the acquisition of equipment abroad, such as light multi-role wheeled armored vehicles (LMVs) from the Italian firm Iveco[562] or the purchase of MISTRAL frigates from France,[563] as a sign of the weakening of Russian industry.

In reality, Russia has done exactly what Western countries have done, and sought to buy less expensive "off-the-shelf" equipment. This is because Russia is developing highly sophisticated weapons systems, such as hypersonic weapons, the ARMATA platform for armored vehicles, robotic systems and control networks using artificial intelligence. Russia therefore reserves investment for the domestic production of sensitive, high-tech equipment, preferring to turn abroad for simpler systems. This is exactly what happened with Iran's SHAHID-136 drones (known in Russia as GERAN-2). It's worth noting in passing that a large proportion of these purchases were made from NATO countries, indicating that Russia had no intention of getting involved in a conflict with the Europeans.

In the same vein, Gina Raimondo, US Secretary of Commerce, told a Congressional hearing in May 2022 that the Russians were collecting

---

561. https://www.lemanbleu.ch/fr/Emissions/189661-Geneve-a-Chaud.html
562. https://defence-blog.com/italian-made-iveco-lmvs-tactical-vehicles-spotted-during-milita-ry-parade-rehearsals-in-russia/
563. https://sldinfo.com/2023/02/the-french-mistral-the-case-of-the-russian-sale-and-its-aftermath/

microprocessors from washing machines and refrigerators to obtain the microprocessors needed for their weaponry.[564] That's all it took to fuel European silliness. Ursula von der Leyen, President of the European Commission,[565] and Annalena Baerbock, German Foreign Minister,[566] echoed the message over and over again. Why do our female politicians insist on proving Françoise Giroud's prediction right: *"Women will truly be equal to men the day they appoint an incompetent woman to an important post."*

According to French TV channel *TF1*, Russia does not produce semi-conductors. As you'd expect from a conspiracy media outlet, this is a lie. In fact, Russia produces 25 percent of its requirements, including military ones, which mainly use 100-150 nm microprocessors and medium-nanometer processors (30-65 nm). It can count on China for the lower-nanometer microprocessors (20-60 nm) used in military equipment. Low-very low-nanometer micro-processors (4-12 nm), found in tablets and cell phones, are not generally used for weaponry, as they are difficult to "harden." As if to contradict our muses, the Ukrainians themselves declared that the Russians have no shortage of micro-processors.[567]

That said, sanctions have highlighted a vulnerability, and Russia has decided to implement a program aimed at creating the capacity to produce 7nm microprocessors by 2030.[568]

Thus, despite the rumors propagated by the Western media, there is no evidence that Russia has had to buy weapons systems from outside players to compensate for a deficiency in its defense industry. There are several reasons for this. The first is that the Russian defense industry is in very good shape. It is innovative and extremely competitive on the international market. Unlike Western countries, the Russian arms industry, like that of Ukraine, has continued to export military equipment. Today,

---

564. Jeanne Whalen, "Sanctions forcing Russia to use appliance parts in military gear, U.S. says," *The Washington Post*, May 11, 2022 (https://www.washingtonpost.com/technology/2022/05/11/russia-sanctions-effect-military/)

565. https://www.youtube.com/shorts/eMGN-l3VHAE?feature=share

566. https://twitter.com/mazzenilsson/status/1695478885196935255

567. Chris Livesay & Erin Lyall, "Russia is bombarding Ukraine with drones guided by U.S.-made technology, and the chips are still flowing," *CBS News*, January 4, 2023 (https://www.cbsnews.com/news/ukraine-war-russia-iranian-drones-us-made-technology-chips/)

568. Simon Lüthje, "Russia wants to manufacture its own chips using the 7 nm process", *Basic-Tutorial*, October 24, 2023 (https://basic-tutorials.com/news/russia-wants-to-manufacture-its-own-chips-using-the-7-nm-process/)

its arms exports have been significantly reduced, as most of its production has been redirected to domestic needs.

Russian Microprocessor Acquisitions by Country

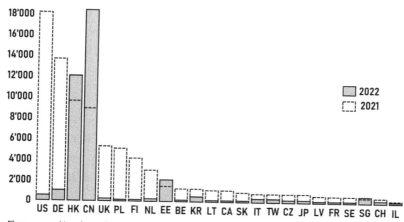

Figure 49—Number of transactions per country for the acquisition of microprocessors, according to the work of Ukrainian researcher Elina Ribakova.[569] As can be seen, China and Hong Kong have largely replaced the United States. We note that Estonia, which never misses an opportunity to show its hatred of the Russians, seemed to be talking out of both sides of its mouth, as did the husband of Prime Minister Kaja Kallas, who doesn't seem to shine either in integrity or intelligence. [Source: Elina Ribakova].

Russia's armaments industry represents around 800 companies and almost half a million jobs. Whereas during the Communist era, the industry operated on the principle of a planned economy, today it operates on the principle of a market economy. In fact, the architecture of the Russian arms industry is very similar to that of Europe in the 1960s-1980s: the companies are virtually all state-owned. Unlike Western military-industrial complexes, whose interests may diverge from those of the state, in Russia there is convergence.

After the Cold War, the arms industry in the West, and especially in Europe, gave way to civilian production in order to reap the "peace dividend." Many people, particularly in France, have been upset by this situation, seeing it as a strategic error. But this is not true. The situation in Europe and good relations with Russia (until 2014 at least) meant that the absence of a mili-

---

569. https://twitter.com/elinaribakova/status/16082603620042055569

tary threat was a reality, and did not objectively justify maintaining a large production capacity. This is probably the underlying reason why the United States has done everything to maintain a continuum of threats since the end of the Cold War. Even today, only neo-Nazis maintain the narrative of a Russian threat to Europe, to justify our policy towards Ukraine.

Electronic Warfare

Electronic Combat

A field systematically ignored by our "experts" and virtually always confused with cyberwarfare is *electronic warfare* (EW). Although the two disciplines may intersect, they are technically distinct. Simply put, electronic warfare is the war of waves in the so-called ether, while cyberwarfare is the war of software.

As society has become increasingly computerized, the scope of EW activities has expanded exponentially, particularly in a country as vast as Ukraine, where military communications use highly computerized satellite systems, similar to the GSM networks used in the civilian sector.

Designated "Radio-electronic Combat" (радиоэлектронная *борьба*) (REB) in Russia, this is a field in which it excels and probably has a greater lead than the West. It's also an area of quiet success, as the *BBC* acknowledges:[570]

> *Russia is not only outnumbering and outgunning Ukrainian forces, it also has extensive experience in electronic warfare. Russia has blocked and jammed Ukraine's military communications systems.*

On May 25, 2023, the British Ministry of Defense reported that, according to *Geollect*, since May 14, 2023, the Russians had hacked the automatic identification system (AIS) to make it appear that commercial ships were moving, by creating the impression of a 65 km long "Z" symbol on the Black Sea,[571] visible on open-source tracking software.[572]

---

570. https://www.bbc.com/news/world-europe-62090791
571. https://www.tradewindsnews.com/technology/ship-ais-data-spoofed-to-draw-pro-war-russian-z-symbol-in-black-sea/2-1-1456329
572. https://twitter.com/DefenceHQ/status/1661607073803640833

At the start of its intervention in February 2022, Russia was able to neutralize all Ukrainian military transmission systems.

The destruction of *Starlink* terminals forced command posts to exchange firing data by voice, via the *Iridium* satellite telephone network. This slowed down artillery reaction times, making them more vulnerable to counter-battery fire.

One of GE's main efforts is the fight against drones. In *The Economist*, a Ukrainian official states:[573]

> *The Russians are very, very good at what they do [...] They do black magic when it comes to electromagnetic warfare. They can jam frequencies, fool the GPS system, send a drone to the wrong altitude so that it just falls out of the sky.*

System 1L269 KRASUKHA-2

Figure 50—The Krasukha-2 is a system designed to jam distant warning systems such as the E-3 SENTRY AWACS used by NATO up to a range of 250 km. It can also jam radar-guided missile systems. This is why it is also used to protect ISKANDER-type missile launch sites, for example. It transmits false data to the attacking missile, throwing it off course.

---

573. "Ukraine is betting on drones to strike deep into Russia," *The Economist*, March 20, 2023 (https://www.economist.com/europe/2023/03/20/ukraine-is-betting-on-drones-to-strike-deep-into-russia)

6. A Technological War

In August 2023, the Ukrainian army was taken by surprise in the Kupiansk sector,[574] despite the American E-8 J-STARS and RQ-4 GLOBAL HAWK keeping a constant watch on the area from the Ukrainian border and the Black Sea. The reason why the preparations for this attack went undetected is that the Russians are able to make themselves "invisible," thanks to electronic warfare, which blinds Western radars. It is the KRASUKHA family of systems deployed in Crimea that enable the Russians to operate as if behind an "electronic screen."

System 1RL257 KRASUKHA-4

Figure 51—The Krasukha-4 is a jamming system for American J-STARS-type onboard radars, used to track enemy movements on the ground. Such systems are used in the Crimea, for example, to divert Ukrainian attacks guided by American control systems.

The War against Satellites

From the start of the SMO, Ukrainian control structures were severely damaged by Russian strikes. Ukraine had to fall back on the *Starlink* network, with some 20,000 terminals financed by the American, British and Polish governments. Implemented by Elon Musk's SpaceX company,

---

574. Dan Sabbagh, "'I couldn't take it any more': holdouts quit Kupiansk after renewed Russian shelling", *The Guardian*, August 29, 2023 (https://www.theguardian.com/world/2023/aug/29/holdouts-quit-kupiansk-after-renewed-russian-shelling-ukraine)

the *Starlink* system enables data transmission via a network of satellites, and has rapidly become instrumental for the transmission of operational data, including drone piloting and target designation. It has thus become one of the priority objectives of Russian electronic warfare. Operating this network in Ukraine costs around 400 million USD per year.

Starlink thus quickly became one of the priority targets of Russian electronic warfare. Initially, SpaceX succeeded in preventing jamming of its satellites,[575] but by October 2022, massive *Starlink* failures were having "catastrophic" consequences on Ukrainian operational transmissions.[576] According to General Valerii Zaluzhny, head of the Ukrainian forces, the Russians were destroying 500 *Starlink* terminals a month.[577] This forced command posts to exchange firing data by voice via the *Iridium* satellite telephone network, slowing down artillery reaction times and making them more vulnerable to counter-battery fire.

The use of civilian satellite networks for military purposes could lead Russia to consider satellites as legitimate targets.[578]

Anti-Drone Systems

The Russians have developed a whole range of tools to eliminate the Ukrainian drone threat. The most obvious of these is air defense. The problem with Western anti-aircraft systems is that they rely on a limited number of systems for all airborne threats. This is the case with the PATRIOTs used by Ukraine, which become extremely costly when used against cheap drones with limited effect. The Russians have a different philosophy, adopting a multi-layered defense system, with more systems and partially overlapping performance.

575. Michael Kan, "Pentagon Impressed by Starlink's Fast Signal-Jamming Workaround in Ukraine," *PC Magazine*, April 21, 2022 (https://www.pcmag.com/news/pentagon-impressed-by-starlinks-fast-signal-jamming-workaround-in-ukraine)

576. Elizabeth Howell, "Elon Musk says Russia is ramping up cyberattacks on SpaceX's Starlink systems in Ukraine," *Space*, October 14, 2022 (https://www.space.com/starlink-russian-cyberattacks-ramp-up-efforts-elon-musk)

577. Xander Landen, "Starlink Outages Put 'Dent' in Ukrainian Counteroffensive Against Putin," *Newsweek*, October 8, 2022 (https://www.newsweek.com/starlink-outages-put-dent-ukrainian-counteroffensive-against-putin-1750116)

578. "Russia Says U.S. Satellites Assisting Ukraine Are 'Legitimate' Targets," *The Moscow Tmes*, October 27, 2022 (https://www.themoscowtimes.com/2022/10/27/russia-says-us-satellites-assisting-ukraine-are-legitimate-targets-a79208)

The linchpin of our anti-drone program is the PANTSIR SM system, the latest iteration of the system created in the early 1990s. It is a point defense system, optimized for combating small drones whose trajectories are difficult to anticipate. The PANTSIR system is distributed at tactical level and contributes to the air cover of BTGs. It can detect targets measuring 15x15 cm, and is equipped with short-range missiles (<7 km) to shoot down small tactical UAVs. The sensitivity of its radar system makes it an effective weapon system against tactical missiles, such as the TOCHKA-U (SS-21) or HIMARS.

The PANTSIR System

Панцирь-СМ
PANTSIR-SM
Armement: 4 canons de 30 mm
12 missiles sol-air
Distances: Detection – 75 km
Interception – 40 km

Figure 52—The PANTSIR-SM is one of the most effective tactical-operational anti-aircraft systems.

The second anti-UAV tool is the Mi-28NM combat helicopter. It is optimized for drone warfare. Its NO25E radar makes it a kind of "mini-AWACS," capable of monitoring airspace and detecting very small objects. It is also capable of hunting drones at night. However, its weak point is the sensitivity of its missiles, which cannot lock onto small drones with insufficient heat signature. It is integrated into the RUK control systems, enabling rapid response to the needs of ground troops.

The Mi-28NM

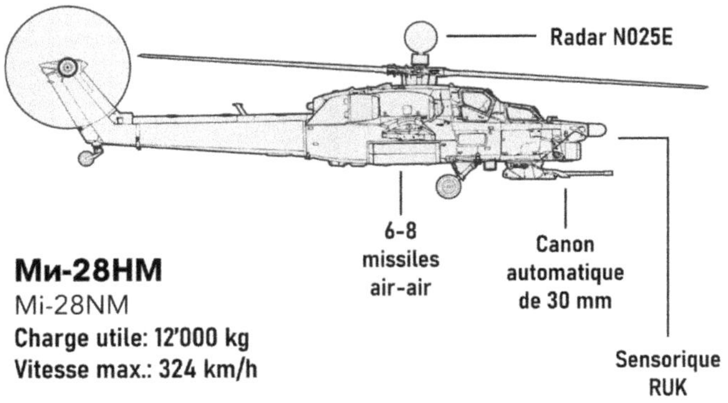

Radar N025E

Ми-28HM
Mi-28NM
Charge utile: 12'000 kg
Vitesse max.: 324 km/h

6-8
missiles
air-air

Canon
automatique
de 30 mm

Sensorique
RUK

Figure 53—The Mi-28NM has been specially designed to combat drones, particularly at night.

The most important element in Russia's arsenal against drones and aerial missile attacks (ballistic missiles, HIMARS or cruise missiles) is the set of electronic measures. The Russians have created a set of systems that form a multi-layered defense from the strategic to the tactical level.

These systems operate in a wide variety of ways. The most common is GPS signal jamming. According to the American magazine *Forbes*, Russia is able to shoot down 90 percent of Ukrainian drones with its electro-magnetic systems.[579]

It's important to understand that these "layered" systems mean that the granularity of the interception increases as you get closer to the target of the attack, rather like a spider's web. This explains why medium-sized Ukrainian drones were able to penetrate Russian airspace and were only intercepted close to their targets.

The Russians have introduced tactical jamming systems on a large scale, known as "trench jamming" systems, such as the STRIJ, which provides automatic drone suppression. The system lets the drone approach, then automatically switches on, jamming the signal and taking control.

---

579. David Axe, "Russia's Electronic-Warfare Troops Knocked Out 90 Percent of Ukraine's Drones," *Forbes*, December 24, 2022 (https://www.forbes.com/sites/davidaxe/2022/12/24/russia-electro-nic-warfare-troops-knocked-out-90-percent-of-ukraines-drones/?sh=2b8c98a9575c)

STRIJ Anti-Drone System

Figure 54—The Russians have developed a whole range of electronic systems to neutralize drones before they become a threat. The STRIJ is one such system, designed to protect tactical units.

The problem with drones is that they are often too small to be detected and fought effectively by air defense. The answer is EW, which neutralizes drones. According to the UK's *Royal United Services Institute*, the Russians neutralize some 10,000 Ukrainian drones a month.[580] By their own admission, by March 2023, the Ukrainians were losing 10-15 drones a day, and released a credit of 800 million euros[581] for the purchase of drones.[582]

The Russians seem to be able to decrypt in real time the Motorola 256-bit encryption systems used to guide small drones.[583] When a DJI drone loses radio contact with its operator, due to interference or other causes, it attempts to return to the last known location where it was able to communicate. If communication cannot be re-established, the *"Failsafe Return-to-Home"* function is activated and the drone automatically returns to its starting point. If GPS navigation is jammed—as is often

580. https://static.rusi.org/403-SR-Russian-Tactics-web-final.pdf
581. https://youtu.be/qQ2kCDBYY6I
582. https://t.me/dsszzi_official/5621
583. Jack Watling & Nick Reynolds, "Meatgrinder: Russian Tactics in the Second Year of Its Invasion of Ukraine", *Royal United Services Institute for Defence and Security Studies (RUSI)*, May 19, 2023 (https://static.rusi.org/403-SR-Russian-Tactics-web-final.pdf)

the case over much of the front line—and the drone cannot return home, it lands softly wherever it is.[584]

The Russians also have the means to jam GPS signals and thus disrupt the use of drones and guided missiles. According to *Forbes* magazine, Russia is able to shoot down 90 percent of Ukrainian drones with its[585] electromagnetic systems.

The Wunderwaffen

At the end of the Second World War, with the German army retreating on all fronts, Hitler and his personal staff continued to believe that the situation could be turned around through the use of new weapons. Germany was at the forefront of the development of new technologies and weapons, which it was believed could "change the game." Jets, missiles, new armored vehicles—these were later known as *Wunderwaffen* ("wonder weapons"). But German industry, under bombardment, was no longer able to ensure regular production, and human resources were dwindling. The *Wunderwaffen did* not prevent the defeat of the Third Reich. Eighty years later, Ukraine is going through the same experience as those masterminds.

From March 2022, as Russian coalition forces advanced in Ukraine, the Western discourse asserted that Russia was losing the war. The new weapons deployed by Russian forces, notably hypersonic missiles, were dubbed *Wunderwaffen* by the extremist Western propaganda press, in order to present them as Russia's last resort in the face of inevitable defeat.[586]

In fact, by May-June 2022, Ukraine had literally been "demilitarized," and Vladimir Putin's stated goal had been achieved. Ukraine swapped a promising peace plan for Western aid *"for as long as it takes."* Initially, the main concern was the number of weapons. That's why some weapons,

584. David Hambling, "New Report: Ukraine Drone Losses Are '10,000 Per Month'", *Forbes*, May 22, 2023 (https://www.forbes.com/sites/davidhambling/2023/05/22/ukraine-drones-losses-are-10000-per-month/?sh=799a1320384a)
585. David Axe, "Russia's Electronic-Warfare Troops Knocked Out 90 Percent of Ukraine's Drones," *Forbes*, December 24, 2022 (https://www.forbes.com/sites/davidaxe/2022/12/24/russia-electronic-warfare-troops-knocked-out-90-percent-of-ukraines-drones/?sh=2b8c98a9575c)
586. Volker Pabst, "Moskau zeigt auf seine 'Wunderwaffen'", *Neue Zürcher Zeitung*, March 20, 2022 (https://www.nzz.ch/international/russlands-wunderwaffe-erster-kampfeinsatz-von-hyperschall-rakete-ld.1675519)

6. A Technological War

such as the JAVELIN missile, are literally *Wunderwaffen,* whose effectiveness will be rapidly reduced by Russian countermeasures.

"Wonder Weapons" Literally and Figuratively

Figure 55—Saint Javelin, who literally became a Ukrainian icon in the first hours of the Russian operation. It shows that right from the start of the SMO, Ukrainians were dependent on Western weapons, which tended to contradict the repeated discourse of a Ukrainian victory. It also testifies to the "miraculous" nature of Western aid, seen as the only recourse against a predicted defeat (by honest commentators!).

For their part, the Russians are seeking to make better use of the strengths of their various weapons systems, including those that appear obsolete, as we shall see. Miracle weapons such as JAVELIN, HIMARS, PATRIOT or STORM SHADOW are losing their effectiveness in the face of the adaptability of Russian technicians, who are finding parries that they can quickly bring to the battlefield.

Hypersonic Weapons

The Russians have a whole range of missiles, which Ukrainian air defenses are still having trouble stopping. These include the 9M723 ISKANDER-M and Kh22 BOURYA missiles. According to Yuriy Ignat, spokesman for the Ukrainian Air Force, this is one of the reasons why Ukraine would like to have F-16s to combat the Kh-22.[587]

Hypersonic missiles have entered the Ukrainian conflict with a vengeance. Their operational significance in the Ukrainian theater is less than the change they herald in the strategic balance of forces between Russia and the West. Undergoing testing since December 2017, the Kh-47M2 KINJAL missile was first engaged in combat on March 18, 2022, to strike Ukrainian logistics sites. This was probably both a first test in combat conditions and a signal to the West.

Not all the characteristics of these missiles are precisely known. Nevertheless, they appear to pose a major challenge to Western air defense systems, such as the American MIM-104 PATRIOT, the Norwegian NASAMS or the German IRIS-T SLM. On May 8 2023, *RTS* announced that Ukraine had successfully shot down a hypersonic missile for the first time on May 4.[588] Yet three days earlier, the Ukrainian Air Force spokesman had told a Ukrainian media outlet[589] that Ukraine had not shot down such a missile.[590]

Primarily deployed on MiG-31K and MiG-31I aircraft, the KINJAL can also be operated on the Su-34 platform. The advantage of this diversification is that it frees up MiG-31s for engagement with cruise missiles, which its radar can effectively combat.

587. Joseph P Chacko, "Here is a list of Russian missiles that are too powerful for Ukrainian air defences to shoot down", *Frontier India*, March 7, 2023 (https://frontierindia.com/here-is-a-list-of-russian-missiles-that-are-too-powerful-for-ukrainian-air-defences-to-shoot-down/)

588. https://www.rts.ch/info/monde/13999930-le-chef-de-wagner-dit-avoir-eu-la-promesse-de-moscou-de-recevoir-les-munitions-demandees.html#timeline-anchor-1683373528352

589. "Ukraine's Air Force denies ballistic missile shot down over Kyiv on May 4," *The Kyiv Independent*, May 5, 2023 (https://kyivindependent.com/ukraines-air-force-denies-ballistic-missile-shot-down-over-kyiv-on-may-4/)

590. Olena Bohdanyok, "Повітряні Сили спростували збиття над Києвом гіперзвукової ракети 'Кинжал' вночі 4 травня Ексклюзивно," *suspilne media*, May 5, 2023 (https://suspilne.media/466841-ci-bula-zbita-nad-kievom-giperzvukova-raketa-vnoci-4-travna-so-pro-ce-vidomo/)

The KINJAL Kh-47M2 Hypersonic Missile

Figure 56—The KINJAL hypersonic missile, deployed mainly by MiG-31K aircraft.

While our media are constantly telling us that Russia has no capacity for technological development, we can see that it has succeeded in developing a whole range of hypersonic missiles (with speeds of between 10,000 and 30,000 km/h). For example, Russia has begun deploying ZIRCON hypersonic missiles on its ships.[591]

Since they are difficult to intercept, these missiles pose a considerable threat to US aircraft carriers; that is, to America's force projection capability. The geostrategic significance of these new weapons does not yet seem to be understood in the West, which remains trapped in its own narrative. But Vladimir Putin has been talking about them for several years now, about new-technology weapons that are—indeed—years ahead of the West.[592] The USA, for example, has not yet been able to develop equivalent systems.

591. Brad Lendon & Anna Chernova, "Putin deploys Russian warship with Zircon hypersonic missile, TASS says," *CNN*, January 5, 2023 (https://edition.cnn.com/2023/01/05/europe/russia-warship-hypersonic-missile-deployed-intl-hnk-ml/index.html)

592. Nick Mordowanec, "Putin Brags New Weapons Are 'Decades' Ahead of Rest of the World's," *Newsweek*, August 15, 2022 (https://www.newsweek.com/vladimir-putin-brags-russian-new-weapons-decades-ahead-other-countries-1733754)

Armored Vehicles

Balance of Force

At the start of the SMO, both sides had roughly the same number of tanks. Ukraine had some 800 T-64 tanks and around 100 T-72 tanks. Russia, with around 80 BTGs according to the Pentagon,[593] had around 800-1,000 battle tanks. Thus, there was a certain balance.

Since February 24, 2022, if our media and brilliant military "experts" are to be believed, the Russians have lost nothing but tanks. Ukraine, on the other hand, is said to have captured hundreds,[594] plus those received from the West in 2022-2023, for a total of around 2,700 battle tanks. However, as we shall see during the 2023 counter-offensive, the Ukrainians were short of battle tanks and had to rely on Western aid.

Russian Tanks versus Western Tanks

The Western narrative emphasizes the effort to help Ukraine and the far superior quality of the equipment supplied, while the Russians seem to be fighting with antiques. Yet the course of events seems to belie our experts and other disinformers. Are the Russians better at getting the best out of their wrecks than the Ukrainians, or are our experts lying? It's the latter.

Our TV "experts" seem to have turned into hucksters (more "liars" than "hucksters," in fact), extolling the merits of Western tanks over Russian ones, which they say are poorly designed, obsolete and poorly served by poorly trained, demotivated soldiers. As for modern tanks, according to "expert" Alexandre Vautravers, they have only had a *"sample presence,"* and the Russians do not have the capacity to produce new ones.[595]

We are used to hearing that Russian equipment is of inferior quality to Western equipment. This is not entirely true. The Russians, like the Soviets, have a different philosophy from the West when it comes to modernizing their armed forces.

---

593. "Senior Defense Official Holds a Background Briefing, April 18, 2022," *defense.gov*, April 18, 2022 (https://www.defense.gov/News/Transcripts/Transcript/Article/3002867/senior-defense-official-holds-a-background-briefing-april-18-2022/)

594. "Attack On Europe: Documenting Russian Equipment Losses During The 2022 Russian Invasion Of Ukraine," *Oryx*, February 24, 2022 (https://www.oryxspioenkop.com/2022/02/attack-on-europe-documenting-equipment.html)

595. https://www.club-44.ch/mediatheque/

Weapons systems in the West are extremely expensive, and strive to incorporate the latest and even emerging technologies. The result is that our equipment is technologically advanced, but arrives on the battlefield at a relatively slow pace.

Conversely, the Russians (and formerly the Soviets) prefer to deploy proven technologies. They work more closely than the West on "families" of devices, using many common components. In other words, the gap between generations of weapons is shorter in Russia than in the West, and their equipment is less expensive. As during the Cold War, the number of generations of their major equipment is higher than in the West. As a result, the average technological level of their systems is higher than in the West, at a lower cost.

This explains why, after giving Ukraine recently produced equipment, the West had to fall back on equipment from the 1960s. On the Russian side, destroyed equipment can easily be replaced by equipment from the previous generation, with inexpensive upgrades.

Obsolete and Unusable Tanks

Even a cursory analysis shows that what we delivered to Ukraine was nowhere near the level of what the Russians have. For, in reality, the West did not give us their best equipment, but their junk. At a meeting in April 2023 at the Ramstein base in Germany, one of General Zaluzhny's aides told his American counterparts:[596]

> *We're sorry, but some of the vehicles we've received are unsuitable for combat... The BRADLEYs and LÉOPARDs have broken or missing tracks. The radio is missing from the German MARDER fighting vehicles, which are nothing more than iron boxes with caterpillar tracks.*

The weapons supplied to Ukraine were more a political choice than an operational one. Such is the case with the AMX-10RCs that France

---

596. Alona Mazurenko, "US and the West insisted on Ukraine's targeted counteroffensive to cut off Russia from Crimea", *Ukrainska Pravda*, December 4, 2023 (https://www.pravda.com.ua/eng/news/2023/12/4/7431593/)

decided to send in January 2023, just before the Ramstein conference.[597] This is not in itself bad equipment, but it was designed for a different use, period and terrain. In July, Ukrainian military officials declared it unsuitable for the current counter-offensive.[598] The AMX-10 RC is a reconnaissance vehicle; but the Ukrainian army didn't really need a reconnaissance vehicle whose functions could be performed by simpler, less vulnerable vehicles, or even drones. In November, the first series of vehicles sent by France was destroyed. However, Ukraine is apparently looking forward to receiving a new series.[599] In fact, in November, after the world's attention was focused on Israel and Palestine, Ukraine felt—probably justifiably—forgotten. The Ukrainians therefore like to boast about the equipment they receive, even though this will not lead to victory, but will only prolong the conflict.

In September 2023, Annalena Baerbock, German Foreign Minister, confessed to *CNN*[600] that weapons supplied by Berlin *"are obsolete and unusable."*[601] A few days earlier, Ukraine had simply rejected 10 LEOPARD 1A5 tanks offered by Germany as unusable, while 10 tanks of the same type supplied in July suffered from the same problems.[602] The Ukrainian press reports that the LEOPARD 1A5s offered by Denmark also have the same defects.[603]

597. "France's sending AMX-10RC light tanks to Ukraine is an important decision before next Ramstein meeting", *The New Voice of Ukraine*, January 5, 2023 (https://english.nv.ua/nation/france-s-sending-amx-10rc-light-tanks-to-ukraine-is-an-important-decision-before-next-ramstein-meet-50295680.html)
598. "Ukrainian commander warns French tanks are inadequate for counteroffensive", *Euronews / AFP*, July 2, 2023 (https://www.euronews.com/2023/07/02/ukrainian-commander-warns-french-tanks-are-inadequate-for-counteroffensive)
599. David Axe, "Ukrainian Marines Almost Wasted Their First Batch Of French AMX-10RC Scout Vehicles. Now They're Getting A Second Batch", *Forbes*, November 1, 2023 (https://www.forbes.com/sites/davidaxe/2023/11/01/ukrainian-marines-almost-wasted-their-first-batch-of-french-amx-10rc-scout-vehicles-now-theyre-getting-a-second-batch/?sh=77d5525048da)
600. https://edition.cnn.com/videos/tv/2023/09/25/amanpour-annalena-baerbock-ukraine-unga.cnn
601. Dinara Khalilova, "German foreign minister acknowledges some of Berlin's weapons are outdated, inoperational", *The Kyiv Independent*, September 26, 2023 (https://kyivindependent.com/german-foreign-minister-acknowledges-issues-with-weapons-delivered-to-ukraine/)
602. Martin Fornusek, "Ukraine refused 10 Leopard 1 tanks from Germany due to poor condition", *The Kyiv Independent*, September 19, 2023 (https://kyivindependent.com/media-ukraine-refused-10-leopard-1-tanks-from-germany-due-to-poor-condition/)
603. Dinara Khalilova, "Danish Leopard 1 tanks donated to Ukraine have defects", *The Kyiv Independent*, September 22, 2022 (https://kyivindependent.com/media-danish-leopard-1-tanks-donated-to-ukraine-have-defects/)

The American magazine *Forbes* even reports that to train Ukrainian LEOPARD tank crews, Denmark even had to get tanks out from museums![604] The problem is that our narrative was that we were doing our utmost to give Ukraine modern weapons that would enable it to be victorious. But we knew, including our brilliant military "experts," that this was not true.

The LEOPARD 1A5 is a tank designed in the 1950s, equipped with a 105 mm cannon. During the Cold War, this tank was adapted to the standards of the time in terms of armament, protection and mobility. Since the 1990s, the 120 mm caliber has become the norm, with corresponding protection. With these tanks, the Ukrainians will be a generation behind.

Comparison of the Age of Russian Tanks and Tanks Supplied to Ukraine (2023)

Russie		Ukraine	
Type	Âge (ans)	Type	Âge (ans)
T-72B/BA	27	M-55S	14
T-72B3	8	M1A1 ABRAMS	38
T-72B3 obr. 2016	3	LEOPARD 1A5	36
T-80BV/U	20	LEOPARD 2A4	38
T-80BVM	4	LEOPARD 2A6	22
T-90A	20	Strv 122A	25
T-90M	3	LEOPARD 2PL	35
Âge moyen	13,4	Âge moyen	29,7

Figure 57—An urban legend, propagated by some so-called military "experts," is that the Russians have no modern equipment. In fact, Russian equipment is generally modern and high-performance.

Western equipment arrives with major logistical constraints. Some systems are obsolete in the West, and some spare parts are simply no longer manufactured, as in the case of the LEOPARD 2A4 tank. For others, such as the German GEPARD anti-aircraft tank, ammunition is difficult to obtain.

---

604. David Axe, "To Train Ukrainian Troops, the Danish Military Had To Borrow Leopard 1 Tanks From Three Museums," *Forbes*, September 8, 2023 (https://www.forbes.com/sites/davidaxe/2023/09/08/to-train-ukrainian-troops-the-danish-military-had-to-borrow-leopard-1-tanks-from-three-museums/)

However, Ukrainian logistics and its industrial base were organized around weapons of Soviet and Russian origin. The supply of thousands of Western vehicles of various origins in the space of a few months did not allow this industrial base to adapt, particularly under Russian strikes. Far from simplifying life for Ukrainians, the Westerners complicated it and even made it more vulnerable.[605]

Combat logistics can be carried out relatively easily by exchanging modules, such as the engine block or gearbox, for example. But more complex repairs can only be carried out by specialized personnel from NATO countries. This means setting up repair centers outside Ukrainian territory, which brings the "repairing" countries into Ukraine's operational logistics chain (and thus as co-belligerents).

As for STRYKER wheeled armored vehicles, leaked Ukrainian documents show that 76 percent are unusable because of frequent breakdowns!

Russian Tanks Conceptually Worse?

First of all, it should be remembered that there is no such thing as an absolute weapon, and that perfection in the field of battle tanks is illusory. Tanks are designed to meet specific needs that are difficult to replicate from one country to another. That's why, for the same type of battle tank, each user country adapts it to its own specific conditions.

One example is the number of crew members, which some "experts" seem to see as a new problem. In fact, it's a debate that's been going on for over 60 years. Most Western tanks have a 4-man crew (tank commander, loader, gunner, pilot), while Russian tanks have a 3-man crew (tank commander, gunner, pilot). A 4-man crew has certain advantages, particularly if one of the crew members has a problem. However, 3-man crews allow more electronics and weapons to be packed into the same volume, or—as is the Russian design—reduce the tank's silhouette and thus its vulnerability.

In the early 1970s, the German-American MBT-70/Kpz-70 project (from which the M1 ABRAMS and LEOPARD 2 were derived) had its own 3-man crew (all located in the turret). Future Western tank projects, such as the

---

605. David Axe, "Ukraine's 2024 Problem: How To Repair Thousands Of Western-Made Combat Vehicles," *Forbes*, September 5, 2023 (https://www.forbes.com/sites/davidaxe/2023/09/05/ukraines-2024-problem-how-to-repair-thousands-of-western-made-combat-vehicles/)

6. A Technological War

Polish PL-01, the M1 ABRAMS X or the German KF-51, as well as the new Russian T-14 ARMATA battle tank, are all designed for 3-man crews. Despite these drawbacks, this seems to be the solution of the future.

In reality, we're seeing the same phenomenon as during the Cold War. Western tanks are often more technologically advanced, but appear on the battlefield at a very slow pace. Conversely, Russian tanks are generally technologically simpler solutions, but arrive more quickly on the field. What's more, they use standardized platforms that can be easily upgraded on an ongoing basis, even in the event of war, as is the case in Ukraine.

Western Tanks Designed for a Different Operating Environment

Western tanks are designed for use in Central Europe, with irregular terrain that requires the tank to be high enough to fire while benefiting from the natural protection of the terrain. Russian tanks, designed for much flatter terrain, offer a lower silhouette, which would be a disadvantage in Central Europe, as it would require the tank to be more exposed to fire. There is therefore no universally perfect solution; only solutions that are more or less well adapted to the operational context.

Tanks Designed for Different Environments

Figure 58—Comparison of the silhouettes of a Russian T-90 tank (gray) and a German LEOPARD 2A6 tank (black). Western tanks are generally designed to fight in Central Europe, with its slightly hilly terrain. They are therefore taller, to allow greater gun travel for scrolling fire. Russian tanks are designed to operate on Russian territory, which is much flatter, and are therefore generally lower. In Ukraine, this means that Western tanks are easier targets to acquire and therefore more vulnerable than their Russian counterparts.

Vehicles that were largely obsolete for this conflict, such as the American M113 troop carrier, the French VAB or the American M2/3 BRADLEY, whose development was so chaotic that it was made into a film comedy (*The Pentagon Wars*[606]), reappeared close to the front line.

On the ground, as noted by *Forbes* magazine, Ukraine is losing its equipment.[607] The AMX-10 RC supplied by France, which are essentially reconnaissance vehicles designed in the 1970s, are unsuited to the war in Ukraine.[608] The M2/3 Bradley infantry fighting vehicles, including the M2A2 ODS-SA version, reputed to be invincible, are dropping like flies.[609] And that's not even mentioning the M113s, which are destroyed by almost any infantry weapon.

In fact, the Westerners got rid of their old equipment by giving it to the Ukrainians. One example is the MRAP MaxxPRO, designed for the Iraq war. Very high, they are easy targets for anti-tank missiles at very great distances, and are not designed for muddy terrain. Many of them got stuck in the mud, making them easy targets for the Russians.[610]

In fact, it seems that the Ukrainians prefer to engage their tanks in pairs in support of infantry platoons rather than in tank duels.[611]

The tanks supplied by the West generally come from reserves that were mothballed in the early 1990s and have deteriorated. This equipment must undergo a complete overhaul before being sent to Ukraine.

In October 2023, LEOPARD 2s were reported to be *"dropping like flies."* In fact, even obsolete equipment is still very good, provided it is in the hands of experienced crews.[612] But that's not the crucial point. In fact, the propaganda surrounding Western tank deliveries has made them a symbol and a priority for the Russian military. Here again, the Western narrative has been detrimental to the effectiveness of the Ukrainian army.

---

606. https://en.wikipedia.org/wiki/The_Pentagon_Wars
607. https://www.forbes.com/sites/davidaxe/2023/06/13/as-losses-pile-up-ukraine-needs-a-lot-more-tanks-and-fighting-vehicles/
608. https://www.forbes.com/sites/davidaxe/2023/06/14/the-ukrainian-marine-corps-amx-10rc-recon-vehicles-didnt-last-long-in-a-frontal-assault-on-russian-defenses/?sh=41f2c254103f
609. https://youtu.be/vP6NdM5hEPk
610. Jack Watling & Nick Reynolds, "Stormbreak: Fighting Through Russian Defences in Ukraine's 2023 Offensive, *RUSI*, September 2023 (https://ik.imagekit.io/po8th4g4eqj/prod/Stormbreak-Special-Report-web-final_0.pdf)
611. Michael Kofman & Rob Lee, "Perseverance and Adaptation: Ukraine's Counteroffensive at Three Months", *War On The Rocks*, September 4, 2023 (https://warontherocks.com/2023/09/perseverance-and-adaptation-ukraines-counteroffensive-at-three-months/)
612. Clément Poursain, "Les chars Leopard 2 ukrainiens tombent comme des mouches, et c'est encore à cause des drones", *korii.fr*, October 31, 2023 (https://korii.slate.fr/et-caetera/chars-leopard-2-ukraine-tombent-comme-mouches-drones-fpv-kamikazes-pertes-vehicules-blindes-guerre-russie)

Vehicles Designed for Different Uses

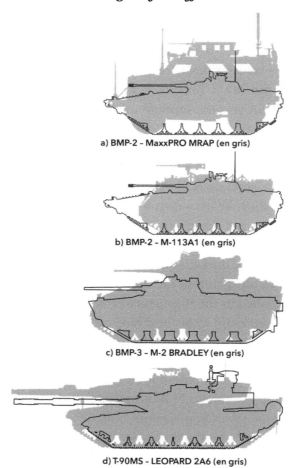

a) BMP-2 – MaxxPRO MRAP (en gris)

b) BMP-2 – M-113A1 (en gris)

c) BMP-3 – M-2 BRADLEY (en gris)

d) T-90MS – LEOPARD 2A6 (en gris)

Figure 59—Russian armored vehicles are generally more compact in shape than their Western counterparts. This is because they were designed to operate on Russia's great plains, whereas NATO vehicles are designed for the more rugged European theater of operations. What's more, vehicles like the MaxxPRO were designed for a counter-insurgency environment, where higher ground is required.

According to *Ukrainska Pravda*, fighter detachments (*okhotniki*) in surveillance zones (or coverage zones) received a bonus of 5 million rubles for the first M1 ABRAMS or LEOPARD tank destroyed, and 500,000 rubles for subsequent ones.[613] These bonuses made LEOPARDs and

---

613. https://www.pravda.com.ua/eng/news/2023/01/30/7387083/

CHALLENGERs priority targets. This is why Ukrainian commanders are reluctant to use them. The German magazine *Der Spiegel* even reported that LEOPARD 2 crews invent problems for their tanks to avoid going into battle,[614] or even abandon them before they are even engaged in combat.

When we compare the silhouettes of the vehicles supplied by the West with those used by Russian forces, we see that they are generally unsuited to conventional conflict on flat terrain. Too massive, they are quickly detectable and difficult to escape the tense trajectory of Russian tanks, which apparently manage to destroy Ukrainian tanks from a distance of 7,370 m.[615]

Delivery of LEOPARD 2 Tanks to Ukraine (Status: August 2023)

Pays fournisseur	Type	Nombre
Allemagne	LEOPARD 2A6	18
Canada	LEOPARD 2A4	8
Espagne	LEOPARD 2A4	10
Norvège	LEOPARD 2A4	8
Pologne	LEOPARD 2PL	30
Portugal	LEOPARD 2A6	3
Suède	Strv 122A	10
Total		87

Figure 60—When talking about the LEOPARDs received by Ukraine, our media avoid mentioning the problems associated with integrating systems that look similar, but have different operational capabilities and logistical requirements. Yet this is part of the difficulty the Ukrainians have in committing their forces.

A closer look at the types of tanks supplied by Western manufacturers leads to a number of conclusions. Firstly, it can be seen that the machines supplied are not of the latest generation. For example, there is a significant difference between the LEOPARD 2A6 and the LEOPARD 2A4. The A6 version is equipped with a system enabling it to be integrated into a battlefield management system (BMS), whereas the A4

614. https://www.spiegel.de/international/world/on-the-front-in-ukraine-going-into-battle-in-a-leopard-2-tank-a-9baffb53-1e5b-4a18-8ec5-173d067721af
615. https://www.bitchute.com/video/MLqVGHxfxnED/

version is not. Furthermore, their ammunition is apparently ineffective against Russian T-90s.[616]

Comparison of the Main Western Tanks Delivered to Ukraine

M1A1 ABRAMS

Année de mise en service: **1980**
Armement principal: **Rheinmetall 120 mm (âme lisse)**
Masse en ordre de combat : **57 t**
Puissance spécifique: **20.05 kW/t**
Autonomie (terrain): **150-200 km**

LEOPARD 2A4

Année de mise en service: **1985**
Armement principal: **Rheinmetall 120 mm (âme lisse)**
Masse en ordre de combat : **62 t**
Puissance spécifique: **17,7 kW/t**
Autonomie (terrain): **220 km**

LEOPARD 2A6

Année de mise en service: **2001**
Armement principal: **Rheinmetall 120 mm (âme lisse)**
Masse en ordre de combat : **62 t**
Puissance spécifique: **17,7 kW/t**
Autonomie (terrain): **550 km (route)**

Figure 61—Main battle tanks supplied to Ukraine. All are excellent machines, but their diversity makes them ill-suited to Ukraine's current needs. Moreover, although the tanks may look very similar, the main differences are in electronics, optronics and fire-control systems. These elements are critical to "making the difference" on the battlefield.

The Western Myth Challenged

LEOPARD 2 tanks have been captured by the Russians, who will be able to study them in detail.[617] To avoid this situation, the British imposed such strict conditions on the use of their CHALLENGER 2s[618] that the Ukrainians can hardly use them at all.

---

616. Thorsten Jungholt, "Bundeswehr-Kampfpanzern fehlt wirksame Munition," *Die Welt am Sonntag*, April 26, 2015 (https://www.welt.de/politik/deutschland/article140083741/Bundeswehr-Kampfpanzern-fehlt-wirksame-Munition.html)

617. https://www.thedrive.com/the-war-zone/russian-capture-of-ukrainian-leopard-tank-bradleys-seen-in-video

618. Inder Singh Bisht, "UK Planning to Avoid Challenger Tank from Falling into Russian Hands," *The Defense Post*, January 30, 2023 (https://www.thedefensepost.com/2023/01/30/uk-challenger-tank-russian/)

The British feared that the *Chobham* armor of their CHALLENGER 2 tanks might be of interest to the Russians. After lengthy discussions, the government agreed to deliver 14 of them, on condition that the Ukrainians do everything in their power to prevent the Russians from capturing them. They therefore imposed constraints on the Ukrainians. For example, the CHALLENGER 2s cannot be used in a sector where the front line threatens to be breached by the Russians.[619] As described by a British official:[620]

> *The first step is to train and work with mission planners to ensure that CHALLENGERs are not used in scenarios where they think collapse is a realistic possibility.*
>
> *The second step is to make sure, at the tactical level, that the Ukrainians are trained to recover a tank under enemy fire. They certainly don't lack courage.*
>
> *Other extreme options are being considered, including the use of private military contractors to recover damaged tanks.*

That's why Ukraine has received American M-88 armored recovery vehicles specially designed for combat towing.[621] Not only does this equipment require logistics for which Ukraine is not prepared, but each piece of equipment requires its own logistics chain, with the added requirement of preventing these weapons from falling into Russian possession.

From the very first engagements, images of CHALLENGERs in flames, hit by Russian anti-tank missiles, not only went round the world, but shattered their reputation for invincibility. But as they had already done

---

619. Inder Singh Bisht, "UK Planning to Avoid Challenger Tank from Falling into Russian Hands," *The Defense Post*, January 30, 2023 (https://www.thedefensepost.com/2023/01/30/uk-challenger-tank-russian/)

620. Jerome Starkey, "SHOCK & ROLL Army hammering out emergency plan to keep Putin's hands off top secret British armour if tanks are damaged in Ukraine", *The Sun*, January 27, 2023 (https://www.thesun.co.uk/news/21191872/army-emergency-secret-british-armour-tanks-war-ukraine/)

621. Christopher Woody & Jake Epstein, "Ukraine is getting a new heavy-duty armored vehicle to haul its damaged tanks off the battlefield, US officials say," *Business Insider*, January 25, 2023 (https://www.businessinsider.com/ukraine-getting-m88-armored-recovery-vehicles-along-with-abrams-tanks-2023-1?r=US&IR=T)

6. A Technological War

with the LEOPARD 2A4 tanks they had just received, the Ukrainians set about reinforcing the CHALLENGER's armor.[622]

This is why the M-1 ABRAMS, which officially arrived in the Ukrainian theater on September 25, 2023,[623] may well be employed more sparingly. Thus, Kyrylo Budanov, head of military intelligence, noted that these tanks are arriving against the clock, and that without considerably greater firepower, they will be little more than targets on the battlefield.[624]

Ukraine as a Testing Ground

The arrival of Western equipment on the TVD Ukraine enabled Russia to test and improve its own equipment. A case in point is the T-14 ARMATA battle tank, a few examples of which were briefly seen on the TVD Ukraine. Their small number was interpreted by our "experts" as Russia's inability to produce and deploy this new tank, prototypes of which had already been shown at military parades in May 2015 and 2016.

In reality, the T-14 is a completely new tank design which is still under development. It has only been deployed in Ukraine for evaluation purposes. Our military pseudo-experts generally forget that in the West, it usually takes 10-15 years to develop a battle tank of traditional design. This is the case for the LECLERC tank (developed from 1977 to 1992) or the LEOPARD 2 (1967-1979).

Traditionally, Russian tanks, designed for fighting on flat terrain (and not for the hilly terrain of Central Europe!), are very compact and therefore offer a smaller surface area. Yet the ARMATA's silhouette and volume are closer to its Western counterparts than to its predecessors.

622. Alia Shoaib, "Ukraine appears to be modifying the UK Challenger 2 battle tanks to protect a 'notorious' weak spot, report sa," *Business Insider*, September 30, 2023 (https://www.businessinsider.com/ukraine-modifying-challenger-2-tanks-to-address-weakness-report-2023-9?r=US&IR=T)
623. https://www.reuters.com/world/europe/abrams-tanks-arrive-ukraine-zelenskiy-2023-09-25/
624. Howard Altman, "Exclusive Interview With Ukraine's Spy Boss From His D.C. Hotel Room," *The Drive*, September 22, 2023 (https://www.thedrive.com/the-war-zone/exclusive-interview-with-ukraines-spy-boss-from-his-dc-hotel-room)

The ARMATA System

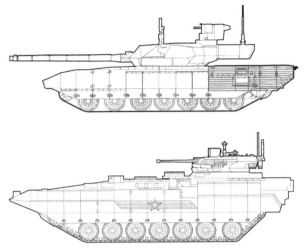

Figure 62—The ARMATA system is a family of combat vehicles, of which the T-14 (top) is the battle tank version and the T-15 (bottom) is an infantry fighting vehicle.

T-14 ARMATA Compared to its Peers

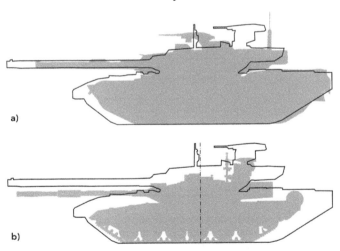

a)

b)

Figure 63—Comparison of the T-14 with the M-1 ABRAMS (a) and with the T-90 (b). For a similar volume, the T-14 weighs almost 13 t less than the American tank. On the other hand, it is considerably larger than the T-90, for an equivalent mass. This suggests lower ground pressure, and therefore greater mobility in difficult terrain.

The General Concept of the T-14 ARMATA

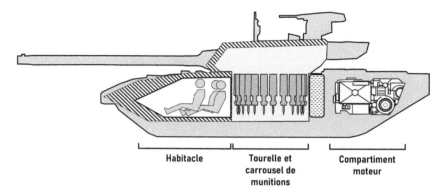

| Habitacle | Tourelle et carrousel de munitions | Compartiment moteur |

Figure 64—The T-14 was designed around crew survival.

Volumes for the American M1 ABRAMS Tank and the Russian T-14 ARMATA

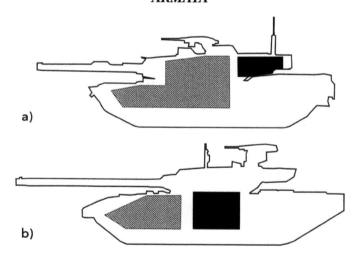

a)

b)

Figure 65—Comparison between the American M1 ABRAMS tank and the Russian T-14 ARMATA tank. As can be seen for a similar silhouette (a), the interior layout is radically different. The crew compartment (hatched) is essentially located in the turret for a conventional tank like the M1 or LEOPARD 2 (b), whereas it is completely protected in the tank body for the ARMATA (c). Similarly, the ammunition compartment (in black) is located in the turret for conventional tanks and in the middle of the tank, in the least vulnerable position, for the ARMATA. In modern western tanks (ABRAMS or LEOPARD 2), the ammunition compartment is separated from the cockpit by a bulkhead designed to protect the crew.

The special feature of the ARMATA is that it places the crew and ammunition in the most protected part of the tank, whereas traditional tanks have them in the most vulnerable part: the turret. This means that all turret functions are remotely controlled from the tank body. Should the turret be rendered unusable, crew survival would certainly be better than in a traditional tank.

Developing New Concepts

Soviet BMP-1 infantry fighting vehicles were designed for mechanized combat in defense of Soviet territory. For this reason, they were equipped with a 73 mm cannon and anti-tank missiles. In Afghanistan, the problem was different—infantry had to fight at height. For this reason, the BMP-2 was equipped with a 30 mm rapid-fire cannon, with a higher elevation than the BMP-1. As for the anti-tank missile, it became "optional."

During the war in Chechnya, Russian forces had to intervene against an adversary solidly protected by buildings. This required greater firepower, which only battle tanks had at the time. But tanks are highly vulnerable in urban environments, and tank losses were massive. The Russians therefore began to design an infantry escort vehicle for mixed terrain, sufficiently protected against direct impact and with sufficient firepower to fight targets at height and distance.

This gave rise to the BMPT concept, prototypes of which were tested on the TVD Syria. The vehicle is based on the chassis of a T-72 tank, and features a turret with remote-controlled armament. The entire crew is housed inside the vehicle body, and the turret contains only the weapons and fire-control system.

The main threat to tanks on the battlefield comes from remote-controlled drones, or drones that detect and select their own targets using artificial intelligence modules. Protection against this threat can take various forms. The simplest is a wire mesh "parasol" placed over the turret, which detonates the charge prematurely (similar to the "Schürzen" that the Germans used on their tanks during the Second World War). More sophisticated, the Russians have developed the 3VD35 munition, which disperses an aerosol that blinds optronic, thermal and electro-magnetic systems.

The BMPT-2 TERMINATOR

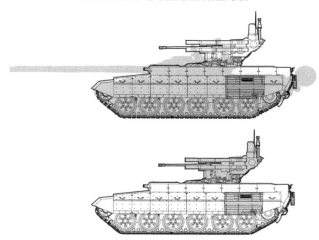

Figure 66—Top: Comparison of the silhouette of the T-72 (in gray) and the BMPT TERMINATOR. As can be seen, the BMPT is taller, as its armament has an elevation enabling it to combat targets located on top of buildings, as seen in Ukraine. Below: The crew is protected inside the vehicle body, and the turret contains only the weapons and fire control system.

Recycling Old Tanks

In February-March 2023, videos of T-54/55 and T-62 tanks being transported by rail to Russia were circulating on social networks. On the French channel *LCI*, "journalist" Jean Quatremer concluded that Russia was no longer able to produce tanks.[625] Swiss military "expert" Alexandre Vautravers laughed at these tanks, which he described as "collectors' items," and asserted that modern tanks have only a *"sample"* presence in the Russian army, as it can no longer afford to buy them.[626] In the *NZZ*, Marcus Keupp, a military "expert" from the Swiss Federal Institute of Technology in Zurich, calculated the attrition rate of the Russian army's tanks and concluded that it would simply run out of them by October 2023[627] and that this will lead to Russia's defeat.[628]

---

625. https://youtu.be/7bh1ZX0H0E4?t=460

626. https://www.club-44.ch/mediatheque/

627. Thomas Zaugg & Benedict Neff, "Deswegen sage ich: Russland wird den Krieg im Oktober verloren haben", *NZZ*, March 27, 2023 (https://www.nzz.ch/feuilleton/marcus-keupp-deswegen-sage-ich-russland-wird-den-krieg-im-oktober-verloren-haben-ld.1731488?reduced=true&mktcval=Twitter&mktcid=smsh)

628. "War in Ukraine: 'Putin's army will be defeated by October at the latest'", *La Libre*, April 4, 2023 (https://www.lalibre.be/international/europe/guerre-ukraine-russie/2023/04/04/guerre-en-ukraine-larmee-de-poutine-sera-vaincue-au-plus-tard-en-octobre-B252W43RBBGDPB5YSCBUNFDY7Y/)

It's with experts like that that we lose wars. First of all, our pseudo-experts are contradicted by *The Economist*, which claimed a month earlier that the Russians were producing 20 new tanks and upgrading 90 a month,[629] which matched the *Wall Street Journal*'s estimates.[630]

In fact, our "experts" were predicting a drastic drop in tank production because of the embargo on certain components from Europe. In fact, there was a small crisis situation in 2018 because of the unavailability of SOSNA-U rifle scopes, whose thermal vision module manufactured by Thales, in France, was embargoed.[631] But according to *Forbes* magazine, the Russians have decided to produce this component themselves in a new rifle scope designated PNM-T.[632]

Furthermore, our "experts" obviously failed to note that since August 2022, the Ukrainians have been running out of battle tanks and are starting to put a modernized version of the T-55 back on the battlefield, produced in Slovenia under the designation M-55S.[633]

For the Russians, the problem is different—they have no shortage of tanks, and their production capacity is intact, as we have seen. The arrival of refurbished T-54/55/62 tanks on the TVD Ukraine has nothing to do with the losses suffered, but with the nature of the fighting in Ukraine.

Traditionally, battle tanks are designed to fight other battle tanks. It's a duel, fought at distances ranging from 1500 to 3000 m. You need to be able to neutralize your opponent's tank on the first strike. This implies a high probability of being hit and destroyed in a single shot. This is why tanks have sophisticated fire-control systems and projectiles with a very taut trajectory, giving them a high hit probability. These are solid tungsten arrows 2-3 cm in diameter and 80-100 cm long, projected at

629. https://www.economist.com/the-economist-explains/2023/02/27/how-quickly-can-russia-rebuild-its-tank-fleet
630. Daniel Michaels & Matthew Luxmoore, "Russian Military's Next Front Line: Replacing Battlefield Equipment Destroyed in Ukraine," *The Wall Street Journal*, April 25, 2022 (https://www.wsj.com/articles/russian-militarys-next-front-line-replacing-battlefield-equipment-destroyed-in-ukraine-11650879002)
631. David Axe, "A Shortage Of Optics Was Holding Back Russian Tank Production. That Shortage May Have Ended", *Forbes*, August 7, 2023 (https://www.forbes.com/sites/davidaxe/2023/08/07/a-shortage-of-optics-was-holding-back-russian-tank-production-that-shortage-may-have-ended/)
632. https://crib-blog.blogspot.com/2021/04/a-new-sight-for-modernized-t-90.html?m=1
633. Oleg Danylov, "The M-55S tank: a deep modernization of the Soviet T-55 for the Armed Forces", *Mezha*, September 20, 2022 (https://mezha.media/en/2022/09/20/the-m-55s-tank-a-deep-modernization-of-the-soviet-t-55-for-the-armed-forces/)

6. A Technological War

speeds of 1600-1800 m/s and stabilized by fins. Designated APFSDS,[634] these non-explosive projectiles deliver enough energy on impact to pierce even the thickest armor.

The problem is that the Russians have found that there are no real tank duels in Ukraine, for two reasons:

- The Ukrainians no longer have any battle tanks.
- The Ukrainians use their tanks in pairs, to support infantry assaults.

Secondly, they noted that, as the majority of battles are infantry battles, the role of armor is less to combat opposing tanks than to support infantry assaults. The smooth-bore guns used for APFSDS projectiles are much less effective at firing explosive projectiles (HE) against protected infantry positions at long range.

It was therefore necessary to find a kind of mobile artillery that fulfilled the function of the "assault guns" (*samokhodnaya ustanovka*) of the Second World War. Thus, as London's *Royal United Services Institute (RUSI)* noted, the Russians are not using T-54/55/62 tanks to fight Ukrainian tanks, but to support infantry with explosive shells (HE) against protected or fortified Ukrainian positions, up to a distance of 4000 m.[635] These "collector item" tanks thus provide infantry with considerable firepower at low cost on the outskirts of urban areas, to fire on protected positions in buildings, for example.

The Use of Old T-54/55/62 Tanks by the Russian Army in Ukraine

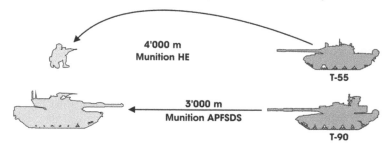

Figure 67—Although obsolete for tank duels, T-54/55s can be used as "assault guns," providing fire support for infantry with explosive shells (HE). More modern tanks (T-72, T-80 and T-90) can be reserved for use against Ukrainian battle tanks.

---

634. APFSDS: *Armour Piercing Fin-Stabilized, Discarding Sabot*

635. Jack Watling & Nick Reynolds, "Meatgrinder: Russian Tactics in the Second Year of Its Invasion of Ukraine", *Royal United Services Institute for Defence and Security Studies* (RUSI), May 19, 2023 (https://static.rusi.org/403-SR-Russian-Tactics-web-final.pdf)

The Artillery

Russian Artillery

Russia has always maintained a strong artillery system. Already during the Second World War, the famous KATYUSHA, ancestors of today's TORNADO-S, had acquired a terrible reputation among German forces.

In Afghanistan, the Russians came to understand the benefits of integrating artillery into highly responsive control systems. Fire is the fastest-moving element on the battlefield. But it needs to receive target designations and orders quickly enough. That's why the Russians are keen to network their artillery. These are the ROK/RUK systems seen above, which they were able to test in Syria.

Comparison of Large-Caliber Artillery in Ukraine

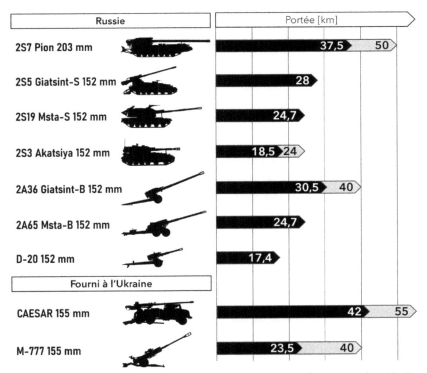

Figure 68—Comparison of ranges for large-caliber artillery pieces (152-203 mm). In black, the range with conventional ammunition; and in grey, the range with rocket-assisted propulsion (RAP) ammunition. The availability of RAP projectiles is clearly to Russia's advantage.

The Russians still acknowledge weaknesses in their driving systems, notably the lack of satellite surveillance systems and strategic UAVs, which would provide better visibility of the theater of operations.

The Russians need 2 minutes between the detection of a Ukrainian shot and the triggering of counter-battery fire.[636] However, moving an M-777 howitzer requires 2-3 minutes for a trained crew in optimal conditions.[637] In theory, this means not only that a Ukrainian artillery piece can fire only one shot in each firing position, but that it can be destroyed each time before it can even move. In addition to counter-battery fire, M-777s are particularly vulnerable to Russian LANCET 1 and 3 drones, which have reportedly destroyed or damaged some 200 artillery pieces, including many M777s, according to the Ukrainian General Staff.

In comparison, the Russians still have around 750 2S19 MSTA-Bs.

That said, even if the Russians have succeeded in adapting their counter-battery and air defense systems to combat HIMARS missiles, they do not yet have the capacity to track launchers, which can conduct a kind of *"hit and run"* and fire missiles before the Russians can act on the launcher.

The 10 to 1 superiority enjoyed by Russian artillery certainly goes a long way towards explaining the difference in casualties with Ukraine. Nevertheless, even if Russia had fired some 12 million shells by 2022 and produced 2.5 million per month, according to *RUSI*,[638] this is likely to represent a significant logistical burden. This undoubtedly explains the shift towards precision artillery, with increasing use of laser-guided projectiles such as the 152 mm KRASNOPOL-M and KRASNOPOL-M2, production of which will increase 25-fold by 2024.[639]

---

636. https://eng.mil.ru/en/special_operation/news/more.htm?id=12449739@egNews
637. http://www.military-today.com/artillery/m777.htm
638. Dr Jack Watling & Nick Reynolds, "Meatgrinder: Russian Tactics in the Second Year of Its Invasion of Ukraine", *Royal United Services Institute*, May 19, 2023 (https://rusi.org/explore-our-research/publications/special-resources/meatgrinder-russian-tactics-second-year-its-invasion-ukraine)
639. Inder Singh Bisht, "Russia to Ramp Up Upgraded Artillery Shell Production 25-Fold," *The Defense Post*, August 24, 2023 (https://www.thedefensepost.com/2023/08/24/russia-increased-artillery-shell-production/?expand_article=1)

Guided Artillery Ammunition

2K25 Краснополь-М

2K25 Krasnopol-M
Calibre: 152 mm
Portée: 26 km
Guidage: Laser

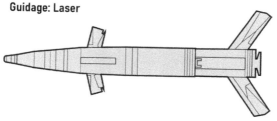

Figure 69—Russian 152 mm KRASNOPOL-M guided ammunition.

This trend can also be observed with the increasing integration of UAVs and artillery. *RUSI* notes that the Russians are *"actively improving"* their equipment, and that the complexity, density and diversity of UAVs are "worryingly" increasing.[640] Clearly a far cry from Ursula von der Leyen's "micro-processors recovered from washing machines!"

The evolution of firepower towards precision is accompanied—quite logically—by that of control systems. Extensive use of ROK/RUK, with UAVs for target detection, has created a capacity to exploit the use of precision artillery ammunition. The Russians have realized that it's not enough to have precision weapons, but that they need to be integrated into control systems that enable them to respond rapidly, and to assign the right target to the right projectile. This means networked control systems.

Westerners tend to project Ukrainian weaknesses onto Russia, because there is absolutely no evidence that the Russians are short of ammunition. A study by the *Jamestown Foundation* shows that by 2021, their annual production of artillery shells was four times greater than that of the Americans.[641]

---

640. Jack Watling & Nick Reynolds, "Stormbreak: Fighting Through Russian Defences in Ukraine's 2023 Offensive, *RUSI*, September 2023, p. 22 (https://ik.imagekit.io/po8th4g4eqj/prod/Stormbreak-Special-Report-web-final_0.pdf)
641. Hlib Parfonov, "Russia Struggles to Maintain Munition Stocks (Part Two)", *The Jamestown Foundation, Eurasia Daily Monitor*, Volume 19, No. 186 (https://jamestown.org/program/russia-struggles-to-maintain-munition-stocks-part-two/)

6. A Technological War

Russia's Annual Production of 152 mm Artillery Ammunition

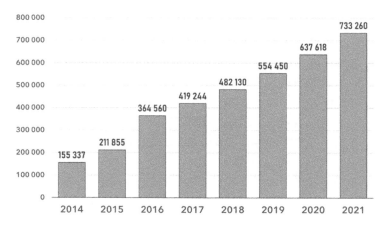

Figure 70—Estimated production of 152 mm ammunition by Russia between 2014 and 2021, according to the Jamestown Foundation, an American institution strongly opposed to Russia. These figures, which seek to demonstrate that Russia does not have the means to produce its ammunition, nevertheless manage to show that Russian capacity was more than four times greater than that of the USA.

Ukrainian Artillery

The Myth of the Ukrainian Advantage

By early June 2022, Ukraine had lost most of its military potential. Its 152 mm artillery of Soviet origin is either destroyed or out of ammunition. It is therefore dependent on Western supplies and must rely on 155 mm artillery provided by NATO countries.

In order to sustain the hope of success in its counter-offensive, our media sought to demonstrate that Ukrainian artillery is better than Russian artillery. There's no doubt that equipment like the French CAESAR or the American M-142 HIMARS is good. But comparing the capabilities of the two protagonists on the basis of the performance of their[642] artillery pieces is a little simplistic.

As we have seen, Russian artillery is remarkably powerful. While a comparison of artillery pieces such as the CAESAR with those used by Russia would seem to give Ukraine an advantage in terms of range, the

---

642. https://youtu.be/sgY0k4eZJXI

sheer quantity of this equipment must not be overlooked. Compared with the few dozen pieces supplied by the West, Russia can line up hundreds of pieces of equivalent range. What's more, it's quite rare for weapons to be fired at the limit of their maximum range.

From a technical point of view, the Western systems have weaknesses stemming from the Ukrainian context—the very high intensity of artillery exchanges, very long logistical chains and personnel unfamiliar with their use. A few weeks after their arrival in Ukraine, the CAESARs proved incapable of keeping up with the high rates of fire imposed by the Russians.

The problem is not so much the quality of the weapons as the context in which they are used. The weapons supplied by the West are not designed for this type of warfare. Since the 1990s, the "great" Western armies have been equipped to wage colonial-style wars against adversaries with little in the way of heavy equipment. Ukraine is therefore caught between two different conceptions of artillery: the traditional Russian conception, based on massive fire, and a more tactical Western conception, based on *sniping artillery*. The idea is to reduce the number of shots needed to destroy a target, and therefore the logistical burden.

Designed to be used more sparingly than their Russian counterparts, Western systems are also more fragile, making them extremely difficult to maintain. Without adequate logistics, these systems have to be taken back to neighboring Poland to be overhauled in workshops close to the border. In the Spanish newspaper *El Pais*, a Ukrainian soldier noted that the accuracy of the 155 mm M-109 PALADIN howitzers supplied by the USA fell from 7 m to 70 m because of wear on the tubes.[643] In contrast, the Russians can replace worn tubes directly on the battlefield, which is considerably simpler and prevents the weapons from being used to the point of failure. As early as 2022, France was planning to deploy a workshop close to the Ukrainian border for repairs, as reported by the Ukrainian military website *Militarnyi*.[644] As for the American M777 howitzers, according to Brigadier General Volodymyr Karpenko, head

643. Cristian Segura, "En el asedio al frente ucranio de Avdiivka: 'Los rusos están más preparados para la guerra y para morir'", *El Pais*, November 13, 2023 (https://elpais.com/internacional/2023-11-13/en-el-asedio-al-frente-ucranio-de-avdiivka-los-rusos-estan-mas-preparados-para-la-guerra-y-para-morir.html)
644. https://mil.in.ua/en/news/the-ministry-of-defense-wants-to-create-a-service-center-for-caesar-self-propelled-howitzers/

of logistics for the Ukrainian land forces, they are subject to frequent malfunctions and 30 percent have to be systematically withdrawn for repair after being engaged.[645]

The Ukrainians received a large number of artillery systems from all over Europe. But the most talked-about were the 190 M-777 155 mm howitzers supplied by Australia, Canada and the USA, and the 49 CAESAR systems (30 in 6x6 version from France and 19 in 8x8 from Denmark). Presented as "game-changers," they were celebrated by our media. But this also posed a problem for Ukraine. It now had to deal with Western 105 and 155 mm ammunition, in addition to the "traditional" 122 and 152 mm ammunition of Soviet origin.

Western equipment is undeniably good. But its diversity makes it very difficult to integrate into a compact, coherent control system. EXCALIBUR 155 mm precision ammunition[646] only achieves its full effectiveness with integrated control systems. What's more, their range is only really superior with[647] *power-assisted* ammunition, which the Ukrainians have only received in small quantities. On the Russian side, on the other hand, these munitions seem to be widely available. Thus, the advantage that the performance of a weapon system can bring is counterbalanced by the small number of systems available. Moreover, as the American magazine *Forbes* reveals, their guidance system can be jammed by systems such as the POLYE-21.[648]

Contrary to what the official narrative claims, the West—despite their best efforts—did not give Ukraine superiority in terms of artillery.

The Problem of Ammunition

But by the end of 2022, Ukraine was running out of ammunition and the West was struggling to supply it.

---

645. Stew Magnuson, "Ukraine to U.S. Defense Industry: We Need Long-Range, Precision Weapons," *National Defense Magazine*, June 5, 2022 (https://www.nationaldefensemagazine.org/articles/2022/6/15/ukraine-to-us-defense-industry-we-need-long-range-precision-weapons)

646. "Ukraine to receive new precision-guided 155-mm artillery rounds from USA," *Ukrainian Military Center*, July 9, 2022 (https://mil.in.ua/en/news/ukraine-to-receive-new-precision-guided-155-mm-artillery-rounds-from-usa/)

647. RAP: Rocket Assisted Projectile.

648. https://www.forbes.com/sites/vikrammittal/2023/11/19/new-technologies-could-help-re-solve-ukraines-artillery-challenges/?sh=89747f638d68

In Afghanistan, the United States fired around 300 rounds a day.[649] Logically enough, their production capacity is adapted to this consumption. At the end of 2022, Christine Wormuth, Secretary of the U.S. Army, stated that it amounted to 500 shells per day, or around 14,000 155 mm shells per month.[650]

According to the *New York Times*, Ukrainian forces fire 2000 to 4000 shells a day.[651] The *Kyiv Post* even put the figure at 6000 to 7000 shells a day.[652] According to classified documents "leaked" in April 2023, the Ukrainians are firing an average of 3500 155 mm shells a day.[653] In other words, the Ukrainians fire in 2 to 7 days the equivalent of the American monthly production. The Ukrainians admit that their consumption of artillery shells exceeds US production capacity.[654]

In reality, it's the West that's struggling to find the ammunition to keep Ukraine on track. On March 20, 2023, the EU decided to finance 1 million shells over 12 months,[655] for which it had managed to mobilize 2 billion euros, one of which would be used to compensate countries that had dipped into their stocks to help Ukraine. The remaining billion was to be used to finance shell production. The problem is that this production capacity does not really exist in the EU, and we will have to turn to an external source: Turkey.[656] Predictably, this triggered the ire of France, Greece and Cyprus, who dug in their heels. France wanted the money to stay within the EU, while Greece and Cyprus refused to finance Turkey's defense

649. Steven Erlanger & Lara Jakes, "U.S. and NATO Scramble to Arm Ukraine and Refill Their Own Arsenals," *The New York Times*, November 26, 2022 (updated November 29, 2022) (https://www.nytimes.com/2022/11/26/world/europe/nato-weapons-shortage-ukraine.html)

650. "Ukraine's artillery shell expenditure outstrips US production", *The New Voice of Ukraine*, December 24, 2022 (https://english.nv.ua/nation/ukraine-s-artillery-shell-expenditure-outstrips-us-production-war-news-50293094.html)

651. John Ismay & Thomas Gibbons-Neff, "Artillery Is Breaking in Ukraine. It's Becoming a Problem for the Pentagon", *The New York Times*, November 25, 2022 (https://www.nytimes.com/2022/11/25/us/ukraine-artillery-breakdown.html)

652. https://www.kyivpost.com/post/51

653. Russia/Ukraine Joint Staff J3/4/5 Daily Update (D+369) (February 28, 2023) (SECRET/NO FORN)

654. Oleksandr Syrskyi, "Ukraine's artillery shell expenditure outstrips US production", *The New Voice of Ukraine*, December 23, 2022 (https://english.nv.ua/nation/ukraine-s-artillery-shell-expenditure-outstrips-us-production-war-news-50293094.html)

655. "Боррель уточнив деталі 'історичного рішення' ЄС про закупівлю боєприпасів Україні", Європейська правда, March 20, 2023 (https://www.eurointegration.com.ua/news/2023/03/20/7158323/)

656. "EU cannot agree on how to spend €1 billion on ammunition for Ukraine", *Ukraïnska Pravda*, April 5, 2023 (https://www.pravda.com.ua/eng/news/2023/04/5/7396641/)

industry.[657] Finally, in October, *Bloomberg* and *Ukrainska Pravda reported* that the EU had only been able to meet 30 percent of its objectives.[658]

Western production capacity for 155 mm artillery ammunition is unable to keep pace with Russia. Today, total Western production capacity per month is equivalent to what Russia fires in a single day. The explosives produced in the USA are no longer sufficient to keep pace with artillery shell production, so we have to buy them from Japan.[659] The West is at the end of its tether.

Western Artillery in Ukraine

Obusier M-777 (USA)
Calibre: 155 mm
Masse: 4200 kg
Cadence de tir: 2-4 cp/min
Portée maximale: 21-30 km

Canon automoteur CAESAR
Calibre: 155 mm
Masse: 29 t (8x8)
Cadence de tir: 6 cp/min
Portée maximale: 40-55 km

Figure 71—The West has supplied a whole range of artillery to Ukraine, much of it from old stocks in Eastern European countries. The most high-profile were the American M-777 and the French CAESAR. Their main quality is that they can be deployed rapidly and are accurate enough not to require group firing. The ranges indicated here can be extended by the use of guided ammunition.

657. "Cyprus worried EU's Ukraine ammunition grant could end up in Turkish arms industry", *In-Cyprus*, April 7, 2023 (https://in-cyprus.philenews.com/news/local/cyprus-worried-eus-ukraine-ammunition-grant-could-end-up-in-turkish-arms-industry/)
658. "EU falls behind schedule to provide Ukraine with shells", *Ukrainska Pravda*, October 26, 2023 (https://www.pravda.com.ua/eng/news/2023/10/26/7425770/)
659. https://euromaidanpress.com/2023/06/02/japan-will-supply-tnt-explosives-to-the-us-to-increase-the-155mm-artillery-shells-production/

Our media have presented them as "wonder weapons," but in reality, these weapons do not have the desired effect, because they cannot be engaged in the way they were designed.[660] Despite enormous assistance from Western countries, these weapons cannot be integrated into battlefield management systems and are therefore used inefficiently.

Multiple Rocket Launchers

With the destruction of Ukraine's artillery potential in the spring of 2022, the West was forced to supply multiple missile launchers. Their performance is not radically different from that of their Russian equivalents.

The effectiveness of the M-142 HIMARS comes mainly from its 227 mm GMLRS missiles, which have a non-ballistic trajectory, making them difficult to combat. The Americans have only supplied Ukraine with M-31 rockets with a range of 70 km.[661] Presented as "wonder weapons," they have not radically changed the situation. The Russians quickly learned to decentralize their ammunition depots. What's more, it would appear that a system was sold by Ukrainians to the Russians, enabling them to adapt the software of their anti-aircraft systems to respond effectively against these missiles. As noted by the *Ukrainian Military Pages* website in July 2023:[662]

> *The Russians seem to have a fairly good level of intelligence (ISR) on the battlefield. They did not need to deploy operational reserves to repel the Ukrainian attacks. There is also evidence that the effectiveness of the HIMARS strikes was reduced by effective Russian countermeasures.*

---

660. Alex Hollings & Sandboxx News, "Ukraine's troops have been highly effective with the M777 howitzer, but US troops can turn it into a 'giant sniper rifle'", *Business Insider*, September 18, 2022 (https://www.businessinsider.com/us-targeting-system-makes-m777-howitzer-highly-accurate-2022-9)

661. Howard Altman, "Are There Enough Guided Rockets For HIMARS To Keep Up With Ukraine War Demand?", *The War Zone*, July 27, 2022 (https://www.thedrive.com/the-war-zone/are-there-enough-guided-rockets-for-himars-to-keep-up-with-ukraine-war-demand)

662. https://www.ukrmilitary.com/2023/07/analysis-of-ukraines-counteroffensive-from-the-front.html

6. A Technological War

The M-142 HIMARS (like the M-270 MLRS) can also fire the GBU-39 GLSDB flying bomb, using a thruster.[663] The radars of Russia's S-300 and S-400 anti-aircraft systems can detect a HIMARS missile at a range of 80 km, and a GLSDB at 30-40 km, given its smaller size. On the other hand, the speed of a GLSDB is three times lower than that of a HIMARS missile, making it easier to intercept. On March 28, 2023, the first GBU-39 bomb launched on Russian territory was intercepted by air defense.

American classified documents "leaked" in April 2023 indicate that at the end of February the Ukrainians were firing just 17 missiles a day. As Ukraine had then received 38[664] systems, we can conclude that a majority of M-142s or a large part of the ammunition had been destroyed, which would confirm the statements made by the Russian General Staff.

GBU-39 Ground-Launched Small Diameter Bomb (GLSDB)

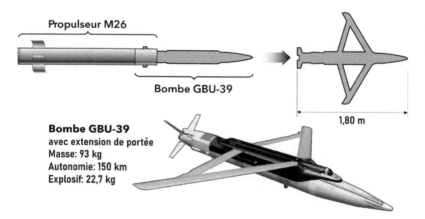

Figure 72—The GLSDB from Boeing and Saab is still under development. However, according to the Russian authorities, it has already been deployed in the Ukrainian theater in March 2023. The M26 booster pushes the bomb 32 km, after which it detaches and glides to a total distance of 150 km.

663. David Axe, "Ukraine's New Rocket-Boosted Glide-Bombs Can Turn Around and Hit Targets on The Backs of Hills, 90 Miles Away," *Forbes,* February 3, 2023 (https://www.forbes.com/sites/davidaxe/2023/02/03/ukraines-new-rocket-boosted-glide-bombs-can-turn-around-and-hit-targets-on-the-backs-of-hills-90-miles-away/)
664. "U.S. Security Cooperation with Ukraine—Fact Sheet," *Bureau of Political-Military Affairs, State Department,* April 19, 2023 (https://www.state.gov/u-s-security-cooperation-with-ukraine/)

The M-142 and M-270 are perhaps more sophisticated than the equivalent Russian systems. Like the rest of the Western armaments produced since the late 1990s, they were designed for projected operations. They are modular and can be adapted to different operational requirements, but they are very expensive and complex to produce. Today, Lockheed-Martin produces 10,000 GMLRS missiles a year. With further investment, it will reach 14,000 units by 2024, but will not double production until 2026[665]. In fact, the United States simply does not have the material and personnel capacity to increase production and meet the needs of both Ukraine and its other customers.

Equivalent Russian systems are more numerous, but simpler and therefore less costly to produce. As a result, Russia can easily increase its production and play on a greater density of systems deployed in the field.

Multiple Rocket Launchers

M142 HIMARS
Missiles: 6
Portée: 90 km

9K515 «Торнадо-С»
9K515 «TORNADO-S»
Missiles: 12
Portée: 120 km

Figure 73—The American M142 HIMARS and the Russian 9K515 TORNADO-S. Although the American system has been celebrated in our media, the TORNADO-S is the latest Russian multiple rocket launcher and has superior characteristics. It fires 300 mm missiles with a nominal range of 120 km, but has been tested with a range of 200 km.

---

665. Sam Skove, "Why It's Hard to Double GMLRS Production," *Defense One*, March 30, 2023 (https://www.defenseone.com/business/2023/03/why-its-hard-double-gmlrs-production/384646/)

The Russian equivalent of the M-142 HIMARS is the 9K515 TORNADO-S. Like its predecessors, the BM-21, BM-24 and BM-27, it can fire ammunition in bursts. However, its missiles can also be programmed independently, and can reach separate targets thanks to the GLONASS navigation system. It takes just a few minutes to set up the battery, and the missiles are fired by remote control, to avoid exposing the crews to counter-battery fire. TORNADO-S missiles change position every seven minutes to reduce this risk.

Counter-Battery Systems

The conflict in Ukraine sometimes seems to have become an artillery battle.

The Russians have developed particularly effective counter-battery fire capabilities, and are able to destroy Western equipment almost as soon as it arrives in the theater of operations.

Counter-Battery Systems

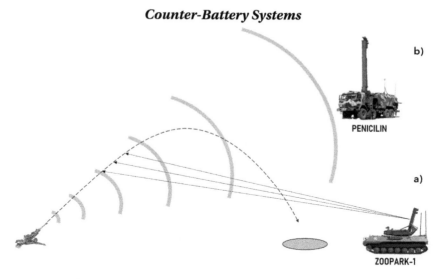

Figure 74—The Russians use a variety of counter-battery systems. The aim is to detect the location of the enemy's fire, in order to respond as quickly as possible. A distinction is made between active systems, such as the ZOOPARK-1 artillery radar (a), which detects a projectile and tracks it by calculating its trajectory, and passive systems, which detect fire using a combination of thermal and acoustic signals, such as the PENICILIN system (b). The former are easy to detect, while the latter are undetectable by the enemy.

The Russians need two minutes between the detection of a Ukrainian shot and the transmission of its coordinates to trigger counter-battery fire.[666] On the Ukrainian side, moving an American 155 mm M777 howitzer requires two to three minutes for a trained crew in optimal conditions.[667] In theory, this means not only that a Ukrainian artillery piece can fire only one shot in each firing position, but that it can be destroyed each time before it can even move.

This ability to instantly fire counter-battery fire has considerably limited the capabilities of Ukrainian artillery. With the gradual advance of Russian troops, Ukrainian artillery is almost no longer able to reach the city of Donetsk. What the West was unable to stop through negotiation, the Russians have achieved by force.

Cluster Munitions

On July 7, 2023, Volodymyr Zelensky's advisor Mykhailo Podolyak tweeted:[668]

> ...the number of weapons counts. So, weapons, more weapons and always weapons, including cluster munitions.

Cluster munitions are literally containers projected by artillery shells or rockets, which open above their target to deliver several dozen small explosive devices. These submunitions can be anti-personnel, anti-tank or a combination of both. They can explode above or on contact with the target, acting as small grenades or shaped charges capable of piercing the upper armor of armored vehicles. They can also be anti-personnel mines, such as the infamous Soviet PFM-1.

---

666. https://eng.mil.ru/en/special_operation/news/more.htm?id=12449739@egNews
667. http://www.military-today.com/artillery/m777.htm
668. https://twitter.com/Podolyak_M/status/1677253680880336897

The PFM-1 Anti-Personnel Mine

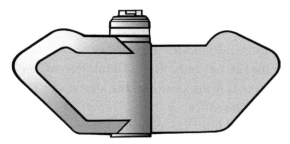

Figure 75—The PFM-1 mine is the Soviet copy of the American BLU-43 DRAGONTOOTH mine, widely disseminated in Laos during the Vietnam War. Used by the Soviet army in Afghanistan, it was the source of a mine clearance manual I wrote for Ahmed Shah Massoud during the war against the Soviets, and of my commitment to the fight against anti-personnel mines.

The PFM-1 mine contains only 37 grams of explosive, enough to seriously injure one person. Both Russia and Ukraine have them. Unlike Russia, Ukraine is a party to the Ottawa Convention on the prohibition of anti-personnel weapons. On July 27, 2022, thousands of these mines were scattered in a populated area of Donetsk, in the Russian zone.[669] But not *a single* Western country or media outlet expressed its disapproval.

This type of ammunition was developed as early as the late 1970s, as part of the ASSAULT BREAKER project, which aimed to develop technologies to combat Soviet *Operational Maneuver Groups* (OMGs) in the depths of the NATO system.

At a time when artillery fire was time-consuming to fine-tune, sub-munition projectiles made it possible to deploy a large quantity of explosive devices very quickly against a moving adversary. Proportionately speaking, it was the equivalent of the machine gun against infantry in the First World War.

The problem with these weapons is that submunitions are produced at low cost and leave a very large number of duds that can explode at any time. According to *RTS*, the dud rate is as high as 2 percent;[670] but

---

669. David Hambling, "Who Dropped Thousands Of Antipersonnel 'Butterfly' Mines On Donetsk? (UPDATE: UK Blames Russia)," *Forbes*, August 4, 2022 (https://www.forbes.com/sites/davidhambling/2022/08/04/who-dropped-thousands-of-antipersonnel-butterfly-mines-on-donetsk/)
670. https://www.rts.ch/play/tv/redirect/detail/14160304

in Israel, the rate is actually as high as 40 percent.[671] This is why they are considered a danger to civilian populations, and why 111 countries have signed up to the *Convention on Cluster Munitions* (CCM).[672] Neither Russia, Ukraine nor the United States are parties to the CCM.

That said, these are weapons designed to enable a defender to fight an attacker, not an attacker to attack a defender. This means that these are weapons that are used in areas that you don't want to occupy quickly. This is why Ukraine used them in 2014 and 2022 in the regions of Donetsk,[673] Kharkov[674] and Izyum,[675] but accused Russia—without providing proof).

Cluster Bombs

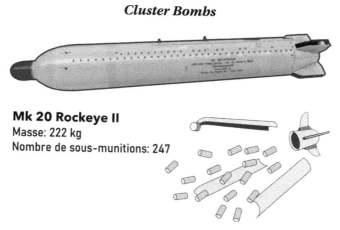

Mk 20 Rockeye II
Masse: 222 kg
Nombre de sous-munitions: 247

Figure 76—The Mk 20 Rockeye II cluster bomb is one of the types requested by Ukraine from the USA.

Russia had two reasons for not using such weapons at the start of the SMO. First, the SMO was undertaken for the benefit of a population it seeks to protect. Second, it is in the position of the attacker who would put its own troops at risk.

---

671. http://www.haaretz.com/news/idf-commander-we-fired-more-than-a-million-cluster-bombs-in-lebanon-1.197099
672. https://www.clusterconvention.org/
673. Andrew Roth, "Ukraine Used Cluster Bombs, Evidence Indicates," *The New York Times*, October 20, 2014 (https://www.nytimes.com/2014/10/21/world/ukraine-used-cluster-bombs-report-charges.html)
674. Thomas Gibbons-Neff & John Ismay, "To Push Back Russians, Ukrainians Hit a Village With Cluster Munitions," *The New York Times*, April 20, 2022 (https://www.nytimes.com/2022/04/18/world/europe/ukraine-forces-cluster-munitions.html)
675. https://theintercept.com/2023/07/05/ukraine-cluster-bombs-biden/

But these conditions changed in 2023—while the USA gives Ukraine cluster munitions for its counter-offensive, the Russians are the defenders.[676] The pretext was that these munitions would be good for dislodging the Russians from their trenches or for clearing mines. In reality, this decision was due to the fact that the Americans no longer have any alternatives, as they have run out of ammunition.[677] But its effect is to legitimize the use of this same type of ammunition to break up the Ukrainian counter-offensive. This is why the Americans specified on July 13:[678]

> *The Ukrainian government has given us written assurances on the responsible use of these weapons, notably that they will not use them in urban areas populated by civilians.*

But, as usual, the Ukrainian government does not keep its word: one of the first use of these new munitions was—on a civilian area, and it killed a journalist.[679]

Thus, not only was this delivery by the Americans literally "against the clock," but it legitimized Russia in committing such weapons to combat the Ukrainian counter-offensive. One sometimes gets the impression that the West is doing everything in its power to ensure that the Ukrainians fail.

Long-Range Missiles

In the summer of 2023, as its counter-offensive stalled, Ukraine began attacking long-range targets on Russian territory or in the Black Sea, and requested long-range missiles. Until then, the West had refused to supply

676. Eric Schmitt, "Ukraine starts using American-made cluster munitions in its counteroffensive, U.S. officials say," *The New York Times*, July 20, 2023 (https://www.nytimes.com/2023/07/20/world/europe/ukraine-cluster-munitions.html)

677. Mark F. Cancian, "Cluster Munitions: What Are They, and Why Is the United States Sending Them to Ukraine?", *Center for Strategic and International Studies*, July 10, 2023 (https://www.csis.org/analysis/cluster-munitions-what-are-they-and-why-united-states-sending-them-ukraine)

678. "Cluster munitions can disperse several hundred small explosive charges", *Euronews / AFP*, July 8, 2023 (https://fr.euronews.com/2023/07/08/armes-a-sous-munitions-en-ukraine-quel-danger-pour-les-civils)

679. "War reporter's death prompts Russian outrage over Ukraine's alleged use of cluster bombs," *Reuters*, July 22, 2023 (https://www.reuters.com/world/russian-journalist-killed-three-wounded-near-ukraine-frontline-2023-07-22/)

weapons that could reach Russian territory, as Crimea was not considered Russian territory. The British supplied STORM SHADOW cruise missiles. France followed suit with the supply of SCALP missiles, which are similar to the British STORM SHADOW, although some sources claim a slightly longer range.

American missile launchers can launch several "small" *Guided Multiple Launch Rocket Systems* (GMLRS) missiles or a larger *Army Tactical Missile System* (ATACMS) missile. The ATACMS has a range of 300 km and an explosive charge of 200 kg, and could enable Ukraine to reach targets on Russian territory, with a high destructive capacity. However, the Americans were initially reluctant to supply Ukraine with ATACMS missiles, fearing an escalation.[680] In fact, according to the *Wall Street Journal*[681] and *The Hill*,[682] the HIMARS delivered to Ukraine have even been secretly modified so that they cannot fire long-range missiles capable of reaching Russian territory.

Long-Range Missiles

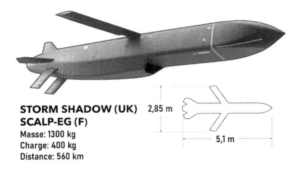

STORM SHADOW (UK) 2,85 m
SCALP-EG (F)
Masse: 1300 kg
Charge: 400 kg   5,1 m
Distance: 560 km

Figure 77—The British STORM SHADOW missiles and their French version SCALP-EG are produced by the German firm MBDA. Their range allows them to reach Russian territory. This shows that the Europeans are not seeking to resolve the conflict but to prolong it, which they can afford to do because they are not paying the price in blood.

680. John Ismay, "The Missile Ukraine Wants Is One the U.S. Says It Doesn't Need," *The New York Times*, October 6, 2023 (https://www.nytimes.com/2022/10/06/us/ukraine-war-missile.html)

681. Michael R. Gordon & Gordon Lubold, "U.S. Altered Himars Rocket Launchers to Keep Ukraine From Firing Missiles Into Russia," *The Wall Street Journal*, December 5, 2022 (https://www.wsj.com/articles/u-s-altered-himars-rocket-launchers-to-keep-ukraine-from-firing-missiles-into-russia-11670214338)

682. Brad Dress, "US secretly modified HIMARS for Ukraine to prevent Kyiv from shooting long-range missiles into Russia," *The Hill*, December 5, 2022 (https://thehill.com/policy/defense/3762042-us-secretly-modified-himars-for-ukraine-to-prevent-kyiv-from-shooting-long-range-missiles-into-russia/)

On September 22, 2023, Ukraine struck the Black Sea Fleet headquarters in Sevastopol with cruise missiles. The Ukrainians launched a first volley of decoys.

Figure 78—Range of the SCALP-EG cruise missile supplied to Ukraine by France. The USA did not want to supply long-range missiles to prevent the war spreading to Russian territory. The French have no such scruples. This is exactly why Africans no longer want them on their territories.

Guided Bombs

Since December 2022, the USA has been supplying Ukraine with JDAM-ER guided bombs, which have a range of 80 km and use a GPS signal to steer towards their target. But secret documents "leaked" in April 2023 indicate that they malfunction and are susceptible to Russian jamming.[683] Moreover, these bombs hover at a relatively modest speed

---

683. Ellie Cook, "Russian Glider Bombs Spark New Air Defence Woes for Ukraine," *Newsweek*, April 13, 2023 (https://www.newsweek.com/russia-glider-bombs-ukraine-air-defense-jdams-1794155)

and are vulnerable to Russian PANTSIR-SM anti-aircraft systems, which can hit very small targets such as drones or HIMARS missiles.

For their part, the Russians have developed a number of systems equivalent to those delivered to Ukraine. These include the GROM, which is the equivalent of the JDAM-ER.

Russian Glider Bomb GROM

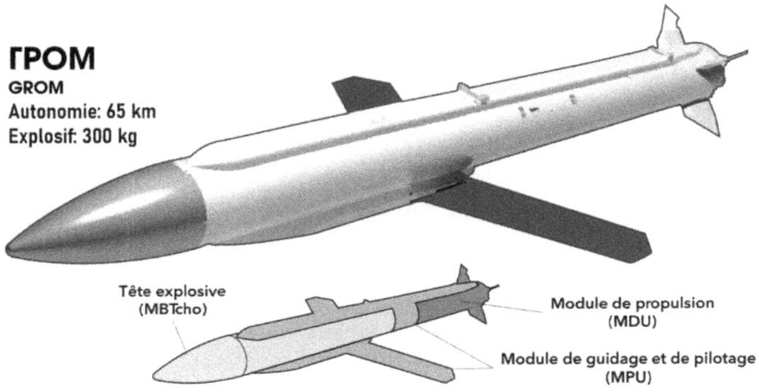

ГРОМ
GROM
Autonomie: 65 km
Explosif: 300 kg

Tête explosive
(MBTcho)

Module de propulsion
(MDU)

Module de guidage et de pilotage
(MPU)

Figure 79—The GROM bomb is the Russian equivalent of the American JDAM-ER bomb. It is a gravity bomb with retractable wings and a guidance mechanism.

The Russians have found that when it comes to fighting ground targets aviation bombs are more effective (and probably less costly) than missiles. To this end, they have developed a whole line of "intelligent" glider bombs, which can autonomously direct themselves at their target.

This explains the apparent reduction in Russian artillery fire in the Donbass since March 2023. The Russian air force is much freer to engage its FAB-500[684] bombs and, above all, its UPAB-500B and UPAB-1500B glide bombs. Introduced for the first time in 2019, the UPAB-1500B can be engaged from a distance of 40 km, out of range of Ukrainian tactical anti-aircraft systems. Improved after the Mariupol fighting to combat protected targets, these bombs were used at Avdiivka and Bakhmut, and are widely engaged to combat the Ukrainian counter-offensive in the Zaporizhzhia sector.

---

684. Andrew Stanton, "Ukraine Issues Warning About New Modified Russian FAB-500 Aerial Bombs," *Newsweek*, April 8, 2023 (https://www.newsweek.com/ukraine-issues-warning-about-new-modified-russian-fab-500-aerial-bombs-1793298)

6. A Technological War

UPAB-500B and UPAB-1500B Guided Bombs

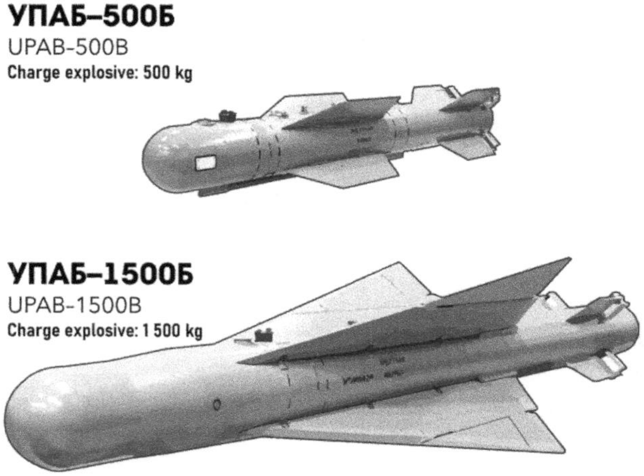

УПАБ–500Б
UPAB-500B
Charge explosive: 500 kg

УПАБ–1500Б
UPAB-1500B
Charge explosive: 1 500 kg

Figure 80—Designed to combat heavily protected infantry, the UPAB-500B and UPAB-1500B bombs can be dropped beyond the range of Ukrainian anti-aircraft defenses, autonomously and precisely targeting their targets.

Air Defense

The purpose of Russia's armed forces is to defend its national soil. This explains why, for the past thirty years, while Western countries have been looking for solutions to their wars overseas, the Russians have been concentrating their efforts on the needs of their national defense. This is true of their air defense, which is one of the most advanced in the world, even if it remains imperfect.

One problem is the proliferation of drones that function as mini cruise missiles, flying at low altitude and only detected by radar at a late stage. This explains the success of the Ukrainian strikes against Sevastopol in September 2023.

The A-50U MAINSTAY, stationed at the Machulishchy military airfield near Minsk, is an essential part of Russia's air warfare system. But apparently, the Russians didn't have enough of them to monitor the entire airspace, especially around Crimea. A new version of the A-50U has been optimized to detect "new types of aircraft,"—obviously drones.

A-50 MAINSTAY

Figure 81—A-50 MAINSTAY early warning aircraft. This is the Russian equivalent of the AWACS used by NATO countries in Romania and Poland. It can simultaneously detect and process some 150 targets up to a range of 650 km in the air and 300 km on the ground.

Drones and Robotic Weapons

The use of drones in combat is not new. The first prototype "aerial torpedo" dates back to 1918 (Kettering Bug), and the use of small recreational drones to observe or throw grenades has been widely seen in Syria, for example. The use of drones on the battlefield is not new, either. Right from the start of the SMO, Ukraine engaged Turkish-origin BAYRAKTAR drones, which appeared to be a "wonder weapon," but which did not escape Russia's formidable anti-aircraft defense and were quickly forgotten by our media.

The novelty lies rather in the distribution of their use across all levels of engagement, from lower tactical to strategic. Reconnaissance and/or air strike capabilities are now available at all these levels, significantly increasing insecurity on the battlefield. The testimonies of Ukrainian soldiers who are tired of this constant threat overhead bear witness to the anxiety-inducing nature of these aircraft.

From the very start of the Russian offensive, drones made their presence felt on the battlefield. The Ukrainians were quick to see their potential for enhancing their tactical reconnaissance capabilities. But their use quickly evolved. Inspired by techniques developed in Syria by the Islamic State, small commercial drones, home-made to carry a small explosive charge or grenade, provide strike capability down to the lowest tactical level. Small and relatively inexpensive, they can be engaged in swarms, which is one of the technological revelations of this conflict.

279

Widely used by Ukrainian troops at the start of the conflict, their use has been reduced by supply difficulties (partly due to the sanctions on such equipment applied to China by the United States) and above all by the rapid proliferation of Russian jamming systems.

Main Drones in the Ukrainian Theater

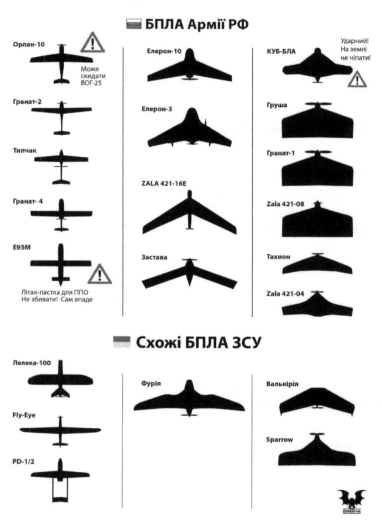

Figure 82—The proliferation of drones in the theater of operations has necessitated the distribution of an identification card for Ukrainian servicemen. [Source: https://en.defence-ua. com/weapon_and_tech/how_to_distinguish_between_russian_and_ukrainian_uavs_in_the_ sky_photo_comparison-3180.html, June 2022]

Use by Ukrainians

Aerial Drones

The conflict in Ukraine has seen the immoderate use of drones for every possible purpose. The novelty lies not so much in the use made of drones, nor even in the inventiveness that accompanies them, but in their sheer number.

The Ukrainians use three categories of drones:

- TB-2 BAYRAKTAR and equivalent operational UAVs supplied by the West. They can carry out observation and surveillance missions, or attack missions. Highly effective in the hands of Azerbaijan against Armenia, which had only rudimentary anti-aircraft defenses, TB-2s were quickly eliminated by Russian anti-aircraft defenses.
- Drones designed or modified for long-range strikes. These are the Soviet-era Tu-141 STRIZH operational drones, designed for aerial reconnaissance, but converted by Ukraine into makeshift cruise missiles. One of these aircraft crashed in Croatia in March 2022, and others have been fired against Russian territory. For the same role, but of a more modern design, the Ukrainians obtained the GPS-guided BOBER, which distinguished itself in attacks on the city of Moscow.
- Commercial drones, modified in Ukraine for reconnaissance or combat missions. They are guided using FPV (*First Person View)* goggles, which enable them to observe their surroundings prior to an attack, or to direct artillery fire. Among these are the lightweight DJI MAVIC 3 drones, converted to carry a grenade or small explosive charge. Nothing new here, this is what the Islamic State did on an almost industrial scale in Syria in 2015 to 2016.

Drones are widely used at senior tactical and operative levels to monitor the battlefield and coordinate actions on the ground. But the UK's *RUSI* has found that rapid changes in leadership have meant that operational commanders don't always trust the reports of subordinate commanders, and want to have visual control of the action themselves. This has led to a decline in the use of smoke ammunition to cover the movement of infantrymen towards the Russian lines. Commanders preferred their own view of the battlefield to smoke cover to conceal their troops' movements. The use of smoke ammunition accounts for only 3 percent of fire missions.[685]

While the flexibility and ingenuity of the Ukrainians is to be commended, the military effectiveness of these systems remains highly uncertain. For example, to detect the DJI MAVIC 3, the Russians use the DJI AeroScope platform, which can detect communications between the drone and the control unit in real time and thus neutralize them.[686]

The Ukrainian BOBER Drone

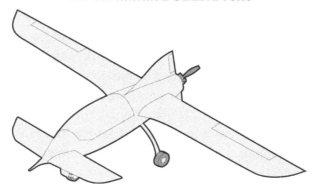

Figure 83—The BOBER drone is a local development. Very simple in design, it is designed to carry an explosive charge. Drones of this type were used to carry out attacks on Moscow in July-August 2023.

Naval Drones

A semi-new development is the use of naval drones against Russian ships and installations in the Black Sea. In fact, while the technological solution is new, the concept is not. Even during the Second World War, the Italian *Incursori* of the famous *Xa Flottiglia MAS* unit used manned torpedoes against British ships. The idea was taken up by others, the most recent example being the *Sea Black Tigers* unit of the *Liberation Tigers of Tamil Eelam* (LTTE).

Wrongly called "suicide boats," they were explosive devices, but their crews didn't sacrifice themselves: they jumped from the boat before

685. Jack Watling & Nick Reynolds, "Stormbreak: Fighting Through Russian Defences in Ukraine's 2023 Offensive", *RUSI*, September 2023, p. 22 (https://ik.imagekit.io/po8th4g4eqj/prod/Stormbreak-Special-Report-web-final_0.pdf)
686. https://www.bbc.com/news/world-europe-62090791

impact. The main difference with the Ukrainian devices is that today, GPS has replaced the pilot.

The Ukrainians have developed a whole range of these drones, some of which have become famous for their attacks, notably the attack on the Kerch Bridge in July 2023. This attack was carried out by an autonomous SEA BABY-type device carrying 860 kg of explosives, against one of the bridge's pillars.

August 24, 2023, President Volodymyr Zelensky formalized the creation of the *Ukrainian Navy's 345th Independent Brigade of Unmanned Naval Systems* (*385-ï окремої бригади морських безпілотних комплексів Військово-Морських сил* ЗСУ).[687] As Vasyl Malyuk, its leader, pointed out, this is a project steered by the *Security Service of Ukraine* (SBU),[688] which is also behind the development of the drones and its production in secret underground workshops.[689]

Drone naval «Микола-3»

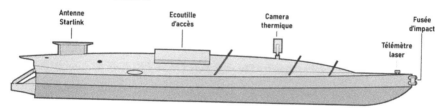

Drone naval «SEA BABY»

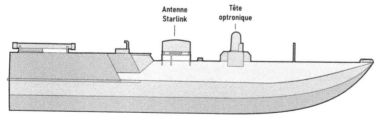

Figure 84—Ukrainian naval drones. Top: The Mykola-3, used in attacks on the port of Sevastopol, Crimea, and on Russian vessels monitoring the TURKSTREAM gas pipeline in the Black Sea, after the NORD STREAM incident in September 2022. Below: The SEA BABY engaged against the Kerch Bridge during the attack on July 17, 2023.

687. https://novynarnia.com/2023/08/24/385-brygada/
688. https://youtu.be/UoHACsoQBxM
689. https://ssu.gov.ua/novyny/morski-drony-unikalna-rozrobka-sbu-vasyl-maliuk-rozkryv-detali-rezonansnykh-spetsoperatsii-sluzhby-bezpeky-ukrainy

Underwater drones seem to be a new weapon in the Ukrainian arsenal. The TOLOKA 1K-150, introduced in April 2023, is one of the developments proposed by young Ukrainian engineers.[690] It's a kind of guided torpedo whose performance is not yet known. Nevertheless, we may well ask what is the use of these weapons, which cannot have a decisive effect on the course of the conflict?

The Suicide Boat Concept

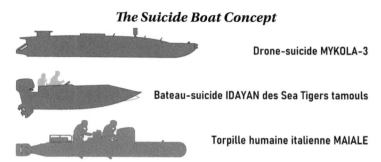

Figure 85—Comparison of the size of Ukrainian MYKOLA-3 drones, Tamil Tiger IDAYAN suicide boats and World War II Italian Incursori MAIALEs.

Ukrainian Drone TOLOKA 1K-150

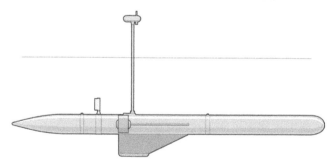

Figure 86—The TOLOKA 1K-150 underwater drone, designed by the Ukrainian BRAVE1 group, is 1.5 m long. It operates just below the surface of the sea, thanks to its mast-mounted camera, and can cover distances of up to 1200 km.

---

690. "Ukraine's 'Toloka' Underwater Maritime Drone Is a New 'Headache' for russians in the Black Sea," *Defense Express*, April 27, 2023 (https://en.defence-ua.com/weapon_and_tech/ukraines_toloka_underwater_maritime_drone_is_a_new_headache_for_russians_in_the_black_sea-6531.html)

Use by Russians

Aerial Drones

A particularly important development is the systematic use of "small," inexpensive drones, which can be deployed *en masse* to saturate enemy defenses, and which function as mini cruise missiles. These are known as "suicide drones." In particular, the Russians use the Iranian-built GERAN-2 and the Russian-built LANCET-3.

GERAN-2 originates from Iran, where it is produced under the name SHAHEED-136. Its adoption by Russia has fueled the narrative of a *"tattered industry"*[691] and given a new pretext for applying new sanctions on Iran.[692] In reality, the GERAN-2 is produced under license in Russia, where it has undergone a number of modifications—its navigation system has been hardened and works with the Russian GLONASS satellite system. Its latest versions are derived from the SHAHED-131, but are powered by a turbojet, making them quieter.[693] It is therefore highly resistant to electronic countermeasures, and is difficult to detect by radar, thanks to its fiberglass hull. It is a kind of "mini cruise missile," which can be used in large quantities on poorly protected targets up to a distance of 2500 km.

Made largely from commercial components, the GERAN-2 is extremely economical, and its destruction requires very costly means, making it an attrition weapon par excellence. Its production cost is estimated at around $20,000, whereas the Ukrainians have to fight them with S-300 missiles of Soviet origin, whose unit cost is estimated at $130,000, or American NASAMS missiles at $500,000 each. A Ukrainian pilot even sacrificed a MiG-29 to shoot down a GERAN-2.[694]

---

691. https://youtu.be/R9n3s3CyZ9o
692. "Switzerland sanctions supply of Iranian drones to Russia," *Swiss Government*, November 2, 2022 (https://www.admin.ch/gov/fr/accueil/documentation/communiques.msg-id-91102.html); Daphne Psaledakis & Arshad Mohammed, "New U.S. sanctions target supply of Iranian drones to Russia," *Reuters*, January 6, 2023 (https://www.reuters.com/business/aerospace-defense/us-targets-supply-of-iranian-drones-russia-new-sanctions-2023-01-06/)
693. Maksim Panasovskyi, "The Shahed-136 kamikaze drone got a turbojet engine instead of the piston-powered MD550 and now it won't buzz like a scooter," *gadget.com*, September 27, 2023 (https://gagadget.com/en/uav/323974-the-shahed-136-kamikaze-drone-got-a-turbojet-engine-instead-of-the-piston-powered-md550-and-now-it-wont-buzz-like-a-s/)
694. Girish Linganna, "Historic! A kamikaze drone downs a fighter aircraft, Ukrainian MiG-29 crashes trying to shoot an Iranian Shahed-136 drone", *Frontier India*, October 13, 2022 (https://frontierindia.com/historic-a-kamikaze-drone-downs-a-fighter-aircraft-ukrainian-mig-29-crashes-trying-to-shoot-an-iranian-shahed-136-drone/)

Drone GERAN-2

Герань-2
Geran-2
Vitesse: 185 km/h
Autonomie: 2000–2500 km
Charge explosive: 30–50 kg

Figure 87—The GERAN-2 (Geranium) drone is the Russian version of the SHAHEED-136 produced by Iran. Its guidance system has been modified to make it invulnerable to electronic countermeasures.

The LANCET-3 is the latest iteration in a line of drones that appeared in 2018, and was tested in Syria as early as 2020. The LANCET-1, its predecessor, had a mass of 5 kg and an explosive charge of 1 kg, which was sufficient against troops, but not against "hard" targets such as armored vehicles.

Its cruciform canopy makes it highly maneuverable, and it can be used for reconnaissance, surveillance or strike missions. It can monitor an area, search, find and select a target, and destroy it autonomously. Its "brain" is of commercial origin[695] and uses NVIDIA's JETSON TX2, a graphics processing unit (GPU) used on game consoles. It's a very fast artificial intelligence device, and one of the most energy-efficient on the market. It is abundantly available on the market and can be easily obtained at a modest price. It can carry out pre-programmed or autonomous missions thanks to on-board artificial intelligence.

It's a versatile, intelligent weapon, particularly effective against moving targets. Its modular warhead and multiple guidance systems enable it to be used in a variety of configurations—as an FPV (*First Person View*) drone guided by vision goggles, for laser target marking and image transmission for *Battle Damage Assessment* (BDA). It uses an encrypted

---

695. David Hambling, "Russia's Smartest Weapon May Have An American Brain," *Forbes*, March 28, 2023 (https://www.forbes.com/sites/davidhambling/2023/03/28/does-russias-smartest-weapon-have-an-american-brain/)

transmission module and is resistant to electronic countermeasures. In October 2023, the American magazine *Forbes* reported that Russian FPV drones are increasingly equipped with thermal cameras, making them particularly devastating.[696]

RUSI noted the interest of this type of weapon, its versatility and the speed with which the Russians are able to operationalize product improvements. Such is its effectiveness that the Russian manufacturer, ZALA, claims to have increased production by a factor of 50.

In its "suicide" configuration, it can be networked with other UAVs for target detection. It has thus become an important component of the ROK/RUK. Apparently, according to the Ukrainian General Staff, Russian LANCET 1 and 3 drones have destroyed or damaged some 200 artillery pieces, mainly M777s. Silent, small and difficult to detect, they are particularly effective at night.

Since November 2023, Russian forces have been receiving the SCALPEL, which has broadly the same characteristics and performance as the LANCET-3, with a cruciform wing, but is less expensive to produce.[697]

Russian Suicide Drone LANCET-3

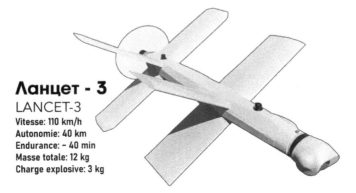

Ланцет - 3
LANCET-3
Vitesse: 110 km/h
Autonomie: 40 km
Endurance: ~ 40 min
Masse totale: 12 kg
Charge explosive: 3 kg

Figure 88—One of the most effective drones of the Ukraine campaign. Produced by Kalashnikov, the Lancet is a low-cost suicide drone that can provide information, before slamming into its target and destroying it with its 5-6 kg of explosives.

696. David Hambling, "Russia Adds Thermal Imaging To FPV Kamikaze Drones," *Forbes*, October 11, 2023 (https://www.forbes.com/sites/davidhambling/2023/10/11/russia-adds-thermal-imaging-to-fpv-kamikaze-drones/)
697. https://bulgarianmilitary.com/amp/2023/11/18/russian-army-received-15-scalpel-uavs-this-is-the-new-lancet/

The KUB-BLA[698] is an attack drone developed by the Russian firm ZALA. First presented in 2019, it was tested on the TVD Syria. With its small dimensions (1.210 m x 0.95 m x 0.165 m) and powered by a small electric motor that makes it very quiet, it is very discreet. It is equipped with software, enabling it to work in swarms with other similar devices.

It uses Artificial Intelligence Visual Identification (AIVI) technology for real-time target recognition and classification. It entered service in August 2022.

KUB-BLA Suicide Drone

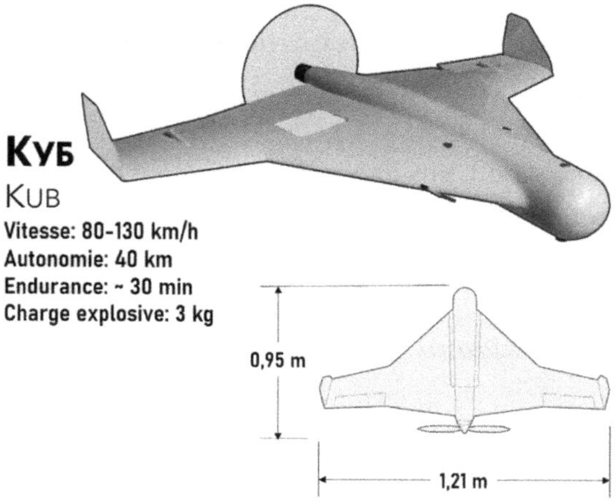

КУБ
KUB
Vitesse: 80-130 km/h
Autonomie: 40 km
Endurance: ~ 30 min
Charge explosive: 3 kg

0,95 m

1,21 m

Figure 89—The KUB-BLA drone is used for the Reconnaissance-Rapidization Complex (RUK).

That said, we are seeing a resurgence in the use of small commercial FPV drones at the tactical level. Lightweight, inexpensive, easy to use and highly flexible, they offer a solution that is just as effective as, but more efficient than, the LANCET-3.

On the operational front, the Russians have introduced the ORION drone, which is comparable to the American MQ-1 PREDATOR or MQ-9 REAPER. With an endurance of 24 hours and a range of 1400 km, it can carry out aerial surveillance and reconnaissance missions. It can launch 50 kg gravity bombs (KAB-50 and FAB-50) or guided bombs (UPAB-50) in

---

698. BLA: Беспилотный Летательный Аппарат or "Unmanned flying machine".

combined reconnaissance and strike missions. It has been deployed on the Ukraine TVD since at least March 2022. However, its 7500 m ceiling makes it vulnerable to Ukrainian S-300 anti-aircraft missiles.

The ORION Drone

ОРИОН
ORION
Vitesse max: 200 km/h
Autonomie: 1400 km
Endurance: 24 h
Masse totale: 1150 kg
Charge utile: 250 kg

Figure 90—The ORION UAV is one of Russia's latest operational UAVs. It was tested in Syria in 2019 and has been deployed on the Ukraine TVD since March 2022.

The latest development in Russian drones is the appearance of "transparent" drones. Made of non-metallic materials, they are invisible to radar waves and can therefore largely evade detection systems.[699]

Robotic Weapons

The idea of robotizing the battlefield goes back a long way. The Russians have several projects, some of which are operational, such as the PLATFORMA-M and NEREKHTA systems, which are used for surveillance missions at certain Russian bases. These systems were tested in Syria, alongside combat systems such as the URAN-9.[700]

The latter was tested during the ZAPAD-2021 maneuvers and implemented in the Donbass, but more to validate software solutions and the networking of these weapons within the ROK/RUK framework than for operational commitments.

---

699. Boyko Nikolov, "Russia unveils foamplast FPV UAV with max-radio transparency," *Bulgarian Military*, October 15, 2023 (https://bulgarianmilitary.com/amp/2023/10/15/russia-unveils-foamplast-fpv-uav-with-max-radio-transparency/)
700. https://youtu.be/d0qG64xao6s

The results of these engagements are not known, but apparently the idea of a combat vehicle that can act autonomously on the battlefield is still a distant prospect.

The URAN-9 Robotic Combat Vehicle

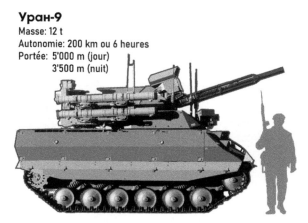

Уран-9
Masse: 12 t
Autonomie: 200 km ou 6 heures
Portée: 5'000 m (jour)
3'500 m (nuit)

Figure 91—The URAN-9 is a combat system capable of autonomous anti-tank actions. The use of such systems is beginning to form part of a doctrinal corpus built up from experience in Ukraine.

The PLATFORMA-M and NEREKHTA machines are simpler systems capable of carrying out programmed actions in a simpler context than the URAN-9.

Платформа-М
Platforma-M
Masse: 800 kg
Charge utile: 300 kg
Endurance: 10 h

Нерехта
Nerekhta
Masse: 1 t
Charge utile: 500 kg
Autonomie: 20 km

Figure 92—PLATFORMA-M and NEREKHTA are systems capable of carrying anti-tank systems.

7. Information Warfare

Cyberwarfare

Cyberwarfare is generally considered to be the war of the 21st century, and as early as 2021, our "experts" were predicting a Russian cyberwar against Ukraine, which would neutralize the economy or even destroy it to such an extent that military intervention would not be necessary. But a study by the *Center for Security Studies* (CSS) at the Swiss Federal Institute of Technology in Zurich has brought us back to reality. Entitled "Farewell to Cyberwar: Ukraine's Reality Check", it shows that cyberwar played only a minor role in the Ukrainian conflict:[701]

> *We contend that experts who believe that cyberwar is a reality continue to underestimate the practical limits of cyberattacks (also known as cyber-effects operations) and, consequently, to overestimate their strategic significance—despite ample empirical evidence showing that cyberattacks are not very effective in carrying out coercive and destructive actions.*

CSS concludes:

> *Overall, there is no evidence that Russian-sponsored operations or, indeed, all operations related to this conflict (including those of the various hacktivist "armies" that have emerged) have had a*

---

701. Lennart Maschmeyer & Myriam Dunn Cavelty, "Goodbye Cyberwar: Ukraine as Reality Check", *ETH Zurich—Center for Security Studies*, May 2023 (https://css.ethz.ch/content/dam/ethz/special-interest/gess/cis/center-for-securities-studies/pdfs/PP10-3_2022-EN.pdf)

measurable impact on the course of the conflict, provided obser-
vable tactical advantages—such as sabotaging military equipment
or disrupting enemy communications in combat—or generated a
strategic advantage.

The real problem with warfare in cyberspace is that we are unable to determine with any certainty the origin of attacks. So-called cybersecurity firms are materially unable to do so, and their opinions on our media come almost exclusively from third-party sources. Clearly, these forms are usually part of the problem.

In December 2016, *CrowdStrike* claimed that the hacker entity FANCY BEAR (allegedly associated with Russian military intelligence) had penetrated the Ukrainian artillery fire control network to implant malware, causing major losses.[702] The information was hardly much, but some mainstream media, more guided by Russophobia than by a concern for honest reporting, such as *Swiss Radio-Television*[703] or the newspaper *Libération*,[704] relayed it all the same. As it turned out, the information was totally false.[705]

In fact, since the early 2000s, what we call "cyberwar" has been more a war between "*trolls*" than a means of destabilizing countries, as Hollywood likes to predict. Our media like to amplify cyber events and take advantage of the fact that their perpetrators are difficult to identify, to attribute them to Russia. What's more, while it's certain that attacks are coming from Russia, that doesn't mean the government is involved.

For example, when Estonia was attacked on April 27, 2007, our media immediately accused Russia,[706] claiming that even if the government wasn't directly involved, the action couldn't have taken place without the Kremlin's approval. Some evened raised the specter of NATO Article 5.[707]

---

702. "Use of FANCY BEAR android malware in tracking of Ukrainian field artillery units," *CrowdStrike*, December 22, 2016.

703. "Russian Democratic Party hackers targeted Ukrainian military," *rts.ch*, December 22, 2016.

704. Amaelle Guiton, "Les Russes donnent des sueurs froides sur le front numérique", *liberation.fr*, December 30, 2016

705. The old report was published on December 22, 2016, and the corrected report on March 23, 2017 (Oleksiy Kuzmenko & Pete Cobus, "Cyber Firm Rewrites Part of Disputed Russian Hacking Report," *Voice of America [VOA]*, March 24, 2017).

706. Sylviane Pasquier, "Estonie: la main de Moscou", *L'Express*, May 16, 2007; Kertu Ruus, "Cyber War I: Estonia Attacked from Russia", *European Affairs*, volume IX, Nr 1-2, Winter/Spring, 2008; Benoît Vitkine, "L'Estonie, première cybervictime de Moscou", *Le Monde*, March 14, 2017

707. James A. Lewis, "The 'Korean' Cyber Attacks and Their Implications for Cyber Conflict", *Center for Strategic and International Studies*, October 2009

Radio-Télévision Suisse unreservedly denounced the responsibility of the Russian government.[708] However, of the 3700 IP addresses that triggered the attack, 2900 were Russian, 200 Ukrainian, 130 Latvian and 95 German.[709] According to Mikko Hyppönen, an expert with the Finnish IT security firm *F-Secure*:

> *In practice, there is only one IP address that leads to a government computer. It is, of course, possible that an attack was also launched from there, but the person involved could be anyone from the janitor of a government department to the very top.*[710]

Thus, we don't know. There is no evidence of Russian official involvement[711] and everything points to civil society action. Moreover, neither the European Commission nor NATO[712] confirm Russia's involvement. In the end, only one culprit was identified: a young Russian activist from the "Nachi" youth movement—a Russian patriotic organization that fights against *"oligarchs, anti-Semites, Nazis and liberals"*—who acted independently. It's clear that our journalists always haul up the usual suspects.

A study by the University of Adelaide (Australia) on cyber activity in early 2022 in Ukraine shows that the Ukrainians were clearly prepared for an intensification of military operations. As early as February 24, cyber activity by Ukrainian bots was immediately at a very high level, and it was only a few days later that Russian cyber activity began.[713] This indicates that Ukrainian networks had already prepared their cyber-attacks before February 24, and were ready to unleash them very quickly on that day.

708. "Russian-Estonian cyberwar triggered", *rts.ch*, August 6, 2007 (updated January 31, 2013)

709. Santeri Taskinen, Mari Nikkarinen and Shankar Lal, "The Estonian Cyberwar," April 21, 2017 (https://mycourses.aalto.fi/pluginfile.php/457047/mod_folder/content/0/Kyber%20Crystal.pdf?forcedownload=1)

710. Nate Anderson, "Massive DDoS attacks target Estonia; Russia accused", *arstechnica.com*, May 14, 2007

711. Sean Michael Kerner, "Estonia Under Russian Cyber Attack?", *internetnews.com*, May 18, 2007

712. Les cyberattaques—repères chronologiques (https://www.nato.int/docu/review/2013/Cyber/timeline/FR/index.htm) (accessed October 1, 2019)

713. Bridget Smart, Joshua Watt, Sara Benedetti, Lewis Mitchell & Matthew Roughan, "#IStandWithPutin versus #IStandWithUkraine: The interaction of bots and humans in discussion of the Russia/Ukraine war," *The University of Adelaide*, August 15, 2022 (updated August 20, 2022) (https://arxiv.org/abs/2208.07038)

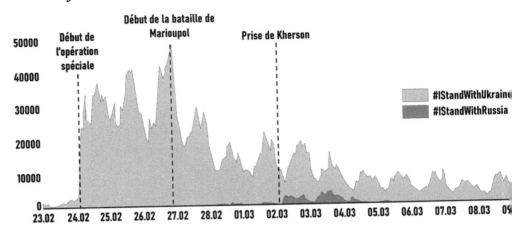

Cyber Activities at the Start of Russia's Special Military Operation

Figure 93—Source: Bridget Smart, Joshua Watt, Sara Benedetti, Lewis Mitchell & Matthew Roughan, "#IStandWithPutin versus #IStandWithUkraine: The interaction of bots and humans in discussion of the Russia/Ukraine war," The University of Adelaide, 15 august 2022 (https://arxiv.org/abs/2208.07038)

As we saw with *TV5 MONDE*, with regard to what they call the "hybrid war," our media and our experts embroider from events that nobody is in a position to know precisely, as a responsibility of Russia. Technically speaking, they are engaging in conspiracism, i.e., the creation of a narrative from elements that are often real, linked by an arbitrary logic, for a presumed malicious purpose.

According to CSS, the vast majority of known events attributed to Russia (most often without any evidence) have had only limited and localized effects, with little or no impact on the conflict. It's a safe bet that a large proportion of these events attributed to cyberwarfare are actually problems with installation software management (as we've seen in the USA, where electricity supply companies hide their management problems behind so-called Russian attacks).

Here again, the official narrative about these Russian attacks, by artificially amplifying their impact for propaganda purposes, contributes to minimizing Russia's capabilities in this area.

Propaganda and Misinformation

Propaganda and disinformation are two terms used indiscriminately by our media. Yet they represent distinct activities.

Propaganda is literally "that which is worth spreading." It usually focuses on our own positive points (as in a commercial) or on the opponent's weak points. But the information itself is (usually) not false. This was the dominant strategy of the USSR during the Cold War. The same philosophy applies today.

Disinformation is the deliberate misleading of an adversary by means of false information. Unlike our media, which see disinformation as an end in itself, the Russians understand it as a means to an end, as part of a given strategy.

Generally speaking, in a conflict, the defender emphasizes propaganda to highlight his defensive capabilities for the purpose of deterrence. The attacker, on the other hand, emphasizes disinformation to conceal his intentions. Yet, in this conflict, literally the opposite is true.

Propaganda and Disinformation from the West and Ukraine

The official narrative is at the heart of Western and Ukrainian strategy. Its aim is not only to instill confidence in the Ukrainian population, but also and above all to destabilize the Russian population and its support for its government. But its primary function is to maintain the material support of the West.

In early November 2023, Oleksei Arestovitch, Zelensky's former advisor, confessed to lying to his fellow citizens in order to promote a narrative:[714]

> *A large part of the responsibility for creating the average citizen's faith in our swift and magnificent victory lies with me personally. Back then, I created this illusion so we could survive. Today, I'm destroying it so we can survive.*

There's nothing really new here, as much of the information I've already given in my previous books has now been confirmed. As far as Ukraine is

---

714. https://twitter.com/djuric_zlatko/status/1720923003742036309

concerned, it was no doubt fair game to spread disinformation, but it was both immoral and criminal to amplify these lies in our own countries and thus consciously encourage the development of a form of Russophobia. There is no doubt that our journalists should be held to account in court for deliberately inciting hatred.

With a certain childishness, the West waged a war of narratives, thinking that this would be enough to bring about political change in Russia. Particularly in Europe, this has resulted in the total exclusion of information that deviates from the Western narrative. Those who venture off the beaten track are accused of "relaying the Kremlin's discourse" and therefore of being "agents of Vladimir Putin's networks." Even when relaying information from Ukraine that contradicts the Western narrative.

What the Russians say is invariably described as "propaganda," whereas when the Ukrainians give false information, it's more likely to be described as "storytelling."[715]

On numerous occasions, our media has immediately accused the Russians of deliberately targeting civilians in Ukraine, when the pattern of incidents shows that they could have been caused by Ukrainian anti-aircraft missiles having missed their target. Thus, instead of showing some restraint, our media sought to add fuel to the fire.

On September 6, 2023, a missile hit a market in Konstantinovka. *RTS* immediately reported that the Swiss government "*condemned the Russian raid,*" pointing out that "*attacks on civilians are prohibited by international humanitarian law.*"[716] Yet less than a fortnight later, the *New York Times* reported:[717]

> *But the evidence gathered and analyzed by the New York Times, including missile fragments, satellite images, witness accounts and social networking posts, strongly suggests that the catastrophic strike was the result of an errant Ukrainian air defense missile fired by a BUK system.*

715. https://youtu.be/bEv4-IJsl9k?t=270
716. https://www.rts.ch/info/monde/14293014-les-dix-premiers-chars-leopard-1-arrivent-en-ukraine.html#timeline-anchor-1694033722199
717. https://www.nytimes.com/2023/09/18/world/europe/ukraine-missile-kostiantynivka-market.html

This is one of many examples of our media and governments deliberately accusing Russia before waiting for more substantial information. In fact, this is a common practice in the West, allowing false accusations to be made without the need for justification. It's a problem I identified when I was in charge of the doctrine for the protection of civilians at the United Nations. I noticed that this practice tends to encourage crimes against civilians (action under a false banner). Here we have an example of governments and the media encouraging crimes against civilians.

As the American magazine *Newsweek* noted in an article entitled, "What Ukraine learned from the Islamic State"[718] (the title changed a few hours later to "How Ukraine is applying the Islamic State scenario"), Ukraine adopted the Islamic State's techniques for communicating:[719]

> *For Ukraine, the motive behind creating polished videos of battlefield scenes is to attract enough viewers worldwide to ensure that the country's struggle against Russia is not forgotten, and to prove that the West's financial and military support for Kiev has not been, and will not be, in vain.*

The target of Western communication is the Russian population. It's not really about supporting the Ukrainian people (indeed, none of our mainstream media has taken issue with the fact that Kiev has been shooting at its own population since 2014), but about provoking a political crisis in Russia. That's why our media don't inform us about the situation as it is, but as we'd like Russians to perceive it.

For example, on April 13, 2023, *RTS*[720] refered to Russia's *"degraded conventional military capabilities."* Yet less than two weeks later, General Christopher Cavoli, Commander-in-Chief of *US European Command* (SACEUR), asserted before a US Congressional committee that "Russia's

718. Isabel van Brugen, "What Ukraine Learned From ISIS," *Newsweek*, May 31, 2023 (https://web.archive.org/web/20230531073952/https://www.newsweek.com/what-ukraine-russia-war-learned-isis-surveillance-drones-strikes-videos-1803199)

719. Isabel van Brugen, "How Ukraine Followed the ISIS Playbook," *Newsweek*, May 31, 2023 (https://www.newsweek.com/what-ukraine-russia-war-learned-isis-surveillance-drones-strikes-videos-1803199)

720. https://www.rts.ch/info/monde/13940354-des-documents-classifies-decrivent-des-luttes-intestines-dans-les-cercles-de-pouvoir-russes.html

7. Information Warfare

air, naval, space, digital and strategic capabilities have not been significantly degraded during this war."[721]

So not only are our media lying to us, they're lying to the Ukrainians themselves. For example, Ukrainian POWs explained that they had been bolstered to go into battle by being told that the *"Russians were weak, ill-equipped and tired."*[722] As a sergeant from the 32nd Ukrainian Independent Mechanized Brigade put it: *"Everything is different from what you read in the daily press releases and in the media."*[723]

Of all the European media I consulted for my books, virtually none even attempted to provide objective information on the conflict. It is accepted that a conflict always has an emotional component, and that a degree of subjectivity is inevitable. As I have shown in my books, the media that have systematically downplayed Russia's capabilities are: *RTBF* (Belgium), *LCI, TF1, BFM TV* and *France 5* (France), *RTS, SRF, Le Temps, Neue Zürcher Zeitung* and the tabloid *Blick* (Switzerland). Our media live off the blood of others. It is therefore logical—if not acceptable—that they seek to inflame tensions rather than calm them.

More worrying are their military experts (Nicolas Gosset in Belgium; Pierre Servent, Michel Yakovlev, Michel Goya and Dominique Trinquand in France; Alexandre Vautravers in Switzerland). They represent a form of unenlightened despotism, where analysis is carried out without knowledge, and judgment is made without knowledge. Military personnel must have a realistic image of their adversary, not of an imaginary entity. Anyone who believes his opponent is weak is afraid of him.

This discourse leads to a number of paradoxes. For example, while Russia is said to have been defeated by Ukraine, is on its last legs, and *"its industry is in tatters,"*[724] Russia is seen as the main threat to Europe.[725] As we shall see in this book, the Ukrainian media, under pressure and heavily controlled, nevertheless manage to give us more objective information than the Western

721. https://armedservices.house.gov/sites/republicans.armedservices.house.gov/files/04.26.23 Cavoli Statement v2.pdf

722. https://twitter.com/MyLordBebo/status/1672196798297899010

723. Igor Kossov, "New brigade bears heavy brunt of Russia's onslaught in Kharkiv Oblast", *The Kyiv Independent*, September 1, 2023 (https://kyivindependent.com/new-brigade-bears-heavy-brunt-of-russias-onslaught-in-kharkiv-oblast/)

724. https://youtu.be/R9n3s3CyZ9o

725. Stefan Grobe, "Russia is the 'main and most direct threat to Alliance security'", *Euronews*, July 1, 2022 (https://fr.euronews.com/my-europe/2022/07/01/la-russie-est-la-menace-principale-et-la-plus-directe-pour-la-securite-de-lalliance)

media. This underscores the importance of narrative in Western communication, and explains why this narrative must be framed by strict censorship.

In October 2023, on the Ukrainian media outlet *Strana*, a battalion commander declared:[726]

> *At the start of the war, all Ukrainians were ready to defend the country and [there were] many volunteers. But after the withdrawal of Russian troops from the Kiev area, the situation changed.*
> *Immediately afterwards, I noticed that the media were broadcasting theories to the effect that we were fighting with bums, that the Russian army didn't know how to fight, that in principle, victory would come in a week or two, a month at the most. That in spring, then summer, then autumn, then winter, without specifying which, we would enter Crimea. That the war was in principle victorious. So, people were put in a hot bath. We had a break in our vision of reality. But in Russia, that wasn't the case. The Russians began to understand that the war would not be easy for them. They understood that they would have to fight for a long time.*

As I said in my previous books, the turning point was the misinterpretation by Ukraine and the West about the Russian withdrawal from Kiev. It was a *withdrawal*, not a *retreat*—but our media, eager to see a Russian defeat, fed a narrative that today weighs heavily on Ukraine. In addition to weakening the will to defend inside Ukraine, the effect of Western disinformation is to stimulate hatred. In mid-October 2023, *RTS* accused Russia of trying to influence the parliamentary elections, based on a video posted on X (Twitter) showing a black man urinating on a sidewalk. The accusation is said to be justified by the fact that "*the accounts that broadcast this video are most likely fake and 'Russian-influenced.'*" In other words, we know absolutely nothing about it, and the expression "Russian influence" in no way implies that the Russian government is involved, not to mention that this kind of video is proliferating on social networks. Here, *RTS* was creating a conspiracy out of thin air, based on suspicions and elements that we don't know to be related. It's technically and literally conspiracism, aimed

---

726. https://strana.news/news/449257-kombat-vooruzhjonnykh-sil-schitaet-ch-to-stratehicheski-ukraina-proihryvaet-rossii.html

both at stirring up hatred against Russia and at influencing a democratic process in Switzerland. To the media's credit, a confidential Swiss intelligence report is said to be the basis of this fantastic accusation.[727]

Russian Propaganda and Disinformation

The West's main weakness in today's complex world is that it perceives situations only through its own prejudices. Since the Cold War, everything that comes from Russia (and the USSR before that) is presented in the West as propaganda or disinformation (which are synonyms in the minds of our journalists). The problem with analyzing Russian propaganda and disinformation is that it doesn't reach us. Westerners have put up so many barriers and censors that we're reduced to believing they exist, without being able to prove it.

In the midst of the Ukrainian conflict, Swiss journalist Jean-Philippe Schaller found no better example to convince us that Russia is disinforming us than the KGB's INFEKTION operation, dating back to—1985.[728] Confessed to by the Soviets themselves in August 1987,[729] this operation aimed to attribute the creation of the AIDS virus to the USA.[730] It is symptomatic that our "journalist" has been reduced to going back to the 1980s to demonstrate Russian disinformation today. His choice proves that examples of Soviet (or Russian) disinformation are rare, whereas the Swiss journalist, for his part, lines up an average of 1 piece of false information every 3:20" on his show.

Thus, *trolling* on social networks originating in Russia is automatically attributed to the Russian government and qualified as disinformation. By contrast, examples of Western disinformation are ostensibly implausible ("Putin takes bloodbaths"). What is described as "disinformation" for Russia becomes mere *"storytelling"* Ukraine.[731]

The information available on Russian websites shows that Russia does not place much emphasis on mind control in the conduct of its

727. "According to an SRC document, Russia would try to influence elections in Switzerland", *rts. ch*, October 15, 2023
728. https://youtu.be/bEv4-IJsl9k?t=1337
729. Thomas Boghardt, "Operation INFEKTION—Soviet Bloc Intelligence and Its AIDS", *Studies in Intelligence,* Vol. 53, No. 4, CIA, December 2009
730. https://cia.gov/resources/csi/studies-in-intelligence/volume-53-no-4/soviet-bloc-intelligence-and-its-aids-disinformation-campaign/
731. https://youtu.be/bEv4-IJsl9k?t=285

operation. In fact, the opposite is true. The Russians try to convince by deed. Unlike the Ukrainians, they have acquired a solid reputation for treating their prisoners well. As a result, Ukrainian units surrender in large numbers without even fighting. Conversely, the Russians are afraid to surrender because of the way prisoners of war are treated. As a result, the Ukrainians don't have enough prisoners to trade with the Russians.[732] The mistreatment of Russian POWs has been known for a long time, but our media, like the Swiss *RTS* or *LCI* in France, gloss over these issues so as not to undermine the official narrative Thus, on March 20, 2022, on the *Ukraïna 24* channel, Dr Gennadiy Druzenko declared that he had given the order to castrate all Russians *"because they are cockroaches and not men."*[733] This information was neither commented on nor condemned by the media supporting neo-Nazi ideas. That said, this kind of propaganda tends to encourage Russians not to surrender. Here again, we see the asymmetrical effects of the Western and Ukrainian narratives.

The Reason the Russians won't Surrender

Figure 94—Ill-treatment. On March 20, 2022, Dr. Gennadiy Druzenko declared on Ukraïna 24: "I have always been a great humanist and said that a wounded man is no longer an enemy, but a patient, but I have given strict orders to castrate all men because they are cockroaches and not men." A remark very similar to Heinrich Himmler's: "We Germans, who are the only ones in the world to have a decent attitude towards animals, will also adopt a decent attitude towards these human animals." [Sources: Daily Mail; https://www.jewishvirtuallibrary.org/ remarks-by-himmler]

---

732. https://svidomi.in.ua/en/page/ukraine-has-problems-with-the-exchange-fund-ukraines-ombudsman

733. Will Stewart, "Ukrainian doctor tells TV interviewer he has ordered his staff to CASTRATE Russian soldiers because they are 'cockroaches'", *Daily Mail*, March 21, 2022 (updated March 22, 2022) (https://www.dailymail.co.uk/news/article-10636597/Ukrainian-doctor-tells-TV-interviewer-ordered-staff-CASTRATE-Russian-soldiers.html)

We can see that Russian communication sticks to the facts, probably to avoid being too easily singled out by the Western media. The technological means of geolocating communications on social networks show a good correlation between Ministry of Defense announcements and the actual situation on the ground. This is a further argument for claiming that our media are talking nonsense about Ukrainian successes, for example. While the material losses announced by Russia can be relatively well verified, this is not the case for human losses.

That said, for Ukrainians and Russians alike, counting casualties is sometimes complicated, and the figures announced are not necessarily misinformation. For example, when a vehicle is targeted by two different snipers, each will report one hit. That's why sites like *Oryx*[734] are unreliable, as they often count the same casualties several times over, photographed from different angles or in a different context; but our media take this site as their main source on Russian casualties.[735] It's probably for this reason that the site closed its doors at the beginning of October 2023.

The logic of Russian communication is diametrically opposed to that of Ukraine. While the latter multiplies victorious communiqués, Russia has not sought to magnify its successes. For example, the push on Avdievka, which Russian forces were slowly but surely carrying out from late summer 2023, was not the subject of any communiqués. Nor did our media mention it. In November 2023, we realized that, contrary to what our media had said, all Ukrainian offensives had failed, including the rather crazy amphibious operation across the Dnieper. On a more serious note, we might have expected Russia to play down its own capabilities and apply the principle laid down by the Chinese strategist Sun Tzu over 2000 years ago: *"Appear weak when you are strong."*

However, this disinformation work was not carried out by Russia itself, but by the West. Immediately after the outbreak of the SMO, it was declared that Russia had already lost the war.[736] The systematic underestimation of Russian capabilities by our media (in French: *LCI, BFM TV, Le Monde, RTBF, RTS, Le Temps*, etc.) ultimately led the Ukrainians

---

734. https://www.oryxspioenkop.com/2022/02/attack-on-europe-documenting-equipment.html
735. https://www.rts.ch/info/monde/13492719-en-ukraine-de-plus-en-plus-dhelicopteres-russes-sont-abattus.html
736. https://legrandcontinent.eu/fr/2022/02/27/pourquoi-poutine-a-deja-perdu-la-guerre/

302

The Russian Art of War

to overestimate their own capabilities. They committed themselves to a conflict they had been promised would be short and won in advance.

The Western narrative made an essential contribution to Ukraine's destruction in two ways: by minimizing Russia's capabilities, and by pushing Ukraine to hold on to the ground. Significantly, our media happily talked about square meters taken back, but systematically ignored the human cost of these "gains," and the square meters lost a few days later. We were given the impression that the Ukrainian army was only advancing; whereas overall it was retreating, as the *New York Times* showed at the end of September 2023, while the "counter-offensive" was underway.[737]

The information disseminated by Russian media such as *RT* and *Sputnik* focuses—logically enough—on the elements that work against Ukraine. However, we can see that the information given is very often accurate, unlike official Ukrainian information, which is very often false. Paradoxically, Russia tends to favor propaganda, while Ukraine uses disinformation.

Losses

From the outset of the Russian intervention, the Western narrative has revolved around the Russian defeat, Ukraine's unexpected resistance and Vladimir Putin's inability to assess the risks rationally. It was said that the Russians are losing more men than the Ukrainians in this operation. Human losses thus become one of the main indicators of success, and thus a central element of narratives. And while both sides made statements about the losses suffered by their opponents, in Ukraine these figures had a central political significance. A case in point is the projection of the Russian death toll (100 K) on one of Kiev's tallest buildings[738] reported by *Newsweek at the* end of December 2022.[739]

---

737. Josh Holder, "Who's Gaining Ground in Ukraine? This Year, No One", *The New York Times*, September 28, 2023 (https://www.nytimes.com/interactive/2023/09/28/world/europe/russia-ukraine-war-map-front-line.html)

738. https://t.me/tymoshenko_kyrylo/3160

739. https://www.newsweek.com/ukraine-marks-russian-100000-troop-death-milestone-100k-light-projection-kyiv-library-building-1769193

Our media tried to hide their bias behind platitudes such as *"Ukraine and Russia overestimate the death toll on the opposing side."*[740] Scientific-seeming "studies" attempted to lend credibility to Russian casualty estimates, without questioning the figures given for Ukraine.[741] The total absence of serious research into the mortality of Ukrainian forces seems to be the fear that real figures will destroy the official narrative. From then on, estimates became facts and facts become language.

That said, this information war is only possible because the real figures are unknown, and the two countries involved—Russia and Ukraine—do not share them. It should be noted, however, that neither the Russians nor the Ukrainians are likely to know the exact number of their dead in real time. This is what is known as the "fog of war": between an event (the death of a soldier) and its consideration at command level, hours or even days can pass. The situation becomes even more complicated when there are deserters, as is the case mainly on the Ukrainian side.

On the whole, there are very few means of accurately counting the dead on either side. The two main ones are tracking the evolution of military cemeteries using satellite imagery, and monitoring mortuary announcements in the media and social networks.

Russian Losses: Misinformation as an Editorial Policy

The first thing is to know what you're counting. We distinguish between *"casualties," which is* a generic term that includes the dead, wounded and missing, and *"fatalities."* Our media deliberately maintain a permanent confusion between these two terms, which they use as synonyms.

On August 22, 2022, *Radio-Télévision Suisse (RTS)* declared:[742]

> *Russia, in particular, has conceded very few casualties since the start of its invasion (1300 dead, last count established in March), while the United States estimates Russian losses at around 80,000 dead and wounded, recalled French senior civil servant Cyrille Bret on the Tout*

740. "Ukraine and Russia overestimate deaths on opposing side, study finds," *Le Temps*, August 15, 2023 (https://www.letemps.ch/monde/russie-12-morts-dans-une-explosion-dans-une-station-service-au-daguestan)

741. David Laitin (ed.) *et al*, "Estimating conflict losses and reporting biases", *PNAS*, Vol. 20, No. 34, *Stanford University*, Stanford, CA, August 14, 2023 (https://doi.org/10.1073/pnas.2307372120)

742. https://www.rts.ch/info/monde/13323492-larmee-ukrainienne-concede-9000-morts-en-six-mois-dinvasion-russe.html

un monde program. "Between 80,000 and 1300, we can measure the extent of possible manipulations" on both sides, he stressed.

The Swiss state media manipulates figures and cheats on three counts: time, sources and the nature of the figures:

- The figure of 1300 was derived from the balance sheet published in March by the Russian Ministry of Defense, which is actually 1351[743] (so higher than *RTS* claimed), while the estimate of 80,000 was published in August 2022, five months later.[744] The Swiss media was already dishonest when it comes to time.
- The figure of 80,000 came from the Pentagon, based on Ukrainian information, according to the American website *military.com*.[745] Significant detail: while the English-speaking media mentioned a range of 70,000-80,000 dead, *RTS* automatically took the higher figure. Yet another example of dishonesty.
- The figure of 1351 published by Russia represented "deaths," while that of 80,000 represented "losses" ("dead + wounded + missing"). *RTS* was therefore comparing apples and oranges here. CQFD!

One way of counting them is to follow the trail of deaths on social networks and in the Russian media. This is what the Russian opposition media *Mediazona,* which teamed up with the *BBC* at the start of the SMO, is doing to estimate the number of Russian deaths in Ukraine. As the media outlet is vehemently anti-Putin, it's not hard to imagine that its figures are overestimated and tend to be unfavorable to the Russians. But its methodology seems reliable, unlike our media, which has none.

That said, in France at least, pro-Ukrainians and pro-Russians have the same difficulty in basing their information on data they have researched and verified themselves. For example, on the *Institut des Libertés*

743. "Some 1,351 Russian troops killed since start of special operation in Ukraine—top brass", *Tass,* March 25, 2022 (https://tass.com/politics/1427515)

744. Caroline Anders, "Russia has lost up to 80,000 troops in Ukraine. Or 75,000. Or is it 60,000?", *The Washington Post,* August 9, 2022 (https://www.washingtonpost.com/politics/2022/08/09/russia-has-lost-up-80000-troops-ukraine-or-75000-or-is-it-60000/)

745. Travis Tritten, "Russia Has Suffered Up to 80,000 Military Casualties in Ukraine, Pentagon Says," *military.com,* August 8, 2022 (https://www.military.com/daily-news/2022/08/08/russia-has-suffered-80000-military-casualties-ukraine-pentagon-says.html)

medium, which aims to re-establish honest information, Jacques Sapir claimed that *Mediazona* was announcing 60,000 Russian deaths at the beginning of August 2023.[746] However, at the end of October, the site announced a *casualty* count of 34,857 (as of October 20). Even allowing for the fact that these were casualties, our expert was unreasonably doubling the Russian death toll, which in August stood at just over 30,000. As we can see, there is a profound lack of rigor in our approach to this conflict.

The *Mediazona* website is well known, but our media avoid referring to it, as the figures it gives are much lower than their own. For August 22, *Mediazona* and the *BBC* gave a death toll of 5185 (as of July 29).[747]

In fact, the Russian Ministry of Defense officially announced the death toll only twice: on March 25 (1351 dead) and September 21, 2022 (5937 dead).[748] It has not mentioned Russian deaths in subsequent communiqués. The figures announced by the Ukrainian Ministry of Defense were 15,000 Russian deaths on March 24, 2022[749] and 55,510 deaths on September 22.[750]

But on the dates of the official Russian announcements, the *Mediazona* website announced figures of 1,316 and 6,219 dead (counted as at September 9, 2022).[751] There is therefore a fairly good correlation between the official figures and those of the opposition.

Assuming that *Mediazona* does a serious job, there are two obvious conclusions:

- The figures given by the Russian Ministry of Defense were most probably correct;
- The Ukrainians (and therefore our media) tend to report Russian losses that are ten times higher than the reality.

746. https://youtu.be/89vMt9tsPxQ?t=434
747. https://zona.media/casualties
748. https://meduza.io/en/news/2022/09/21/shoigu-says-5-937-russian-soldiers-have-died-in-ukraine
749. https://www.reuters.com/technology/ukraine-uses-facial-recognition-identify-dead-russian-soldiers-minister-says-2022-03-23/
750. https://kyivindependent.com/general-staff-russia-has-lost-55-510-troops-in-ukraine-since-feb-24/
751. https://web.archive.org/web/20220921032116/https://en.zona.media/article/2022/05/20/casualties_eng

Comparison of the Russian Death Toll according to our Media and according to Mediazona

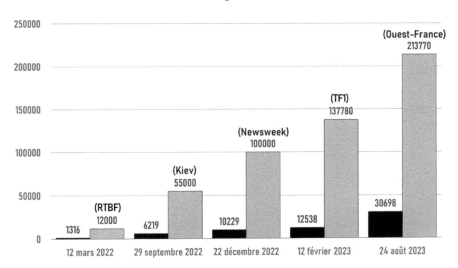

*Figure 95—Comparison of figures given by various media (in grey) and the Russian opposition media Mediazona in collaboration with the British BBC (in black).
Our media give us figures that come directly from Ukrainian propaganda, without any verification. In fact, they confirm their figures with information from other media.
It's information that goes round in circles. In technical terms, they don't base their conclusions on independent information. [Sources: Mediazona,[752] RTBF,[753] Libération,[754] Newsweek,[755] TF1,[756] Ouest-France)[757]*

As for the ratio between Russian and Ukrainian fatalities, this is largely based on speculation. In March 2023, according to one NATO "official," casualties would amount to 1 Ukrainian for every 5 Russians killed or

752. https://en.zona.media/article/2022/05/20/casualties_eng
753. https://www.rtbf.be/article/la-guerre-en-ukraine-est-aussi-une-guerre-des-chiffres-mos-cou-et-kiev-ne-saccordent-pas-sur-le-nombre-de-morts-10953528
754. https://www.liberation.fr/checknews/guerre-en-ukraine-y-a-t-il-eu-6000-morts-russes-comme-laffirme-moscou-ou-55000-comme-le-revendique-kiev-20220923_AL4JKOEZ-4BFQDJWMEKPJSFZYEI/
755. https://www.newsweek.com/ukraine-marks-russian-100000-troop-death-milestone-100k-light-projection-kyiv-library-building-1769193
756. https://www.tf1info.fr/international/guerre-ukraine-russie-avec-plus-800-morts-par-jour-en-moyenne-les-pertes-russes-au-plus-haut-en-fevrier-2023-2247923.html
757. https://www.ouest-france.fr/europe/ukraine/guerre-en-ukraine-la-contre-offensive-com-mentee-lourdes-pertes-russes-le-point-sur-la-nuit-34004d91-be82-45b4-a577-2c2bf8776bd5

wounded; while Oleksiy Danilov, Secretary of the Ukrainian Security and Defense Council, puts the ratio at 1:7.[758]

Looking at the figures for Russian losses, we can see that Ukraine systematically applies the technique of "projection" or "mirroring" to communicate. In this way, the numbers announced by Ukraine on the losses of each side have to be inverted to give an image closer to reality.

Number of deaths per week in Russian Forces according to **Mediazona**

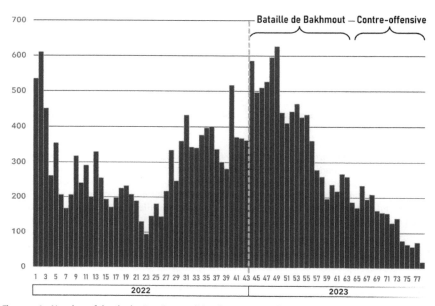

Figure 96—Number of deaths by Russian coalition forces per week, according to the opposition media, Mediazona, with the British BBC. It is difficult to pinpoint the fluctuations in these figures. We can recognize the impact of the Battle of Bakhmut in early 2023, but we can also see that Russian losses are falling during the Ukrainian counter-offensive. On the x-axis, the number of the week of conflict.

On September 30, 2023, the media outlet *Ukrinform reported that* according to the Ukrainian General Staff, the number of dead in the ranks of the Russian army in Ukraine was around 278,130.[759] On the

758. Roman Olearchyk, Ben Hall & John Paul Rathbone, "Bakhmut: Ukrainian losses may limit capacity for counter-attack", *The Irish Times/The Financial Times*, March 9, 2023 (https://www.irishtimes.com/world/europe/2023/03/09/bakhmut-analysis-ukrainian-losses-may-limit-capacity-for-counter-attack/)

759. https://www.ukrinform.net/rubric-ato/3767984-russian-military-death-toll-in-ukraine-rises-to-about-278130.html

same date, the *Mediazona* website gives a total figure of 32,656 dead on the Russian side (count as of September 22, 2023).[760] This figure mainly included combat troops, but also the deaths of personnel from specialized formations:[761]

Deaths in Russian Specialized Formations

Troupe	Nombre
Forces aéroportées	1872
Infanterie de marine	720
Détachements spéciaux de la garde nationale	486
Spetsnaz du GRU	345
Pilotes militaires	178
Officiers du FSB	55
Total	**3656**

Figure 97—Table of specialized training deaths. [Source: BBC News, August 4, 2023]

In June 2023, "expert" Alexandre Vautravers claimed that Russian airborne forces had been reduced from 15,000 to 5000, and had therefore lost 60 percent of their strength.[762] In fact, their numbers were between 45,000 and 60,000[763] and in August, *BBC News* reported losses of 1872 men, i.e., around 4 percent. The estimate was therefore wrong by a factor of 15.

Ukrainian Losses

Military Losses

The number of dead Ukrainian servicemen is unknown. Fearing—with good reason—that if Western public opinion knew the number of dead, it would oppose its governments' support for the war, Ukraine gives no figures.

Observations on the ground and testimonies from returning Western volunteers tend to confirm that Ukrainian forces are suffering consi-

---

760. https://en.zona.media/article/2022/05/20/casualties_eng
761. https://www.bbc.com/russian/features-66401153
762. https://www.lemanbleu.ch/fr/Emissions/189661-Geneve-a-Chaud.html
763. https://en.wikipedia.org/wiki/Russian_Airborne_Forces

derably higher losses than the Russians. Significantly, while our media have attempted to estimate Russian losses, they have not done so for the Ukrainians, reiterating official Ukrainian statements—no doubt too afraid of what they might discover.

The Ukrainian strategy of defending every square meter of territory to the bitter end only leads to the destruction of its own forces. This is what the French and Germans did in 1914-1918. But this time, the Russians are mobile. To use a historical comparison, we therefore have the situation of a 1914 defense and a 1940 attacker. The result—by the summer of 2022, Ukraine's military potential had been destroyed.

The West took fright and began to supply Ukraine with arms, hoping to turn the situation around. The Russians realized that the West would not allow the Ukrainians to negotiate, and would seek to prolong the conflict until Russia was exhausted. Thus, they changed their approach—if they couldn't stop the flow of weapons, they would have to destroy those who were using them.

A different kind of war began. The objective was still military potential, but instead of destroying the weapons, those using them were destroyed. Thus, in early June 2022, President Zelensky reported daily losses of 60 to 100 men.[764] On June 9, Zelensky's adviser Mykhailo Podoliak told the *BBC* that Ukrainian forces were losing 100 to 200 men a day.[765] In mid-June, David Arakhamia, Zelensky's chief negotiator and close adviser, spoke of 200 to 500 dead a day, and put total losses (dead, wounded, captured, deserters) at 1,000 men a day.[766] According to *Business Insider*, Ukraine would then have lost the equivalent of the entire British infantry, or more than 18,000 men.[767]

Whether these figures are accurate is unclear. On the one hand, experts close to the intelligence services believe that these figures are far below reality. On the other hand, the Ukrainian figures are higher than the

764. Mazurenko Alona, "Подоляк: Щодня гине 100-200 українських захисників," *Ukrainska Pravda*, June 9, 2022 (https://www.pravda.com.ua/news/2022/06/9/7351600/)

765. "У війні гине 100—200 українських військових щодня—Офіс президента", *BBC News*, June 9, 2022 (https://www.bbc.com/ukrainian/news-61752749)

766. Dave Lawler, "Ukraine suffering up to 1,000 casualties per day in Donbas, official says", *Axios*, June 15, 2022 (https://www.axios.com/2022/06/15/ukraine-1000-casualties-day-donbas-arakhamia)

767. Katie Anthony, "Ukraine has lost more troops during the Russian invasion than there are infantry in the British army, defense expert says," *Business Insider*, June 28, 2022 (https://www.businessinsider.com/ukraine-has-lost-more-troops-than-there-are-in-the-british-army-expert-2022-6)

estimates given by the Russian army. Some claim that Ukrainian forces suffered 60,000 dead and 50,000 missing. By June 2022, former US general Stephen Twitty estimated Ukrainian army losses at 200,000 men.[768]

In September 2022, according to a Ukrainian soldier in the *Washington Post*, the Russians were losing one man for every five Ukrainians.[769] This is exactly the opposite of what NATO told us, as we have seen.

On November 30, 2022, Ursula von der Leyen, President of the European Commission, declared[770] that *"more than 20,000 Ukrainian civilians and over 100,000 military personnel have been killed to date.[771]"* This immediately aroused the ire of Kiev, which demanded that this figure be withdrawn. This was done on the spot.[772] But this indicates several things. Firstly, the sensitivity of the death toll for internal stability in Ukraine. Secondly, Mrs. von der Leyen certainly did not invent this figure, which is probably circulating confidentially in Western halls of power. Thirdly, given Mrs. von der Leyen's tendency to play down Ukrainian losses, the figure of 100,000 dead is probably underestimated.

This hypothesis seems to be confirmed by Israeli Mossad estimates published at the end of January 2023 by the Turkish media *Hürseda Haber*,[773] which mentioned 157,000 Ukrainian deaths. Unverifiable, but realistic.

Accounting for 65 percent to 75 percent of casualties, artillery is one of the main causes of death on the battlefield.[774] The number of shells fired is therefore probably a good indicator of the ratio of losses on either side of the front line. According to Ukrainian and Western military officials, the Ukrainians are firing around 2000 to 4000 shells a day and the Russians around 40,000-50,000, a ratio that varies between 1:10

---

768. "US-General verwundert: "200.000 ukrainische Soldaten verschwunden"", *Exxpress.at*, June 8, 2022 (https://exxpress.at/us-general-verwundert-200-000-ukrainische-soldaten-verschwunden/)
769. John Hudson, "Wounded Ukrainian soldiers reveal steep toll of Kherson offensive," *The Washington Post*, September 7, 2022 (https://www.washingtonpost.com/world/2022/09/07/ukraine-kherson-offensive-casualties-ammunition/)
770. https://t.me/wartearsorg/79
771. https://twitter.com/AZgeopolitics/status/1597913370023579648
772. "Von der Leyen statement about death of 100,000 Ukrainian soldiers cut from speech", *The New Voice of Ukraine*, November 30, 2022 (https://english.nv.ua/nation/von-der-leyen-statement-about-death-of-100-000-ukrainian-soldiers-cut-from-speech-50287771.html)
773. "ddia: MOSSAD'a göre Ukrayna ve Rusya kayıpları", *Hürseda Haber,* January 25, 2023 (https://perma.cc/FD7T-LQU8)
774. https://matthew.krupczak.org/2021/04/10/medical-department-u-s-army-wound-ballistics-causative-agents-of-battle-casualties-in-wwii/

and 1:25. According to the Spanish newspaper *El Pais*, this ratio is 1 to 10;[775] thus, we can estimate that the Ukrainians have 10 to 11 times more dead than the Russians. For February 2023, the calculation would give between 140,000 and 350,000 deaths on the Ukrainian side. Difficult to confirm, but more likely than the far-fetched figures thrown around by the media without justification.

We can see that the Russian loss figures announced by Ukraine—and therefore our media—are systematically 10-11 times higher than those observed by *Mediazona*. It is likely that Ukraine is artificially inflating the figures so that they are higher than its own losses. This means that, if we accept the figure of 14,000 dead announced by the site for Russia in February 2023, it is not incongruous to estimate the number of Ukrainian dead at over 150,000 men. This would confirm the figure mentioned by the Israeli Mossad at the end of January.

The fact remains that these figures are still estimates. However, despite what our media tell us (without ever proving anything), testimonies from Ukrainian soldiers seem to confirm considerably higher losses on the Ukrainian side.

In early 2023, an American ex-volunteer on the Ukrainian side told *Newsweek* magazine that life expectancy in Bakhmut for Ukrainians is around 4 hours.[776] In March 2023, a Ukrainian military officer reported that his forces were losing 1-2 companies a day and around one battalion a week.[777] In March 2023, the *Washington Post* quoted the testimony of a commander of the 46th Ukrainian parachute brigade in Bakhmut, who claimed that he was the only survivor of his original unit and that it was now made up of new conscripts with no experience.[778] He was dismissed three days later.[779]

---

775. https://english.elpais.com/international/2023-03-01/ukraine-outgunned-10-to-1-in-massive-artillery-battle-with-russia.html

776. Anna Skinner, "Bakhmut Life Expectancy Near Four Hours on Frontlines, Fighter Warns," *Newsweek*, February 20, 2023 (https://www.newsweek.com/bakhmut-life-expectancy-near-four-hours-frontlines-ukraine-russia-1782496)

777. https://www.bitchute.com/video/WFZMB0E15Yl7/

778. Isabelle Khurshudyan, Paul Sonne & Karen DeYoung, "Ukraine short of skilled troops and ammunition as losses, pessimism grow," *The Washington Post*, March 13, 2023 (https://www.washingtonpost.com/world/2023/03/13/ukraine-casualties-pessimism-ammunition-shortage/)

779. Olga Kyrylenko & Olena Roshchina, "Battalion commander of 46th Brigade demoted after Washington Post interview and resigns", *Ukrainska Pravda*, March 26, 2023 (https://www.pravda.com.ua/eng/news/2023/03/16/7393733/)

On July 17, 2023, Roman Revedjuk, a well-known Ukrainian journalist, revealed on his Facebook account that the Ukrainian army had more than 310,000 dead.[780] Difficult to verify, but this corresponds to around 11 times the total of 28,652 dead stated by *Mediazona* for Russia on July 28, 2023.[781] The Ukrainian site *Wartears.org* does a similar job to *Mediazona*, but for Ukrainian forces, filling in the missing data with a mathematical model. By the end of September 2023, it estimated 285,000 deaths.[782]

In September 2023, The *Times* of London painted a tragic picture of the situation around the village of Rabotino, where losses were said to be as high as 90 percent. This is undoubtedly an exaggeration, although one of the officers interviewed admitted that he had lost 75 percent of his troops.[783] It does, however, give an idea of the level of Ukrainian losses, which our media play down in order to keep Ukraine fighting.

These are just figures, of course, but a June 29 report by the *Kiev International Institute of Sociology* shows that 63 percent of Ukrainians know at least 3 people who have been killed in the fighting, and 78 percent know at least 7 people who have been killed or wounded.[784]

What is pompously referred to as "OSINT" (*open source intelligence*) has grown in importance with the Ukrainian conflict. But the methodology and professionalism of these amateur "analysts" very often leave much to be desired, which is why their figures should be treated with caution. Perhaps it's because fiction has failed to surpass fact that the *Oryx* website will ceased operations on October 1, 2023.[785]

Furthermore, it should be noted that no Western organization has attempted to do the same job as the *BBC* and *Mediazona* in assessing the number of dead Ukrainians. Testimonies from Ukrainian soldiers are systematically ignored so as not to compromise the Western narrative, and military and financial support for Ukraine. This indicates that the figures given by our media are most likely underestimates, as they do everything to keep Ukrainians fighting—and keep getting killed.

780. https://youtu.be/0uAh19aQF58
781. https://web.archive.org/web/20230801021222/https://en.zona.media/article/2022/05/20/casualties_eng
782. https://wartears.org/posts/math-model/
783. Anthony Loyd, "Ukraine counteroffensive: 'I'm ready to die... 90% of the guys here will die too'", *The Times*, September 5, 2023 (https://archive.ph/IGjVe#selection-851.0-915.25)
784. https://www.kiis.com.ua/?lang=eng&cat=reports&id=1254&page=1&y=2023&m=6
785. https://twitter.com/oryxspioenkop/status/1670723829713215489

The *BBC* reports a Ukrainian military officer as saying that the "Marines" newly arrived to reinforce their bridgehead at Krinky, on the Dnieper, could not even swim.[786]

Ultimately, Ukraine is in a situation where the mobilization of new fighters risks affecting the country's economic life. In other words, Zelensky's decision in March 2022 to abandon his own proposal for resolving the conflict now comes up against the physical limits of his population, which Western material aid cannot compensate for. With his decision, Zelensky has made Putin the master of the clocks.[787]

Civilian Losses

On March 22, 2022, on the set of *RTS*, Gennady Gatilov, the Russian ambassador, explained that Russia is trying to conduct the SMO "delicately" and minimize collateral damage. But Philippe Revaz, the Swiss journalist who interviewed him, accused the Russian military of massacring women and children[788] (without providing any supporting evidence).

Yet on the same day, in the American magazine *Newsweek*, a Defense Intelligence Agency (DIA) analyst declared:[789]

> *I know it's hard to swallow that the disaster and destruction could be much worse than it actually is. [But that's what the facts show. It suggests to me, in any case, that Putin is not intentionally attacking civilians, that he may be aware that he needs to limit the damage in order to preserve a way out for negotiations.*
>
> *The heart of Kiev was barely touched. And almost all the long-range strikes were directed against military targets.*

In January 2023, Oleksei Arestovitch, then an ex-personal advisor to Volodymyr Zelensky, interviewed on the Ukrainian media *Mriya*, used

---

786. James Waterhouse, "Ukraine war: Soldier tells BBC of front-line 'hell'", *BBC News*, December 4, 2023 (https://www.bbc.com/news/world-europe-67565508)

787. Robert Clark, "Ukraine's army is running out of men to recruit, and time to win," *The Telegraph*, August 22, 2023 (https://www.telegraph.co.uk/news/2023/08/22/ukraines-army-is-running-out-of-men-to-recruit/)

788. https://www.rts.ch/play/tv/redirect/detail/12960214

789. William M. Arkin, "Putin's Bombers Could Devastate Ukraine But He's Holding Back. Here's Why", *Newsweek*, March 22, 2022 (https://www.newsweek.com/putins-bombers-could-devastate-ukraine-hes-holding-back-heres-why-1690494)

almost the same words as Ambassador Gatilov to describe the Russian intervention:[790]

> *They [the Russians] didn't want to kill anyone... They tried to wage an intelligent war... A special operation as elegant, as beautiful, as quick as lightning, where polite people, without causing any harm to the kitten or the child, liquidated the few resistance fighters. And not even eliminated, but offered to surrender, to defect, to understand, and so on. They didn't want to kill anyone. All they had to do was sign a waiver.*

Philippe Revaz was therefore spreading disinformation and contradicting the statements made by the Ukrainians themselves, simply on the basis of unverified information.

The Russians' aim is not to destroy or occupy the country, but to destroy its potential threat to the Donbass. This is why they have not accompanied their advance with massive bombardments that could affect the population, as the West did in Iraq or Afghanistan:[791]

> *In 24 days of conflict, Russia carried out some 1,400 strikes and launched almost 1,000 missiles (by way of comparison, the United States carried out more strikes and launched more missiles on the first day of the Iraq war in 2003).*

For Ukrainians, the situation is very different. Those in power and those around the power-mongers have a problem with their minorities, whom they consider inferior. Fighting in Russian-speaking areas is not really a problem. This is why Ukrainian forces have few qualms about endangering their population, who are not ethnically Ukrainian.[792] Between 2014

---

790. https://en.mriya.news/58331-they-didnt-want-to-kill-anyone-arestovich-spoke-about-the-beginning-of-the-nwo

791. William M. Arkin, "Putin's Bombers Could Devastate Ukraine But He's Holding Back. Here's Why", *Newsweek*, March 22, 2022 (https://www.newsweek.com/putins-bombers-could-devastate-ukraine-hes-holding-back-heres-why-1690494)

792. https://www.amnesty.org/en/latest/news/2022/08/ukraine-ukrainian-fighting-tactics-endanger-civilians/

and 2022, the Ukrainian government fought its own population, driving them to organize militias.

On October 18, on *TV5 Monde*, Pascal Boniface, director of IRIS, attempted to compare Russia's strikes in Ukraine and Israel's strikes in Gaza.[793] Israel's response to the Hamas operation launched on October 7, 2023 provides us with an element of comparison on the question of civilian protection. Between February 24, 2022 and October 8, 2023, in 591 days, 9806 civilians lost their lives in Ukraine, including 560 children and 7649 in Kiev-controlled territory, an average of 13 per day.[794] In Gaza, between October 7 and 31, 2023, Israel killed 8,525 Palestinians. As the civilian or combatant nature of these Palestinians is not specified, we will take into account the mortality of women and children, according to the United Nations Office for the Coordination of Humanitarian Affairs (UN OCHA). It appears that during these 25 days, some 5729 (67 percent) were women and children, and at least 3542 were children,[795] i.e., 379 per day.[796]

Thus, the Russians (and Ukrainians) caused the death of 0.94 children per day, while Israel killed 141.7 per day. Beyond the numbers, this indicates fundamentally different strike policies. The figure for Ukraine tends to indicate collateral damage; whereas for Gaza it is more a question of deliberate policy, confirmed by Israeli officials who have stated that they prefer *"damage and destruction"* to the precision of strikes.[797]

To these deaths, however, must be added those which accumulated between 2014 and 2022, and which could have been avoided if Ukraine, France and Germany had agreed to implement the Minsk Agreements and if Britain and the USA had respected their UN Security Council mandate. What's more, if Britain, the USA and France had let Zelensky negotiate his mid-March 2022 proposal, all these victims would still be alive today.

793. https://youtu.be/0pleiz2H4T4
794. https://ukraine.un.org/en/248799-ukraine-civilian-casualties-8-october-2023
795. https://www.ochaopt.org/content/hostilities-gaza-strip-and-israel-reported-impact-day-25
796. https://ochaopt.org/content/hostilities-gaza-strip-and-israel-flash-update-13
797. James Rothwell, "Israel abandons precision bombing in favour of 'damage and destruction'", *The Telegraph*, October 11, 2023 (https://www.telegraph.co.uk/world-news/2023/10/11/israel-abandon-precision-bombing-eliminate-hamas-officials/)

8. Conclusions

Ukraine and the West have approached the Ukrainian conflict like a pedestrian crossing the street without looking.

Despite the specious arguments of our politicians and other pencil-pushers, the West is at war with Russia. It's a conflict that primarily serves the interests of the United States. This is why the West has done nothing to implement the Minsk Agreements, and has opposed all negotiating solutions proposed by Ukraine in February,[798] March[799] and August[800] 2022.

The West pushed Ukraine to keep fighting, promising aid for "as long as it takes." Convinced by its own narrative, it overestimated Ukraine's strengths and underestimated those of Russia. This led the West to predict a rapid collapse of Russia. This is why Zelensky agreed to provoke Russia.

Russia, for its part, no doubt thought it too would carry out a short-term military operation. But unlike the West, Russia achieved its objectives in a matter of weeks—as early as February 25, Ukraine was ready to negotiate. But at the insistence of the Europeans, these negotiations were broken off a few days later. In mid-March 2022, Zelensky returned to the negotiations with a proposal. In essence, Russia withdrew from Ukraine and the latter agreed not to join NATO. At this point, Russia had achieved its two objectives: denazification (achieved on March 28) and demili-

798. Maïa de La Baume & Jacopo Barigazzi, "EU agrees to give €500M in arms, aid to Ukrainian military in 'watershed' move", *Politico*, February 27, 2022 (https://www.politico.eu/article/eu-ukraine-russia-funding-weapons-budget-military-aid/).

799. https://www.pravda.com.ua/eng/news/2022/05/5/7344206/

800. Tom Balmforth & Andrea Shalal, "UK's Boris Johnson, in Kyiv, warns against 'flimsy' plan for talks with Russia", *Reuters*, 24 August 2022 (https://www.reuters.com/world/europe/uks-johnson-kyiv-warns-against-flimsy-plan-talks-with-russia-2022-08-24/)

tarization (with Zelensky's proposal). The intervention of Great Britain and the European Union in the bilateral dialogue between Ukraine and Russia ruined Zelensky's efforts and postponed the achievement of the demilitarization objective. It was achieved at the end of May, by which time Ukraine had lost most of its resources and was dependent on the West. Demilitarization, which could have been achieved by negotiation at the end of March, was achieved by force at the end of May.

But Russia is more resilient than expected and is not collapsing. Ukraine is continuously supplied by its Western allies, which means that Russia is no longer just demilitarizing Ukraine, but NATO itself—because slowly, the West can no longer sustain its effort—its resources are exhausted.

The problem is that we knew we were heading for a dead end. The intelligence services and a few honest commentators had analyzed the situation and identified the weaknesses in Western discourse right from the start of the SMO. It was our media that systematically dismissed any information indicating that these analysts were right, in order to keep up the pressure on Ukraine.

The West's involvement has become a trap for itself—for after asking Zelensky to withdraw his March 2022 peace plan with the promise of a victory we knew to be illusory (because the aim was not to win, but to destabilize Russia), we've put him in a much worse situation today. As I pointed out in my book *Ukraine Between War and Peace*, Ukraine and the West are captives of the "sunk cost fallacy" theory.[801] As we know from common practice, persisting with a bad project simply to justify the investments already made is an open door to disaster.[802] This is what we are seeing today in Ukraine.

You can't win a war with prejudice—you lose it. These prejudices have been fostered by our media. For our politicians, as we have seen with the example of the Canadian parliament, are generally uneducated, ill-informed, more attached to their careers than to the well-being of the population they represent, and are therefore vulnerable to unverified and biased information, such as our media feed us on a continuous basis.

---

801. https://youtu.be/GCmfXMMhRzk
802. Caeleigh MacNeil, "Sunk costs: a trap influencing our decisions?", *asana*.com, January 10, 2022 (https://asana.com/fr/resources/sunk-cost-fallacy)

As Ukrainian MP Gerachenko put it in the *Washington Post*, October 2023:[803]

> We all want it all. But this is the real world, and we have to make decisions based on real options. We don't have unlimited time or an unlimited number of citizens.

While my analyses of the conflict showing Ukraine's weaknesses were labeled "Russian disinformation" and dismissed outright, in November 2023, General Zaluzhny confirmed these analyses almost word for word.[804]

This is why we (i.e., our media and politicians) have thus become—*volens nolens*—the main architects of the Ukrainian defeat that is taking shape. Paradoxically, it's probably because of a few self-proclaimed experts and hobby strategists on our screens that Ukraine finds itself in this situation today.

Reasons for Russian Success

At the end of September 2023, Russia was clearly on the road to success—the objectives set out by Vladimir Putin in February 2022 have been achieved, while Ukraine is living on Western aid, which is getting weaker by the day. We use the word "success" here—not "victory," as the terms of the latter are still unknown. Yet even those who were fiercely opposed to Russia are beginning to speak of a Russian victory. In December, the British daily *The Telegraph* headlined "Putin's Russia nears devastating victory. Europe's foundations tremble."[805]

803. David Ignatius, "A hard choice lies ahead in Ukraine, but only Ukrainians can make it," *The Washington Post*, October 5, 2023 (https://www.washingtonpost.com/opinions/2023/10/05/ukraine-kyiv-russia-war-united-states-support/)
804. "Ukraine's commander-in-chief on the breakthrough he needs to beat Russia", *The Economist*, November 1, 2023 (https://www.economist.com/europe/2023/11/01/ukraines-commander-in-chief-on-the-breakthrough-he-needs-to-beat-russia)
805. Daniel Hannan, "Putin's Russia is closing in on a devastating victory. Europe's foundations are trembling", *The Telegraph*, December 9, 2023 (https://www.yahoo.com/news/putin-russia-closing-devastating-victory-170326959.html)

The main reason for Russia's success is that we only know it through prejudice and the blindness in which our "elites" and journalists have imprisoned us.

On December 7, 2022, before a Senate committee, General Bruno Clermont analyzed the conflict and referred to a *"totally erroneous analysis by the Russians on three points:"*[806]

- *"The first is the existence of a Ukrainian nation.* Not true. Unlike Clermont, the Russians have in-depth knowledge of the situation in Ukraine. For it is Ukraine's policy towards its minorities that has resulted in Russian-speakers (and Magyar-speakers) no longer feeling Ukrainian. The starting point for Donbass autonomism was the repeal of the Kivalov-Kolesnichenko law on February 23, 2014 on official languages. An ultra-nationalist policy extended by the Law on the Rights of Indigenous Populations of July 1, 2021, which is somewhat equivalent to the Nuremberg Laws of 1935, giving different rights to citizens depending on their ethnic origin.[807] This is what prompted Vladimir Putin to write an article on July 12, 2021, calling on Ukraine to consider Russian speakers as part of the Ukrainian nation and not to discriminate as proposed by the new law. Incidentally, Clermont should note that there is no popular resistance in Russian-occupied areas. Significantly enough, as reported by the American media outlet *Forbes*, in the Russian-occupied Kherson oblast, the Ukrainian language has been maintained as the official language, while on the Ukrainian side, Russian has lost this status.[808]

- *"The second is the overestimation of the power of the Russian army."* Here again, Clermont's thinking is based on prejudice. We have attributed objectives to Russia that it has never sought to achieve. For example, Russia has never sought to "take over" Ukraine. In fact, Russian objectives were achieved very quickly—by February 25, 2022, Ukraine was ready to negotiate; by March 28, the objec-

---

806. "War in Ukraine: 'It's a 20th-century war'", *Public Sénat/YouTube*, December 7, 2022 (https://youtu.be/kIJtZmzK1mc)

807. "Нардеп від 'Слуги народу' Семінський заявив про 'позбавлення конституційних прав росіян, які проживають в Україні'", *AP News*, July 2, 2021 (https://apnews.com.ua/ua/news/nardep-vid-slugi-narodu-seminskii-zayaviv-pro-pozbavlennya-konstitutciinikh-prav-rosiyan-ya-ki-prozhivaiut-v-ukraini/)

808. https://www.forbes.ru/society/490766-vlasti-hersonskoj-oblasti-priznali-ukrainskij-azyk-oficial-nym-naradu-s-russkim

tive of "denazification" had been reached; and by early June 2022, the objective of "demilitarization" had *de facto* also been reached. Since June 2022, Western intervention has prolonged the conflict. Russia had probably underestimated the West's determination to sacrifice the Ukrainian military to satisfy its own objectives.

- *"The third is the underestimation of the power of the Ukrainian army.* Once again, this is false. It was precisely because the Ukrainian army was building up its strength in the Donbass with a view to implementing Volodymyr Zelensky's decree of March 24, 2021 for the reconquest of Crimea and the south of the country, that the Russians attacked. By the general's own admission, the Russians were not fully prepared for this conflict, which clearly shows that they were pushed into action. Secondly, Ukraine's material capabilities were destroyed in May-June 2022 and it is now dependent on the West, while its personal capabilities were exhausted in December. What the Russians have probably underestimated is the West's determination to keep the conflict active, despite Ukraine's lack of human and material resources, which has been bled it dry.

Clermont is a perfect illustration of why Westerners lose wars—they judge their adversaries on the basis of their own prejudices, not on the facts. Clermont is repeating the same mistake made by his predecessor, General Gamelin, on August 23, 1939—mistaking his desires for realities. A true military man knows that the worst mistake you can make in war is to underestimate your adversary.

Our "experts" systematically refer to what NATO forces would have done in a similar situation. The problem is that Russians don't think about war in the same way. Westerners are incapable of thinking outside the box. This explains their repeated failures in North Africa and the Middle East.

By December 2022, the Ukrainian army of February 2022 no longer existed. It had been replaced by less experienced forces, and its major equipment was largely of Western origin.

The West saw the Kharkov (September 2022) and Kherson (October 2022) episodes as an indicator of Russia's weakness and inability to regenerate its forces. Russian disinformation couldn't have done a better job. Thanks to analyses dictated by propaganda and obsessed by a chimerical

Ukrainian victory, the West has concentrated its arms deliveries on offensive equipment (armor and artillery) and neglected the supply of defense equipment.

The nature of Russia's objectives is essentially qualitative, so they cannot be represented on a map, nor can they be used to determine where Russian forces will end their combat actions. The end state they seek is initially a set of security guarantees for the Russian populations of Ukraine and for the security of Russia. This objective could have been achieved without intervention, had Ukraine and Western countries honored their commitments. It could also have been achieved in March 2022, if the West had not pressured Zelensky to withdraw his conflict settlement proposal. This reaction showed Vladimir Putin that the West does not want a political solution. It is therefore likely that the conflict will only end when the military threat is physically neutralized, either by reducing its territorial presence, or when it no longer has human resources. Since March 2022, these resources have been gradually eroded, whereas the agreement proposed by Zelensky could have preserved them, since Russia did not intervene to make territorial gains.

Another factor that favored Russia's success was the strategic coherence in which it conducted its operation. Thanks to the sanctions it had been under since 2014, Russia has built up an environment that makes it less dependent on the West. This form of economic robustness has a decisive effect in making the decision-making process independent of outside influences.

Conversely, European countries have only limited decision-making independence, as they are dependent on political and economic constraints. Thus, by pushing Russia to consolidate its economy while increasing pressure on the populations of the Donbass, the West has created a lose-lose context.

The real problem is the image that Westerners have of Russia—underestimating your opponent is the best recipe for losing. We can argue about the nature of Russian democracy, but if we refer to the *Democracy Perception Index 2023*, we see that the gap between expectations of democracy and the reality of its application exceeds our prejudices.[809] This gap, known

---

809. https://www.allianceofdemocracies.org/initiatives/the-copenhagen-democracy-summit/dpi-2023/

as the "democratic deficit," is 11% in Switzerland, 18% in Russia (as high as in Sweden, Denmark or Canada), 29% in Belgium and 32% in France. Admittedly, expectations are lower in Russia than in France or Belgium, but this shows that the system is adapted to what the population expects.

In other words, instead of worrying about improving the governance of others, we should first look at our own problems.

Reasons for the Ukrainian Defeat

The main reason for the Ukrainian failure is that Zelensky played the role of commander-in-chief and led the operations himself. He played the role of commander-combatant in military fatigues, which our media have assigned him. He therefore exposed himself, rather than relying on his military. Yet he clearly lacks the skills to lead military operations, creating tensions with the armed forces. Since the end of 2022, the troops have lost confidence in their command. Zelensky's insistence on holding on to Bakhmut against the advice of his staff has been disastrous.[810] It's amusing to note that, like *The Kyiv Independent,* I had already pointed out this problem in my previous works, but this was labeled "conspiracy" by our media.

In other words, it was well known that there were problems with the Ukrainian leadership, and that this could lead to failure. In early December 2023, the Ukrainian media outlet *Strana* referred to Zelensky's responsibility for the disaster of the Dnieper crossing operation at Krinky, and quoted the *Financial Times* as saying that Zelensky saw reality through rose-colored glasses.[811]

In military terms, Ukraine has suffered from a doctrinal shift that has created a gap between different generations of military cadres. The transition from a Soviet-inspired doctrine to a NATO-inspired one has created a vulnerability. For example, the notion of superiority, a key element in NATO concepts, has never been fully applied by Ukraine.

---

810. Kate Tsurkan, "Zelensky, Zaluzhnyi have conflicting views on Bakhmut," *The Kyiv Independent,* March 6, 2023 (https://kyivindependent.com/bild-zaluzhnyi-and-zelensky-have-conflicting-views-on-bakhmut/)
811. https://strana.today/news/452665-itohi-656-dnja-vojny-v-ukraine.html

As *Ukrainska Pravda* declared in December 2023:[812]

> *According to a senior Ukrainian military official, war games "don't work". The war being fought by Ukrainian soldiers is unlike any other that NATO forces have faced. This is a major conventional conflict without the air superiority that American armed forces have enjoyed in every recent conflict in which they have been involved. Trenches worthy of the First World War are blocked by ubiquitous drones and other futuristic tools.*

The problem is that *all* our TV "experts" have been incapable of thinking outside the box. In France, journalists became military "experts" and the military became political commentators. Neither has rigorously applied the principles of their profession—throughout the Ukrainian crisis, both have presented the image of amateurs whose incompetence has proved deadly for Ukraine.

The hearings of these "experts" before parliamentary representatives in France illustrate two conceptual weaknesses that affect NATO armies—and therefore the Ukrainian army—in the way they conduct operations:

- The tendency to ignore the opponent in their tactical planning. This may come as a surprise, but it stems from the fact that for thirty years, our armies fought with overwhelming superiorities, rendering the opponent's reactions insignificant.
- The inability to think of operational success as the product of operational synergies. Our generals continue to see operational/ strategic success as the sum of tactical successes.
- The inability to develop real strategies, resulting from the other two weaknesses.

The main factor in Ukraine's failure was the overriding role of politics and communication in military decision-making. As we have seen, Ukraine thought it was engaging in a short-term conflict with massive NATO involvement. The discourse and role of politics were therefore

---

812. Alona Mazurenko, "US and the West insisted on Ukraine's targeted counteroffensive to cut off Russia from Crimea", *Ukrainska Pravda*, December 4, 2023 (https://www.pravda.com.ua/eng/news/2023/12/4/7431593/)

decisive in Kiev. The problem is that this discourse was self-sufficient. Our journalists relayed it without even questioning whether it was realistic or not. Obviously, materially supporting a winning protagonist is very different from helping a loser. In early 2023, France decided to double its support for Ukraine, supplying 2000 155 mm shells per month. In November 2023, General Zaluzhny asked Lloyd Austin, US Secretary of Defense, for 17 million shells and $350 to $400 billion in aid.[813] This illustrates the disconnection of our military and politicians from the realities on the ground, confirming my observations following the mediocre hearings of "experts" by French MPs.

But the West has not really lived up to Ukrainian expectations.

At the beginning of December 2023, the *Washington Post* noted what I had already announced in my previous books, namely, that the West had considerably underestimated Russian capabilities. On the same day, the *BBC* reported the words of Ukrainian soldiers involved in the attempted breakthrough at Krinky on the Dnieper. They revealed that they had not planned any major logistical resources, as they had assumed that the Russians would flee as soon as they approached.[814]

By underestimating the adversary, and thus influencing our policies, our media have undoubtedly become the architects of the Ukrainian defeat. As early as February 2022, we could see that Western and Ukrainian objectives were wavering between desire and reality. But whatever one might think of the merits of the SMO, it was clear that Ukraine had no interest in prolonging the fighting. The problem had been identified as early as February 2022 (and mentioned in my previous books); but obsessed by their own narrative and hatred of the Russian, the West deliberately let Ukraine go under.

Of course, it's easier to wage war with the blood of others, safe in the comfort of a newspaper in Paris, Brussels or Geneva.

The Russians have perfectly understood that a war is not fought exclusively on the battlefield; it can also be fought on diplomatic terrain. That's why they tried in September 2014, February 2015, December

813. Alona Mazurenko, "Commander-in-Chief Zaluzhnyi asked Pentagon chief for 17 million rounds of ammunition", *Ukrainska Pravda*, December 4, 2023 (https://www.pravda.com.ua/eng/news/2023/12/4/7431543/)
814. "Ukraine war: Soldier tells BBC of front-line 'hell'", *BBC News*, December 4, 2023 (https://www.bbc.com/news/world-europe-67565508)

2021, February, March and August 2022. Each time it was our media and politicians who opposed a solution. Josep Borrell, head of EU foreign policy, had himself said that *"this war must be won on the battlefield.*[815]*"* It probably will be.

Thus, on September 25, 2023, Vyacheslav Volodin, Speaker of the Russian Parliament (Duma), declared that the conflict would end either with *"the surrender of the Kiev regime to the conditions of the Russian Federation, or [with] the end of Ukraine's existence as a state."*[816]

At the end of November 2023, the positions could be summarized as follows:

- Zelensky and his entourage probably know that their political (and probably physical) survival is linked to the continuation of the fight and therefore seek nothing less than the unconditional surrender of the Russian forces;
- The Americans have sought a "freeze" in the conflict and have urged Zelensky to open a dialogue with the Russians, but also have refused to compromise;
- The Russians have understood that freezing the conflict is just a way of taking a break that would allow Ukraine to rearm, without resolving any of the problems that led to the confrontation in the first place.

The Ukrainians are beginning to realize that they are on a dead-end street, and that they have not provided themselves with a way out. The failure to define what might be a "victory" offers options, but nobody in Kiev seems to have the political courage to seize them. David Arakhamia's statements to the Ukrainian media *1+1*, showing that there was a solution in March 2022[817] and that Zelensky brushed it aside only to be in a worse situation a year and a half later, are bombshells. It's interesting that none of our media covered this interview in Europe. However, it was picked up by the Russian opposition media *Meduza*, which added the testimony of Oleksei Arestovitch, a former adviser to Zelensky, who confirmed that

---

815. https://www.courrierinternational.com/article/vu-de-russie-l-ue-veut-balayer-la-diploma-tie-au-profit-de-la-guerre-estime-moscou

816. http://duma.gov.ru/en/news/57887/

817. "Interview with David Arakhamia, head of the Ukrainian delegation at the peace talks", *1+1*, November 25, 2023 (https://youtu.be/0G_j-7gLnWU)

the war could have ended at the beginning of April 2022 and thus *"spared the lives of several hundred thousand Ukrainians."*[818] Note the "several hundred thousand" of lives Westerners have wasted.

Both men are just stating what I mentioned in my book, *Operation Z*, and which a professor at the Université Libre de Bruxelles, a so-called "expert" on Ukraine, considered a lie during a debate in June 2023.

At the front, Ukrainian commanders began to refuse Zelensky's orders to advance.[819] Criticism exchanged between Zelensky and General Zaluzhny, his commander-in-chief, seems to be turning into a power struggle. The assassination of one of General Zaluzhny's aides-de-camp,[820] followed by an attempt on the wife of the head of military intelligence (GUR),[821] appear to be manifestations of this struggle.

On the one hand, Zelensky continues to rule out any strategy against Russia other than fighting, without really defining the desired objective. He roundly criticizes General Zaluzhny for the catastrophic situation on the ground,[822] despite the fact that the conduct of the war has been more political than military on the Ukrainian side. The Ukrainian army was understaffed and women had to be sent to the front, while rumors of a forthcoming general mobilization have been multiplying. In the field, the military has lost confidence in the country's political leadership.

On the other hand, General Zaluzhny now confesses that waging a war of attrition against Russia was a mistake[823] and that *"a prolonged conflict*

---

818. "'We had to buy time' A Ukrainian negotiator said Moscow offered peace in exchange for Kyiv ending its NATO bid. Russia's propagandists were thrilled", *Meduza*, November 28, 2023 (https://meduza.io/en/feature/2023/11/28/we-had-to-buy-time)

819. Matthew Dooley, "Ukraine's top commanders refuse orders to advance against Putin in major blow to Zelensky," *Express*, November 2, 2023 (https://www.express.co.uk/news/world/1830656/ukraine-refuse-zelensky-vladimir-putin-russia)

820. Veronika Melkozerova, "Aide to Ukraine's top general killed by explosive in birthday present", *Politico*, November 6, 2023 (https://www.politico.eu/article/aide-to-ukrainian-armed-forces-commander-killed-by-explosive-in-birthday-present/)

821. Luke Harding, "Ukraine spy chief's wife recovering after being poisoned", *The Guardian*, November 28, 2023 (https://www.theguardian.com/world/2023/nov/28/ukraine-spy-chiefs-wife-recovering-after-being-poisoned)

822. Dinara Khalilova, "Zelensky's administration official criticizes Commander-in-Chief Zaluzhnyi's comments in press", *The Kyiv Independent*, November 4, 2023 (https://kyivindependent.com/presidential-office-on-zaluzhnyis-article-military-should-refrain-from-disclosing-front-line-situation/)

823. "It was mistake to hope for exhaustion of Russian Federation, situation reached dead end,— Zaluzhnyi," *Censor.NET*, November 2, 2023 (https://censor.net/en/news/3453121/it_was_mistake_to_hope_for_exhaustion_of_russian_federation_situation_reached_dead_end_zaluzhnyi)

benefits the enemy rather than [Ukraine]."[824] He criticized his president and seems to have the confidence of the military and the Americans.

Zelensky is in power, but cannot dismiss his general because of Zaluzhny's great popularity in the military. Unlike the Europeans, the Americans realize that they have reached an impasse with Ukraine. In November 2023, a year after covering Zelensky as "Man of the Year," *TIME Magazine* called him *"messianic"* and *"delusional"*[825]—the same terms used for Vladimir Putin.[826]

As for the situation on the ground, the fact that the front line is moving very little does not mean that we are in a stalemate, as our "experts" claim. It simply means that Russia is advancing cautiously—because, unlike Ukraine, Russia has the material, human and economic resources to continue fighting. As *The Economist* puts it: *"The war is not a stalemate. Russia clearly has the advantage because it is free to maneuver all along the front line and attack wherever it chooses."*[827]

The problem is that Volodymyr Zelensky doesn't have a realistic picture of his desired end outcome. It's easy to understand his aspiration to see the Russians withdraw and thus re-establish Ukrainian sovereignty over the entire territory. But as things stand, it's hard to see how this can be achieved. The idea of a total victory over Russia that he, his entourage and the media continue to evoke seems far-fetched and unrealistic. The fall in his popularity, at the end of 2023, is commensurate with the successes attributed to him up to that point. The Tarpeian Rock is close to the Capitol. Today, Zelensky must be kicking himself for not having seized every opportunity to improve the situation since he came to power. He is now in the worst possible situation, with an adversary who is victorious

---

824. "'It was my mistake': Ukrainian Commander-in-Chief on counteroffensive and 'gunpowder' for victory", *RBC-Ukraine*, November 2, 2023 (https://newsukraine.rbc.ua/news/it-was-my-mistake-commander-in-chief-on-counteroffensive-1698929719.html)

825. Simon Shuster, "'Nobody Believes in Our Victory Like I Do.' Inside Volodymyr Zelensky's Struggle to Keep Ukraine in the Fight", *TIME Magazine*, October 30, 2023 (https://time.com/6329188/ukraine-volodymyr-zelensky-interview/)

826. Taras Kuzio, "Putin weaponizes history with new textbook justifying Ukraine invasion," *The Atlantic Council*, August 22, 2023 (https://www.atlanticcouncil.org/blogs/ukrainealert/putin-weaponizes-history-with-new-textbook-justifying-ukraine-invasion/)

827. "Ukraine's commander-in-chief on the breakthrough he needs to beat Russia", *The Economist*, November 1, 2023 (https://www.economist.com/europe/2023/11/01/ukraines-commander-in-chief-on-the-breakthrough-he-needs-to-beat-russia)

and no longer interested in negotiating with him, because the Russians have understood that he is not in control of his decisions.

Confronted too late with the prospect of not being victorious, both the West and the Ukrainians have failed to define a clear, concrete and realistic picture of what might constitute a victory. Foreign Minister Dmytro Kuleba asked, *"If the West cannot win this war, who can?"*—thus admitting that Ukraine was fighting for the West.[828]

What the Ukrainians don't seem to have understood (or don't want to admit) is that the West wasn't trying to help them, but to weaken Russia. That's why Congress has doubts about the usefulness of continuing to invest in this conflict. In December 2023, Zelensky went to the United States to convince Congress to release the $61 billion promised by Joe Biden. But instead of responding to Congress' concerns about how the money would be used, or what strategy he intended to use to achieve victory, he accused them of supporting Vladimir Putin through their indecision.[829] Calling your allies traitors is hardly a winning diplomatic strategy.

That said, we can understand Zelensky's bitterness at having been made to give up peace in exchange for aid that was supposed to be for "as long as it takes," but became for "as long as we can" in December 2023.[830]

In Ukraine, the moment is ripe for calling everything into question. After the euphoria of a promised victory, reality is hitting Ukrainian society hard. Political assassinations are on the rise, with former socialist MP Ilya Kiva (who had claimed that the Bucha massacres had been staged by the SBU and British MI6) was murdered by Ukrainian services, according to *NBC News*.[831]

On December 14, 2023, Vladimir Putin took part in a four-hour question-and-answer session in Moscow. Olekseï Arestovitch, Zelensky's former advisor, commented on X (Twitter):

---

828. Iryna Balachuk, "If the West cannot win this war, then what war can it win?—Ukraine's Foreign Minister", *Ukrainska Pravda*, November 6, 2023, (https://www.pravda.com.ua/eng/news/2023/11/6/7427407/)

829. Paul McLeary, "Zelenskyy says Putin is 'inspired' by Capitol Hill deadlock on Ukraine," *Politico*, December 11, 2023 (https://www.politico.com/news/2023/12/11/zelenskyy-says-putin-is-inspired-by-capitol-hill-deadlock-on-ukraine-00131145)

830. https://www.whitehouse.gov/briefing-room/speeches-remarks/2023/12/13/remarks-by-president-biden-and-president-zelenskyy-of-ukraine-in-joint-press-conference-2/

831. https://www.nbcnews.com/news/world/ukraine-assassinated-ilya-kiva-moscow-traitors-russia-rcna128479

Putin holds a press conference with a yellow-blue background. If Zelensky had spoken against a white-blue-red background, he'd have been toast by now.

Putin calls us brothers and a united people, and we call them pigs and orcs.

On screen, Putin is confronted with embarrassing questions from Russians.

Who do you think has the edge: us or them?

Arestovych ☑
@arestovych

\- Путин дает пресс-конференция на желто-синем фоне.

Если бы Зеленский выступил на бело-сине-красном, его бы уже сожгли.

Путин называет нас братьями и единым народом, а мы их - свиньями и орками.

На экране у Путина - неудобные вопросы от россиян.

Как вы думаете - у кого преимущество:

\- у нас, или у них?..

Translate post

11:38 AM · Dec 14, 2023 · **206.1K** Views

Figure 98—Tweet by Oleksei Arestovitch—In Ukraine, opinions are beginning to change...
[Source: https://twitter.com/arestovych/status/1735247972252664208]

The West continues to talk of a possible victory, but are they still credible?

This crisis has shown that Europe has not only lost its global political and industrial leadership, but is deeply divided on a wide range of issues. In fact, the only thing that unites Europe is Russophobia.

At the end of the Cold War, our arms industry reshaped itself around a more cooperative approach to international security, in which diplomacy regained its rightful place. By trading in a law-based international order for a rules-based one, we have created a more confrontational environment for which this industry is no longer suited.

The mediocrity of our journalists and politicians has long been known. Now we've discovered the mediocrity of our military. Lack of courage, lack of imagination, inability to understand an adversary or lack of empathy seem to have become the hallmarks of modern officers—to the point of giving the Ukrainians inadequate training for the war they are waging. All these qualities are compounded by a profound stupidity. Recall here that in its April 2019 strategy for the US government to weaken Russia using Ukraine, the *RAND Corporation* warned that this could:

> *have a significant cost for Ukraine, as well as for the prestige and credibility of the United States. It could result in disproportionate human and territorial losses for Ukraine, as well as refugee flows. It could even lead Ukraine to a disadvantageous peace*[832].

We knew this—and yet here we are.

A handful of fanatical Western politicians and journalists have deliberately sacrificed Ukraine.

---

832. James Dobbins, Raphael S. Cohen, Nathan Chandler, Bryan Frederick, Edward Geist, Paul DeLuca, Forrest E. Morgan, Howard J. Shatz, Brent Williams, "Extending Russia: Competing from Advantageous Ground", *RAND Corporation*, 2019 (p. 100)

Table of contents

1. Introduction 7

2. Russian Military Thought 13
Russian Military Doctrine 16
  Doctrinal Elements 16
    Principles of Military Art 16
    Force Correlation 17
    Nuclear War 19
    Hybrid Warfare 33
    The Link Between Politics and War 39
  Doctrine Structure 41
  Strategy 44
  Operative Art 47
    The Essence of Operative Art—Synergy 47
    Operational Control 51
    Offensive Operations 57
    Defensive Operations 61
  Tactics 64
    Defense 65
    The "Pocket of Fire" 68
    The Battalion Battle Group (BTG) 70
Russian Conduct 75
  A Pragmatic Philosophy of Conduct 75
  Grades and Functions 78
  The "Lack of Non-Commissioned Officers" 78

3. Special Military Operation (SMO) in Ukraine 81
Correlation of Forces 81
Russian Forces 88
    The Numbers at the Start of the SMO 88
    Russian Armed Forces Personnel 91
        Partial Mobilization 92
        Conscription 94
        The "Wagner" Military and Private Security Company 95
        Chechen Forces 100
    Integrating Ukrainian Defectors 100
Russia's Objectives and Strategy 101
The Operative Concept and Russian Leadership in Ukraine 104
    Phase I 108
        The Objectives 109
        Assessment of Phase 1 114
    Phase 2 115
        The Objectives 116
        Operations Management 116
        Assessment of Phase 2 122
    Phase 3 123
        The Objectives 125
        Operations Management 125
        The Aerial Campaign Against Electrical Infrastructure 128
        Clandestine Warfare 131
        Assessment of Phase 3 132

4. Ukrainian Military Thinking 133
Ukrainian Forces 134
    The Ukrainian Army Faced with Attrition 139
    Poorly Trained Soldiers 142
Ukrainian Conduct 144
Ukrainian and Western Strategies 145
    Western Strategy 145
    The Ukrainian Strategy 153
        Western Aid 157
        Sanctions 164

NATO Intervention 165

The No-Fly Zone 167

The Spring Counter-Offensive (2023) 170

Western and Ukrainian Objectives 172

Strategic Objectives 172

Operational Objectives 176

The Conduct of Ukrainian Operations 178

A Hesitant Start 179

The Counter-Offensive Proper 181

Reasons for Failure 186

Strategic Reasons 186

Operative Reasons 189

Tactical Reasons 190

Western Critics 192

The Question of Co-Belligerence 195

Recourse to Terrorism 196

Attacks on Civilians 197

Attacks on Infrastructure 201

Wet Actions 203

The Drone Campaign 205

Zelensky's Threats 207

5. Strategic Analysis 209

The Center of Gravity 209

Terminology 209

Critical Factors 210

Centers of Gravity in Russia and Ukraine 212

Comparison of Strategic Factors 217

The Notion of Victory 223

6. A Technological War 227

The Russian Defense Industry 227

Electronic Warfare 230

Electronic Combat 230

The War against Satellites 232

Anti-Drone Systems 233

The Wunderwaffen..237

Hypersonic Weapons 238

Armored Vehicles 241

Balance of Force 241

Russian Tanks versus Western Tanks.................................241

Obsolete and Unusable Tanks 242

Russian Tanks Conceptually Worse? 245

*Western Tanks Designed for a Different Operating
Environment* 246

The Western Myth Challenged 250

Ukraine as a Testing Ground 252

Developing New Concepts 255

Recycling Old Tanks 256

The Artillery 259

Russian Artillery 259

Ukrainian Artillery 262

The Myth of the Ukrainian Advantage..........................262

The Problem of Ammunition 264

Multiple Rocket Launchers 267

Counter-Battery Systems...270

Cluster Munitions 271

Long-Range Missiles 274

Guided Bombs 276

Air Defense..278

Drones and Robotic Weapons 279

Use by Ukrainians 281

Aerial Drones...281

Naval Drones 282

Use by Russians 285

Aerial Drones...285

Robotic Weapons...289

7. Information Warfare 291

Cyberwarfare 291

Propaganda and Misinformation..295

Propaganda and Disinformation from the West and Ukraine........295

Russian Propaganda and Disinformation 300
Losses 303
Russian Losses: Misinformation as an Editorial Policy 304
Ukrainian Losses 309
   Military Losses 309
   Civilian Losses 314

8. Conclusions 317
Reasons for Russian Success 319
Reasons for the Ukrainian Defeat 323

Best sellers Max Milo Editions

Hitler's banker, Jean-François Bouchard

Confessions of a forger, Éric Piedoie Le Tiec

The Koran and the flesh, Ludovic-Mohamed Zahed

Governing by fake news, Jacques Baud

Governing by chaos, Collectif

A political history of food, Paul Ariès

Mad in U.S.A.: The ravages of the "American model",
Michel Desmurget

Mondial soccer club geopolitics, Kévin Veyssière

Putin: Game master?, Jacques Baud

Treatise on the three impostors: Moses, Jesus, Muhammad,
The Spirit of Spinoza

TV Lobotomy, Michel Desmurget